The Geopolitics of Hunger

The Geopolitics of Hunger

by Josué de Castro

with an Introduction
by Jean-Pierre Berlan

Monthly Review Press
New York and London

Library of Congress Cataloging in Publication Data
Castro, Josué de, 1908-1973.
    The geopolitics of hunger.
    Published in 1952 under title: Geography of
hunger.
    1. Food supply.   2. Nutrition.   3. Hunger.
I. Title.
HD9000.5.C29   1977   338.1'9   74-2140
ISBN 0-85345-357-8

First printing

Monthly Review Press
62 West 14th Street, New York, N.Y. 10011
21 Theobalds Road, London WC1X 8SL

Manufactured in the United States of America

Contents

A Note
from the Publisher

This book was first published in English in 1952 under the title *The Geography of Hunger.* It was subsequently revised and expanded for the French editions of 1964 and 1973, and the author was in the process of making further revisions when he died in 1973. Because the unfinished manuscript was a combination of old and new material, with no indication as to the date of the data used, we decided to take the 1952 edition as the basic text. We then used typographical notations to indicate the new material that has been added to the French edition, as follows:

—Updated statistical data, where given, appear in footnotes at the bottom of the page.

—Material added to the text—whether sentences, paragraphs, or whole sections—has been indicated by the use of brackets.

In addition, we have included the reference notes that were added to the French edition, and enlarged the bibliography accordingly. Sections that were written specifically for this edition are so indicated in footnotes.

Finally, we have restored the original title, which the book bears in other languages, as more fitting and accurate.

Introduction
by Jean-Pierre Berlan

"Some people are going to have to starve,"
said the U.S. Secretary of Agriculture to a
congressional committee. "We're in the position of a family that owns a litter of puppies:
we've got to decide which ones to drown."
—*Fortune*, May 1946

Average World Energy Intake
(in cal/person/day)

1934-38	1961	1972
2,380	2,380	2,440

The most striking feature of the figures given above is not
so much the absolute numbers of calories per person per day
as the constancy of these averages over the last four decades.
What they suggest is that since the 1930's, there has been
little change in the world food situation.

We know a great deal more about nutrition today than we

I want to thank Mrs. de Castro for the documents she provided for the biography
of her husband, Prof. Michel Cépède and my colleagues J. P. Bertrand, J. P.
Chabert, and P. Spitz for their help in preparing this introduction.

did ten or fifteen years ago, but our knowledge is still sketchy. It is difficult to give a precise definition of physiological needs, for the cultural and symbolic aspects of human nutrition, the various ecological and social structures within which human beings live, must also be taken into account. Crass commercial interests intrude on scientific considerations, consciously or unconsciously. A balanced diet is possible at a number of different levels of food intake, with varying results; no absolute optimum for health can be defined. Any nutritional norm, in short, reflects not only scientific findings but complex political, economic, and ideological considerations.

Thus, it makes sense to begin this discussion of Josué de Castro's masterpiece, *The Geopolitics of Hunger,* with some preliminary observations on the current status of nutritional knowledge and on hunger in the world today.

I

Our understanding of energy and protein needs has come a long way since Baron Justus von Liebig's theory, in the nineteenth century, that proteins are the fuel of the body. Yet even though a broad consensus may now exist among scientists, as reflected in the latest United Nations Food and Agriculture Organization-World Health Organization report,[1] recent statements issued by these organizations also contain certain inconsistencies and misconceptions. The basic issue is the specificity of protein hunger, once widely believed to be, and publicized as, the most challenging and difficult of all nutritional problems.

Energy and protein needs correspond to two different functions: energy fuels the body; protein fulfills its plastic needs, i.e., supplies the elements necessary to build up the body's tissues or replace them when they are worn out.

Today it seems generally agreed that "when the energy supply is insufficient, some of the proteins are diverted to supply energy and are not available to cover the plastic needs."[2] Conversely, when their caloric intake is adequate, people are unlikely to suffer from protein deficiencies.

This statement is in sharp contrast to the manner in which the question of hunger was previously conceived. This somewhat reluctant reversal, as reflected in the official publications of various agencies of the United Nations occurred about 1972; hence, de Castro could not take it into account in the latest edition of his book. As recently as 1971, the idea of a "protein gap" was being widely publicized by F.A.O. experts as the most challenging nutritional problem. For example:

In May 1971, a U.N. panel of experts issued a document entitled "Strategy Statement on Action to Avert the Protein Crisis in the Developing Countries." This Statement recognized "that any significant degree of caloric deficiency can exacerbate protein deficiency, because the protein in the diet is then used in part for energy purposes." It did not, however, assess the degree to which protein deficiency could be cured simply by people eating larger amounts of their present diets. Instead, action is proposed to "Avert the Protein Crisis," ignoring the possibility that the problem is not specifically one of protein—hardly surprising, perhaps, in light of the document's title, which undoubtedly reflects the panel's terms of reference.[3]

The effort to establish the existence of an impending "protein crisis" required some tortuous statistical manipulations:

The final misconception deserving comment in this context is the statistical fallacy inherent in the [very] calculations that lead the U.N. to talk about a "protein crisis." Such a description grossly exaggerates the protein problem. Worse, it leads to the proposal of dangerously unrealistic standards. The fallacy is embodied in the following argument: since there is considerable variation in individual protein needs, individuals whose intake is equal to minimum requirements run the risk of getting less than they need; consequently, recommended levels of intake for individuals should, for safety's sake, be above the level of minimum requirements. On this basis it is mistakenly argued that the standard for national supplies, given ideal distribution, would need to be the sum of recommended individual allowances (i.e., minimum requirements plus 20 percent).

If this sounds like an expensive national insurance policy, consider the next stage of the argument: since the distribution of intakes covers a far broader range than the distribution of needs, national standards have to be raised enough to ensure that everybody's requirements will be met.[4]

To confront the "protein crisis," it is necessary not only to increase the production of proteins from conventional sources but also to promote research for the development of unconventional sources, particularly of protein-rich food mixtures.[5] To support such developments, it is recommended that underdeveloped countries levy a "protein development tax."[6]

The terms used by the panel—"conventional" and "unconventional"—belong to the lexicon of international organizations and require explanation.

"Conventional sources" refers to the production of animal proteins and calories through the conversion of plant calories and proteins; in the developed countries—where animals are no longer used for draft purposes—livestock breeding has become the technical process whereby this conversion is effected. Modern feeding technologies consume huge amounts of plant resources, particularly cereals (see pp. 31-38 for a more detailed discussion of this), because the efficiency of the conversion process is so low: to produce a single gram of poultry protein requires 5 grams of plant protein; to produce a single gram of beef protein, 12 to 15 grams. In caloric terms, the ratio is similar. Even in the most modern agricultural systems (such as in the Netherlands) the overall yield of livestock breeding is only 12 to 15 percent of the plant intake.[7]

In the case of "unconventional sources," on the other hand, shortcuts are taken to eliminate the "waste" involved in the usual process of conversion: proteins are extracted directly from the raw material—the plants, particularly protein-rich legumes—and are then processed, concentrated, mixed, colored, flavored, and packed for shipment. A technologically inferior but gastronomically superior version of this process has in fact been in use all over the world for centuries, if not tens of centuries, in the preparation of many sorts of beans, lentils, and peas. The use of "unconventional sources," however, does not imply the refinement of these already existing techniques. Rather, to put it plainly, it refers to the development of advanced technologies by a dozen financially powerful multinational corporations, most of them based in the United States, as a means of opening up new markets for themselves.[8]

To sum up, the first solution involves an extension of the more conventional aspects of agribusiness, those that retain some agricultural basis; the second implies the accelerated growth of its most modern and concentrated sector, the food-processing industry. There is, however, no difference in substance between the two. For decades, such remedies have dominated the policies of both governments and international organizations.

The shift in what we might call the world food paradigm—from an emphasis on protein deficiency to an emphasis on overall caloric deficiency—cannot be attributed solely to scientific advances in the field of nutrition. Other factors have contributed to the change: the fact that the previous conception of a "protein crisis" reflected the meat-eating biases of only a tiny percentage of the world's population; the pressures of the Western agribusiness complex;[9] the fear of overproduction. The new, more realistic conception reflects a certain mood of disenchantment and resignation: "If they cannot have meat, let them eat cereals." It remains to be seen, however, whether the practical measures that logically follow from this new conception, i.e., increasing the production of cereals and giving them to human beings rather than to animals, will be implemented.

We now turn from the production to the consumption side of the relationship between proteins and energy, where the vital question is one of distribution. According to F.A.O. experts, "if social factors do not have influence [but they do, don't they?] individual consumption will be dictated by needs."[10] According to the same experts, either an excess or a deficiency of energy intake is deterimental to health. As for protein, although a deficiency may likewise be harmful, "there is no evidence that a much higher intake than necessary has any effect, good or bad."[11] Excessive consumption of animal protein—which tends to be monopolized by the richer and more powerful sectors of the population—may in fact have an adverse effect because it implies a large intake of fats, and of late it has become the subject of a great deal of research. The risk of overweight, circulatory problems, and heart disease may thus provide at least some sort of physiological barrier to the appropriation of too large a share of the world energy supply by the greedy populations of the rich capitalist world and the voracious upper classes of underdeveloped countries.[12] We cannot expect them to fatten themselves to death the way the ruling class of the Roman Empire poisoned itself with lead. But as far as proteins in general are concerned—as well as other nutrients associated with qualitative aspects of diet—there is no absolute physiological limit to consumption, and the rich countries and their retainers around the world have an enormous appetite.

Consumption of animal protein is not distributed in accordance with physiological needs. If it were, those who are weakest—including infants, particularly at weaning time, children, and pregnant and nursing women—would receive priority. Rather, it tends to be the privilege of wealth. Even in terms of energy, where the distribution is less skewed than in the case of protein, the problem remains. It seems, in short, that the problem of hunger is inseparable from the problem of distribution.

There is a plentiful food supply in all developed countries, yet substantial sectors of their populations still suffer from some form of malnutrition. The case of the United States, as de Castro demonstrates, is particularly illuminating. In this "granary of the world," where domestic food production is potentially more than equal (126 percent) to consumption needs, at least 7 percent of the population suffers from energy and/or protein deficiencies. On the Asian continent, China and India provide an interesting study in contrasts. Both are at about the same overall nutritional level (producing approximately 95 percent of their consumption needs), yet hunger is endemic in one country and has disappeared from the other. No great nutritional or economic expertise is required to draw the obvious conclusion: a society that stresses equality can very rapidly eliminate the most extreme manifestations of hunger and ride out periods of shortages without famine. It is useless to think that an increase in the production of food will solve the problem of hunger; there must also be a change in distribution.

Let us carry this analysis a bit further, comparing the availability of food in different areas of the world. In developed countries, the energy supply ranges as high as 126 percent of consumption needs; in developing regions it may go as high as 110 percent, though in three such regions (Africa, the Far East, the Asian socialist countries) it falls short of 100 percent. Altogether, the energy supply in developing areas is estimated at 95 percent of needs; in developed countries it is approximately 30 percent higher. As for proteins, the supply in developed areas is 65 percent higher than in developing regions (96 grams/person/day as against 58 grams/person/day).

At first glance, such inequalities may not seem so appalling. But figures can be misleading. For example, there appears to be a sufficient protein supply in both developed and developing regions, but this is only apparently the case. For one thing, part of the protein supply is diverted to supply energy; for another, as per the preceding discussion, there is no automatic correspondence between a satisfactory average supply of protein in a country and an adequate protein intake per person. Moreover, if we compare the five countries with the highest energy intake with the ten lowest, the gap between the two groups is 80 percent. In the case of proteins, it rises to 250 percent; for animal protein consumption it exceeds 1,000 percent. A person living in Mozambique, for example, consumes 3.8 grams a day; in Nigeria, the figure is 5.3 grams. In France or the United States, however, average consumption per person is more than 60 grams a day. And if we compare groups within countries, a similar maldistribution appears, with the richer classes tending to get the lion's share of the supply of animal proteins. Even within families, in fact, often it is the breadwinner who gets the largest and best portion of the foods that are in short supply.[13]

Inequalities between countries in terms of calories, rather than animal proteins, seem, predictably, to be somewhat less acute. But in this case as well, appearances are deceptive. Since animal proteins and calories are themselves the result of the conversion of plant calories and proteins, any meaningful comparison of nutritional levels must be based on a concept of original proteins or calories, i.e., the plant resources directly consumed as well as those used for the production of animal protein. If we compare the level of original energy and protein consumption in developed countries and underdeveloped ones, the ratio is on the order of three or four to one.[14]

These figures could be even further elaborated, but in general they show that the world food situation can best be described as characterized not by scarcity but by inequality.[15]

This inequality of distribution means, according to F.A.O. estimates, that 462 million people are suffering from an inadequate protein/energy supply. This figure calls for some brief comments. First of all, it is, in the F.A.O.'s own words, a "weak" estimate, calculated for a year labeled "average," even though it was the best yet in terms of per-capita food supply. The "poor crops" of 1972 and the subsequent monetary crisis have added tens if not hundreds of millions of people to the ranks of the underfed.[16] Second, the assumptions on which the computation is based are rather questionable. It is assumed, for example, that there is no problem of inequality of consumption if the energy supply of a country exceeds 110 percent of its needs—an assumption that would rank Brazil among the hunger-free countries! The estimate also fails to take into account the fact that a whole range of necessary technical operations intervene between food needs and consumption—storage, transportation, cooking—all of which entail some degree of loss. These operations, moreover, are controlled by a powerful class of tradesmen and speculators whose interest—especially in times of shortages—is not in maximum efficiency but in maximum profit. Finally, the criterion adopted to estimate the number of people likely to be underfed is such that "it is extremely unlikely that an individual will be classified among the underfed if in fact his food supply is higher than a limit fixed at a very low level."[17] That limit, indeed, is set at a level of caloric consumption—between 1,900 and 2,000 a day, depending on the area of the world—which under normal conditions seems inadequate to sustain any productive activity. What it represents, therefore, is a bare minimum level of consumption under favorable conditions.

J. Klatzmann has arrived at the following tentative estimates of the world food situation, based on a careful appraisal both of current methodologies and available statistical evidence:

15 percent of the world population is overfed;
10   "   is well fed;
15   "   belongs to an
               intermediate category;
50   "   is underfed to varying
               degrees;
10   "   suffers from serious
               nutritional deficiencies.[18]

Half of infant deaths are the result of malnutrition, and 200 million children suffer from nutritional deficiencies. Although there has been a decrease in the incidence of beriberi, pellagra, and scurvy, due to advances in public health, endemic goiter or endemic cretinism (which fifteen years ago claimed 200 million sufferers), as well as vitamin A and iron deficiencies, are still widespread. (Estimates show that 100,000 children in the Far East alone are going blind each year due to a lack of vitamin A.[19])

Whatever the estimates, they all point to an appalling situation. There has been no appreciable quantitative change in this overall situation in the last few decades: the majority of humanity has yet to get rid of hunger. The facts that originally moved de Castro to write *The Geopolitics of Hunger* are still very much with us—but our political, economic, and ideological environment has undergone some momentous changes.

II

Josué de Castro was born in Recife, Brazil, in the heart of one of the worst hunger areas of the world. "Recife is the city of the 'cycle of the crabs,' crabs which feed the inhabitants of the swampy slums, whose bodies in turn feed the crabs;[20] it also stands at the junction of two explosive hunger areas: the *sertão,* where drought causes periodic famine, and the sugar-growing Nordeste, where large *fazendas* were established with slave labor and where growing staple foods was prohibited so as to free the land for cane and, above all, to keep the workers in bondage."[21]

As a medical doctor and founder of the Nutrition Institute of Brazil, de Castro came into close contact with the symptoms of hunger and so, undoubtedly, did many of his colleagues. By the early years of World War II, de Castro's broad scientific and social experience had led him to produce a number of works—most notably *Living Conditions of the Working Class in Recife* (1935), *Minimum Wages* (1935), and *Brazilian Nutrition in the Light of Human Geography* (1937)—which broke through the taboos surrounding the subject of hunger and began to expose the social roots of the problem. He, along with John Boyd-Orr, André Mayer, W. R. Aykroyd, and others, was a pioneer in the study of the relationship between human nutrition and social conditions in various parts of the world.[22]

The scientific investigations of these medical doctors, biologists, or nutritionists appeared at a time when economists were asserting confidently that the Depression was due to overproduction, particularly of agricultural products. Out of the works of these men grew the foundations—and, we might add, the illusions—of the Food and Agriculture Organization of the United Nations, which was established at the Hot Springs Conference of 1943, as well as of the general movement of reconstruction and development during the postwar period.

De Castro was closely associated with the F.A.O.; as president of the Brazilian committee, he participated in the third session of the organization (in 1947) and in 1951 was elected to a four-year term as independent president of the Executive Council. He played a major role in the movement toward greater international awareness of the world food situation, a process in which *The Geopolitics of Hunger* exerted broad political and ideological influence.*

It is paradoxical that this masterpiece had its genesis in a quite different project for a whole series of books on hunger. In 1946, de Castro published *The Geography of Hunger: Hunger in Brazil,* which he intended to be the first of a number of volumes dealing with hunger in various areas of the world, including Africa, Asia, Europe, and Central and South America. Events did not run according to plan. De Castro was asked by Little, Brown & Co. of Boston to write a book providing a comprehensive view of hunger in the world and its "political implications." He intended it to be a work that condensed into one volume "all the regional particularities of hunger," extending his perspective by "linking the phenomenon of hunger to the political developments of the contemporary world. The book had to be more than a geography of hunger. It had to be a political geography of hunger that would bridge the gap between the current biological and political crises."

In 1952 the book was published under the ambiguous English title *The Geography of Hunger,* but in almost thirty other languages it bears the title *The Geopolitics of Hunger.* The book was an immediate success, awarded both the prestigious Roosevelt Prize by the American Academy of Political Science and, in 1954, the no less pretigious Lenin Prize. At

---

* After the military coup of 1964 in Brazil, de Castro lived in France, where he taught in various universities.

the height of the Cold War, both camps attempted to claim the work and the man for their side.

In its various editions (the French has been substantially revised and expanded, notably in 1964 and 1973), *Geopolitics* spans the entire post-World War II era and reflects "a unique historical experience born amid contradiction and dissolved in ambiguity—the experience of decolonization and development."[23] Yet the original core of ideas developed by de Castro has retained its power through all the political and ideological changes of this period and has only been strengthened by the revisions and additions he made to it over the years.

III

The modern definition of hunger is the lack of one or more essential nutrients. Here, it is analyzed by de Castro as "the biological manifestation of underdevelopment," and underdevelopment, in turn, is approached not as the result of a flawed relationship between man and nature but as the outcome of a historical and political dynamic.

The book develops two related theses. The first is that "hunger is a man-made plague"; "hunger due to the inclemency of nature is an extraordinary catastrophe, while hunger as a man-made blight is a 'normal' condition in the most varied parts of the world" (p. 75). The second challenges the Malthusian notion that demographic pressure on subsistence levels is responsible for human misery and hunger. De Castro demonstrates that it is starvation that causes overpopulation, not the reverse.

In developing the first of these theses, de Castro focuses on locating the social roots of so universal a phenomenon as hunger. In most areas, he finds, hunger can be traced back to the effects, direct or indirect, of the system of colonial exploitation: latifundism and minifundism, underexploitation of resources (particularly land), monoculture, stunted industrialization, exploitation of peasants, and feudalism. Case studies of Latin America, the southern United States, pre-revolutionary China, India, Hungary, southern Italy, and Japan provide ample evidence for his point of view.

In the case of pre-revolutionary China, for example, after identifying the natural causes of famine—floods, drought, locusts, earthquakes, typhoons—he goes on to point out:

> An analysis of the problem of hunger as a whole makes clear at once that the so-called natural causes are only the immediate factors and are themselves the result of social causes in the background, of factors inherent in the structure of the Chinese economy. It is the tragic and absurd economic organization of the country that leads to its state of permanent nutritional poverty and exposes it to periodic crises of hunger. (p. 274)

Colonial powers in search of quick profits, of course, served only to reinforce this "tragic and absurd economic organization," leading to his conclusion that hunger is the product of imperialist exploitation. In India, colonial exploitation "cut short India's economic revolution and forced the country back to a medieval economy and into permanent starvation" (p. 328). Whatever crafts or nascent industrial development existed were promptly crushed by the British, who used the most reactionary class of feudal landlords as the social base of their power.[24]

The wealth of evidence amassed by de Castro demonstrates conclusively that hunger and underdevelopment are not to be relegated to the realm of natural phenomena. Rather, they represent the legacy of years of colonial plunder, economic exploitation, and political oppression.

More controversial, at least for some shortsighted critics, is the second of de Castro's major theses, and the one he considers the "crucial point" (p. 77) of the entire book: his claim that starvation is the cause of overpopulation and that, indeed, there is a correlation between increased protein intake and a lower rate of fertility. He starts with the fact that countries with high nutritional standards and high per-capita protein intake have low rates of demographic growth, buttresses his argument with the results of experiments done with rats and even with human beings (pp. 129-134), and goes on to offer a physiological explanation for this phenomenon when dealing with the Far East (pp. 283-284). Throughout the book he maintains a strict anti-Malthusian position, opposing all forms of birth control.

Critics have been quick to contest the validity of the evidence offered by de Castro. They point out that a statistical correlation does not necessarily reveal a causation, citing experimental results and estimates that contradict de Castro's biological interpretation. The low rate of demographic growth in Western industrial societies probably cannot be attributed to a single cause, be it protein intake or anything else. A recent article in Le Monde, for example, suggested that contributing factors might include the psychological stress of life in capitalist society (competition, insecurity, and tensions of all sorts) and the development of the underwear industry!

De Castro's approach is far more sophisticated, however, than his insistence on a biological explanation suggests. His critics fail to make a dent in the argument that hunger is rooted in social relations. For example, in the section on China de Castro followed up his biological analysis of the relationship between starvation and fertility with the following statement: "Parallel with these biological mechanisms, there is a complex social mechanism through which chronic hunger works powerfully toward speeding up population growth" (p. 285). And a few pages earlier he made the very modern observation that:

> There is no way of limiting the growth of the Chinese population
> without first changing the whole economic and social structure of
> the country.... Any attempt to prescribe neo-Malthusian
> measures as a means of alleviating Chinese hunger will be lacking
> not only in scientific justification but in social effect, since it will
> not awaken the slightest response in the Chinese masses. (p. 279)

The wealthy members of the Indian Rotary Club who organize sterilization drives in rural areas and their imperialistic
backers from large foundations would do well to ponder this
statement. In fact, the merit of de Castro's argument is not so
much its scientific truth—whose validity, de Castro himself
admits, is narrowly limited by the interventions of numerous
social, economic, and cultural factors—as its practical, political, and human consequences. In this respect, de Castro's
passionate anti-Malthusianism is both a voice of hope and a
call to action.

IV

Today, twenty years after the original publication of *The
Geopolitics of Hunger*, one is still struck by its remarkable
qualities, by the honesty and generosity of its author. Yet
one must also recognize that the book's phenomenal success
has not been due solely to intrinsic merits. It must be placed
in its proper historical perspective.

When the book first came out, a new economic order was
emerging in the wake of World War II, one dominated by a
country—the United States—that had rejected a direct
colonial policy. Elsewhere in the world, the enlightened bourgeoisie of various countries had already recognized that the
collapse of the old colonial empires was inevitable. They were
counting on independent India to demonstrate the superiority of the "free" development model to an "enslaved"
communist China (a theme which now seems to have van-

ished from the economic literature). The American ruling class, with its relative lack of experience and expertise in the field of international affairs, was confronted with the enormous task of reorganizing the world capitalist system. Above all, it had to channel the upsurge of nationalism in colonial countries into movements for formal independence and to "develop" these new territories—a task the former colonial masters had been too weak to accomplish. The other superpower, the U.S.S.R., was too weakened and devastated by the war to pursue an expansionist policy at that time.

Even before the war ended, awareness of the wretched legacy of the colonial past was becoming widespread. As early as 1941, the Atlantic Charter had included "Freedom from Want" among the four freedoms promised to the people of the world. The Charter of the United Nations was drafted along the same lines, with specialized agencies created to combat hunger and underdevelopment, which were identified as prime causes of war and international tensions.

A wave of idealism emerged out of the ruins and massacres of World War II, and with it came the progressive notion that the answer to world problems lay in development through international cooperation, aid, and technological advances and exchanges. By 1951, the Marshall Plan had already demonstrated that such a policy was feasible. In retrospect, of course, it is clear that the new ruling order regarded these ideas as little more than a smokescreen for the advancement of its commercial and political interests. The World Bank and the International Monetary Fund, for example, were to be tied to the reign of the dollar and run in strict accordance with conventional banking methods. Subsequent events—the Cold War, the independence of India and of Indonesia (after the Netherlands' unsuccessful attempt to reconquer its former colony), the "loss" of China, the first Indochina war, the Korean War, the coup in Prague—eliminated any of the postwar idealistic spirit that remained. Foreign policy considerations came to play a dominant role in the shaping of attitudes and the adoption of economic policies toward the former colonies.

Although de Castro shows that colonialism and, in a more general way, systematic exploitation and plunder (in Puerto Rico, for example) are at the root of hunger and under-development, the solutions he suggests are largely technical: cultivation of vast areas of the world that lie idle or are inefficiently used; corrective measures to combat erosion (although de Castro perceptively observes that erosion stems from problems in human relationships and not from a faulty relationship between man and nature);[25] and, finally—turning from these to more traditional methods of increasing agricultural output—the application of scientific resources to develop new plants, produce synthetic foods (plankton, yeast, or algae), improve fishing techniques, etc.

All these measures, if correctly implemented, would provide resources sufficient to feed the world. Yet the postwar era was still haunted by the familiar specter of rising surpluses in the midst of starvation—in other words, by the problem of effective distribution of agricultural products. As de Castro stated it, inadequate distribution would lead to surpluses and under-consumption. This, indeed, was the primary problem of U.S. agriculture. Due to the country's pervasive influence, agricultural and economic power, it also became the primary focus of the policies of international organizations. It is hardly surprising that the various proposals drafted after the war meshed perfectly with the needs of the new ruling order. These proposals, despite certain superficial variations, were fundamentally alike in their emphasis on free trade and the free flow of capital—in other words, the free flow of U.S. capital to vast new areas. Whatever development took place would be geared to and directed by the interests of the dominant power. De Castro wrote optimistically in the last chapter of his book that "As colonial areas develop into great consumer markets, they will be in a position to contribute substantially to the consolidation of a more balanced economy by absorbing certain surplus products of the more highly developed areas" (p. 493). Little did he know that the Foreign Trade and Assistance Act would be passed two years later by the U.S. Congress. Under this act, large amounts of surplus would be disposed of, serving the "national security goals" of U.S. foreign policy and allowing the United States to be the real decision-maker in agricultural policy in underdeveloped areas. Neither could he have foreseen, when he suggested that raw material prices be fixed in accordance with the prices of consumer goods in the producing country, how unpopular this proposal would prove to be!

From the foregoing it should be clear that much of de Castro's book could be accepted by both the United States and the U.S.S.R. The United States was attempting to expand its influence by reaping the spoils of the former colonial empires. De Castro's anti-Malthusianism, meanwhile, found favor in the Soviet Union, a country that is sparsely populated in the best of times and had suffered devastating population losses during the war. Everyone could agree on the necessity of developing the productive forces—as long as the social content of that development was left vague. Now, of course, we can more readily see the similarity between the models of development—in their organization, mode of control, and goals—the two sides had in mind. Both countries evidenced the same messianic drive toward an integrated and unified world system; they differed only on the question of who would control it. Both tended to select from de Castro's book only those points that conformed to their own goals and to neglect the spirit in which it was written and the warnings it contained.

Events took a different course from the one originally envisioned by de Castro. The hopes raised by decolonization were progressively eroded until the "poor crops" of 1972, and the famines that resulted, shattered whatever illusions remained.

This progressive disillusionment, as well as other changes in the world picture, were reflected in various new editions of the book that appeared over the years. In the French edition of 1956 some minor corrections were made and a few pages devoted to developments in China. With remarkable foresight, de Castro wrote that "socioeconomic developments since 1949 justify the belief that the new China's struggle against hunger can be victorious, that it will be able to vanquish forever the thousand-year-old specter of starvation." Among those "socioeconomic developments" were the restoration of peacetime conditions; the breaking of links with imperialist powers, including the revocation of treaties and repudiation of foreign debts; agrarian reform; and fantastic strides in public health, even the hygienic recycling of human excrement. In 1957 de Castro visited China and saw for himself that "the population showed almost none of the classic symptoms of hunger," signs he was used to encountering in the other underdeveloped countries of the world—a striking success indeed.

The 1973 French edition, the most recent and the last before de Castro's death, was much more extensively revised and expanded than previous editions. Not only did it contain most of the material added earlier, but there was also a great deal of entirely new data, providing an update on conditions in some important areas of the world: the new China, where hunger has been wiped out thanks to a mass movement respectful of the country's past and to the implementation of methods "that involved neither miracle fertilizers nor automation"; India, symbolic of "the illusions of independence," where the program of intensive agriculture known as the "Green Revolution" remains suspect, to de Castro, despite its apparent success; Cuba and Brazil;* and black Africa, "where political independence has not been followed by economic independence."

The new material—ranging from the simple addition of a sentence or paragraph to the insertion of whole new sections —continues to stress de Castro's original thesis that the problem of hunger is rooted in imperialist, colonial, neocolonial, or class domination and has nothing to do with natural causes. Indeed, the very areas on which he focuses—the contrasting cases of Brazil and Cuba, of India and China—bear out this point. In the concluding sections, however, it is the technical rather than the social aspects of hunger that are emphasized, providing interesting overviews of scientific advances in various fields.

This shift in emphasis is made quite explicit. He begins as follows:

> Technically, there are no obstacles. The knowledge that man now possesses, if intelligently applied, would provide humanity with enough food of the necessary quality to insure its nutritional balance for many years to come, even if the population were to double, quadruple, or increase tenfold. The difficulties in resolving what is known as the Malthusian dilemma are not technical; they are political difficulties of much greater complexity (p. 466).

But then, surprisingly, he goes on to write: "This chapter, however, is limited to an analysis of technical resources."

There are two possible explanations, in my view, for this apparent disinclination to deal further with the political aspects of hunger. First of all, de Castro did not want to issue political prescriptions. The lessons of his book were self-evident, and he was not, after all, a revolutionary activist. Second, his prime target was the neo-Malthusians, and if he

* Material written mostly in 1962.

stressed the contrast between what was technologically possible and what had actually been achieved, it would more effectively serve to undermine their position.

Such an approach, however, is not devoid of ambiguities. Although de Castro is right to point out the great technical potential for increasing world agricultural production, there are dangers in his emphasis on the latest achievements of science and technology. Single-cell proteins, enriched foods, and the like are no more than gadgets; they are to the problem of hunger what "dream cars" are to the problem of transportation, serving only to conceal the basic nature of the problem and leading people to believe that "more of the same" will solve it. These new technologies are controlled by multinational corporations whose interest is in gaining a monopoly over the preparation of legumes and cereals—an activity people, on their own, have been carrying on for centuries all over the world.

An emphasis on science and technology tends to encourage people to approach the problem of hunger essentially in terms of food production, even though we have seen that "social factors," in the delicate phrasing of the F.A.O., "influence" the distribution of both energy and protein, particularly when foodstuffs are in short supply, and that the problem, on a world scale or within countries, is one not so much of absolute scarcity as of inequality. It is unrealistic to expect that the problem can be solved by increasing the size of the "pie," when the very economic and technological forces marshalled to make this increase possible merely widen the gap between wealth and poverty.

The development of agricultural production in Third World countries during the postwar years was largely a matter of the extension of the system of Western agribusiness. It was the dissemination of this model, under the leadership of the United States and with the sponsorship of international organizations, that led to the monopolization of the world food supply by a few capitalist countries and, most recently, to the food crisis of 1972-74. The next section, therefore, will be devoted to a brief examination of the main features of this model. Such an analysis will, I hope, prove a useful complement to de Castro's book.

V

Even before World War II, agricultural production in the United States was undergoing technological changes of immense and far-reaching importance. Since the war, this new agricultural model has spread to other developed countries and has established some powerful enclaves in the underdeveloped world as well. Such developments have affected all aspects of agricultural production and have brought about a marked separation between the two traditionally interdependent spheres of animal and plant production. Structurally, moreover, this transformation has been marked by the rise of a powerful agribusiness complex which encompasses all aspects of food production and distribution and is controlled by huge, diversified corporations operating in tandem with the state apparatus. Since this development is most advanced in the United States, our discussion will begin with some brief observations on that situation.

Agriculture, as traditionally defined, now seems to be an insignificant, marginal sector of the U.S. economy, representing barely 3 to 4 percent of the gross national product. All the activities involved in the production, processing, and marketing of agricultural products in 1966 employed 30.4 percent of the total U.S. work force—down from 41 percent in 1947. The overall employment figures for the same period, however, remained fairly stable; the rapid decrease in farm employment (down 44 percent) was offset by the growth of input-producing industries (up 16 percent) and above all of the processing and marketing sectors (up 26 percent). For every job in the agricultural sector, there are three in the industrial sector.[26]

The industrial sector is an integral part of U.S. monopoly capital. Within this system powerful corporations, highly concentrated and diversified, work hand in hand not only with the financial establishment but with the state itself, which has, since the Depression, served as the primary stabilizer of the entire system. Thus, corporations seeking foreign expansion receive the backing (if not the active encouragement) of the national government. Similarly, federal agricultural policy has evolved into an agribusiness policy in which two somewhat contradictory goals have been pursued: on the one hand, to provide the marketing and processing sectors—and, almost incidentally, the American consumer—with cheap raw materials and, on the other, to stabilize farm income so that agricultural outlets remain available to manufacturers of industrial inputs. (This might be viewed as a more general and systematic application of the inducements offered to farmers by machinery manufacturers in the early Depression years—a guaranteed price for their produce in return for the purchase of equipment.) The resolution of this dilemma has had far-reaching implications: an acceleration of the "modernization" of agriculture through the elimination of smaller farmers and the concentration of land, capital, and credit in the hands of the most "efficient" producers; a continuous flow of new agricultural technology through a complex network of research institutions; agriculture's growing dependence upon the suppliers of its industrial inputs; a heightened specialization and division of labor; and an incessant search for new markets under the rhetorical guise of "free trade" and "mutual advantage."

In terms of these goals, U.S. agricultural policy has been extremely successful. The number of farms has decreased from 6.5 million in the mid-1930's to 2.9 million today. Most of these, moreover, are almost "ghost" farms; 50 percent are so marginal that they provide less than 13 percent of family income. At the other end of the spectrum, 150,000 farms—5 percent of the total—account for 50 percent of sales. It is these few farms—the larger, more powerful, more efficient ones—that constitute the economically significant core of U.S. agriculture. They are geared to the market, capable of swift reactions to fluctuations in price, and they are flexible enough both to survive long periods of underemployment of their productive capacity and to take advantage of any new opportunity arising on the market. The space they occupy is specialized, empty, socially and culturally bankrupt. They operate in the context of a carefully designed system of state planning and rely on the expansion of U.S. multinational corporations, and the related foreign activities of the state (aid, military intervention, etc.) to ensure access to existing markets or to open up new ones.

The modernization of agricultural production, and the accompanying tendency toward overproduction, means that the system must constantly be expanded. On the domestic market, eating habits are manipulated to encourage higher consumption of animal products and processed foods. The drive for higher meat consumption was based on the implementation and extension of new technologies in livestock breeding, which intensified the division of labor on the farm level and tended, as noted before, to break up the previously interdependent processes of raising animals and raising crops.

These new technologies are characterized not only by careful genetic selection of livestock but also by intensive feeding methods involving the use of computer-calculated rations in specialized units. The rations are basically composed of cereals, whose "inadequate" protein content is offset by the addition of a concentrated protein source, usually an oil-seed meal (soybean, peanut, rapeseed, etc.) and, occasionally, fish meal.* Control of the process of converting plant into animal products has thus shifted from the hands of farmers into those of large corporations—companies that usually began as grain dealers, millers, or oil-seed processors and later expanded their operations into the related fields of feed production, breeding, specialized-equipment manufacture, processing, etc.

The National Commission on Food Marketing gives quite a full summary of the methods used in achieving this corporate control:

Development of the basic breeding stock, a highly specialized, large-scale business, has been concentrated in the hands of a few leading firms. They have maintained an effective barrier to entry by continuously striving to improve their product through extensive research and by keeping high-performance breeding lines within their control. The products of these firms thus became clearly differentiated by their superior performance and the differentiation was maintained through continuous advanced genetic research and careful control of products at current stages of development. . . .

There is one more question: why the system of coordination that developed was not one of ownership integration at all stages, including that of poultry production. At this [latter] stage, coordination was achieved by contract instead. The answer is to be found in the fact that many underemployed farmers with unused facilities were willing to sell their labor at very low rates [even at negative rates, the commission should have added] because they had little or no alternative. Also, contracts were attractive to the large combines because they involved no social security, work-

---

* The term "inadequate" does not refer to the natural or physiological needs of farm animals. Under capitalism, the inadequacy implies a slower rate of rotation of the invested capital because animals grow more slowly, and in the rate of production of surplus value. It is therefore opposed to the fundamental goal of capitalist production: the production of surplus value and its accumulation on a continually enlarged scale.

man's compensation, and other employee costs. The capital of feed companies and poultry processors could earn higher returns when put to other uses.[27]

This process of technical innovation (and, at times, of technical obsolescence) is not limited to livestock breeding but is also apparent in such related fields as nutrition (marketing complicated rations with esoteric ingredients of doubtful value to mislead farmers and beat out the competition), machinery, and the use of drugs to control disease. It is also a process not limited to the United States but international in scope. In France, for example, only one breeder is left; his survival is due to his exclusive access to the results of government research. Multinational corporations are active in Brittany where the social structure bears a striking resemblance to that of the southern United States, the current center of American poultry production.

A fantastic concentration of production, in fact, has occurred in the wake of these technical developments. Poultry production in the United States, for example, had a broad geographical distribution in the early 1940's; now it has become concentrated in the South through "contract integration." Although these contracts may take many forms, their basic effect is always the same: the farmers are turned into powerless appendages of the large corporations (or large co-ops, which amount to the same thing), which become their sole source of supplies and equipment, the organizers and supervisors of their work, and the exclusive markets for their products. Under the clauses of the contracts it is the farmers who actually bear most of the risks of production. The firms keep pouring in new technology and equipment, which demand an increase in the farmers' scale of operations; the farmers must run faster and faster to pay back their loans, a goal that always seems to elude them. In the end they go bankrupt, and if they organize to fight back, as they did recently in the South, swift action is taken to crush their efforts.

Although this concentration has reached an extreme in the poultry industry, it can also be found, in various guises, in other sectors of livestock breeding. Cattle-raising, for example, once a small-scale activity localized in the Midwest, has shifted to other areas and become a big business, with animals packed into huge feedlots.

The expansion of this model, domestically and worldwide, has provided needed market outlets for U.S. grain manufacturers and multinational agribusiness corporations. Today, 35 percent of the world production of cereals—432 million tons, enough to feed the combined populations of India and China —is fed to animals. The use of cereals for livestock feed, moreover, takes place almost exclusively in the developed countries, where cereal consumption by animals is enough to feed 1.072 billion people, which is almost on a par with what is consumed in the underdeveloped world.[28]

Together the U.S. government, American farm groups (U.S. Feed Grain Council, American Soybean Association, etc.), and multinational corporations have pushed the international propagation of this model. Generations of scientists all over the world have been trained to believe in its unique virtues; in fact, it became implanted in people's minds even before taking root in the fields. The model also serves to popularize Western styles of eating, as part of a more general dissemination of Western culture and ideology. In Japan, any burger stand named McDonald's or Burger Chef is assured of instant success.

The model's major "advantage"—to U.S. agriculture, to agriculture in certain other developed countries, and to multinational agribusinesses—is that it is enormously wasteful of primary resources—cereals and meals—and thus provides limitless opportunities for market expansion. In underdeveloped countries the only beneficiaries of such a model are the local bourgeoisie and middle classes, for whom cars and steaks represent the pinnacle of capitalist development. Otherwise, it only increases inequality of food consumption in these areas, depriving the poorer classes (and countries) of any chance of reaching an adequate nutritional level in the foreseeable future. Thus, most of the catch of the fishing industry developed in Peru—which de Castro mentions as a positive achievement—is turned into fish meal to supplement the animal feed of the developed countries. This is all the more ironic and absurd given the fact that the protein contained in the fish meal is of excellent nutritional quality, far better than that of the end products, pork or poultry. The same could be said of the peanut meal produced in Senegal or India.

The basic irrationality of such a system of production-consumption is concealed by a sort of magic recipe cooked up with the implements of economic analysis. "Consumer preferences," combined with a sprinkling of Engels' law, show that as incomes rise the consumption of "higher foods" (oils, fats, meat products, sugar) also tends to rise, while the consumption of "lower foods" (potatoes, for instance) declines. This correlation is so convincing, this "truth" so firmly established, that the whole topic is no longer subject to debate but has attained the status of a natural phenomenon.

But as we have tried to show, this system of production-consumption, far from being the "prime mover" of the development of the agribusiness system, far from resulting from any innate human need or desire, is the fruit of a historically determined form of economic development, the model of capital accumulation.

This capitalist model of development is sharply at odds with some of the traditional systems described by de Castro in his book. For example, it is worth contrasting his discussion of the role of hogs in China with the image presented by modern hog factories in the Midwest: burning up high-value products such as cereals and soybeans and generating huge amounts of unrecyclable waste which ends up polluting the rivers and streams. In the same vein, his discussion of the theories of the English scientist Sir Albert Howard—who, perhaps, goes too far in his condemnation of Western technologies—indicates alternative methods of developing agricultural production. In China, for example, some of the technologies proposed by Howard have been implemented on a large scale.

VI

The main features of the colonial system are analyzed in *The Geopolitics of Hunger*. The methods employed in colonial exploitation depended on the "rationalization" of the socioeconomic (agricultural) system—which in fact meant its "destruction" and integration into a market economy that had already been attained. However such methods might vary according to circumstances, they had one thing in common: the use of violence.

It was no easy task to turn peasant subsistence farmers into producers of agricultural commodities for the world market. Nor was it a simple matter to go on to uproot them entirely, transforming them into urbanized jobseekers in their own countries or the colonial metropolises. This disruption of peasant societies and their economic bases led to the monopolization of international markets by a few capitalist countries, with the United States playing the leading role. In fact, the current trend in the international market for staple food products represents a reversal of the previous flow of commercial exchanges. The industrialized world, in pre-World War II days a net importer of cereals and oil-seed products, is now a net exporter of the same products.

The shifting of the food balance to the disadvantage of the underdeveloped world is a result of the colonialist policies of the former imperialist countries. For, despite the "independence" of the former colonies, they have actually become neocolonial states. Let us focus for a moment on the policies being implemented in the Sahel regions of Africa, keeping in mind that they are only the specific manifestations of a more general process of capitalist development.

At the end of World War II, France did away with impressed labor, the most blatantly exploitative feature of its colonial system.[29] Formerly, administrative or military power had been used to force men into building roads, railways, and ports, or into working on plantations or collective fields, raising crops for the colonial power. Taxation—first in kind, later in money—had a powerfully destructive effect on social organization, compelling the peasants to seek out sources of money within the capitalist sphere of production. Agricultural development projects were devised, which aimed at supplying goods for export (cotton, for example) and involved the resettlement of peasants on developed lands; but the peasants repeatedly tried to escape and rejoin their communities and villages. "The main feature of labor exploitation during this colonial period is the tendency to separate the laborer from his environment. . . . Thus, colonization did not favor the reproduction of the labor force. On the contrary, it applied the same policy to this resource as it had to other natural resources, the policy of destructive exploitation. It could exploit the labor force only through the separation of the laborers from their means of production and reproduction, without giving them anything in exchange."

The neocolonialism of the post-World War II era was based on a different principle: "the use of the productive and reproductive capacity of the community to bear the cost of the production and reproduction of the labor force." Thus, "hidden unemployment," normally viewed with alarm by bourgeois economists, could be turned into a means of profitable exploitation for the capitalist sector. The village or the family unit is made responsible for basic subsistence needs, for the production and reproduction of a labor force which is then made available to the capitalist sector of the colonial economy. Since the colonial economy bears no responsibility for production and reproduction which takes place within the subsistence economy—and therefore outside of the sphere of capitalist relations—the cost of such a labor force can be extremely low. Under such an arrangement, the subsistence economy can be left to take care of itself while exclusive emphasis is placed on the development and expansion of production for the capitalist economy. Thus the export-goods sector receives priority, since the colonial or neo-colonial "independent" states derive a high proportion of their income from levies on exports.

Taxes force peasants to become involved in the capitalist sector of the colonial economy, since there alone is cash to be found. This paves the way for all the cynical manipulation and abuse so common in underdeveloped countries, particularly since "for peasants money has no [intrinsic] value. There is no way to measure the relative productivity of domestic activities and of paying commercial activities. And such a measurement is especially difficult given the fact that it would mean comparing a use value (labor power used for subsistence purposes) with an exchange value (money derived from the sale of commodities)."

Such a system is highly unstable, tending toward an expansion of the commercial sector and, at the same time, toward a deterioration of conditions in the sphere of subsistence agriculture. The fate of subsistence agriculture, in fact, is sealed, caught as it is in the specific contradiction of the system. On the one hand, the colonial economy is opposed to any investments or improvements that would increase the cost of producing and reproducing the domestic labor force. All its resources are devoted to the commercial sector, condemning the subsistence economy to stagnate at a low level of productivity. The encroachments of the capitalist economy and its development at the expense of the subsistence economy, as well as the unfolding specific contradiction of the system, result in endemic food shortages which jeopardize the very existence of the system.

On the other hand, faced with food shortages, peasants will tend to withdraw from the production of export goods and go back to subsistence agriculture. Such a possibility frightens the huge class of bureaucrats which lives off the surplus product of the peasants' labor. The obvious answer is to get staples or cereals from foreign sources or from Food for Peace surpluses. The result, no less obvious, is to make the neocolonial countries dependent on the world market. Their commercial sectors expand to include trade in those staples formerly produced by their own subsistence agriculture, thus further exacerbating the crisis in the agricultural sector.

At this stage, the process of primitive accumulation is almost complete. Drought, a natural phenomenon, leads to mass starvation, a social phenomenon rooted in the process of capitalist development. Humanitarian concern for the victims of Sahel should not overshadow the fact that they are victims of capitalist development and not, as the media would have us believe, of a natural disaster. For capitalist countries, international organizations, and local bourgeoisies or bureaucracies, the depopulation of vast areas of land, the extermination of nomadic peoples, means new opportunities for profit. New frontiers, purged of their "Indians," are being opened up and it is easy to guess who the "ranchers" will be.

The decline in subsistence agriculture has not been offset by a boom in export crops, such as peanuts. Countries producing peanuts and tropical oil seeds in general have run into formidable competition from U.S. soybeans and cottonseeds, not only on the world market but within their own economies. Soybean oil, once foreign to the eating habits of the people of North Africa, is now being widely consumed in this area, thanks to the passage of the Foreign Trade and Assistance Act of 1954 and the dumping of large quantities of this oil by philanthropic organizations. Olive oil, meanwhile, has been diverted toward the markets of developed countries.

Competitive pressure from developed countries has also been felt in other areas; fiber production and rubber, for example, have had to compete with synthetic fibers and U.S. cotton. The impact of this competition is particularly grave given the fact that whereas the developed countries have erected a number of barriers—tariffs, subsidies, quotas—to the importation of goods from underdeveloped areas, the underdeveloped countries, in turn, are unable to protect their own markets, to subsidize their own agriculture, and are thus powerless to control the activities of the corporations which trade in and transport their crops.

The growth of international trade, one of the most prominent features of the world economic picture since 1958, has tended to generate increasingly fierce competition between commodities and crops produced by very different economic and social structures. The Senegalese peasant with his hoe competes with the American farmer and his 100-horsepower tractor.

The expansion of a powerful agribusiness complex in the Western world and the decline of traditional agriculture, even of some export crops, in colonial and neocolonial countries has led to a reversal of trade patterns between the underdeveloped and developed areas of the world. As noted previously, before World War II the developed world as a whole was importing cereals and oil seeds; the United States, for example, imported soybean oil from Manchuria.[30] Now the developing countries are the importers; their raw grain imports soared from 12.4 million tons between 1949 and 1951, to 34.4 million tons from 1966 to 1968, and up to 36 million tons in 1972. (These figures do not include China.) The F.A.O. estimates that by 1985 the developing countries, the satellites of the capitalist world, will show a deficit of 85 million tons, as against 16 million tons from 1969 to 1971.[31] The financial drain on the limited resources of these countries has been immense, with costs increasing from one billion dollars in 1955, to four billion in 1972-73, and ten billion in 1973-74.

The world market is controlled by a small group of capitalist countries, dominated by the United States. In 1973 the United States accounted for 44 percent of world wheat exports, Canada for 17 percent, Australia for 9 percent, and France for 13 percent. Together, these four countries made up 83 percent of world exports, a situation even the most conservative economist would describe as monopolistic. The largest wheat producer, the U.S.S.R. (25-30 percent of world production) has traditionally been a small-scale exporter, focusing mainly on markets in other socialist countries. Trade in feed grains shows a similar pattern: in 1973, the United States supplied 60 percent of world exports (primarily corn), the other exporters being Canada (barley), France (corn, barley), Argentina, and Australia.

The United States is also the largest rice exporter—between one quarter and one third of world exports. (Thailand is the next largest, and Pakistan and Italy also carry some weight.) Although it is the biggest exporter of rice, the United States actually produces very little rice, a negligible percentage of world tonnage.

Finally, the United States has a monopoly over the export of soybeans. This is a commodity of crucial importance, since soybeans supply more than 50 percent of all edible oil exports and a much higher proportion of world exports of high-protein meal. The recent development of soybean pro-

duction in Brazil—a rapid, even explosive development remi-
niscent of the sugar-cane, rubber, gold, and coffee cycles
described by de Castro—has just begun to chip away at the
U.S. share of world exports (currently about 70 percent). We
might add, however, that the growth of the Brazilian soybean
industry—its expansion from almost nothing in the mid-
1960's to an output of 9 to 10 million tons (about a quarter
of U.S. production) in 1975—has taken place partly at the
expense of the production of black beans, one of the dietary
staples of the Brazilian people.

The monopolistic structure that characterizes the export
markets of the world is also typical of world trade in general.
Control is in the hands of a few multinational corporations,
most of them based in the United States, which have extended their operations to include the storage, transportation, and processing of grain, oil seeds, and other agricultural
products. The power of these companies is based on a number of factors: an extensive network of computerized data;
close ties with the state apparatus (is there such a scarcity of
managerial and administrative talent in the United States that
the same people divide their time between the corporations
and the Department of Agriculture?); easy access to the
enormous amount of working capital needed to finance their
operations; and finally, as we have already mentioned, the
material base—grain elevators, barges, trucks, freight cars,
ships, and factories—without which there can be no genuine
power.

The most crucial factor in the control of world markets is
the building up of reserve productive capacity (which only
rich countries can afford), particularly in domestic operations. Such reserves can provide an important element of
adaptability. Those that can be mobilized on the spot (the
diversion of cropland acreage, for example, or the genetic
diversification of breeding strains) offer the same sort of
short-term flexibility as do ordinary reserves of working

stock. In the long run, other sources of productive capacity can be tapped. For instance, there are still huge areas of land that could be cultivated more intensively or subjected to more extensive double-cropping. The result of all this is a powerful, dynamic agribusiness complex, capable of rapid adjustment to various levels of aggregate demand and working in close cooperation with the federal government, which establishes goals for agricultural production on the basis of various factors, including foreign policy considerations, expansion of commercial markets, and domestic conditions. Thus, when India was on the verge of famine, large quantities of U.S. wheat were shipped and the production in the U.S. was adjusted accordingly: all acreage restrictions on wheat were suspended in 1967 and 1968.

The world food crisis that started in 1972 has once again put the problems of agricultural production and nutrition in the forefront. The crisis should be envisaged in the perspective of important trends already described rather than in terms of weather vagaries. It should be pointed out that the term world food crisis is inadequate. If masses of people have starved in underdeveloped countries, if the low-income classes of developed countries suffered badly from price increases for food, the United States and its agribusiness complex were the great beneficiaries of the crisis. The export of agricultural products, for instance, rose from $8 billion in 1972 to $21.3 billion in 1974 (year ending in June). This excess in the agricultural trade balance almost matched the increase in oil prices.

The sales of wheat to the Soviet Union, which triggered the crisis, are a good illustration of the control exercised by the United States government and the multinational corporations of the grain trade:

> All the contracting parties received substantial benefits:
> World prices remained stable during the negotiations and rose rapidly thereafter.

Unaware of the deal, some of the farmers sold their crops at a relatively low price.

The companies were able to collect large subsidies making up the difference between domestic prices and a world price.[32]

The operation, in short, first "suspended the law of supply and demand within a small circle of friends, then let it run wild on a world scale."

Other points in *The Geopolitics of Hunger* are worth discussion. De Castro's views and criticisms of foreign aid, for instance, remain liberal. His analysis of the Green Revolution is technical even if he is rather circumspect as to what could really be expected in the long run. In fact, all this is in line with the task de Castro had in mind: to destroy on a scientific basis the position of the neo-Malthusians. In so doing, de Castro has gone much further and has given us a masterpiece, which stands as an extraordinary document of its era. More important still, the book has withstood the test of time; readers of this welcome new edition will find that its fundamental message—that "hunger is a man-made plague"—is, tragically, just as relevant today as it was thirty years ago.

—J.P.B., 1975

Part I
The Universal
Phenomenon
of Hunger

1
The Taboo of Hunger

The history of man from the beginning has been the history of his struggle for daily bread. It is very difficult to understand how this pretentiously superior animal, this lord and master of the universe who has won so many battles against the forces of nature, should have failed to obtain a decisive victory in his struggle for subsistence. For we know from scientific observation that even after some hundreds of thousands of years of striving, at least two thirds of the world's population live in a permanent state of hunger.[1] A billion and a half human beings* can still not find the means of escaping this most terrible affliction of society.

Is it possible to consider hunger as a phenomenon inherent in life itself, a natural and inevitable contingency like death, or should it be regarded as a social evil, a plague of man's own making? It is with this dangerous and delicate question that my book will deal. Because of its explosive political and social implications, the subject until very recently has been one of the taboos of our civilization. It has been our highly vulnerable Achilles' heel, a subject that could not safely be discussed in public. Like sex, hunger was shameful, indecent, unclean. It was made untouchable, taboo.[2]

* Two billion.

Buddha, in antiquity, said that "hunger and love constitute the germ of all human history," and much later Schiller observed that "hunger and love rule the world." Nevertheless, until the end of World War II very little had even been written about the phenomenon of hunger. The number of books on the subject in any language was shockingly scanty—especially in view of the abundant literature on matters of obviously secondary social importance. What were the hidden motives that led our culture to abstain from dealing with the problem of hunger, from trying to get at the root of it? It is strange to find that its narrow sensual aspect had been ignored, what Spinoza called the impulse and instinct that has served as the motive force of human evolution; but it is even more curious to observe the oppressive silence that had always surrounded its broader influence as a universal calamity.

The disparity is most surprising when we compare the case of hunger with other calamities that have repeatedly devastated the world—with, for example, wars and epidemics. It then becomes painfully clear that hunger was the least studied and discussed, the least understood in its cause and effects. For each study of the problems of hunger there were a thousand publications on the problems of war. A ratio of more than a thousand to one! Yet, as this book abundantly demonstrates, the human waste that has resulted from hunger is considerably greater than that produced by wars and epidemics combined.[3] The damage has been more extensive in the number of victims and a great deal more serious in its biological and social consequences. In the last century the Swiss scientist Waser pointed out that the loss of life brought about by the plague or by war was usually made up in an average period of ten years, while the survivors of great famines were broken for the rest of their lives. But to dissipate any remaining doubts as to the unquestionable leadership of hunger's destructive powers, it is sufficient to emphasize the universally recognized fact that hunger has been the most common and effective cause of war and that it has been the advance agent that prepared the ground for the outbreak of the great epidemics.[4]

Hunger, then, has unquestionably been the most potent source of social misfortunes, but our civilization has kept its eyes averted, afraid to face the sad reality. War has always been loudly discussed. Hymns and poems have been written to celebrate its glorious virtues as an agent of selection. In this civilization of ours, which began mercantilist and ended militarist, an attempt was even made to demonstrate by scientific theory that the existence of war was necessary and in accord with the natural law of life. Thus, while war became a leitmotiv of Western thought, hunger remained only a vulgar sensation, the repercussions of which were not supposed to emerge from the realm of the subconscious. The conscious mind, with ostentatious disdain, denied its existence.

The Prejudices of Western Civilization

There were several motives for this conspiracy of silence. First, there was the question of morality; the phenomenon of hunger, whether hunger for food or sexual hunger, is a primary instinct, and there was something shocking about this to a rationalist culture that tried by all possible means to make reason dominate instinct in human conduct. Instinct was held to be animal, while reason alone had social value, and our civilization attempted systematically, though unsuccessfully, to deny the creative power of instinct, treating it as low and indecent.

Since the end of the eighteenth century Western culture, with its Encyclopedists and idealist philosophers, has put forward a concept of man and his behavior that renders him virtually angelic—a being who, from cannibal beginnings, soared on wings of culture to the purest intellectualism, free of animal impulses. But in reality each arrogant optimist of that infatuated nineteenth century, as he spoke of man's magnificent rise and his perfection, felt the indiscreet needling, in his most intimate being, of hunger and sexual desire, the remnants of his primitive bestiality. These cultural idealists thought that they could master the impulses by hiding and smothering them; European civilization made it a point not to mention these subjects. "And for a whole century, an extremely long century," said Stefan Zweig, "this cowardly moral conspiracy of silence dominated Europe."[5] Until one day a genius, inconveniently and providentially, broke the oppressive quiet.

To the pretended astonishment of official science and contemporary morality, Sigmund Freud declared sex to be a force so intense that it extends to, and indeed dominates, the consciousness. Man, before everything else, is sex. This view of mankind was not entirely surprising, but it was inconvenient. Each of Freud's learned colleagues had felt the conflict of sexual instincts in himself, like a hidden abscess he dared not lance publicly for fear of revealing the pus. Freud broke open the abscess. Singlehanded, with opposition and disapproval on all sides, he carried out the lifesaving operation. Since then, it has been possible to speak of sex in a voice above a whisper.

Hunger and Economic Imperialism

There were reasons even stronger than prejudice, reasons rooted in the shrouded world of economic interest, for suppressing discussion of hunger. Dominant and privileged minorities used their deftest sleight of hand to keep the question of hunger from the attention of the modern spirit.

It was to the advantage of economic imperialism and international commerce, both controlled by profit-seeking minorities, that the production, distribution, and consumption of food products be regarded as purely business matters rather than as phenomena of the highest importance to society as a whole.

The world's geography expanded in the sixteenth century, and colonial economies followed the extending horizon, raising European civilization toward its zenith of splendor. In the seemingly fine world of imperial Europe there was no place for ugly relevations of starvation, particularly since hunger, too, was a product of the colonial system. Hunger has been chiefly created by the inhuman exploitation of colonial riches, by the latifundia and one-crop cultures which lay waste the colony, so that the exploiting country can take too cheaply the raw materials its prosperous industrial economy requires. For economic misery was hidden from the world's eyes; tragedies like that of China, where in the nineteenth century some one hundred million individuals starved to death, or like that of India, where twenty million people died of hunger in the last thirty years of the century, were glossed over.[6]

Western literature, inheriting Western culture, bent to its interests and blinded by its splendor, was an accomplice in its silence. A very few authors dared break the taboo and communicate their dark visions of the subterranean world of starvation and suffering: Knut Hamsun, in his masterly novel *Hunger*, a detailed report of the confused and contradictory sensations produced by his own hunger; Panait Istrati, wandering famished across the glimmering plains of Rumania; Felekov and Alexander Neverov, describing dramatically the intense black hunger of Russia in convulsion; George Fink, starving in the gray and sordid suburbs of Berlin; and John Steinbeck telling, in *The Grapes of Wrath*, the story of the Joad family's epic journey of hunger across the richest lands of the richest country in the world. These and a few others were voices crying in the wilderness of indifference.

Science, then, was catastrophically unprepared for the Allied liberation of the Nazi concentration camps. On April 12, 1945, Allied medical men and Red Cross technicians entered the horror camp of Bergen-Belsen to find thousands of people in the last stages of starvation. They did not know what to do for them. They began medical treatment by feeding, orally, predigested foods or, in the graver cases, by giving intravenous injections. The results were disastrous. Ingestion by mouth was very poorly tolerated, and injections increased the edema that had come from starvation. Doctors and nurses had to watch the horrible reactions of their patients, who thought that this was a new form of torture. It took time and the sacrifice of many lives to learn that the best nourishment for such cases was skim milk.

Jack Drummond, the great English specialist on nutrition, published an account of the Bergen-Belsen episode in 1946. In spite of the enormous progress that had been made in the science of nutrition, he said, and "although in our lifetimes millions have died from starvation in Russia, China, India, and elsewhere, it was not possible to find clear-cut advice how to resuscitate people who are near death from this cause. That fact," he commented, "is a terrible reflection on our lack of concern for the human race as a whole."[7]

The story of Bergen-Belsen's liberation constitutes a tremendous accusation against our Western civilization. It was necessary for famine to return and ravish Europe itself before Western science took an interest in combating it. Two terrible world wars were necessary, as well as a great social revolution—the Russian Revolution, in which seventeen million people perished, twelve million of them from starvation —before Western civilization was persuaded that trying to conceal the reality of hunger was like trying to shut out the sun with a sieve.

The force of inexorable circumstance finally began to overcome the taboo on hunger. Scientists became interested, and they were permitted to study the subject objectively. Nations were urged to publish statistics on the real living conditions of their populations, and there was a move to stimulate publication of reports and essays on the forbidden subject. [Today it is different. The fight against hunger has become one of the fundamental concerns of our time. It has inspired a great many publications, and the world campaign against hunger organized in 1959 by the Food and Agriculture Organization of the United Nations gave rise to what could be termed an "outpouring" of works on the subject. The outpouring is most welcome and in dramatic contrast to the silence of twenty years ago.]

The World and the Social Revolution

The underlying reason for such a radical change of attitude is that the world is now passing through a revolutionary phase in its history. The two world wars and the Russian Revolution were no more than visible symptoms of the developing world revolution, cataclysmic manifestations of the impact of social forces seeking to remove obstacles from their path. But in order to make the dangerous statement that we are living in a world revolution, it is necessary to define "revolution."

The word "revolution" is used here not in the sense of violent overthrow of constituted authority and the seizure of power but as meaning a process of transformation of the whole, a historical transmutation that replaces one world of social beliefs by another in which the former social values no longer have meaning. I use the term "revolutionary phase of history" to refer to what Ortega y Gasset calls the "historical crisis." The Spanish philosopher explains the historical process as taking place in two ways: by the successive change of things within our world or by a change in the world as a whole. The former is a question of "historical evolution," while the latter represents a "crisis" or "historical revolution." In our times we are witnessing a complete overhauling of the social systems and ways of life that were in effect at the beginning of the century; we are passing from one social era to another.

Julian Huxley attempted to characterize the two eras of our age by calling that which is past the "era of economic man" and that of the future the "era of social man."[8] And, indeed, the most noticeable feature of the violent contrast between these two worlds (both embraced by the life of one generation) is a shift in the center of interest. Until World War I, Western civilization, with its exaggerated economism, was exclusively preoccupied with the technical domination of the forces of nature. And while it was thus engaged with the problems of economic exploitation and the creation of wealth, man and his problems were almost entirely forgotten. In the postwar world, however, what we see on all sides—in both the capitalist West and the sovietized East—is a concentrated interest in biological man as a concrete entity, a sort of priority conceded to human problems over strictly economic problems. This does not mean that in the "era of social man" economics will be relegated to a secondary level but rather that, at least in the minds of theoreticians of development, it will be oriented to function in the interest of human welfare. The democracies in our day have shown themselves to be deeply concerned with the protection and biological revalorization of man, while the U.S.S.R. still articulates its five-year plans in accordance with the principle of a Communist humanism, even if this idea is not always respected in action. Present-day economic activity can no longer be simply the art of establishing lucrative enterprises; it must also be a science that teaches methods of promoting "a greater quantity of economic welfare." In this new era an attempt must be made to have money serve man, instead of making man the slave of money and to organize production to satisfy the fundamental needs of various groups of human beings, rather than let men go on killing each other in an attempt to slake their insatiable thirst for the profits of production.

An interest in man and in the rehumanization of culture is theoretically the common denominator of both of the great economic systems that are now struggling for universal supremacy. It seems to me that capitalist democracy and Russian "democracy" must not represent two worlds in irreconcilable struggle but rather two poles of a single world. As social poles they have their differences and peculiarities, but the growing interest of man in man himself and the anxious search for means of collective betterment mark an area where the two systems must converge. As they come closer together they must necessarily resolve their conflicts, since they must both face the circumstance that men who live together have to get along with each other. [Unfortunately, despite the dawning consciousness of these problems on political leaders in recent years, the industrial and post-industrial civilizations produced by the technological explosion are a long way from bringing man the benefits that he can justly expect from economic expansion.]

The Violation of the Taboo

As our taboos were broken and our social goals started to change, interesting studies of hunger began to appear. In 1928 the League of Nations put the problem of alimentation on its permanent agenda; the League's Organization on Hygiene sponsored investigations in several countries and a series of valuable reports was published. The very first inquiries, carried out by strictly scientific methods in the most varied regions of the world, revealed the alarming fact that more than two thirds of humanity live in a permanent state of hunger.

This shocking situation, at a crucial moment of history when our only hope of finding the way to survival is to recognize the great errors of our civilization, has led the conscience of mankind to a radical change of attitude toward the problem. We have set out to face it with courage and to solve it with energy.

Evidence of this new spirit was the first conference on the process of postwar reconstruction, the Food Conference called by the United Nations at Hot Springs in 1943. There the experts of forty-four nations frankly confessed the nutritional facts of their countries' lives and planned the joint steps necessary to fulfill their needs. They proposed to erase, or at least to lighten, those black areas that represent, on maps of qualitative demography, the nuclei of undernourished and starving populations. These groups, in their physical and cultural inferiority, in their alarming death rates and their incidence of deficiency diseases like beriberi, pellagra, scurvy, xerophthalmia, rickets, osteomalacia, endemic goiter, and anemia, show their organic lacks, their total or specific hungers for one, for several, sometimes for all the elements indispensable to human nourishment.

Hunger is the most degrading of adversities; it demonstrates the inability of existing culture to satisfy the most fundamental human necessities, and it always implies society's guilt. To combat and exterminate it, as the Food Conference hoped to do, it will be necessary to have broader and more intense studies of nutrition throughout the world. Every student's observations ought to be published, as contributions to the preparation of a universal plan.

One great obstacle to adequate planning is our lack of knowledge of the problem as a whole. The question of feeding the peoples of the world involves a complex of manifestations, biological, economic, and social. Most scientific studies of nutrition limit themselves to one or another of its aspects and give only a unilateral view of its problems. They are almost always written by physiologists, chemists, or economists, specialists whose professional lives are limited to one field. [The world's political leaders and the heads of international organizations make public and generally accept the specialists' work. But theirs is an abstract conception of the problem, an idea formed and accepted so as to ease their consciences.

The real problem, which is political, continues to be pushed out of sight—and therefore remains. In almost all countries of the world, governments represent particular dominant groups and frequently have no real interest in solving the problem of hunger. This is the heart of the matter. Governments have never been seriously interested in developing nutrition policies, sensing vaguely (or sometimes clearly) that to do so would benefit neither themselves nor the groups they represent. Some governments go further and actually pursue "policies of hunger," more or less indirectly, in the interests of large industry. One flagrant example is the destruction of food stocks in many industrialized countries, aimed at maintaining market prices by limiting the supply of produce. A recent United Press International dispatch noted that in the United States in 1968 at least 10 million persons suffered from hunger and malnutrition and that this situation resulted "from a political and economic system that spends millions to remove produce from the market, to limit the amount produced, and to take land out of production in order to maintain and guarantee the profits of the producer."]

The Civilization of the Specialists

Such narrowness of outlook is characteristic of Western civilization. Since the middle of the nineteenth century a kind of university instruction has developed that is no longer interested in transmitting a unified image of the world but rather in isolating, and mutilating, facets of reality in the supposed interest of science. The tremendous impact of scientific progress produced a fragmentation of culture and pulverized it into little grains of learning. Each scientific specialist seized his granule and turned it over and over beneath the powerful lens of his microscope, striving to penetrate its microcosm, with a marvelous indifference to and a towering ignorance of everything around him. Recently in Europe and the United States an extreme development of this type of university education has created within the culture a sort of civilization *sui generis*—a specialists' civilization—directed by men whose scientific outlook is rigorous but who suffer from a deplorable cultural and political myopia. Ortega y Gasset has called them the "new barbarians—men ever more and more learned, and less and less cultured."[9] Worst of all, such men are the dominant type of our cultural elite, representatives of the social dynamic that has brought us to what Rathenau so aptly called "the vertical invasion of the barbarians." The narrow specialists, "men who know more and more about less and less," are one of the most dangerous elements in our cultural life. [If the consumer society produced by this type of culture that mutilates human intelligence and imagination is everywhere under attack today, it is because we have grasped that it can never lead to an authentic social well-being in which the needs of both body and spirit are satisfied.]

As a consequence of the specialists' techniques, we find that even after the cultural barriers were broken few students faced the problem of hunger in its world-wide perspective, its multiple and correlated aspects. Some serious researchers, trying to explain and solve the problem of famine, did direct attention to our classic dilemma of food production in relation to population. The works of John Boyd-Orr, Imre Ferenczi, Frank Boudreau, and a few others can be considered to have a broad outlook and to be genuinely scientific. Some of the reports of the Food and Agriculture Organization, such as the *World Food Survey* published in 1946, have the same objectivity. Unfortunately, the problem of hunger constitutes such a pointed social question that most of the speculative works dealing with it are not free of current political prejudices and superstitions, [or of a deliberate desire to evade the problem because of social or individual pride.]

The Generosity and Stinginess of Nature

Two schools of thought about world hunger are, in my opinion, really dangerous to the future of humanity because they falsify the social reality of the problem. One theory attempts to prove that famine is a natural and incurable phenomenon; the other offers as our only salvation a forced reduction in the world's birth rate. These dispiriting and pessimistic theories can be described as products of a world in transition, speculations of minds formed in a cultural structure that has since been overthrown. Their authors refuse to recognize the social revolution as a *fait accompli* and spin their thoughts out of data that are nothing more than hangovers and phantoms. One characteristic of historical crises, Ortega y Gasset says, is the way old social convictions tend to lose their value before new values, which will give direction to the thought and conduct of the future, are put in order. Many people are left with no way of knowing what to think and withdraw into the past to overcome their inner emptiness.

The contention that famine results from a kind of natural

law has no basis in scientific knowledge. Analysis of certain fundamental statistics will show how artificial that notion is. The oceans cover 71 percent of the surface of the earth, and the remaining 29 percent is the solid part of our planet. This land covers an area of about 36 billion acres of which 30 percent is forested, grassy plains are 20 percent, 18 percent is mountains, and 32 percent desert, either torrid or polar. According to 1940's estimates by United States agricultural specialists such as Robert Salter and Holmer Shantz, only 16 billion acres—half of the land surface of the planet—could then be agriculturally exploited by known methods of soil utilization.[10] Desert and mountainous regions were not considered arable, although more recently there have been notable triumphs of agricultural technique in such areas.[11] Hundreds of thousands of acres of tropical desert have been made fertile by modern irrigation, and the Russians, with their surprising agricultural processes, are adding a wide strip of polar desert to the productive area of their country. [Regions like the Kola peninsula, more than three degrees latitude above the Arctic Circle, are now producing wheat, barley, turnips, carrots, peas, radishes, pumpkins, and cucumbers for the nourishment of their inhabitants. Even farther north, on the Taymyr peninsula (the northernmost territory of the Euro-Asiatic land mass, only 850 miles from the North Pole), selected plants are being cultivated thanks to the methods of vernalization developed by the agronomist Lysenko, methods that adjust the growth cycle to the short period of the arctic summer. Thus oases exist in the middle of the polar desert, producing potatoes, corn, raspberries, and so on—an indisputable victory for technology. And at these latitudes the plants not only produce but produce well: one variety of potato cultivated north of the Arctic Circle yields well over eight tons per acre; in the center of the Euro-Asiatic land mass the average yield is slightly over four tons. In addition, extraordinary progress in genetics has made it possible not only to increase productivity but even to change the composition of the nutritive elements of certain plants, notably cereals; to speed up their growth and effect early maturation; and to increase the number of harvests in certain ecological areas.[12] All this could bring about an amazing multiplication of food produce.]

But even disregarding these experiments, whose economic value may be debatable, the most conservative figures of the American technicians demonstrate that hunger and famine do not result from any natural law. These calculations give mankind some 16 billion acres to cultivate, or 8 acres per individual of the world population. Authorities on agriculture and nutrition, studying the correlation of area cultivated and food supply in the light of modern knowledge of nutrition, have estimated that about two acres per person will supply the indispensable elements of a rational diet.[13] Cultivation according to that ratio would use one fourth of the world's arable land. As yet, the area cultivated has not reached 2 billion acres, an eighth of the earth's natural possibilities.*

Essentially, worldwide hunger is not a problem of production limited by the coercion of natural forces [but of a politics that is based essentially on economic and social inequality and on the premeditated division of the world into ruling and dominated groups. The rulers use hunger as a subtle and effective political instrument.] Frank Boudreau points out that "we have been more successful in producing food than in properly distributing it."[14] War and hunger are man-made. That thesis will be supported in another chapter, but it is worth noting here that anthropologists can find no weapons or signs of organized warfare in the paleontological deposits of the most primitive human groups, nor do their fossilized skeletons show marks of dietary deficiencies. The skeletons of more advanced societies are engraved with the

---

* 3.2 billion acres, one fifth of the possibilities.

evidence of dietary lacks, the biological etchings of hunger. It can be concluded that hunger and war arrived when man had reached a stage in culture when he began to accumulate reserves and to defend his collected wealth; they began, that is, with the difficulties man created in the distribution of natural riches.

The Malthusian Scarecrow

Another theory of hunger accuses nature of provoking this calamity by an indirect mechanism: endowing man with excessive powers of reproduction and thus inviting over-population of the earth. The so-called neo-Malthusians subscribe to this idea. They would revive the doctrines brought forth by the English economist, Thomas Robert Malthus, at the end of the eighteenth century.[15] The first industrial experiments gave the impression that machines could replace men completely, and some people came to feel that the production of human machines must be reduced to keep them from competing with iron ones. In England, which was the cradle of industrialism, Malthus's theories were widely accepted. Then too, as Alfred Sauvy claims, the fear of nascent socialism was responsible for the creation as well as the acceptance of Malthusian theory.[16] Malthus found the increase in world population a great danger to its economic equilibrium, and in defense of this thesis he fathered the hypothesis that population increases in geometrical progression and the food supply in arithmetical progression. Thus as people reproduce, food production becomes irremediably insufficient for their necessities.

Malthus's theory lacked a scientific basis. His first error was to consider the growth of population as an independent variable, isolated from other social phenomena, whereas in fact such increase is strictly dependent on political and economic factors. His notion of a natural law governing the growth of population was challenged by Marx, who pointed out that what really occurs are historical tendencies or cycles which change from one period to another in accordance with changing social organizations. Further, history itself has completely disproved the predictions of Malthus. For a time after the publication of his theories the growth of world population seemed to confirm his predictions, but before the end of the last century the increase had lost its impetus. Fertility began to decline in various countries, and side by side with the specter of overpopulation appeared that of underpopulation.

The central doctrine of Malthus "was thus completely contradicted by historical evolution," says the well-known demographer Imre Ferenczi.[17] Dr. W. R. Aykroyd, then director of the Division of Nutrition of the F.A.O., wrote in 1937 that "now in Western civilization the specter raised by Malthus has been laid."[18] Yet his theory, long buried in the ruins of his frightening predictions, has lately been dug up and used to project new and still more terrifying forecasts, culminating in the prophecy of the end of a world depopulated by famine.

The revival of Malthusian theory has been possible because our period of history generates a collective receptiveness similar to that of Malthus's day. The English economist lived in a time of revolution—the industrial revolution—when people were nervous and doubtful about the future, a state of mind recurring, on a larger scale, in our social revolution. The present world situation involves such a radical transformation of social processes that it is quite impossible to foresee the future of the world. Julian Huxley has said that the present revolution, as among revolutions, is highly revolutionary!

Our blind flight into the unknown tends to frighten prudent spirits, and fear leads them now, as it did when Malthus lived, to attribute social unrest to the sheer number of human beings. When the neo-Malthusians say that mankind is starving and condemned to perish in universal famine because of its inadequately controlled birth rate, they are simply blaming the hungry for the fact that there is hunger. It seems to them that famished populations, raising the demographic pressure of the world by their delirium of reproduction, are criminals.

These criminals are guilty of the crime of hunger, for in the final analysis the neo-Malthusian theory is one of the born starveling, who starves because he is born to starve, just as the criminal, in the old Lombrosian theory, kills and robs because he is born to do so. Like born criminals, the starving deserve an exemplary punishment, and so they are condemned to extermination, either by individual starvation or by controlling reproduction until the born-to-starve disappear from the face of the earth. They are guilty of the masochistic crime of creating hunger and suffering it.

Here is the death sentence that William Vogt, standard-bearer of the neo-Malthusians, serenely pronounced upon those great hunger-makers, the Chinese: ". . . there is little hope that the world will escape the horror of extensive famines in China during the next few years. But from the world point of view, these may be not only desirable but indispensable."[19] Objective data, biological and social facts, will be brought to bear in another chapter on this issue of whether, as Vogt asserts, the famished themselves create the hunger, or whether the guilty are those who go in for neo-Malthusian theories while they defend and benefit from an imperialist economy.

The neo-Malthusians have invented nothing; their theories rest on the same precarious base that supported Malthus. To give a color of reality to their prophecies, they based their predictions on the average annual coefficient of population increase during the last two centuries and calculated that in three hundred years the world would have 21 billion inhabitants. This calculation has as little value as those of Malthus, which have already been disproved by history. The social changes of the next three hundred years are as likely to bring a decrease as an increase in the population.

Another alarmist idea with no basis in fact is that food production cannot be increased because we have reached the practical limits of soil utilization as well as of human saturation. The facts are, first, that of the 50 percent of the globe's soil that can be cultivated, only 10 percent is being used;[20] and second, that production per acre in most of the world could be greatly increased by rational agricultural practices. The special F.A.O. committee which edited the report of the *World Food Survey* in 1946 concluded that even then wheat production in India could be raised 30 percent in ten years: 20 percent by using fertilizers, 5 percent by introducing new varieties, and 5 percent through protection from insects and diseases. They went on to say that after that period additional measures could raise the increase to 50 percent. The same thing could have been done in many parts of the world. Raymond Christensen estimated that half the increase in agricultural production in the United States during World War II was due to the introduction of new techniques.

The crop yield of wartime Britain demonstrates overwhelmingly that necessity can inspire an agricultural expansion far beyond the limits of normal expectation. Before the war, Britain produced only one third of its food needs in calories and imported the other two thirds. Under pressure of the maritime blockade, production climbed until it took care of about 45 percent of the national needs. This came about through an increase of about 60 percent in the area under cultivation, which rose from 8.8 million to 14.5 million acres between 1939 and 1944. And all through the war, surprisingly enough, Britain's nutritional situation, far from deteriorating, improved greatly. At the end of the war the number of its undernourished had sensibly diminished. Considering that the soils of Britain are not among the world's richest, and that they have been farmed for at least two thousand years, it is no exaggeration to say that world food production could be equally increased if economic forces were directed toward that end with the determination that the British showed in meeting and surviving their siege of hunger.

[One need not subscribe to Marx's belief that production can be increased indefinitely to see that it is now a long way from reaching its upper limits. We must not be frightened by the ghost of Malthus, or, as I prefer to call it, the Malthusian scarecrows—for nothing brings his theory more vividly to mind than those grotesque figures that peasants set in the middle of their fields to ward off the birds. In the eyes of the neo-Malthusians, the population of the world is no band of hungry sparrows but a cloud of locusts that threatens to devour the entire produce of their little garden—a garden that, as we have seen, occupies no more than 10 percent of the surface of the globe. To combat this menace to the secure food supply and general standard of living now enjoyed by the rich, the neo-Malthusians of the world raise the scarecrows of their theories of overpopulation—but these theories have no more substance than phantoms.]

The World Carried Away by Water

Another, and growing, set of gloomy prophecies speculates about the effects of soil erosion.[21] There are those who contend that if water continues at its present rate to take up our soil and carry it to sea, the world will soon be a dead planet, its rocky skeleton showing, no flesh of soil or living skin of vegetation covering its ancient carcass. Obviously, there is a great deal of exaggeration and sensationalism in such a statement. No one denies that erosion is a cause of soil impoverishment capable of reducing its fertility and that it might eventually become a universal factor of hunger and misery, but this could happen only in the distant future, and only if no protective measures are taken. To make this perfectly clear, let me point out that there are in the first place two types of soil erosion: the natural process that goes on everywhere and the erosion provoked by man, which is limited to certain geographical areas. Natural erosion is a geological process inherent to the evolution of soils and to their vital equilibrium. It goes on slowly and almost imperceptibly, because as wind and water carry away the top layers of soil, building processes in the lower layers make up for the loss. What happens to the earth's skin is like what happens to our own.

When erosion is provoked by the interference of man, however, the process is different; losing a great deal more of its richness than can be simultaneously replaced, the soil may lose its fertility entirely. It has been estimated, according to Russell Lord, that in the United States alone 50 million acres of productive land have been rendered sterile by erosion.[22] But since it is not an uncontrollable natural phenomenon but rather a consequence of man's intervention, this stripping of the soil can perfectly well be halted by man. Probably, too, there is some exaggeration in the figures cited, the soil's loss of fertility being attributed exclusively to erosion when there are many other factors in its decline. If erosion were the devouring and insatiable monster that some people have painted, much of the world would already be barren and devoid of life. Take for example the Yellow River Valley, cradle of Chinese civilization. Specialists in the matter estimated that before the revolution of 1949 the river bore a cargo of 25 million tons of soil down to the sea every year. [(Now that projects aimed at controlling the problem have been carried out, we have no statistics on the tonnage of dirt annually washed away.)] Yet, for some five thousand years, a human anthill lived there, on a basis of agriculture. The valley, when still subject to this terrific loss from erosion, supported one of the densest rural populations in the world, estimated at more than a thousand inhabitants to the square mile. It can be deduced that erosion is not as black as it is painted; if it were, it would long ago have eaten all the land in China, swept away the "vegetable civilization" without leaving a trace, and long since have dropped it on the bottom of the China Sea.

The truth is that soil erosion and world overpopulation can at most be regarded as capable of causing hunger in future epochs, but never in our era. It seems a contradiction, even a subterfuge, to make so much noise about these latent possibilities and at the same time to pass by in silence the deleterious action of factors that operate before our eyes and that are responsible for the decadence of the world at present.

Hunger and Erosion of the Human Potential

Much more serious than erosion of the soil's riches, a process taking place in slow motion, is the violent erosion of human wealth, the deterioration of human beings through hunger and malnutrition. It is enough to note that throughout the Far East in the 1950's the roll of the undernourished included more than 90 percent of the population, or that in Latin America in the 1940's more than two thirds of the people were ill housed, ill clothed, and ill fed.[23] Or that in prewar England, as reported by the scientist John Boyd-Orr, later general director of the F.A.O., about 50 percent of the population suffered the ill effects of hunger, 40 percent undergoing partial starvation (specific deficiencies), and 10 percent generalized starvation—that is, serious deficiency of all the nutritional elements.

When Hitler's Germany called young Nazis to military service in 1936, only 75 percent of those presenting themselves could be accepted. By 1938, only 55 percent passed muster. The number of the incompetent, the weak-minded, and the deformed was growing alarmingly in the master race itself. In Argentina, a new country, it was found that between 1920 and 1940, among the men called up for military service, the percentage of rejections on physical grounds rose from 30 to 42.2. According to Guillermo Ruse, undernourishment was the principal cause for this increase in the proportion of physically unfit. Even in the United States, thought to be the best-fed country in the world, the Selective Service found during World War II that of the 14 million individuals examined, only 2 million, or 15 percent, really met the required physical standards. [In 1968 a commission of twenty-five experts brought together by the "War on Poverty" published a report in which they stated that 18 million Americans suffered from hunger and another 10 million from undernourishment. The United States Department of Health set the number of those who died of hunger during 1966 at 180,000.] It is not, then, any single group or race or country that is in decadence but all of mankind.

The purpose of this book is to study the terrible erosion that hunger is causing in the human race and its civilization, an erosion that threatens to blot from the earth all the gigantic work of man. If mankind does not try, urgently and on a wide scale, to stop this corrosive action, all the creations of humanity will soon crumble and be buried in the dust of time, and that will happen long before the wind and water have consumed the incalculable potential resources of the soil. The very humanity that is frightened today by the remote danger of a world turned desert through the exhaustion of its natural resources will witness the paradoxical arrival of a world depopulated while still pregnant with fertility and geographical wealth.

I intend no gruesome prophecy of the end of the world; on the contrary, I believe in the biological and social power of necessity [: the principle of teleonomy, the fundamental characteristic of all living systems that has always enabled humanity to survive, even at the most critical moments of history.] Hunger itself will be the guiding force, the mainspring of a social revolution that can gradually draw the world back from the abyss which threatens to swallow our civilization much more greedily than the oceans threaten to swallow our soils. This faith makes me an optimist, interpreting the social agitations and frictions of today as signs of the new era, in which the first requisite for social stability will be fulfilled—the conquest of hunger.

Although I am cheerful about the distant future, I am much more reserved in my optimism concerning the well-being and tranquility of the present generation and those immediately to come. I am afraid that these generations will have to pay too high a price for this magnificent conquest of hunger. Ideas take root in the world of social realities only in response to indisputable necessity at a given historical moment. A large part of the world is not yet entirely convinced of the necessity of doing away with hunger once and for all. There are people who consider it more important to maintain high standards of living for their own regions, and certain social privileges for their own class, than to fight the phenomenon of hunger as such on a world scale. And as long as large groups continue to look at things in this way, the world will go on being menaced by wars and revolutions, until the absolute necessity of survival at all costs forces the privileged to abandon their privileges.

This book was written in the hope that it would speed the maturation of this basic idea: that it is imperative to organize a world-wide campaign for the extermination of hunger. It is offered as a small contribution to our pressing collective task, the preparation of a plan for the revival of our civilization through the physical reconstitution of man. If it seems pretentious to suppose that my modest study can affect, however slightly, the universal fortunes of humanity, let me justify myself in Bertrand Russell's words: "There was never a moment in history when the contribution of individual thought and conscience was so necessary and important for the world as it is in our days." And the English philosopher went on to say that "all men, any man at all, can contribute to the betterment of the world."

Faith in human destiny, in the fruits of the social revolution through which we are living, and in the constructive force of human cooperation, led me into this bold attempt to take the measure of hunger in its universal aspect, to probe its depth and its extension in the various human groups. It is an ambitious plan indeed, requiring a balance of the strictest observation of facts and their most impartial interpretation. [This sort of research is both difficult and dangerous because the author constantly runs the risk of having his intentions misinterpreted and is also continually aware of the vast amount remaining to be done. In truth, even today we do not have an accurate, overall grasp of the problem of hunger. Our awareness is more emotional than rational, more felt than scientific. In terms of the struggle against hunger, we are still, unhappily, in the domain of paternalism, charity, aid, and humanitarianism, when we should be moving toward international economic solidarity and toward a human solidarity that would aim at security for all the world.]

Hunger is a word of many meanings, and I should like to define the way it is used here. The subject of this essay is not individual hunger, either in its physiological mechanism—so well known through the masterly works of Schuff, Luigi Luciana, Ramon Turró, W. B. Cannon, Ancel Keys, and other physiologists—or in its subjective psychological aspects, the material of the magnificent novels of hunger, of endemic or epidemic hunger (famine) affecting great human masses. I shall deal not only with total hunger, the complete debilitation resulting from lack of food which is called starvation and which is generally limited to extremely depressed areas or to exceptional situations, but also with the much more common and more numerically lethal "hidden" hunger which, for lack of certain indispensable nutritive elements, condemns whole population groups to die slowly of hunger although they eat every day. [For example, in 1967 a medical team from the World Health Organization showed how the Indians of Guatemala, whose diet consisted almost exclusively of cassava cakes, exhibited every form of undernourishment and were dying of hunger.]

These partial and specific hungers, which have been identified by modern science in their infinite variety throughout the world, are my chief concern in this study. My conception of hunger, then, embraces everything from the latent deficiencies commonly called conditions of undernourishment and malnutrition to absolute starvation. I have tried to write objectively, with a base in fact and observation, and not merely to speculate abstractly. I have documented my essay from a background that includes more than twenty years' experience in observing the problems of food and nutrition in Brazil—a country that for size and geographical variety is practically a continent—and from activities that brought contact with famous specialists at the successive world conferences of the F.A.O. as well as trips to four continents collecting material on the question of hunger.

Man, Not Parties

This subject is one that is highly charged with emotion, but I shall try, barring accidents, to take sides with no party but that of scientific truth. The English agriculturist C. S. Orwin wrote in the preface to F. W. Bateson's book on agriculture, "I have no politics where the land is concerned."[24] As Orwin studied the land, indifferent to party prejudice, so shall I examine the reality of hunger without preconceived ideas as to what political ideology can solve the problem. I shall attack hunger as the most pressing problem of all humanity, and therefore of all parties. If the reader feels a kind of passion in some passages of this book, it is passion for the truth, which is the poetry of science. The truth I seek is the total vision of a universal human problem.

If I sometimes seem to paint a rather black picture, and if my book is itself a chronicle of calamities, it is the result of writing in the heavy atmosphere that the world has been forced to breathe these last thirty years. The air we live in has been contaminated by corruption, frustration, and fear; it has suffocated us in the smoke of bombs and cannon and smothered us with censorship. Our voices are drowned by the clamor of war victims and the groans of the starving, [and by disputes even among those who know that the accumulation of wealth does not necessarily bring social progress and that the civilization of abundance has been our world's most fertile source of misery].

Hunger, a Man-made Plague

My first aim is to fix certain fundamental relationships that must be appreciated in order to plan a world policy of struggle against hunger. I propose to demonstrate that although hunger is a universal phenomenon, it is not the result of any natural necessity. The study of hunger in different regions of the world will make clear that human societies are ordinarily brought to the starvation point by cultural rather than natural forces, that hunger results from grave errors and defects in social organization, [as ruling groups strive to preserve outdated structures.] Hunger due to the inclemency of nature is an extraordinary catastrophe, while hunger as man-made blight is a "normal" condition in the most varied parts of the world.

Next I shall demonstrate that because all the world's parts are indissolubly linked into one living whole, it is no longer possible to let one region rot and starve without infecting the rest and threatening the whole world with death. These ideas will be developed in the first two parts of the book, where the world of hunger is analyzed as to its universal components and its regional peculiarities. The third section projects a world without hunger, a society freed from its terrible biological slavery. As we investigate ways of combating hunger, it will become clear that there are effective weapons other than a drastic and forcible reduction of the world's population. [The measures that ought to be used are those capable of promoting true economic development, and the sort that stem from changes in institutions and mentality, and also inevitably modify the curve of population growth. Relative overpopulation—for, basically, the idea of overpopulation is relative—is a result of underdevelopment and lack of education. Only the molding of well-developed human beings can re-establish a demographic balance; the partial and badly oriented application of scientific knowledge that now threatens the world cannot do so.[25]] To offset the neo-Malthusian preachment of birth control as our sole salvation, I shall present the point of view of modern geographers and social scientists, who no longer accept any form of rigid natural determinism. To concede that the earth sets a fixed, impassable limit to human population is to revert to the old geographical determination of the times of the nineteenth-century geographer Friedrich Ratzel, according to which nature lays down the law and man is no more than a passive pawn in the play of natural forces, devoid of creative will and powerless to escape the crushing authority of his environment. Nothing could be farther from the truth. Man, with his creative and inventive techniques, is well able to evade the coercion of nature, to free himself of the conception of geographical determinism, and to transform natural limitations into social opportunities.

Hunger as the Cause of Overpopulation

The crucial point of this essay is the argument that overpopulation does not cause starvation in various parts of the world but that starvation is the cause of overpopulation. This idea sounds paradoxical, since hunger, an agent of deterioration and death, seems unlikely to provoke an excessive increase in population. But in reality this is just what happens. Consider that three countries of the world that are held to be absolutely overpopulated are China, India, and Japan; [up until ten years ago these were the hungriest of nations, and the more starvation assailed them the more populated they became.] I shall explain in its proper place how hunger increases the fertility of the depressed groups suffering its permanent action. And from that evidence it is logical to deduce that although it is impossible to eradicate hunger by controlling the growth of population, it is perfectly possible to reverse the process and control the growth of population by doing away with starvation. Simply to retard the birth rate as the neo-Malthusians advocate would, with our contemporary economic framework, only diminish food production and thus increase starvation. The opposite procedure, however, that of protecting the world's demographic possibilities, reestablishing man at a healthier level, is sure to lead to greater food production. [For example, even today in regions where malaria rages, there are hundreds of millions of people too tired and weak to do more than lift food to their mouths. If the world really wanted to stamp out malaria, which is technically possible, this nonproductive group would become new agents of food production, thus improving nutritive conditions in the areas where they live. The same is true with respect to other widespread diseases: gastrointestinal maladies, certain parasites, sleeping sickness, yellow fever, etc.]

The Conquest of Hunger

My survey of the means that are available for overcoming hunger will begin by examining the possibilities of treating domestic plants and animals as food-producing machines whose output can be increased in quantity and quality. There are convincing examples of these possibilities. Between World War I and the 1950's, for instance, scientific breeding increased average milk production in Denmark from 2,000 to 3,200 quarts per capita, in England from 2,700 to 3,200, and in New Zealand from 2,000 to 3,100.[26]

Another and still more effective way to grow more food is to expand agriculture by farming new land and new kinds of soil and by introducing new plants and animals for food purposes. Then, too, there is the recourse of exploiting virtually untapped food reserves like the great wealth of the seas, and there is the possibility of raising living things in ocean waters to provide additional human subsistence.

This study will go on to investigate the problems of food distribution and to discuss the intelligent use of foods in accordance with the findings of the science of nutrition. My text will analyze, in short, both the productive forces and the social relations that must be brought into play in order to effect a readjustment and a fair redistribution of the means of human subsistence.

Only through such readjustment will there be hope for living in a world cleansed of the black and shameful areas of hunger. Only thus will a geography of hunger cease to exist, a tragically strange geography which, instead of describing the earth feeding man, presents man serving simply to feed the earth. What we have now is a map of misery, spotted in Asia, Africa, America, and elsewhere with areas where man apparently is born for no purpose but to die and fertilize the earth. Ours is a geography of ugly scenes like those in [India, where "the land does not belong to man, but man belongs to the land," as H. A. Keyserling said of pre-revolutionary China.] [27]

2
The Gamut of Hunger

Hunger is an extremely variable phenomenon. It can exist as acute starvation, turning its victims into veritable living skeletons, or it can work insidiously to produce subtle chronic deficiencies almost without outward sign. Between these extremes it can attack mankind in many strange and spectacular disguises. There is a whole gamut of degrees of hunger, and its various effects on humankind make up an intricate and complicated history.

The purpose of this study is to draw a map showing the places on our planet where hunger is at work. Since hunger takes so many forms, the first step toward this geographical analysis is to define and characterize the more common types of hunger with which we shall deal.

Ordinarily, when people speak of collective hunger, the images that come to mind are of famished multitudes, physically and mentally devastated by extreme starvation. One thinks of the famine-stricken masses of the Far East, of the human scrap-pile of World War II, of the creatures hovering at the very doors of death in the Nazi concentration camps. To those who know nothing of hunger except what they read in the newspapers, this acute and violent hunger that occurs during wars or in famines resulting from natural cataclysms is the only kind that exists.

Students of nutrition, however, recognize more types than the starvation that chiefly interests reporters and their readers. These other forms are less spectacular, perhaps, but they are of much greater social significance. They affect a greater number of people, and their action is continuous, working from one generation to another.

To take a concrete example, in pre-revolutionary China famines were so frequent that the country was known throughout the world as the "land of famine." A careful historical study carried out at the University of Nanking in the 1920's showed that the Chinese had suffered 1,829 famines during the preceding 2,000 years—an average of almost a famine a year.[1] At these times millions of people starved to death. But in addition to this, one finds in analyzing the vital statistics that China's tragically high rates of general and infant mortality were largely due to hunger and to the chronic undernourishment which was a permanent condition there. It is no exaggeration to say that some 50 percent of Chinese mortality was directly or indirectly caused by chronic malnutrition. Malnutrition works indirectly by reducing the organism to a state of debility in which it is no longer able to resist fatal infections. Thus in a given period of years the number of lives sacrificed to chronic malnutrition, or endemic hunger, is dozens of times greater than the toll of victims claimed by spasmodic episodes of famine, the periods of epidemic hunger.

In New Guinea, according to R. Cilento, eight out of every ten children born before the last world war died before reaching puberty. Investigations showed that this spectacular early mortality was explained by the fact that the children were born already wasted by the starvation of their parents and were unable to develop properly because of their very inadequate diet. Even if a terrible famine had annihilated at one blow the whole population of New Guinea, such a disaster would have been statistically less harmful than the chronic hunger which prevailed in the area. The worst such a famine could have done would be to kill the 20 percent who had survived the depurative effects of hidden hunger, which normally did away with 80 percent of the births in that region.[2]

In India, in New Guinea, and in many other parts of the world, partial or hidden hunger is a social problem much more serious than acute hunger or famine, although it awakens much less sympathy. It is precisely in those areas of the world that are least developed economically that this kind of hunger extorts its highest tribute. The committee of experts engaged by the Milbank Memorial Fund to study living conditions in the undeveloped areas of the world had every reason to arrive at the following conclusion:

> Perhaps the most widespread and serious disease affecting mankind—with the possible exception of some of the less spectacular psychoses—is malnutrition. It predisposes to an impressive array of diseases and ill-health. It is surely quite intolerable that malnutrition should be permitted to continue to prejudice the health of at least 85 percent of the population of the globe.[3]

But just what, after all, is this terrible hidden hunger? In order to understand how it works, we must briefly review the phenomena of human nutrition and see what goes on in the human machine to keep it vitally whole and functioning.

The Human Machine

The human organism is a machine in many ways similar to machines made by man. Whatever work the organism does is the result of a conversion of energy. The fuel utilized is food, which upon combustion in the complicated human motor supplies the energy necessary to the body's vital functioning, just as coal or petroleum feeds the various types of engines.

The living machine has one characteristic that other machines lack: it is able to expand its own mechanisms and to repair its worn parts through its own efforts. This is the apparent miracle of growth and vital equilibrium. It is accomplished by the utilization of food. Food furnishes the indispensable elements for the fabrication, maintenance, functioning, and repair of the living machine. That is the reason for its extraordinary biological importance. That is why food is universally recognized as the most fundamental necessity of life. Through food man obtains the energy necessary to his functions and also the indispensable raw material for the formation of his tissues and the replacement of his physiological losses.

If food did nothing but supply energy, man could live, as Hippocrates imagined, like a machine, on a single food—on one unvarying fuel. But man depends on his food to furnish a whole series of necessary substances that go to make up his complex, living architecture. Since the human organism cannot produce these substances directly, they must be included in the diet if the living mechanism is not to suffer grave deficiencies. A rational alimentation, both sufficient and complete, must be adequate in two senses: it should supply the organism with all the energy it needs and it should furnish all the various substances essential to maintaining its equilibrium. It is believed that some forty elements are necessary for a perfect nutritional balance of the organism. If an individual does not take in as much energy as he expends, then he suffers from general hunger, or energy hunger. If the difference is considerable he suffers semistarvation, and if the deficiency is complete, absolute starvation. That was what happened to the martyrs in the Nazi concentration camps of Europe; their rations gave them only 500 to 1,000 calories, although the average daily need is 3,000.

When, quite aside from the question of energy, the diet is lacking or deficient in one or more of the essential chemical elements, the organism suffers partial or specific hunger. Many of these nutritional deficiencies, as such partial hungers are called, have no external symptoms, although they compromise the health. Others reveal themselves openly as typical diseases—the deficiency diseases. The number of such deficiencies is very great, their intensity is variable, and their possible combinations practically infinite. The commoner deficiencies are those that result from an inadequate supply of proteins, of certain fats, of mineral salts, and of certain vitamins.

Hidden hunger poses complex diagnostic questions. It is often very difficult to identify specifically the missing elements because others are, at the same time, abundantly present. The diagnosis of such states of hunger is indeed one of the most fascinating fields of modern medicine, one that has required great powers of judgment on the part of its investigators, the pioneers of hidden hunger. This book is not a treatise on nutrition, and I have no intention of describing all the various types of clinical deficiency. I shall, however, identify the principal deficiencies and point out their most striking peculiarities, so that the reader unfamiliar with the subject may be better able to appreciate their significance as he finds out where they exist in the present-day world.

The Hidden Hungers

At the same time in history that social progress was making ever more infrequent the famines that had been so common during the Middle Ages, attacks of specific hunger were becoming more frequent and more serious. Today, hidden hunger is the most typical form of man-made hunger.

There are various reasons why latent deficiencies have developed so disastrously among the more civilized human societies. First, there is the dietary monotony which results when civilization leads man to base his alimentation on a restricted number of food elements. If the diet of primitive groups is compared with that of civilized man, the most notable difference is in the variety of foods available.

Primitive man had a vast number of native plants and animals at his disposal, while civilized man limits himself to a mere handful. Maximilien Sorre calls attention to this limitation and cites the following figures: there are some 2 million known species of animals but only 50 have been domesticated and contribute to our food supply.[4] Similarly, out of the world's 350,000 vegetable species, only 600 are cultivated by man. Thus civilized man has confined his basic diet to a small number of products, an insignificant percentage of the natural varieties existing on the surface of the earth. A study of the primitive populations of the Gold Coast showed that the inhabitants of one small community in that region of Africa included in their diet some 114 species of fruit, 46 species of leguminous seeds, and 47 species of greens.[5] This spectacular variety of foods differs sharply from the limited habitual diet of any European or North American group.

The reduced number of food elements used by civilized groups is a direct consequence of the impossibility of supplying great demographic concentrations with a wide variety of products. Little by little, down through the ages, mankind has sacrificed variety to quantity, limiting the regular food supply to those substances of the most concentrated food value which are relatively easy to produce and to preserve. In thus limiting his diet civilized man has increased the likelihood of chronic shortages of certain essential nutritional factors, a situation that a widely varied diet would tend to correct. When many different foods are eaten, specific deficiencies that may develop one day are made up the next, while on a monotonous, never-changing diet the deficiencies are consolidated and grow worse as time goes on.[6]

A second practice that leads to specific deficiencies among

civilized people is the common use of concentrated, purified, and refined foods. Concentrated foods containing a high proportion of energy elements—carbohydrates and fat—have been developed from wild plants by specialized agricultural processes. The cereals, which represent the earliest stage in this conquest of nature, served as the foundation of the first great civilizations—the Indian, Chinese, Mayan, Chaldean, and Egyptian. Because they contain a high energy potential in their easily stored seeds, these agricultural products made possible the concentration of great populations in small areas, such as the valley of the Tigris, the Euphrates, and the Nile.

Although cultivated cereals are rich in energy, they are generally poorer in mineral salts and vitamins than are the seeds of uncultivated native species. In Africa, the Far East, and other relatively primitive areas, seeds are eaten today whose mineral and vitamin content is many times greater than that of the cereal seeds with which the bulk of humanity is fed. This explains, to a certain extent, why deficiencies are rare among primitive populations which continue to be more or less isolated from contact with the white man. Although their food may not be sufficient in quantity, it generally includes native products that are extremely rich in mineral and vitamin elements. It almost always happens that when these aborigines come into contact with white people, their diet, far from improving, grows worse.

In a paper published in 1937, E. J. Bigwood and G. Trolli noted this eloquent fact: the blacks of the Belgian Congo, with their native diet based on millet, sorghum, cassava, sweet potato, and other items practically unknown outside the area, showed no signs of dietary deficiencies when they were examined in their native villages. But as soon as they went to work in the factories and took up a diet under European influence, typical deficiency diseases—beriberi, pellagra, and such—began to destroy large numbers of them. The indigenous population of the Congo has declined about 50 percent since the start of European occupation, and the changes introduced by the colonizers in the eating habits of the people materially contributed to this decline.[7]

The technical processes that eliminate the hull of grains, or other impurities presumed to exist, and give us polished rice, refined sugar, and low-extraction white flour impoverish the foods in vitamins and mineral salts and expose their consumers to specific hungers.

Another cause of the widespread existence of specific hungers among civilized peoples is the fact that a majority in these societies have lost their instinctive ability to recognize this type of hunger. Animals always feel the lack of a given food element and instinctively seek a means of correcting the deficiency, but the nutritional instinct of civilized man has become dulled to such an extent that he is no longer aware of what his organism needs in order to function well. What he feels as appetite is a kind of artificial desire not directly related to his specific necessities; it is a sort of psychical appetite directed more toward the pleasures of eating than toward the satisfaction of nutritional needs.

The instinct of animals, on the other hand, directs their appetite toward substances that can supply specific elements in which the organism feels itself deficient. The hen suffering from a calcium deficiency at laying time will hunt for a supply of the mineral and will pick plaster from the walls or seek grains of limestone in the soil. Pet cats in wealthy houses, kept on an unbalanced diet of sweetmeats, will slip off to the garden to hunt lizards or other animals and will gnaw the bones to supply the calcium denied them in their defective domestic regime. When pampered dogs abandon their sophisticated diet and take to eating lawn grass, as if they were herbivorous, they are obeying an instinct that directs them to a food richer in vitamins. In all these animals, specific hunger gives orientation to their dietary preferences, so as to avoid the onset of serious specific deficiencies.

Man also, in special cases, obeys the instinct of specific hunger. We have the case of the primitive populations of equatorial Africa and of the hot regions of South America; suffering from a deficiency of iron because of an incomplete diet and the robbing of their blood by endemic worm infestation, they seek to overcome the shortage by eating clay. This phenomenon of geophagy is an instinctive defense of the organism in response to a specific hunger. When the Eskimos eat the more tender animal bones or include in their diet caribou dung and the stomach contents of animals killed in the hunt, it is specific hunger for vitamins and mineral salts that leads them to make use of such apparently bizarre foods.

These things happen among the more primitive human groups. Among the more advanced, this instinctive wisdom has been virtually lost.

Protein Hunger

One of the most serious and widespread of dietary lacks, or specific hungers, is protein deficiency. The proteins are the essential elements in the structure of living protoplasm, and thus they represent the underlying base of life itself. They are extremely complex chemical substances, which plants synthesize by combining nitrogen from the soil and carbon from the air with other elements, by means of the energy of sunlight. Plants alone are capable of this creative miracle; animals, although they live much more intensely, cannot create living matter out of inorganic elements. For this reason man and the other animals depend on the vegetable world for their existence. In spite of his ubiquity, man can exist only where he finds a base in vegetable life. In the ultimate analysis man cannot avoid being a vegetarian; he uses vegetable foods either directly or indirectly, by feeding on animals which subsist at the expense of the vegetable kingdom.

Lucien Febvre points out that the boundaries of human occupation in the Arctic are not set, as at first appears, by the presence or absence of the reindeer which serve to feed man but by the occurrence of the lichens and algae that feed the reindeer. Where there is insufficient sunlight for these plants to grow, human habitation becomes impossible. Thus plants constitute the indispensable link between man and his physical environment, and it is through them that the major influence of environment on human groups is exercised.[8] We will have occasion to see that the direct influence of climate on man is relatively slight, since he escapes its effects by various technical means. It is by indirect action, by vegetable resources conditioned by soil and climate, that environment exercises its decisive influence on human society.

Each animal and vegetable species has its own characteristic proteins. These differ in chemical structure, that is, in the proportion and quality of their components, the amino acids. The biological value of a given protein depends on how rich it is in these amino acids, which are the building stones of its molecular structure. Studies of nutrition, in particular those carried out by W. C. Rose and his collaborators, have demonstrated that at least ten kinds of amino acids are absolutely indispensable to human alimentation, some being necessary for growth and others to health in adult life.

Now it happens that all proteins do not include in their composition all these indispensable amino acids. As a general rule, they are found together only in proteins of animal origin, in meat, milk, and eggs, which are consequently referred to as complete proteins. Vegetable proteins are almost always lacking in one or more of the amino acids and are therefore called incomplete proteins. Man, in order to live well, must always take in a certain proportion of animal proteins in his ration.

The experts suggest that, in a perfectly balanced diet, half of the proteins would be of animal origin. Since the foods that furnish these complete proteins are everywhere more expensive, this recommendation represents an ideal that is very difficult to attain. The less privileged classes throughout the world, and all social classes in certain poorer areas, regularly receive less protein than the quantity considered rational for a healthy diet; as a consequence, protein deficiencies are today very widespread, and the results are extremely harmful.

The Italian anthropologist Alfredo Niceforo, at the beginning of this century, made some celebrated studies of the anthropology of the poorer classes, showing that groups of children from these classes were always less developed than children of similar age from the wealthy classes.[9] This was the first objective demonstration of the biological effects of partial hunger caused by shortage of proteins. The retarded growth and substandard weight of the poor children were the primary evidence of protein deficiency. All individuals subject to the partial hunger for proteins, whether their total protein intake is below the minimum or whether their protein ration is lacking in certain amino acids, reveal subnormal physical conditions.

Observations in all parts of the world substantiate the principle of the degrading effect of protein deficiencies on the anthropological character of the individual. Many characteristics formerly thought to be exclusively the result of racial inheritance today are known to depend in greater part on the action of environment, particularly on the type of alimentation the environment affords. McCay pioneered in seeking to relate different types of diet to the physical characteristics of human groups living in India. Robert McCarrison, who continued the studies, demonstrated conclusively that the greater stature, stronger constitution, and superior physical resistance of the Sikhs of northern India, as compared to the Madrassi in the south, were a direct result of the superior Sikh diet and particularly of its greater richness in proteins. The Sikhs made abundant use of meat, milk, and milk derivatives, while the Madrassi ate vegetables.

McCarrison conducted an experiment in which for seven weeks he fed different lots of rats on diets similar to those customarily used by the various population groups of India. At the end of this time, the rats on the Sikh diet weighed an average of 255 grams while those on the Madrassi diet reached only 155 grams. John Boyd-Orr and Gilks observed a like phenomenon in East Africa, where they studied the Kikuyu and the Masai tribes of Kenya. The Kikuyu are farmers, living on a diet of cereals, tubers, and legumes; the Masai, on the other hand, are cattle-raisers, whose diet includes meat, milk, and ox blood, which they take from the animals. These two human groups, living side by side in the same natural environment and the same climate, differ profoundly in their physical measurements. The Masai men are three inches taller and twenty-seven pounds heavier than their Kikuyu counterparts. This difference is a direct result of their fundamentally different diets. The Masai, through an abundant use of foods of animal origin, enjoy a diet balanced in proteins, while the Kikuyu live under conditions of permanent protein hunger.

I have myself had occasion to observe something similar on the American continent. In the course of a study of the distribution, according to stature and predominant constitutional biotypes, of population groups in the northeast of Brazil, I discovered that the tall type predominates in the littoral regions and in the dry backland area far from the coast, while throughout the intervening jungle zone average height is lower than it is in the other two areas. Here is the nutritional situation in each of these three areas of Brazil: along the coast the diet is high in proteins because the inhabitants live by fishing and consume large quantities of marine foods. In the backland also the protein ration is high, since it is a cattle-raising region with abundant production and consumption of meat, milk, and cheese. But in the jungle zone, where sugar-cane monoculture established itself and drove out all other food-producing activities, the diet is very poor, being based on cassava or manioc flour, the protein content of which is extremely low. This difference of proteins in the diet is the key to the mystery of sharp anthropological differences between three human groups living within a fairly small geographical area.

It should not be concluded, from the examples given, that protein hunger is an exceptional phenomenon. Local examples have been cited to furnish documentary proof that protein shortages bring about the physical degeneration of man, but the fact is that protein hunger, in greater or lesser degree, is universal. There is no doubt whatever that the low stature of tropical peoples is not a racial characteristic but is the result of defective diet that is insufficient in proteins. Before the revolution, the average Chinese weighed 121 pounds and the average European 139, a difference due to hunger rather than to race.

In the lands that lie between the two tropics, practically all the inhabitants are of less than average height; this is true of Latin Americans, Pygmies and other black groups of equatorial Africa, of Indians, Filipinos, Indonesians, Indochinese, and others. Now all these peoples live on a predominantly vegetable diet—cereals, tubers, and legumes—because tropical soil and climate are inappropriate to cattle-raising, and therefore to the production of animal products. The only exceptions, the only tall peoples living in equatorial regions, are the pastoral groups that consume large quantities of animal products: the Berber tribes of the Sahara, the Sudanese blacks, cattle-raisers of the African savannas, herdsmen of the upper Nile, the Masai already referred to, and the inhabitants of the Punjab in India. These are the only peoples of the tropical-equatorial region who escape chronic hunger for proteins of high biological value.

But protein hunger not only affects the human animal by worsening the physical appearance of the race; it leads to a whole series of ills. One of the most serious of these is a shocking reduction in organic resistance to disease in general, and particularly to infectious diseases. Since World War I, specialists have been demonstrating the fact that as the quota of proteins in the diet goes down, there is a corresponding rise in the incidence and virulence of such diseases as tuberculosis, pneumonia, dysentery, and typhoid fever. When we attempt today to outline the great areas of human destruction due to tuberculosis, we see that they coincide with the great areas of hunger. This correlation is so clear that we can now safely speak of tuberculosis not only as an infectious disease but equally properly as a disease of malnutrition—a disease of hunger. Just as well-fed individuals, whose diet is rich in iron and other essential elements, can harbor an infestation of worms in their intestines without presenting any symptoms of disease, so can they be carriers of the terrible Koch bacillus without ever becoming tubercular. The only really efficient method of tuberculosis prophylaxis in these areas of misery is to feed the population adequately, because once they are well nourished they will become in effect immunized against the attacks of the tuberculosis bacillus.

The conditions so far described are partial protein deficiencies, in which the lack shows itself only indirectly, in retarded growth or increased tendency to disease. We have still to consider the more striking conditions of extreme shortage, which bring with them typical clinical signs, the unmistakable symptoms of protein deficiency.

One of the most impressive of such symptoms is hunger edema, which gives its victims the grotesque proportions of badly sewn rag dolls. In hunger areas, when protein deficiency grows into famine, it often happens that excessively thin individuals suddenly begin to gain weight and to develop tumefied faces and oversize legs. This happens because of the retention of water in the tissues due to protein deficiency. During the two world wars this phenomenon was widely observed in various European countries. During the Spanish Civil War whole populations exhibited their hunger edema, their deformed bellies and bloated faces. But the phenomenon exists even outside of war areas. In the backlands of the Brazilian northeast it is a commonplace, during the periodic droughts, to see grotesque figures, deformed by hunger edema. Among the fugitives seeking escape there are shrunken children, their little legs like withered twigs, carrying the huge burden of bellies swollen with the dropsy of starvation.

Hunger for Minerals

Another class of specific hungers widely distributed among human beings results from dietary deficiencies in certain mineral elements. Mineral salts are as important to the organism as calories or protein. They have a myriad of functions in the vital mechanism, and they cannot substitute for each other in these functions. An otherwise complete diet which lacks a proper quantity of calcium, for example, or of iron, will seriously upset any living thing that consumes it.

The most recent investigations have revealed that there are thirteen metalloids and sixteen metals always present in living matter. Spectrum analysis has shown that seven other minerals occur occasionally. Although the majority of these mineral elements are widely distributed in nature, and consequently present in sufficient quantities in almost any human diet, there are some which are more or less rare in man's environment, the absence of which frequently causes dietary deficiencies. Such deficiencies can come about in two different ways.

First, the inhabitants of a given area might not take in sufficient quantities of foods that are the natural sources of minerals. Thus, in areas where consumption of milk, greens, and fruits is low—such foods being abundant sources of mineral salts—various evidence of mineral insufficiency is usually to be found. However, such deficiencies may also occur in zones where these foods are habitually consumed, because the foods may be low in minerals in that particular area. The fact is that the mineral content of a given food is extremely variable, depending on a number of factors but principally on the local soil type. Certain deficiencies are associated with certain soils, and a poor soil may in itself be a cause of hunger—specific hunger for particular minerals. The black and extremely fertile soils of temperate and humid regions are generally rich in calcium and phosphorus but poor in iodine. Conversely, humid tropical soils of the red type (laterite) are poor in both calcium and phosphorus. Studies made in various parts of the world show that there are extreme regional and local variations in the mineral content both of the soil and of the foods grown in it.

Through food, soils exert a decisive influence on the health and vital capacity of human societies. Where there is a progressive impoverishment of the soil in a given region, the foods grown in it decline in nutritive value, with consequent deterioration of the local population. Professor E. A. Hooton of Harvard University, studying the skeletons of Pecos Indians who lived on the plains of the southwestern United States, noted that they gradually decreased in height over a period of a thousand years, while at the same time there was an increase in bone deformations and tooth decay. The evolutionary biological decadence of this society is attributed by the anthropologist to the progressive wearing-out of the soil.

Although man may suffer sporadically from shortages of any or all the mineral elements that go to make up his tissues, there are only a few whose deficiency may ordinarily be considered of social significance. They are iron, calcium, sodium, and iodine.

The mineral element most abundant in the human body is calcium, the principal component of the skeleton. For bone building as well as for various other purposes, the human being needs one half to one gram of this element in his diet daily. Because of the very irregular distribution of calcium in the soil, and because natural sources of calcium are very limited in number (foods such as milk, egg yolk, and certain vegetables), calcium deficiency is, of all dietary deficiencies, the most frequent and widespread. Hunger for calcium may be considered a universal phenomenon affecting all climatic zones. Its principal consequences are rickets, softening of the bones, retarded growth, and tooth decay—terrible afflictions capable of causing the decline or even the complete degeneration of a race.

Inasmuch as calcium metabolism is decisively affected by vitamins and hormones, and since the production of these regulating elements depends on environment, chronic calcium hunger manifests itself with extreme variability from one area to another. It is much commoner and much more acute in the cold and temperate zones than in tropical areas, because of the difference in the amount of sunlight; Vitamin D, produced in large quantities by solar radiation, has the function of fixing calcium and phosphorus in the bone structure. That is why larger doses of this mineral are necessary in cold and temperate countries, where sunshine is limited and the body does not make good use of calcium.

Although the consumption of milk in the United States is one of the highest in the world, calcium deficiency is still widespread. Rickets was once so common among children in England that for many years the condition was known throughout the world as the "English disease." In the tropics, on the other hand, where the soils are much poorer in calcium and where consumption of milk and its by-products is generally much lower than in the temperate zones, rickets is rare and tooth decay somewhat less common. The reason is that in these lands of brilliant and year-long sunshine, the human organism, through the action of ultraviolet rays on the skin, manufactures large quantities of Vitamin D. A magnificent equilibrium is thus set up which fixes all the calcium available.

In such areas as the Amazon, the Congo, Mexico, and Puerto Rico, where calcium intake is less than half that prescribed by the specialists, rickets is practically unknown. A Mexican physician, Dr. Rigoberto Aguillar, in the course of a study published in 1944 concerning the nutrition of 10,000 children in Mexico, found that 5,000 of them were suffering from the most varied types of dietary deficiencies but that there was not a single case of rickets.[10] In Puerto Rico, where a whole population constitutes a veritable experimental laboratory of starvation, Dr. Lydia Roberts confirmed the complete absence of rickets.[11] The fact that blacks, who normally inhabit tropical areas, have better teeth than white populations is closely associated with a more efficient utilization of their calcium. No other people are in a position to expose themselves so extensively to the direct action of solar light as are the blacks, who are protected from the harmful extremes of radiation, particularly from heat rays, by the rich pigmentation of their skins. Even blacks, working almost naked on the plantations of Africa and Latin America, cannot expose themselves with impunity to the perils of sunstroke but take refuge in the modest shade of their own skins. In spite of this protection they nevertheless make good use of the capacity for photosynthesis of ultraviolet rays, manufacturing ample doses of Vitamin D and thus fixing their calcium.

So it is seen that even though larger quantities of calcium may be taken into the body in temperate climates, the specific hunger for this element is, nevertheless, more intense and its consequences more apparent in these very regions. What happens in the tropical zones, where available calcium is scarce, is that the skeleton does not develop so fully; the average stature is lower, but the bony tissue is solidly built. In temperate areas, on the other hand, the skeletons are more elongated but more fragile, more subject to abnormalities and deformations. This tendency toward skeletal weakness in the more advanced countries, far from lessening, is apparently increasing progressively with the development of civilization. The anthropologist E. A. Hooton, speaking of the United States, says that the skeletons of grandchildren, as compared to their grandparents, are longer but slighter.

There would appear to be only one way in which civilized peoples might free themselves from the degenerative effects of a relative hunger for calcium. That would be to include in their diet, as the Eskimos do, large quantities of fish oil, a natural source of Vitamin D. Polar peoples, although they get hardly any sunlight and eat neither milk nor vegetables, do not suffer from rickets; they saturate themselves with Vitamin D, which does a very efficient job of fixing the limited amounts of calcium they are able to scrape up by gnawing the bones of animals and eating the fins of fishes.

Phosphorus is the mineral element most widely distributed in the human body; it occurs in the nucleus of every cell and helps to make up the structure of the bones, but there are no known symptoms that mark the hunger for this mineral in man. It is found in so many food substances that any diet at all contains the amount of phosphorus—between one and two grams a day—necessary to the biological equilibrium of the individual. Even in tropical regions where the soils, as we have seen, are poor in phosphorus, the usual diets do not occasion a hunger for this mineral. Osteomalacia, rickets, and other bone disturbances, which can be obtained experimentally in the laboratory by withholding phosphorus, are usually caused by shortages of calcium or Vitamin D when they appear in man, and not by a phosphorus deficiency.

In spite of the rarity, or indeed the nonexistence, of phosphorus deficiencies in the human species, our book must still concern itself with the mineral because the phosphorus-poor soils and plants of certain regions adversely affect human nutrition by hindering the raising of animals, which supply protein foods. This is often the case in tropical regions, where specific hunger for phosphorus has been widely observed in cattle, goats, and sheep. In various areas such as the Congo and the South African Transvaal, the phosphorus poverty of the pastures leads to stunted growth and bone deformations in the animals—phosphorus deficiency, that is. The presence of a type of specific hunger is confirmed when we note that cattle thus attacked develop abnormal appetites, eating the bones of dead animals because they contain phosphorus and calcium. Where soils are poor in phosphorus, or where there is plenty but not in usable form (which is not uncommon), the raising of cattle becomes difficult or even impossible and the whole regional nutrition suffers.

The daily needs of an adult, according to the American nutritionist H. C. Sherman, include between six and sixteen milligrams of iron. It is used by the organism principally to make up the hemoglobin molecules which permeate the red blood corpuscles. The foods that are the usual sources of iron are of both animal and vegetable origin. Among the former the most important are meat—muscles or viscera—and egg yolk. In the vegetable world, the iron content of some plants varies widely with the soil type. Kenneth Beeson has demonstrated that the proportion of iron in lettuce varies from one to fifty milligrams per hundred, according to soil conditions.[12]

The usual sign of iron deficiency is a characteristic type of anemia caused by lack of hemoglobin in the blood. The first cases of this specific hunger were observed in babies, milk being very low in iron. McCay observed some time ago that 50 percent of the babies in London's poverty-stricken East End suffered from nutritional anemia during their first year. Later it was found that this type of anemia, associated with a shortage of iron in the diet, is also very common among adults—just as widespread, in fact, as calcium deficiency.

Unlike calcium deficiency, however, iron deficiency is common in tropical-equatorial regions. Recent studies have demonstrated that the disease, which was always officially known as "intertropical hypoemia," and which affects a majority of the inhabitants of hot regions, is not a direct result of the action of climate, as was thought at the beginning of this century, but is rather a manifestation of specific hunger for iron. The problem is not that these climates provoke a greater expenditure of red corpuscles but rather that the environment does not provide enough iron to make up the normal loss of corpuscles which takes place regardless of climate. Tropical soils, especially those of the laterite type, are among the richest in the world so far as iron is concerned, but the diets of tropical countries are generally very low in this mineral.

The fact is that meat products alone—muscle and viscera—furnish iron in a highly available form, while the iron to be found in vegetables, even in those of high content like spinach, is of very uncertain availability to the human organism. Now it happens that the equatorial-tropical zone is not at all favorable to the production of animal products, sources at once of proteins and of iron. Pastures cannot exist in regions dominated by the tropical forest, and in plains areas the pasturage is so low in nitrogenous products as to make cattle-raising difficult. In the final analysis, then, although tropical anemia may not be a direct result of the action of climate on man, it is nevertheless in large part an indirect result, since the climate creates a type of soil that leads almost invariably to a state of chronic hunger for iron.

There are two different processes that make tropical soils unfavorable to the production of proteins. First, calcium stimulates the action of nitrogen-fixing bacteria; the general poverty of tropical soils in calcium, therefore, restricts the formation of nitrates, which in turn serve as a basis for the elaboration of proteins by plants. Secondly, these soils are constantly being robbed of their nitrates because these materials are excessively soluble and are carried away by the heavy tropical rains.

The indirect action of climate as a cause of anemia due to iron deficiency makes itself felt in still another way. Parasites—great numbers of worms—infest the body of tropical man and aggravate his alimentary anemia. Worm infestation is a terrible thing in these areas because it attacks the population en masse. In the humid tropical regions of Latin America, between 80 percent and 95 percent of the population have worms. In India and other areas the percentage is even greater. In rural areas of Shantung Province, China, before the revolution, Dr. Gerald Winfield found worm infestation in 95 percent of the inhabitants and in the valley of the lower Yangtze, 98 percent.[13] Basing his estimate on the average weight of the ascarids which find a home in Chinese intestines, Dr. Winfield calculated the total mass of these worms at about 130,000 tons—all living on nutritional elements stolen from the slim rations of the Chinese!

Large-scale worm infestation, principally by *Ancilostomus duodenalis* and *Necator americanus,* constitutes a tremendous accessory factor in alimentary anemia. Yet there can no longer be any doubt that, with good nutrition, these worms become quite inoffensive, sharing the regime of abundance like peaceful fellow boarders. They become quiet domestic animals, like any other. The anemias of those with worms are

cured by a good dose of proteins and iron, without eliminating the parasites that live in their intestines. All that is
necessary is to furnish enough food for both man and worm.
Thus in order to satisfy nutritional needs in China in the
1940's, when people insisted on raising worms in such extreme abundance, enough food would have had to be furnished for 400 million Chinese and 8 billion ascarids which,
according to Winfield's estimates, proliferated in the bowels
of coolies and mandarins.

One of the most spectacular manifestations of specific
hunger for minerals is the hunger for iodine, which appears in
the form of endemic goiter or endemic cretinism. Where
water and soil are extremely poor in that metalloid, whole
populations are liable to this terrible scourge that deforms
the body and atrophies the mind. In these regions, goiter is a
horrible deficiency disease that leads to degeneration of the
individual.

Dwarfism, external goiter, deaf-mutism, feebleminded-
ness—such are the most common manifestations of endemic
cretinism, resulting from iodine deficiency.[14] In the course of
this book we will see that on all the continents there are great
human masses ravaged by this deficiency and reduced to
conditions of biological inferiority unworthy of the human
species. Huge areas exist where practically all the inhabitants
have goiters and show other signs of the disease as well. In
the heart of the South American continent and in certain
valleys of the Himalayas there are populations among which
it is difficult to find an adult individual without a well-
developed goiter—as though this deformation of the neck
were a characteristic of the race, a hereditary mark of the
human being. But it is only a mark of hunger, the specific
hunger for iodine.

Under certain climatic conditions a specific deficiency in
sodium may occur. This element is chiefly present in the
body associated with chlorine in the form of sodium chloride

and as such is excreted by the organism. The most important vehicle of elimination of sodium chloride is sweat, which contains between two and three grams of salt per quart. In cold and temperate regions there is so little perspiration that it rarely upsets the balance of sodium chloride; but in tropical-equatorial regions, where the heat often makes individuals sweat as much as ten quarts a day, the heavy drain on the body's sodium chloride is hard to make up in the diet. A drop in the sodium content of the blood and bodily liquids leads to a state of extreme nervous depression and muscular fatigue.[15] Among the causes of tropical neurasthenia and laziness, hunger for salt must be taken into account.

When white Europeans began to colonize tropical regions, one of their difficulties was that any prolonged physical exertion proved to be quite impossible in such climates. In a very short time the colonists felt themselves exhausted. Many of the colonizing peoples, such as the English, French, and Dutch, consistently limited their activity to colonial administration, leaving the labor of production, the cultivation of the soil, and the exploitation of mines to the natives, who showed themselves to be much more resistant to fatigue in these debilitating latitudes. If the natives rebelled against doing the work, the colonists imported blacks from similar climates in Africa and carried out their colonial exploitation with slave labor.

Today, in the light of modern knowledge of nutrition, it is possible to explain this superiority of the black or the Indian over the white man and to explain why these races are capable of hard physical work in extremely tropical climates. One of the secrets of their ability is that blacks, and in slighter degree Indians, lose less salt through perspiration than do whites. Losing less salt, they suffer less fatigue from the same muscular exertion. This is not a biological characteristic of the race but simply the consequences of certain customs in keeping with the environmental conditions. C. A.

Talberg's researches have shown that sweat secreted by skin covered with clothing contains twice as much salt as sweat from bare skin.[16] Since the Indian and the black work almost naked, they lose less salt than the European with his excessive clothing, and thus suffer less from fatigue.

It is interesting that the only European colonizers who succeeded in doing agricultural labor in the tropics were the Portuguese and the Spaniards. The first thing they did in these regions was to shed their excess clothing; they worked naked from the waist up, as blacks work in the cane fields of the Antilles, on Brazilian *fazendas,* or on the cotton plantations of the southern United States. European peoples from the Mediterranean area are better than Nordic peoples at acclimatization in the tropics, less because of race than habits of life—habits of food, clothing, and shelter.

This example shows how the unavoidable deficiency of one mineral—sodium—played an extremely important role in the economic exploitation of a large part of the world's surface. There can be no doubt that this specific hunger, ever since the first colonization of tropical areas, has constituted a terrible handicap to these peoples' economic and social progress.

Vitamin Hunger

The most varied, the richest in nuances, of all the groups of specific hungers is without any doubt the group of vitamin deficiencies. It is also the most familiar to us. The time is long past when vitamins were looked upon as mysterious substances with obscure and miraculous powers. Today every schoolchild knows the names and properties of these essential elements of nutrition, whose absence results in serious disturbances of human health. The field of scientific experimentation on the subject has been wide open ever since the

moment in 1897 when Dr. Christian Eijkman induced poly-
neuritis in birds by feeding them polished rice; it has been
abundantly proved that lack of vitamins causes not only
specific diseases such as xerophthalmia, beriberi, pellagra, and
scurvy but also states of vague indisposition, obscure and
ill-defined disturbances that reveal a hidden or latent hunger.

I am not going to describe the symptoms of each one of
the vitamin deficiences but only to note the most striking
characteristics of this group of specific hungers. In spite of
the fact that the number of known vitamins grows from day
to day as laboratory experimentation advances (it has already
passed twenty), the truth is that only a few of them have
definite social importance. Those whose absence brings about
ill effects on human masses collectively are the vitamins A,
B-1, B-2, C, D, and G.

A great many diseases that have been identified since
remote antiquity, the causes of which have long remained
unknown, are due exclusively to deficiencies of the vitamins I
have named above.

As long ago as the time of Hippocrates, men knew of a
particular disturbance of vision that produced extreme difficulty in seeing at night—nocturnal blindness—accompanied by
serious alterations in the eyeball. At that time the disease was
treated with a degree of success by applying slices of fresh
liver from one or another animal over the eyes. It took
humanity 2,000 years of observation to arrive at the conclusion reached in the early years of our century—that this
disease, now known as nyctalopia, is a manifestation of a
specific hunger for Vitamin A. This vitamin is found in
abundance in liver oil, particularly that of certain fish; there
was consequently a kind of obscure logic in the prescription
of the great Hippocrates.

The natural sources of Vitamin A are animal fats such as
milk and its derivatives, as well as liver oils and certain green
plants. Their deficiency in the human diet, and the ensuing

train of macabre symptoms, are not at all rare. Aside from ocular and visual disturbances, hunger for Vitamin A causes retarded or arrested growth in young people. These ills have always been endemic in the interior of China as well as of Japan, where the disease goes by the name of *hikaw*. In many other areas of the world, Vitamin A starvation has taken a large number of lives; it has stunted a great many children and has led to a great deal of blindness.

The amount of blindness resulting from inadequate nutrition is much greater than might be supposed. Blindness has always increased alarmingly in the wake of great famines; the throngs of blind beggars in European towns of the Middle Ages were in large part a product of the frequent famines of that dark time. The relationship between blindness and hunger was noticed long before anyone suspected the existence of vitamins: an Irish physician, Dr. Emmet, observed that the number of the blind in Ireland increased from 13,000 to more than 45,000 after the famine of 1848,[17] and Sergius Morgulis tells us that the terrible famine that ravaged czarist Russia in 1898 left nearly all the children with eye infections and that a shocking number of persons went blind.[18]

Although hunger for Vitamin A has decreased in Europe in modern times, it continues to exact heavy tribute from humanity in other parts of the world—in the Far East, for example, and in Latin America. Dr. W. R. Aykroyd, who gave many years to a study of alimentation in India, stated in 1948 that nyctalopia was continuing to spread implacably in that country, especially among the lower castes where nutrition is the least adequate.[19]

I had occasion to witness an epidemic of blindness due to nutritional causes. It was right on the American continent, during an acute famine following one of the cataclysmic droughts that periodically desiccate the central part of the Brazilian northeast. This is a region of cattle-raising and subsistence farming, where in normal times nutrition is well balanced, including a good supply of vitamins from milk and cheese and green vegetables on a large scale. But in time of drought all animal and vegetable life disappears, and the local population is left to starve; when all resources are gone various deficiencies begin to appear, including that of Vitamin A. The waves of emigrants who abandon their central highlands for the more humid seacoast regions are mere scraps of human beings, many of them suffering visual disturbances. Examining the human flotsam that such a tropical hurricane of drought had deposited on the beaches of northeastern Brazil, I saw the large proportion of people afflicted by nyctalopia and keratomalacia.

Night blindness, that eccentric disease, has the strange effect of plunging its victims into deep shadow the moment the sun goes down. Its frequent appearance during droughts was noticed at the beginning of this century by a great Brazilian writer who has become universally known—Euclides da Cunha, whose masterpiece, *Os Sertões,* has been translated into English as *Rebellion in the Backlands.* Da Cunha attributed the coincidence of night blindness and droughts to the daily eyestrain induced by the incandescent brightness of the burning air in these tragic periods of dazzling light. Science later confirmed his inspired intuition; night blindness is in fact caused by the inadequate chemical recomposition of visual pigment expended by the action of light—presuming that Vitamin A, which is necessary to its reconstitution, is lacking.

Hunger for Vitamin B-1 also manifests itself in disorders which have been familiar for a long time. The most typical of these is beriberi, which is characterized by muscular paralysis, peripheral nervous perturbations, and other symptoms of nervous or circulatory origin. It flourishes endemically in the Far East and breaks out in sporadic epidemics in other parts of the world. One of the most fascinating chapters in the struggle of science against hunger is the discovery that this malady, which once killed several million people every year in the Orient, is simply a form of hidden hunger.

A Japanese naval physician named Takaki was the first person to suspect that beriberi was caused by a dietary deficiency. Toward the end of the nineteenth century about 20 percent of Japan's seamen were regularly victims of this disease; on big cruisers the mortality rate varied from 10 to 20 percent of the crew. The navies of the Western countries, however, were practically free of beriberi, even in Far Eastern waters. This contrast led Takaki to suppose that beriberi was perhaps due to an inadequate diet on board the Japanese ships, where almost the only food was hulled rice.

Takaki was in charge of the navy's medical service in 1882 when the *Rinjio* returned from a cruise with so few able-bodied men aboard that they had difficulty anchoring it. Of a crew of 276 who had begun the voyage, a 272-day cruise to New Zealand, Honolulu, and South America, 169 were paralyzed and 25 had died. Eighty-two men, most of them weak and ready to drop, brought the ship home. Beriberi had killed 10 percent of the crew, had taken more than 60 percent to the doors of death, and had put the rest almost out of action.

This maritime tragedy alarmed the Japanese people, and there was further consternation when the navy ordered another ship, the *Tsukaba*, to set out immediately on the same cruise, with the same number of personnel. The public would have been horrified to know that the 276 men of the *Tsukaba* were to be guinea pigs for an experiment by Dr. Takaki. They were to carry out a cruise exactly like that of the *Rinjio*, with the difference that their diet would be more varied, including meat, milk, and vegetables. The cruise lasted 287 days; there was not a single death, and only 14 men returned with beriberi. These were the prisoners of habit who had refused to eat the varied foods that were offered.

Takaki proved his point, but he was never able to understand the mechanism by which bad diet produced beriberi, nor could he present a scientific plan to abolish the disease. It was left for a Dutch colonial physician, Dr. Christian Eijkman, to find out how beriberi worked. To Eijkman, too, belongs the honor of having initiated scientific experimentation with animals on problems of alimentation, a method which was to throw light on the deep mysteries of human nutrition.

Eijkman was a medical officer of the Dutch East Indies, stationed at Batavia. He was aware of the shocking incidence of beriberi among the Javanese natives; in the hospital where he worked, two thirds of the patients suffered from it. The island's infirmaries were perpetually full of beriberi, or, as it was called in Java, *kak-ke,* cases. Those victims who were not entirely paralyzed dragged themselves grotesquely along on legs that were dry and withered or swollen and deformed with edema. Their reeling and uncertain walk, with wobbling legs and slack feet, was a daily sight which became engraved on the young doctor's mind.

A startling accident led Eijkman to begin his investigations. He noticed one day through a window that among the chickens pecking in the dusty soil of the hospital's central patio were some who limped and lost balance as though they had beriberi. He hurried out to catch them; their paralysis, on examination, proved to be indeed a perfect duplicate of human beriberi.

In trying to find out how it was that hens and human beings had the same disease, Eijkman managed to raise a corner of the curtain that veiled the mystery of beriberi. He learned that the fowl, as an economy measure on the part of the hospital administration, had the same diet as the patients; they were getting the leftovers of cooked and hulled rice which the beriberi sufferers, with their symptomatic lack of appetite, rejected.

Rice, then, carried the disorder. But how? Eijkman started some scientific experiments. The first possibility was that the rice, contaminated by the patients, transmitted their disease. Eijkman was doubtful of this, since Europeans, with their different living customs, did not catch beriberi even from the closest contact. He proved experimentally that beriberi was not a germ disease by giving separately prepared rice, hulled and cooked like that fed to the patients, to a group of chickens. There was no question of contagion here, and yet he succeeded in producing beriberi in the hens.

The disease, then, was a consequence of mistaken or deficient alimentation. Eijkman fed a second group of fowl on whole, unpolished rice and the signs of paralysis did not appear. He concluded that beriberi was due to the lack of something that existed in the covering of the rice kernel. Indeed, when he gave rice bran to chickens sick with beriberi, they got well as though by magic.

Eijkman's theories were not readily accepted. Official science was reluctant to admit that he was right; consequently, for a long time people went on dying by millions of a perfectly avoidable disorder. The intolerance and fanaticism of official science toward Eijkman's observations brought about the death of some half million people on the American continent in our own century—between 1900 and 1910. These were the adventurers of the Amazon rubber boom, who were struck down just as their latex was bringing them fabulous prices. Without spirit to react or to escape, these hardy pioneers perished along the riverbanks; it is not without reason that "beriberi" originally meant "I can't." When the epidemics ended, no one understood what had happened, but today the causes are plain to see. The disease was over when the American rubber monopoly ended and the workers could no longer afford to import canned European foods, which had been almost all they ate. Driven to planting their own cereals, vegetables, and fruits, they got enough Vitamin B-1 to overcome their specific hunger.

The same sort of thing happened on the rubber plantations

of the Far East, but by the time these were established the science of nutrition had gained enough ground to make itself heard. The doctor and hygienist Victor Heiser, for example, tells of visiting a great rubber plantation in Sumatra and finding a 400-bed hospital to care for the 10,000 laborers of the place.[20] The management wanted to double its working force and planned accordingly to increase the hospital facilities to 800 beds. Since most of the patients were beriberi victims, Dr. Heiser advised the management to develop regional agriculture instead of enlarging its hospital and to see to it that the workers had enough fresh foods. Some time later, although the number of workers had reached 20,000, the original hospital had more room than was needed.

Typical beriberi is today becoming a rarity, but partial deficiencies of Vitamin B-1, on the other hand, are growing more common throughout the world. Countless groups show signs of such deficiency, evidenced by nervousness, lack of appetite, insomnia, tendency to fatigue, and so on.

In 1735 Gaspar Casal, physician at the court of King Philip the Fifth of Spain, described for the first time in clinical detail a terrible disease called *mal de la rosa*, or rose disease. It was so named because one of its common symptoms was red skin splotches which suggested the petals of a fiery rose. It had long afflicted the more miserable inhabitants of Italy and Spain, and it was particularly widespread in the province of Asturias. Casal took it to be a form of leprosy, related to scurvy.

The "Asturian Hippocrates," as this eighteenth-century doctor was called, erred in relating the rose disease to leprosy, but he was correct in setting it beside scurvy. Scurvy and rose disease are both of dietary origin; both are manifestations of hidden, specific hunger. The rose disease has been shown to be endemic in Italy, Rumania, and Bessarabia as well as in Spain, and it is known by several other names—

pellagra, *Lepra asturiensis*, and "Alpine scurvy." Pellagra, an Italian name meaning "rough skin," has been generally adopted as the most expressive.

At the beginning of this century, doctors in the United States began to point out that pellagra was a serious problem in the South, where it was decimating the rural population, particularly the blacks. Its symptoms were the same as those of Casal's day—cutaneous, digestive, and nervous symptoms. The victims suffered first from digestive disorders, later began to exhibit ugly sores, and ended up in the insane asylums with hallucinations and delirium.

For centuries, nobody had guessed the cause of pellagra. It was a glaring fact that the disease attacked only the poor—the unfortunate, poorly fed, and undernourished. Certain observers noted that with better food the patients got better, but they drew no practical conclusions from this fact. At first it was thought that the disease was contagious, that it was caused by an infection; later, since it was endemic to the areas where corn is the principal food, it was considered a poisoning due to some toxic substance in corn.

To an American scientist, Joseph Goldberger, goes credit for the discovery, during the years of World War I, that pellagra is a manifestation of specific hunger. He conducted experiments with animals and with human beings to prove his point. Submitting one group of prison inmates to a special diet, he obtained pellagra experimentally; on the other hand, he injected the blood of pellagra victims into himself and his coworkers to prove that the disease was not contagious. He even went so far as to swallow pills containing pulverized fecal matter and scabs from the sores of pellagra sufferers, without ill effects—thus absolutely eliminating the hypothesis that the disease was contagious. In order to see what could be done through control of the diet, the scientist crowned his experiments by wiping out pellagra in two southern orphanages where the disease was a veritable scourge.

In 1914, when Goldberger began his pellagra studies, statistics registered 11,000 deaths annually caused by this disease in the southern United States. That year 1,192 individuals died of pellagra in the state of Mississippi alone. This was the center of the plague area; as the Amazon, during the rubber boom, became the "river of beriberi," so the Mississippi was a "pellagra river." Along the banks of this river, blooming with white cotton fields and peopled with the descendants of African slaves, pellagra had firmly established its terrorist rule.

Goldberger carried out his decisive experiments in two Mississippi orphanages, one Baptist and the other Methodist. Among the inmates of these two homes in 1914 there were 200 pellagra victims, 130 in one and 70 in the other. The experiment began with the addition of meat, milk, and eggs to the children's diet. In a few days the pellagra splotches began to disappear, the fiery roses faded; tired and depressed children took on life and strength. The following year there was not a sign of the disease to be found in either institution. Thus the hidden cause of the disorder was found, as well as the means of avoiding it.

The cure, scientifically so simple, was from a social standpoint very complicated. To avoid or cure pellagra, all you had to do was prescribe a varied diet containing meat, milk, or eggs. But it happens that pellagra is a disease of poverty and flourishes precisely among the poor, who cannot afford the most fundamental necessities—whereas meat, milk, and eggs are among the most expensive foods everywhere in the world.

When Goldberger arrived at this stage in his research, therefore, instead of enjoying his victory, he fell into profound depression. He was impotent to exterminate the evil; the remedy was not within his reach but depended on complex economic factors. He had his coworker, Edgar Sydenstricker, prepare statistics on the living standards of the southerners, their wages, and purchasing power, and he was forced to the conclusion that these people could not, in fact, afford any other food but the corn and sowbelly they had always eaten. Fresh meat, eggs, and milk were completely out of their reach. They could only go on dying of pellagra. Then it was that the scientist wrote these ironic words: "After all, I am only a simple doctor, and there is nothing I can do to change the economic structure of the South."[21]

The feudal, slave regime of southern agriculture, based on the monoculture of cotton, implanted pellagra in this region of the United States, just as the monoculture of sugar planted vitamin hunger along with the cane in certain of the Antilles and as the mono-exploitation of rubber brought beriberi to the Amazon basin. In each of these cases, hunger has been cultivated by man; it has arisen as a man-made plague.

Ugly cracks in the corners of a child's mouth have always been a badge of poverty and neglect, a kind of insignia of class. They mark not only children but adults too, inhabitants of the tenements, the Hoovervilles, and the rural slums of the world. Long as such cracks have been the sign of a hard and comfortless life, devoid of cleanliness and hygiene, it has been relatively recently discovered that they reveal a type of specific hunger. The condition was thought to mark a transmissible disease which spread easily through the promiscuous life of the less favored classes. This contagiousness explained its wide dissemination. But the work of Howard W. Odum and Dr. William H. Sebrell has demonstrated that mouth cracks are caused by a deficiency of Vitamin B-2— riboflavin—which is found abundantly in liver, milk, and certain vegetables. Other symptoms of riboflavin deficiency are inflammation of the tongue and bloodshot eyes. In certain regions, such as the southern United States and the sugar zones of Latin America, this condition is very widespread. Tom Douglas Spies and his coworkers, indeed, believe it to be the most general of all dietary deficiencies in the southern United States.

In the area of sugar monoculture in northeastern Brazil I have seen many cases of riboflavin deficiency; they were hard-looking individuals, whose cracked lips and congested eyes gave them an evil expression. It is very possible that the legendary evil temper of these hombres with the bloodshot eyes, their irascibility and questionable conduct, all have their base in the dietary deficiencies to which they are commonly subject. A shortage of riboflavin, Vitamin B-2, causes the eye congestion and is generally associated with a shortage of Vitamin B-1, thiamin, which protects the nerves and the deficiency of which upsets the nervous system, making the individual quick-tempered and violent. In the sugar areas of Brazil, many people with bad police records show, upon clinical examination, evident signs of these vitamin deficiencies. It is very possible that the perverse facial expressions of such people, the hostile looks in which Lombroso would immediately discern the born bandit, and their actual criminality as well, may be due in large part to loss of nervous control resulting from specific hunger.

A disease that has been known since the most remote antiquity, and which has martyrized man for centuries, is scurvy. Scurvy is unquestionably one of the most terrible manifestations of specific hunger.

Hippocrates mentions an ugly disease provoking frequent hemorrhages and repulsive ulceration of the gums—cardinal symptoms of scurvy. Wherever man attains a certain degree of civilization and consequently begins to use artificial, preserved, and excessively treated foods, scurvy immediately puts in an appearance. In times of war, on long sea crossings, and during economic crises, scurvy has been one of the more vivid of human miseries, gaudy with blood from the hemorrhages of its victims, the strange bruised appearance of their purple skins, and the ghastly stench of their rotting gums.

Pliny relates that during the war with the Teutons during the first century after Christ, the invading Roman troops were almost exterminated, on the banks of the Rhine, by a horrible illness called *stomacace*, whose description coincides exactly with that of scurvy. Throughout the Middle Ages, scurvy was always to be found in the martyrology of the crusades and in the periodic waste of the great famines. Scurvy's blackest chapter, however, was written during the Renaissance, in the flesh of those intrepid navigators who threw themselves into the mad adventure of discovering seas and shores unknown to European man. During the fifteenth and sixteenth centuries, the crews of sailing ships feared scurvy more than hurricanes. In the long nights of the interminable crossings, tales were told of the historic ravages of this disease, of ships found derelict, floating at random, their crews dead of scurvy. These stories were not mere legends. When the great Portuguese navigator Vasco da Gama led the first maritime expedition to India in 1497, scurvy struck so violently that there were often only half a dozen sailors in condition to work on any one of the four caravels that made up his fleet. Over 100 men were lost during the frightful epidemic.[22] The great Portuguese poet Luiz de Camões, in his famous epic *Os Lusíadas,* gives a perfect description of the disease and attributes it to dietary causes, particularly to the spoiled provisions eaten on board the ships.

On one of the voyages of Christopher Columbus to the New World, in the first years of the sixteenth century, there came about a strange episode. It is said that some Portuguese sailors, seriously sick with scurvy and aware of the dark destiny that awaited them, begged the captain to leave them on a deserted island that came in sight. They wanted to die peacefully and to avoid having their bodies thrown overboard to be eaten by fish. Columbus granted their request. The men, while they awaited their certain death, began to eat some of the leaves, fruit, and woodland sprouts that the fertile island provided. Months later, when the ship returned by the same route, the pilot saw men signaling from the land;

when the ship put in to shore, there were all the sailors who had been left for dead. They were full of life and health, cured by the fresh foods. The island where this miraculous resurrection took place is situated in the tropics at 12° north latitude, and is today called Curaçao. The name is linked to this episode, since *curaçao* means "cure" in Portuguese—it is the island of the miraculous scurvy cure.

Some years later, something similar happened to the crew of the French commander Jacques Cartier, sailing up the St. Lawrence River in Canada. His sailors were all suffering from scurvy when, upon a suggestion of the local Indians, Cartier gave them pine-needle tea. They all recovered as though by miracle. Unfortunately, these occurrences remained practically unknown, and for two more centuries scurvy continued its destructive work upon the high seas.

During the seventeenth and eighteenth centuries Great Britain, queen of the seas, paid the world's highest tribute of lives to scurvy, until the surgeon of the ship *Salisbury* of the Royal British Navy resolved to make an experiment. It was similar to the one carried out by Dr. Takaki. Dr. Lind divided the scurvy victims on board his ship into various groups and submitted each group to a special diet which consisted of the normal ship's fare plus one or another new element. He discovered that the group receiving a supplementary ration of orange or lime juice got well very rapidly. From then on, a daily dose of lime juice was prescribed for the sailors of the Royal British Navy when on voyage, whereupon scurvy beat a strategic retreat, delivering the dominion of the seas over to the British without further argument.

Not until our own century was the mystery of scurvy cleared up and biological explanation given for the cures that saved Columbus's mariners on Curaçao, Cartier's in Canada, and the British Navy on all the seven seas. Doctors Axel Holst and Alfred Fröhlich, in 1907, produced scurvy experimentally in guinea pigs by feeding them dry foods and then cured them with fresh. These investigators got far enough to prove that the disease is caused by the absence of an antiscorbutic principle which exists in citric juices, cole, pine needles, and other foods. Other investigators, among them the Hungarian Albert Szent-Gyorgyi and the American Charles King, succeeded in isolating this element of nutrition and identified it with ascorbic acid, that is, Vitamin C. The richness of various plants in this substance explains the rarity of scurvy in equatorial-tropical regions of the world and its frequency in cold zones where vegetable life is precarious.

Hunger for Vitamin D manifests itself in two typical deficiency diseases: rickets and osteomalacia. Rickets is a children's disease, characterized by crooking of the long bones, particularly those of the legs, by deformation of the skull, which is usually large in proportion, by anemia and chronic fatigue. Osteomalacia is the adult form of rickets, characterized principally by a progressive softening of the bones, which curve alarmingly under the weight of the body, and by the accompanying pain.

There is evidence of rickets having existed in the cold and temperate zones from the earliest antiquity. Skeletons from the period of Roman expansion in the first century after Christ, dug up on the plains of Hungary, show the extreme frequency of the disease in that epoch—such a striking frequency that it led the Hungarian anthropologist Móra to make the picturesque statement that the whole Hungarian people of that period seemed to have been made to serve in the cavalry, because their legs were arched like the letter U.

It was early noted that rickets attacked northern lands in particular, where there is little sun, and that its favorite victims were the children of the poorer classes. In 1660, the English physician Francis Glisson furnished the first complete description of this disease, so widespread in England, and since then it has been known throughout the world as the

"English disease." The fact is, however, that rickets is not a privilege of that people alone. In 1921, the American specialists Hess and Unger showed that two thirds of the children in New York revealed signs of rickets, in one or another degree, and that in the black and Italian sections it affected practically 100 percent. According to Dr. W. R. Aykroyd, out of every two children born in Paris before World War I one was rachitic.

If rickets has long been familiar, so too has been the empirical knowledge that it can be avoided or cured by the use of cod liver oil or by prolonged exposure to the sun. It seems to have been the Norwegians, living in an eternally cloudy climate and hence extremely susceptible to the disease, who first initiated, and with great success, the use of cod liver oil. Some there are who attribute the indomitable energy of the Vikings, who dominated the northern seas in the eighth and ninth centuries and won a great empire, to the power of this miraculous and evil-smelling oil.

Studies made during World War I by the English physician Sir Edward Mellanby, and shortly afterward by the American Elmer V. McCollum, led to the discovery, in certain oils and fats, of an antirachitic vitamin—Vitamin D—which regulates the calcium and phosphorus metabolism, and whose deficiency can cause rickets. Windaus and Stembook demonstrated that the ultraviolet rays in sunlight are capable of producing the vitamin at the expense of other bodies existent in the skin—the sterols. These discoveries explain the distribution of the disease in certain areas and in certain social classes. They make clear the reason for its greater frequency in geographical zones of little sunlight and among the less well-fed classes, who have neither fats such as butter nor fish oils to cover their Vitamin D requirements.

In the tropics, where there is a great deal of sunlight, Vitamin D deficiency can hardly be said to exist, because the sun, activating the sterols of the human skin, pours forth this vitamin like a divine manna from the cornucopia of the heavens. There are, unfortunately, special cases, even in these areas, where for reasons of religious and moral prejudice this great source of life is wasted and Vitamin D deficiency sets in, with its suite of degrading consequences. Osteomalacia is very common in northern India, where it attacks the upper-class women, forbidden by the Mohammedan custom of "purdah" to expose themselves to sun or fresh air. The same thing happened among women of the upper classes in China.

Two centuries ago, the Polynesians of the South Seas enjoyed magnificent constitutions and extraordinary physical resistance; they were the Vikings of the Pacific, the great navigators and fishermen of the Far East. Their habits of living seminaked in the open air gave them as much Vitamin D from the sunlight as the original Vikings got through cod fishing in the northern seas. But the eighteenth-century French colonizers arrived, accompanied by Catholic missionaries who in the name of morality covered those splendid naked bodies with heavy clothing, cutting off their healthful supply of Vitamin D. The result was tragic: that strong and healthy people began suddenly to waste away, to suffer from rickets, and were virtually exterminated. Of the 100,000 people who lived on the Marquesas Islands, no more than 12,000 are left today. In Hawaii, and on Tahiti and Guam as well, white civilization practically did away with the native civilizations. The natives rebelled against the moral impositions of the colonizers only on the islands of Fiji and Samoa, where they went on wearing simple breechclouts and enjoying the benefits of the sun. And on those islands, where there is no hunger for Vitamin D, the populations continue to flourish and increase.

The Signature of Hunger on Body and Soul

We have passed in review the principal forms of hunger, with their individual characteristics. I should like to point out, however, that it is exceptional for any one type of deficiency to appear by itself. What generally happens is that several of them exist together, making up a diagnostic picture of extreme complexity. Certain diseases which until recently have been ascribed to the lack of a single essential food element are today known to be due to the deficiency of a number of elements at once. Pellagra, for instance, is no longer taken to be a specific hunger for nicotinic acid alone but rather for a variety of essential elements. In explaining the pathogeny of certain forms of beriberi, too, there is a tendency to find several deficiencies responsible.

Whether they come singly or in battalions, specific hungers are powerful, and they leave their signatures on the bodies and souls of human beings. The truth is that no other environmental factor acts upon man so despotically, or leaves so deep a mark, as the factor of nutrition.

Man with his technical abilities may escape the direct action of his environment, may create an artificial climate—the human climate—but he cannot escape the indirect influence of nature. Nature exercises its control through the resources that the environment offers, especially the vegetable life. The botanic cover of a region is the indissoluble link that connects a human society with its physical environment—its particular kinds of soil and climate.

The alterations that dietary deficiencies can produce, experimentally, in certain animal strains make clear the extraordinary role that diet must have played in the development and biological evolution of our various racial groups, and in fixing their individual characteristics. We know today that many physical characteristics that have been cited as indications of racial superiority or inferiority have nothing to do with race but are exclusively the results of the molding power of diet. Such characteristics are much more closely related to food resources and eating habits than they are to heredity.

To demonstrate the power of this shaping action of alimentation, Karl Mickey has cited the case of Shetland ponies.[23] On the Shetland Islands, at the northern extremity of the British Isles, 60° north latitude, grew the smallest horses in the world, hardly more than toys for children. It used to be thought that these Shetland ponies constituted a separate race of horses, stabilized by inbreeding—until some businessmen decided to supply the American market by raising ponies in the United States. To their great disappointment, the ponies born under these new conditions got bigger and bigger, generation after generation, until they were the same size as horses of other "races." The fact is, there are no separate races of ponies. Shetland ponies are descendants of English horses, brought to the Shetlands from others of the British Isles; the extreme poverty of the northern soil in certain minerals, and the consequent poverty of the pastures, led to a progressive deterioration of the species. Even after hundreds of generations, when the ponies were taken to areas with richer soil, they regained the characteristics of their ancestors.

Exactly the same sort of phenomenon takes place with certain human groups. The Chinese and Japanese were once considered "human ponies," their height and weight reduced by chronic malnutrition. It cannot be denied that individuals of these races, emigrating to the United States, take only two generations to produce descendants with a significant increase of several inches in height. The anthropologist Emil Torday has observed that another group of human ponies, the Pygmies of equatorial Africa, lose their Pygmy characteristics when transplanted to the plains regions where agriculture and cattle-raising provide much more varied alimentary resources than their customarily extremely limited diet of wild products of the rain forest. Thus the so-called "inferior races" turn out to be starved races; properly nourished, they are in all respects equal to the would-be "superior races."

Not only by acting on his body—degrading him in size, withering his flesh, gnawing at his viscera, and opening wounds in his skin—does hunger destroy the human being. It also acts on his spirit, on his mental structure, and his social conduct.

Starvation itself, as distinguished from the various chronic, latent, and specific hungers, ought first to be considered in studying the effects of hunger on human conduct. No other calamity so damages and shatters the human personality. Lashed by the imperious necessity of eating, a starving man is capable of the most extraordinary actions. His behavior changes as radically as that of any other animal tortured by hunger.

Laboratory workers are familiar with the change that comes about when normally docile rats are put on a starvation regime. They are transformed into wild animals, which bite ferociously. In disaster areas, where there has been wholesale starvation, animal life is similarly altered. During one of the great droughts of the Brazilian northeast, there was a frightful plague of bats; these normally nocturnal creatures became active day and night, and swarms of them invaded houses, sucking the blood of children and even attacking full-grown men. Serpents, too, become frenzied in these Brazilian droughts: rattlesnakes come out of their dens and move in bands through roads, corrals, farmyards, and even houses, searching for prey. During the Spanish Civil War, the depredations of stray dogs in the streets advertised the famine that struck Barcelona.

People subjected to total hunger react as violently as animals. The overwhelming action of hunger dulls all of man's other vital interests and desires, even suppresses them completely. His whole thinking is actively concentrated on finding something to eat, no matter what the means, no matter what the risk. Pioneers and explorers who have fallen into the clutches of hunger have left us full documentation, rich in details, of this tremendous obsession, when the spirit is polarized by one desire, concentrated on a single aspiration: to eat.

In the power of this anguished desire for food man quickly puts aside his other desires, including those of a sexual nature. It is a commonly observed fact that both men and animals subjected to acute and long-continued restriction of food intake lose their interest in sex as well as their reproductive capacity. If at the beginning, in the phase of initial exaltation, hunger sharpens the sexual appetite, as Pitirim Sorokin correctly states, there follows immediately a stage of decline and even complete loss of the reproductive instinct.[24]

Dr. Ancel Keys and his coworkers at the University of Minnesota registered the dramatic decline in sexual interest among a group of boys who submitted voluntarily to an experiment in semistarvation.[25] These investigators state that at the end of six months of hunger sexual interest was extinct in almost all the individuals. Similar phenomena were noted in concentration camps during World War II. Colonel Eugene Jacobs, who studied the effects of hunger during thirty-eight months that he spent in prisoner-of-war camps in Japan, has reported that under the action of hunger there is a rapid and universal loss of libido.[26]

Today we know that the loss of libido through starvation is due in part to the individual's exclusive mental concentration on the search for food and in part to the absence of that stimulus normally provided by the hormones that control sexual reactions. The genital glands of men and women suffer acutely from sharp restriction of nutriment, and their production of hormones is at length paralyzed. During the Russian famine after World War I, it was noted that spermatogenesis ceased entirely in a large number of men, and the number of women with amenorrhea increased alarmingly.

Lack of the male sexual hormone, due to hunger, may go so far as to induce the appearance of female secondary sexual characteristics such as reduction and loss of the beard, smooth, soft skin, or the development of breasts. The great number of such cases observed during the last world war makes me wonder whether the beardless faces and the smooth, feminine complexions of Chinese men may not be related to the fact that this people has been exposed to an interminable series of famines.

Hunger disintegrates the personality by vitiating or suppressing its normal reactions to any and all environmental stimuli not related to satisfaction of the instinct to eat. The other forces that mold human behavior are brushed aside. Attitudes of self-protection and mental control are progressively lost until finally all scruples and moral inhibitions disappear. In this condition more than in any other man appears as the beast of prey to which Spengler refers, given over to "the supreme form of active life, the extreme necessity to assert oneself, fighting, conquering, and destroying."

The sensation of acute hunger is not continuous; it is intermittent, with periodic ups and downs. The first stage of starvation is an abnormal nervous excitement, an extreme irritability, and a violent exaltation of the senses. This is immediately followed by apathy, extreme depression, nausea, and inability to concentrate. Knut Hamsun faithfully describes the cyclical emotional crises of the starving in his famous autobiographical novel *Hunger*, where he shows his hero passing from extreme irritability to morbid indifference, now arrogant, now gentle, now perverse, now magnanimous, all without apparent reason.

In the course of this study, I shall call attention to various social phenomena—banditry and morbid mysticism in certain backward areas, continual revolutions in others, prostitution and moral depravity—all of which are the more or less direct consequences of the dissolvent effects of starvation on the equilibrium and integrity of the human personality. In the experiments of Dr. Keys to which I have referred, there developed in greater or less degree a veritable hunger neurosis, accompanied by dangerous antisocial reactions. And the climax of starvation is accompanied by a state of rage or madness well known to the sixteenth and seventeenth century navigators, who called it "hunger hydrophobia."

The effects on the spirit of undernourishment, or chronic hunger, are less spectacular than those of starvation but more prolonged and persistent in their action. While acute hunger usually causes some form of abnormal excitement, chronic hunger tends to induce depression and apathy. People suffering from chronic hunger soon lose their appetites, no longer feel the sensation of hunger, and thus cease to react to the spur which is man's strongest goad to action.

Chronically undernourished populations are almost insensible to their lack of food; their appetite is scant and sometimes even disappears. To awaken the dulled appetite of undernourished peoples, it is often necessary to stimulate it with appetizers such as pepper and other pungent spices. This is the case, for example, in Mexico, where the anthropologist Ramos Espinosa says that the people "in order to overcome their lack of appetite, cauterize their mouths and stomachs with pepper, so as to produce a reflex secretion of saliva similar to that induced by a good appetite."[27]

Some laboratory experiments I have made confirm the fact that certain types of specific hunger lead to loss of appetite. Rats were fed an apparently normal ration but one from which certain amino acids, substances that form proteins, had been removed. This experimental deficiency brought about an immediate and striking loss of appetite, but the animals again ate voraciously when the same diet was supplemented with a few milligrams of the missing amino acids.

It is the same nutritional phenomenon that satisfies the Mexican with nothing but a *tortilla* and a cup of coffee or that permits the man of the Amazon to go to work among the rubber trees with nothing in his stomach but a little manioc porridge—which he eats again when he gets back to his cabin at night. This kind of hunger explains the loss of all ambition, the lack of initiative on the part of the marginal populations of the world; in diet and not elsewhere are the origins of the fatalism of the lower castes in India or of the alarming improvidence of certain populations in Latin America.

Melancholy is another emotional symptom of chronically hungry peoples. There is no such thing as a melancholy race—as some lyrical and superficial sociologists would have it. But there are melancholy peoples, sad with the sadness brought on by hunger, who are often unable to cheer up even under the influence of alcohol. The sadness of the Mexican Indian, for example, is a result of his scant and deficient diet based on corn; not even his *pulque*, with its high alcohol content, can overcome it.

The celebrated gaiety of the French, on the other hand, is due to their abundant and normally well-balanced diet. A year after the end of World War II I saw that hypothesis confirmed. One beautiful sunny morning, a trainful of children was setting out for the country from one of the Paris stations. From a car alongside I could watch these children for the few minutes before the train pulled out, and I was struck by their odd seriousness, by their silence and lack of spontaneous gaiety. The fine day, and the fact that they were on their way to a picnic, made their solemnity seem incongruous. I looked more carefully, and all became clear—their pinched and pallid little faces, their wan and wrinkled skin, were evidence of the awful hunger that devoured them from within. Those little offspring of the gay Gallic race had lost all their joy of living in the bitter struggle against hunger!

In its sexual effects, chronic hunger, whether specific or latent, operates quite differently from acute starvation. Starvation is known to diminish libido; groups of people subjected to persistent malnutrition, on the other hand, appear to be sexually stimulated. They show a definite increase in fertility over the less badly fed. This intensification of the reproductive capacities in chronically starved people develops through a complex process involving both physiological and psychological factors.

The psychological effect of chronic hunger is to make sex important enough to compensate emotionally for the shrunken nutritional appetite. Under normal conditions, it is universally agreed, the instincts toward reproduction and nutrition compete with each other, and when one retreats, the other advances. When chronic hunger, then, particularly hunger for proteins and certain vitamins, produces chronic lack of appetite and loss of interest in food, the sexual instinct becomes dominant. The chronic starveling, whose appetite for food is dulled and easily satisfied, turns his attention away from his weakened nutritional instincts. The biologically important and psychologically satisfactory activity which presents itself is sexual. Thus one primary need is emphasized to compensate for the diminution of the other.

The exaggerated sensuality of some societies or social classes who live in a state of chronic undernourishment is explained by this mechanism of compensation. Their high fertility index, however, is also due to an important physiological aspect of hunger.

Cattle-raisers have long known that animals which get too fat may become sterile and that reduced rations will re-establish fertility. This empirical evidence has caused no great stir in scientific circles. But there are today experimental data and systematic observations which explain the correlation between food and fertility. They make clear the way in which partial nutritional deficiencies work to accelerate the multiplication of a species.

Hunger for proteins, involving a deficit in certain important amino acids, increases significantly the fertility of animals. Proof of this is in the sensational experiments reported by J. R. Slonaker between 1925 and 1928, which have not yet had the recognition they should and must receive.[28] Slonaker subjected groups of rats to diets which varied in protein content and studied their reproductive indices for six generations. He found that diets rich in proteins, when proteins constituted more than 18 percent of the total caloric intake, were unfavorable on all counts to the reproduction of the species: they increased sterility, retarded the epoch of fertilization of the females, and reduced the number of litters and the number of young in each litter.

Some of Slonaker's figures speak with such eloquence and discrimination that they merit presentation in detail. Slonaker observed that when male rats received a diet with only 10 percent of its total calories in proteins, 5 percent of them were sterile; when the protein content of the ration was increased to 18 percent and 22 percent, the sterility increased to 22 percent and 40 percent respectively. With females, the same increase of protein in the diet lifted the sterility rate from 6 percent to 23 percent and 38 percent respectively. There were impressive differences in the average numbers of offspring of the various groups of rats. Eating 10 percent protein, each rat produced an average of 23.3 offspring; with 18 percent protein, 17.4; and with 22 percent, only 13.8.

These figures clearly suggest that in proportion as the diet increases in protein content, reproductive capacity drops.[29] It is also true, however, that the larger protein rations bring about a better resistance to disease in the young and an increase in the percentage of those that survive. It appears, then, that with a percentage of proteins high enough to guarantee a good survival index among the offspring, the number of these offspring falls off; and that when diets are inadequate in protein, nature multiplies the number of offspring so as to guarantee the continuation of the species.

With the human species, the case is the same. The groups

with highest fertility are those who have the lowest percentage of complete proteins—animal proteins—in their regular diets. The highest birth rates in the world are registered by certain peoples of the Far East, Africa, and Latin America, where the proportion of animal products in the habitual rations does not reach 5 percent of the total food consumed. In contrast to this, the lowest birth rates exist among the peoples of Western Europe, the United States, Australia, and New Zealand, where the average amounts of animal proteins in the diet are the highest in the world: 36 grams per day in Western Europe, 66 in the United States, and 62 in Australia and New Zealand.

Geographically, the countries with high birth rates (above 30/1,000 population) are all tropical countries, whose geographic and economic conditions are ill adapted to either the production or the consumption of proteins of animal origin. The predominantly vegetable diet of these countries is certainly one of the decisive factors in their fertility. If we compare the birth rate with the consumption of proteins, [and especially with the percentage of calories supplied by animal proteins,] we find a correlation between the two, the fertility going down as the consumption of such proteins rises. The table opposite compares two groups of countries— the first with high birth rates, the second with low—in terms of the total consumption of proteins and the percentage of calories furnished by animal proteins.[30]

The table demonstrates a direct correlation between high birth rates and insufficient consumption of proteins. Obviously, there is not an absolute correlation in all cases because many factors besides nutrition affect the mechanisms of fertility and birth.

This aspect of the problem of hunger, the influence of diet on reproduction, has proved the most controversial point of my discussion. Since this book was first published, various criticisms have appeared, most of them inspired by the classic science of nutrition, which has always held that a diet rich in

	Birth rate	Total proteins in grams	Percent of calories in animal proteins
El Salvador	48.4	58	14
Guatemala	47.3	62	8
Costa Rica	45.1	54	14
Jordan	37.0	59	7
Libya	37.0	50	8
Surinam	35.0	47	10
Philippines	34.0	50	9
Taiwan	34.0	65	13
Uganda	25.0	58	7
India	21.0	52	11
Australia	19.3	92	44
Denmark	18.4	95	45
U.S.A.	18.4	92	38
United Kingdom	17.9	89	42
France	17.5	103	41
Sweden	15.8	82	40

proteins is indispensable for high reproductive capacity. Because of the important repercussions that my theory may have in the practical domain of demographic policy, I have done further research on the problem. My results confirm those of Slonaker. I ascertained that a complete lack of proteins leads to sterility in rats but that a partial deficiency always noticeably increases their fertility. Just such states of partial deficiency in certain essential nutritional elements, especially the amino acids, can be observed among badly nourished and highly prolific peoples. The findings of numerous other researchers coincide completely with my own; I shall mention here only the most significant.

In their experiments with rats, Drs. Anton Carlson and Frederick Hoelzel of the University of Chicago found that the highest rates of sterility (76 percent in males and 75 percent in females) appeared in a group that had a relatively rich and plentiful diet, while the lowest rates (19 percent in males and 27 percent in females) showed up in a poorly and sparsely fed group.[31] Dr. Maria A. Rudzinska of New York University established the same relationship between the degree of nutrition and reproductive capacity in studying a protozoan, the *Tokophrya infusionum.*[32] This organism is well fitted for an experiment of this sort because it feeds upon one-celled ciliates such as the *Tetrahymena* and thus its ingestion of food over a given period can be mathematically regulated. Dr. Rudzinska demonstrated that after an optimum point of nutritive intake had been passed, reproductive capacity progressively diminished as ingestion of *Tetrahymena* increased. Overfeeding yielded a giant *Tokophrya,* five times the normal size but completely without reproductive capacity. Dr. Rudzinska concluded that if such a patent relationship could be established both for the one-celled organisms involved in her experiment and for the mammals that served as subjects for Carlson and Hoelzel, a fundamental factor of biology—one that affects the life of every organism, including man—must be involved.

The work of Dr. O. B. Kent, a specialist in bird nutrition, offers a categorical proof of the same relation.[33] By feeding chickens what he called "restricted diets" (as opposed to the extremely rich diets formerly believed best), Dr. Kent obtained a great increase in egg production. His results were so conclusive that the "restricted diet" is now fed on a growing number of American poultry farms. W. H. Grant and H. A. Teitelbaum of Johns Hopkins University demonstrated that dogs subjected to a hunger diet showed their highest fertility rates after five days of deprivation.[34] These experiments, moreover, confirm the natural habits of seals and sea lions, which voluntarily undergo a prolonged period of fasting before the mating season.

Even more significant than the experiments upon laboratory animals is what has been observed of human groups that have exhibited great changes in birth rates following radical modifications of diet. One circumstance that greatly strengthened my theory was the sudden drop in births in Puerto Rico beginning in 1947. From about the turn of the century the island's birth rate had been fluctuating between 42 and 45 births per thousand, but from 1947 onward it fell progressively, and by 1954 it was below 35.[35] This phenomenon can be explained in large part by dietary changes introduced in 1947, a result of Puerto Rico's altered political orientation.

The most dramatic of all confirmations of diet's decisive influence on human fertility may be found in the report on the research of Professor G. E. MacGinitie of the California Institute of Technology, published by the Smithsonian Institution.[36] MacGinitie, working at the Naval Laboratory of Arctic Research at Point Barrow, Alaska, brought to light the highly significant fact that the birth rate has tripled among the area's Eskimos since they turned to a new type of mixed diet that includes vegetables. Eskimo women, whose pregnancies were usually separated by intervals of several years, now have a child almost annually.

Webster Johnson and Raleigh Barlowe established the equally significant fact that between 1936 and 1947 half of the increase in the world's population occurred in the Far East. They wrote: "It is a disconcerting fact that in the areas where population growth has been most rapid, people receive only about 2,000 calories a day. It seems, therefore, that this insufficient diet is related to human fertility."[37]

The exaggerated multiplication of humanity through excessive fertility, then, is partially a problem of specific hunger—one of the strangest aspects of the phenomenon of universal hunger. Hunger is responsible for the overproduction of human beings, excessive in number and inferior in quality, who are hurled blindly into the demographic metabolism of the world.

This manifestation of hunger is of primary importance to my study, since it provides a biological basis for my theory that specific hunger is the cause of overpopulation. The bodily mechanism through which chronic hunger exerts its disturbing and debasing force on the demographic evolution of human societies is involved with their economic and social life and can best be discussed in connection with them. I shall describe its physiology when I take up the problem of hunger in the Far East—an area where relative overpopulation is plainly one of the most peculiar and serious consequences of specific hunger.

Part II
The Regional
Distribution
of Hunger

3
Hunger in the New World

Investigations of living conditions in various American countries have revealed the surprising fact that the Western Hemisphere is one of the great world areas of malnutrition and hunger. This is surprising indeed, because the rest of the world has always thought of the Americas as continents of abundance, endowed with spectacular natural riches. The legend of El Dorado, brought back to Europe by the sixteenth-century conquistadors, created the impression of an earthly paradise, with soil of exceptional fertility and a subsoil pregnant with precious ores. Consequently, it is hard to realize that the immense continental mass that occupies the Western Hemisphere does not produce the food resources needed to supply its own populations. This inadequate food supply cannot be explained on the grounds of an excess of population, since American demographic density is among the lowest in the world. Only Africa and Australia, with their extensive desert areas, have fewer inhabitants per square mile.

It must not be thought that hunger in America is limited to one or two small areas in the poorer regions. Far from it. In all sections of the Americas—northern, central, and southern—in the parts colonized by Latins as well as in those colonized by the British, one finds great human masses who suffer the scourge of hunger. Very different from the glowing accounts of sixteenth-century navigators describing the wealth of Mexico, Peru, and other enchanted and fabulous lands are the somber reports of twentieth-century investigators describing actual living conditions in the various countries of this continent. There are few bright and shining colors in a present-day picture of the continent of abundance; dark blots of malnutrition and hunger are everywhere apparent.

Both the intensity and the causes of hunger vary from one area to another of the Americas. In order, therefore, to get a clear idea of the overall situation, it is necessary to study the differing phenomena in the various areas. An immediate division may be made between two continental areas with distinct characteristics: English-speaking America and Latin America. These two parts of the hemisphere present such well-differentiated features, from their early history down to their current socioeconomic organization, that hunger has quite different characteristics in each of them. Let us begin with Latin America, where the drama of hunger is more violent and involves a larger number of people: some 90 million individuals,* or two thirds of the inhabitants.

The Bankruptcy of El Dorado

Kingsley Davis rightly observed that from a demographic point of view Latin America is one of the most fortunate regions of the world. Its relatively small population inhabits a vast and promising territory—16 percent of the world's habitable land containing only 6 percent of the world's population†—but the economic position of this region is not nearly

---

* 186 million individuals in 1970.
† 7 percent of the world's population.

so favorable.[1] The aggregate annual income of all the Latin American republics totals only $10 to 15 billion, while the national income of the United States is more than $150 billion, over ten times as much. Seymour Harris estimates the annual per capita income of Latin Americans averages less than $100[2]—that is, a tenth of what it is in the United States and an eighth of that in Canada.* The standard of living of the Latin American populations, and particularly their grave dietary situation, speak more eloquently of their real poverty than do these overall figures. But the dietary situation is the principal conditioning factor of the insignificant income of these countries. It is a main cause of their insufficient production, of the incomplete exploitation of their natural resources, of their political instability, and of their technical and educational shortcomings.

If we look closely at the social structure of this region, we find that most of its ills have their roots in the terrible biological misfortune of chronic undernourishment. The fact that a territory of such great potential wealth is occupied by economically second-rate nations is not a result either of racial inferiority or of disintegrating influences in the environment. The evil is neither race nor climate but hunger. All through history, it has been hunger that has hobbled Latin American progress.

The conception of the Latin American native sitting indolently on his doorstep, contemplating with weary eyes a magnificent landscape of luxurious tropical vegetation which he lacks the spirit and energy to dominate, is essentially a

* According to more recent statistics, the aggregate annual income of all the Latin American republics totals only $115 billion, while the national income of the United States is more than $880 billion, approximately seven times as much. Annual per capita income among Latin Americans averages approximately $300—7 percent of the United States figure ($4,200) and 10 percent of the Canadian ($3,000).

picture of hunger. One can see the Mexican Indian starving on the central plateau of Anauac, where the Aztecs and Mayans enjoyed a regime of plenty. One can see the Peruvian Indian deluding his hunger with a few coca leaves, which he chews all day long to anesthetize his appetite, occupying the plateau where the Incas, according to reports of the early navigators, terraced the land and produced food in the greatest abundance. Or one can see the half-breed of the Brazilian northeast wasting away on a hunger diet—beans and manioc meal the year round—in the fertile lands of the cane fields, which brought more wealth to the Portuguese of the seventeenth century than all the luxurious imports of the Orient. Everywhere in Latin America is the native with the somnolent air, mourning his hunger and his misery. And when the foreigner, puzzled to see such poverty in the midst of so much apparent natural wealth, speaks to the native and tries to find out why he is poor, he gets answers that puzzle him still more, unless he is aware of the psychological effects of generations of chronic hunger.

Jeca Tatu, a symbolic character of Latin American fiction, personifies the mental attitude of this land's undernourished inhabitants, broken by hunger, worm infestation, and, frequently, malaria.

Shocked at the way Jeca eats the same thing day after day, the foreigner asks: "Don't beans grow in this country?"

"No, *Senhor.*"

"Rice?"

"No, *Senhor.*"

"Some fruit or other?"

"No, *Senhor.*"

Pausing a moment, with his faraway look, to draw on his pipe or turn over a coca leaf in his mouth, the native returns the same answer to all questions: "No, *Senhor.*"

But the foreigner, unable to imagine that such well-watered lands, covered with such abundant vegetation, should be incapable of producing food, insists and asks once more: "But have you planted some of these things, to see if they'll grow in this country?"

Then the eyes of the half-breed light up momentarily with a malicious sparkle, and he answers with a certain air of surprise, "Ah! *Plantando . . . dá."* That is, "Of course they'll grow—if you plant them!"

The first impression one gets from this human landscape and this dispirited response is that man does not produce on these lands because of indolence, that he is possessed of a tropical laziness to which the climate of the regions condemns the races that live there. But a closer analysis reveals that to call this celebrated tropical apathy the result of climate is a myth. What does exist is an incapacity for activity and a loss of ambition due to ill health, which is in turn a result of the destructive effects of hunger.

When Jeca is well fed he begins to work just as hard and with just as much enthusiasm as does the European farmer in periods of peace and abundance. During a several-year period of heavy internal migration in Brazil, hundreds of thousands of people abandoned the northeastern area of chronic malnutrition and came to the more prosperous coffee-raising and industrial areas of the south. When they went to work in the fields, the men from the north were incapable of keeping up with the Italian colonists or even with the better-fed southerners. They seemed a race of good-for-nothings, unable to exert themselves, lacking both will and ambition. But a short period of good nutrition was all that was needed to transform them into magnificent workers. In certain frontier areas of central Brazil, innumerable towns have sprung up and grown like mushrooms, built by the hands of these northeasterners. Those hands were formerly hardly able to move, but they were capable of superhuman efforts once they received the necessary fuel. [Two-thirds of those who built Brasilia were migrants from the northeast.]

This hunger is nothing new. It comes from the past, from the time of the earliest discovery of these lands, and derives from the uneconomical manner of their colonization and exploitation. Although the history of all the countries to the south of the Rio Grande is largely similar, there are many shades of regional coloration. Instead of attacking the question of hunger in Latin America as a whole, it is best to take it up separately in the two component areas, South America and Central America.

Portrait of South America

There is not a single country in South America in which the population is free of hunger. All suffer from this terrible calamity; the only difference is that it is more intense in some areas, more subdued in others. South America can be divided into two parts according to the degree of hunger: an area (A) of extremely defective nutrition, where quantitative hunger is associated with specific qualitative deficiencies in the diet; and an area (B) of less serious dietary conditions, where there is a lack of certain nutritional elements only and where the diet is in general sufficient in quantity.

Area A embraces three fourths of the land surface of the continent and includes the following regions: Venezuela, Colombia, Peru, Bolivia, Ecuador, Chile, the northwest and the extreme south of Argentina, the western half of Paraguay, and the northern half of Brazil.

Area B lies in the eastern part of the continent between 20 and 40 degrees latitude and includes west-central and southern Brazil, that part of Paraguayan territory that lies to the east of the Paraguay River, Uruguay, and the northeast region of Argentina.

The first of these areas includes a large number of well-defined nutritional zones: the corn zone of the extreme north, the manioc zone of the Amazon basin, the mid-continent corn zone, the potato zone of the Andes, the Chaco manioc zone, the corn zone of northeastern Argentina, and others. In all of these zones we find traditional diets that are insufficient, incomplete, and unbalanced.[3] They are insufficient in calories, unbalanced by an excess of starches, and more or less seriously deficient in proteins, mineral salts, and vitamins.

Caloric deficiency is very widespread and is apparent in all the dietary zones of this area.[4] Thus, in a study I made before the last world war in the region of the Brazilian northeast—an area of cane-sugar monoculture—I found an average daily intake of about 1,700 calories.[5] In the Amazon basin, I estimated the daily ration of the rubber worker who penetrates the jungle to collect the crude caoutchouc to be about 1,800 to 2,000 calories. The Bolivian National Nutrition Commission has set the average daily diet in that country at 1,200 calories,[6] while specialists in Colombia and Ecuador estimated the habitual diets of those two countries at 2,000 and 1,600 calories respectively.* Investigations carried out in Chile make it possible to conclude that 50 percent of the country's population did not manage to get 2,400 calories daily, while 10 percent of them did not even receive 1,500.[7]

All of these figures are alarmingly low and would represent black starvation if we took as our point of reference for the physiological necessities of human beings in this area the universal standard of 2,800 to 3,000 calories daily. The situation, however, is not actually so tragic. In the first place, as we have already seen, the greater part of this South American area has an equatorial or tropical climate, which, generally speaking, forces down the rate of basic metabolism and the metabolism of labor, and thus brings about a perceptible diminution in the individual's expenditure of energy.[8]

* 2,060, 2,280, and 2,020 calories respectively.

Secondly, and again speaking generally, the energy supply of these populations is somewhat higher than the statistics indicate, since the more primitive population groups make habitual use of various food substances the composition of which is virtually unknown to the outside world. For this reason, the specialists take no account of these foods when calculating the energy value of the diet. Again, some of the foods consumed in these countries do not enter into the computations of national statistics because they are produced and consumed locally by isolated population groups which live under semifeudal economic conditions. It is only thus that the apparent miracle of the survival of these populations can be explained. In spite of the fact that their diet, according to statistical data of production and consumption, is not far from that of a concentration camp, they do not show visible signs of extreme malnutrition.

This is well illustrated by the case of Bolivia. When, in the 1940's, the Nutrition Commission estimated the average daily per capita calories at 1,200, it did so on the basis of the food resources of the country and according to statistical calculations. However, such an extremely low energy intake would condemn the whole region to starvation and the population to rapid and unavoidable extinction—a condition not borne out by the facts. There can be no doubt that the normal diet of the Bolivian peasant contains food elements not counted by the specialists or registered by the statisticians. Nevertheless, these dietary regimes supply much less than the total energy necessary to cover the daily needs of the individual, even in a tropical area; and we must not forget that many of those who live on this limited diet inhabit cold or temperate zones, such as the Andean plateau or central and southern Chile.

More serious than this quantitative deficiency, to which the organism seeks to adapt itself by reducing its functional expenditures and limiting its normal appetite, are the qualitative deficiencies. The foremost of these is the shortage of those proteins capable of furnishing the amino acids that are indispensable to the growth and vital equilibrium of the organism. The protein deficiency in these regions is very marked, principally on account of the low consumption of essential foods of animal origin: meat, fish, milk, cheese, and eggs. As a matter of fact, the average consumption of such products in this area is among the lowest in the world, well below the desirable minimum. The average per capita meat consumption does not reach 66 pounds per annum, and in certain regions is is much below this. If the consumption of meat reaches an average of roughly 88 pounds in that part of Brazil which is included in this area, it averages 40 pounds in Ecuador, and only 30 pounds* in Peru.[9] When we compare these figures with those of better-fed regions, such as Canada with 132 pounds or the United States with 130,† or the southern part of Brazil with 154 pounds or Argentina with 300,‡ the inadequate meat consumption of this South American area is thrown into sharp relief.

The average consumption of fish in this area is equally insufficient. Fish has a regular part in the diet of the Amazon region because of the extraordinary piscatory wealth of that river. The inhabitants of some coastal regions and river deltas are practically amphibian—they make their homes almost in the water and devote themselves to catching fish and other marine animals. In these cases the protein deficiency is somewhat lessened—a condition that is apparent in their better physical constitution and greater stature—but it does not disappear completely.

The fact is that the usual methods of fishing, as well as the processes used to preserve the product, are very primitive,

* 92, 50, and 42 pounds respectively.
† 220, 183 pounds respectively.
‡ 228 pounds.

with the result that the supply of this precious food remains precarious even when the waters are full of fish. In Chile, where the consumption of fish is widespread because of that country's 2,500 miles of coast and tremendous reserves of fish, the per capita consumption is only 11 pounds* a year, a quantity obviously insufficient to supply the protein needs of a country that eats little meat and drinks less milk. It is ridiculously small in comparison with the fish consumption of Japan (72 pounds) or even of England (44 pounds).† The failure of South America to take advantage of the nutritional wealth of the sea seems less surprising when we learn from F.A.O. data that fishing has never been an important economic enterprise in the Southern Hemisphere. The southern half of the world accounts for only 2 percent‡ of world production, so that the fishing industry remains almost exclusively an activity of the Northern Hemisphere. [The only exception is Peru, the world's foremost producer.]

When it comes to milk—that other source of complete proteins—the consumption indices of the countries in this area of South America also reveal an alarming deficiency. In the Amazon region of Brazil the consumption of milk is practically nil.[10] In the other countries of the area for which we have statistics, the average consumption everywhere is insignificant: 11 quarts a year per capita in Peru, 14 in Chile, 26 in Ecuador, and 38 in Venezuela.** Only in Colombia and Paraguay are the figures somewhat more liberal, reaching 68 and 126 quarts per capita respectively.†† However, when this is compared with consumption in the United States (110 quarts) or with Denmark and Switzerland in normal times (164 and 263 quarts respectively),‡‡ one sees that milk is a

* 9 pounds.
† 65 and 36 pounds respectively.
‡ 14 percent.
** 69, 106, 73, and 78 quarts respectively.
†† 108 and 68 quarts respectively.
‡‡ 223, 278, and 239 quarts respectively.

very precarious source of proteins in this section of South America. The figures on the consumption of cheese and of eggs are also very low in comparison with other nations.[11] An investigation carried out in 1938 by Dr. Baldo in Venezuela revealed that in the rural districts of the interior, 50 percent of the children got no milk at any time during the year, 59 percent ate no meat, and 89 percent ate no eggs.[12] In the Brazilian northeast, my own study revealed that only 19 percent of the families investigated used milk, while there was practically no consumption at all of cheese and eggs. [Today, despite some progress in the industrial sector of northeast Brazil, nutritional conditions remain the same and essential foods are still missing from the diet of the poor.]

In this area the normal sources of protein are usually corn, beans, and certain tubers and roots, none of which possess the proteins of high biological value capable of furnishing the organism with all the requisite amino acids. In this whole area, there are only a few population points in which animal proteins make up half of the total protein in the diet.

The first biological expressions of protein deficiency in this area are retarded growth and subnormal stature, symptoms displayed by a majority of the population at all stages of life. In Bolivia, where the protein deficit is considerable, children are born markedly underweight. According to a 1940's report of a study by Professor Luis Sotelo, former director of the Department of Nutrition in La Paz, 60 percent of the children born in that city weighed less than 6 pounds at birth (whereas the normal figure is 6¾ to 7¾ pounds).[13] In addition, 35 percent of these children were clearly subnormal in stature. According to anthropological measurements made by Morris Steggaerda during the same period, the average height of the population groups in this area was among the lowest on the American continent.[14]

Many other consequences result from this relative deficit in proteins, though they do not show themselves as openly as they do in those regions of the Far East or Central America where the deficiency is almost absolute. The diarrheas and the partial or complete hunger edemas, so common in areas where nutrition is based almost exclusively on rice as in Indochina,[15] or on corn as in Mexico,[16] are clinical rarities in South America, where dietary monotony is always modified by the use of a variety of nutritional elements. What is common in this area is the appearance of nutritional diseases in children, the etiology of which certainly includes deficiencies of proteins as well as of other nutritional elements. According to a report presented before the first Latin American Conference on Nutrition in 1948, 73.3 percent of the inhabitants of the city of Lima, capital of Peru, presented clinical symptoms of this type. In the Brazilian northeast, the children of the poorer classes, who seemed to be in a good state of nutrition and weighed more on the average than children of the well-to-do classes, were found by laboratory test to suffer from hidden protein deficiencies; the percentage of proteins in the blood was clearly out of balance and their greater weight simply due to a greater retention of water, a dropsical condition of the tissues which precedes the stage of visible edema.[17]

In contrast to the low proportion of proteins is the exaggerated proportion of carbohydrates in the diet of these people. It is the starchy foods—cereals, tubers, and roots—that are most widely consumed in this geographical area, and in many cases several of them are included in one regional diet. This extreme abundance of carbohydrates far overbalances the quotas of proteins and fats. Diets containing more than 80 percent carbohydrates are common. This nutritional imbalance is a decisive factor in the high incidence of beriberi and minor deficiencies of Vitamin B-1 in this area, which occur even when the supply of this vitamin appears to be adequate.[18] It cannot be assumed that there is a greater expenditure of Vitamin B-1 in tropical climates, as was long thought to be the case, nor that there is an exaggerated loss of this nutritional element through abundant sweating.[19] It is simply that the heavy load of carbohydrates to be metabolized requires a proportionately greater intake of Vitamin B-1. When this is lacking, a condition that might be called relative avitaminosis appears, a vitamin deficiency resulting from a lack of balance in the Vitamin B-1–carbohydrate index.

Of the mineral deficiencies, the most common are shortages of calcium, iron, and iodine, and in the lowlands— regions of heat and humidity—a shortage of sodium chloride. The prime factor in deficiencies of this type is the mineral poverty of the majority of tropical soils, as a result of which the plants in this area generally have a lower mineral content than similar species cultivated in other and richer types of soil. In addition, most of the people in this area eat very few green vegetables and fruits, and the poorer classes eat hardly any. The alimentary tradition of the Iberian peoples who colonized these lands has been completely abandoned.[20] Their diet was rich in greens, fruits, and vegetables—the refined and delicate products of intensive garden and orchard culture which was introduced by the Arabs into the Iberian Peninsula and transmitted to the Portuguese and Spanish. In these South American countries, fruits and greens are hardly ever seen on the table of the factory or farm worker. There are even widespread taboos against the use of fruits, popular prejudices that limit their use even when economic conditions would permit it.

Calcium deficiency is general throughout the area and includes all social classes: the average consumption is less than 50 percent of the 0.80 grams daily recommended by nutritionists. In the Brazilian northeast one finds a daily calcium intake of about 0.40 grams, and a similar amount was found in the diet of Colombia. Dr. Santa Maria, Professor of Nutrition at the School of Public Health in Santiago, Chile, estimated in the late 1940's that the daily consumption of this mineral in his country was 0.49 grams per capita,[21] while the nutritionist Emma Reh, through the magnificent researches carried out in Paraguay during the same period, came to the conclusion that the per capita calcium intake in the capital of that country was some 0.29 grams a day, and in a rural section (Piribebuy) 0.36 grams.[22]

In spite of these alarmingly low calcium rations, rickets is a clinical rarity throughout the greater part of the area. Even in the Amazon, where the daily calcium consumption drops to 0.26 grams, there is practically no rickets. The rarity of this disease in tropical-equatorial regions is today a universally recognized fact. We know that Dr. Rigoberto Aguillar, examining 10,000 children of the Mexican plateau in the 1940's, found various kinds of nutritional deficiencies but not a single case of rickets—even though he used clinical methods, including X-ray, capable of detecting its hidden symptoms.[23] The same is true of Puerto Rico—one of the most acute starvation areas in the Americas—where Dr. Lydia Roberts found no trace of rickets among the undernourished children.[24] In the area of South America I am discussing, rickets appears on a socially important scale only in Chile, and there its greatest incidence is among poor children in the south of the country—well below the tropic zone. These regions lack the abundant sunlight of the countries to the north, where the wealth of Vitamin D formed by photosynthesis in the skin prevents the appearance of rickets, even though the diet is deficient in calcium.

If rickets is rare, dental caries are, in compensation, of telling frequency. The only groups to escape tooth decay are certain Indians such as those of the Bolivian uplands; they have magnificent teeth, but we are at a loss to explain the reason for this physiological superiority. In Chile both the Indian and the half-blood populations suffer from a high incidence of dental caries; in schoolchildren it runs from 40 percent to 75 percent. In the rural areas of Paraguay Reh observed that "an adult with good teeth is rarely seen. The young people always have teeth missing, and most of the aged are completely toothless."[25]

Another deficiency that weighs heavily on the health of South Americans is the lack of iron. In the majority of the South American dietary zones the food does not supply the 10 to 15 milligrams of iron necessary to the daily constitution of the hemoglobin pigment. The direct result of this deficiency is a very widespread kind of hypochromatic, microcytic anemia. The so-called "intertropical hypoemia" held by tropicalists at the turn of the century to be an immediate consequence of tropical climates is simply an anemia due to iron deficiency, and therefore of nutritional origin.

In many tropical and equatorial countries, worm infestation is so heavy and common that it is an important contributing factor in deficiency anemia. Intestinal worms rob the blood and hinder the absorption of nutritive elements. According to a report of a former minister of public health in Bolivia, 98 percent of the Bolivian population carries intestinal parasites.[26] According to the data of the Rockefeller Foundation, the incidence in Venezuela is 95 percent.

In Bahia, a city of northeastern Brazil, nearly 40 percent of the schoolchildren were found to be suffering from anemia. When a supplement containing iron was added to their diet, the anemia rate dropped in four months to only 3 percent, confirming the fact that a deficiency was the cause of the disease.[27] In places where this evil is most intense, one finds the strange phenomenon of geophagy, or geomania, the habit of eating earth. This custom, in my view, represents a state of specific hunger. An analysis of the clays that are eaten as food in Brazil confirms the fact observed by Cobert in Tunisia and Batz in the Congo—they are for the most part clays that contain high proportions of iron salts.[28]

Endemic goiter and cretinism caused by iodine deficiency

appear in various sections of this area, all far inland and separated from the coast by mountain barriers. Here the soil and water are extremely poor in this metalloid. The countries most subject to endemic goiter are Paraguay, Bolivia, Ecuador, and Argentina, although the others suffer from it more moderately. In Brazil there is a high rate of cretinic goiter in the southern region, which is a part of area B and will be dealt with later. In Paraguay Reh found that incidence of this disease among students in 35 different towns was 28 percent. In the Itá region the figure rose to 79 percent, while other parts of the country, such as Santo Inacio, were below the national average.[29] In Bolivia the evil is endemic in all provinces; the worst conditions are found in Chuquisara, where some 90 percent of the population is affected. In the Pichincha and Babura provinces of Ecuador, goiter is found in 70 percent of the inhabitants, and among schoolchildren of certain localities the incidence is 100 percent. Another great goiter area is northeast Argentina, where iodine deficiency is associated with innumerable other deficiencies. This, in fact, is one of the worst starvation areas of South America, with 80 percent of the children, according to Ramón Cárcano, showing evidence of malnutrition.[30] It is also a zone of high alcohol and coca consumption, factors which also contribute to the organic decadence caused by cretinic goiter.

In all of these places the victims of this disease show obvious signs of physical and mental degeneration: abnormalities of growth, endocrinous dwarf conditions, partial and general deformities, deaf-mutism, feeble-mindedness, idiocy, and so forth. This, then, is one of the most serious deficiency diseases, capable of causing the complete degeneration of whole groups of the population.

The deficit of sodium chloride may be said to be general throughout the lowlands of the continent's tropical zone, where the hot and frequently humid climate necessarily leads to excessive sweating and to an extreme depletion of the organism's salt reserves. If one recalls that every quart of sweat contains two to three grams of salt and that on the hottest days a person may sweat as much as eight or ten quarts, it will be seen that there is a daily loss of around twenty grams of sodium chloride.

In certain regions, such as the Brazilian northeast, the use of salt, meat, salt fish, and other sources of sodium chloride attenuates the loss from perspiration and prevents the appearance of this particular deficiency. In other zones, however, such as the Amazon, where the consumption of salt is insignificant, the deficiency is a permanent problem. In fact, the Indians throughout the Amazon basin hardly use salt at all; their favorite seasoning is pepper. This dietary imbalance leads to a drop in the sodium content of the blood and bodily liquids and to a compensatory increase in potassium. The nutritional deficiency thus sets up a syndrome in the humors of the body which causes states of nervous depression and muscular exhaustion. The factor of sodium deficiency almost always has a place in the etiology of tropical fatigue in this area.

The problem of sodium hunger is of the highest social and economic importance for people in tropical and equatorial regions. It involves not only climate but racial relations and cultural habits as well. As we have seen, in surveying the various forms of hunger, C. A. Talberg's researches showed that clothed skin secretes sweat almost twice as rich in salt as does naked skin.[31] According to Graham Lusk, this is a decisive argument against the use of clothing in the tropics.[32]

Yet white men, except for the Portuguese, have continued to wear clothes in the hottest climates. Not only have they been ignorant of the advantages of stripping; they have also feared to expose their pale and pigmentless skin, since it is easily penetrated by harmful rays as well as beneficial, by heat as well as ultraviolet. The black, however, is protected from burns and sunstroke by his pigmentation. In Caribbean

or Brazilian cane fields or on North American cotton plantations, wherever he works, in fact, the black goes nearly
naked.[33] And, losing less salt than the white man, he tires less
easily.

The variations of sodium and potassium metabolism provide a logical interpretation of several aspects of South
American life. They undoubtedly account, at least in part,
for the white man's well-known failure at physical work in
the tropics, and thus for his sedentary, bureaucratic functions
and his exploitation of black and Indian labor.[34] They also
demonstrate how a trait representing racial superiority in
polar regions may come to signify inferiority in hot countries
and vice versa, supporting the anthropologists' findings that
there are no biologically superior or inferior races.

In this instance, the question is not mainly one of biological differentiation but rather of the external process of
acclimatization, depending on the customs of the groups
concerned. Thus the details of diet, of clothing, and of work
organization take on great significance in connection with a
scientific exploration of sodium deficiency; these details have
made themselves felt throughout the structure of tropical
life.

The use in this zone of South America of restricted and, to
a certain extent, monotonous diets, limited to only four or
five food substances throughout the year, gives the specialist
in nutrition an impression, at first glance, that a spectacular
variety of vitamin deficiencies will be found there. But repeated investigations of the nutritional state of the people of
various South American countries contradict that assumption
completely. This is not to say that such diets really furnish
the requisite quantities of vitamins, nor that they could
possibly be called balanced diets. They are usually lacking in
vitamins, but the shortage is only partial, so that the organism does not reveal the deficiency in typical clinical symptoms, in frank vitamin diseases.

Only in limited areas and under exceptional conditions do the typical vitamin deficiency diseases appear, in either endemic or epidemic form. The restricted quantity of the diet as a whole and also, to a certain degree, the wide consumption of various spices and sauces made from native plants serve to forestall the more acute states of deficiency.

The lack of fats, of milk, of butter, and of green vegetables in the customary diets of this area necessarily leads to a certain shortage of Vitamin A. Nevertheless, conditions such as xerophthalmia or keratomalacia, eye conditions that reveal this deficiency, are clinical rarities that appear only sporadically. The reason for this is that each area has certain local resources capable to some extent of supplying the organism with this vitamin. In the Brazilian northeast, for instance, the mestizo populations use large quantities of *dendê* (*Elais guineensis*), a palm brought from Africa which produces an oil containing on the average 1,000 units of betacarotene per cubic centimeter.[35] And in Argentina any Vitamin A deficiency is corrected by the widespread use of *maté,* a beverage which has a high content of this element, as analyses carried out under the direction of Professor Pedro Escudero have demonstrated.[36]

Vitamin A deficiency makes itself felt most frequently through retarded growth and through skin disturbances—hyperpigmentation and hyperkeratosis—of the sort once observed by Frazer and Wu in certain parts of China.

Although in the manioc, corn, and rice areas there is an insufficient supply of those elements that make up the Vitamin B complex, the typical deficiency diseases such as beriberi, pellagra, and the conditions due to lack of riboflavin are rare. There was a large-scale epidemic of beriberi in the Amazon basin during the rubber boom from 1870 to 1910. During this period, the productive energy of the region was completely and exclusively absorbed in the latex harvest, with the result that fresh food disappeared entirely.

As rubber rose to represent for a time 28 percent of Brazil's total exports, a great flood of immigrants were attracted to the Amazon.[37] They came in waves, adventurous spirits attracted by the mirage of sudden wealth, seeking the "black gold," the priceless latex that spurted like blood from gashed rubber trees throughout the Amazon Valley. The virgin forest made these pioneers, who tried to snatch this wealth from the breast of the tropical jungle, pay dearly for their daring. And her favorite vengeance was beriberi. A majority of the hard frontiersmen who took part in the rubber rush were struck down by the terrible disease. Most of them came from the arid lands of the Brazilian northeast and were dazzled by the abundance of water in the Amazon region. They usually arrived in good health and full of enthusiasm. They plunged into the jungle along the rubber trails. They bled their trees and collected the precious milk. They smoked their rubber. They sold the product for a fabulous price. And then, just when victory seemed assured, they began to feel the ground falter beneath their feet. Their legs grew weak and lifeless, and a drowsiness crept upward from their feet and into their vitals. A constriction in the chest seized them like a mighty claw. It was beriberi coming on, taking possession of their bodies, gnawing at their nerves and putting an end to vitality. The woodsman who had traveled hundreds of miles on foot, who had come like a conqueror, overcoming all obstacles, along interminable trails, rivers, and inlets, was powerless against the terrible onslaught of beriberi. Then came the swellings, the terrible dropsy with the skin of his arms and legs stretched tight and the shiny, oozing lymph. Or his body dried up, the muscles wasted, and the flesh melted away as though the disease were eating him alive.

No statistics are available to give the precise number of victims. We do not know exactly how many were left as pitiful remains sunk in the swamps of the Amazon or how many came back disabled, carried down the river in litters to gentler lands and milder climates, where they might get over their beriberi and forget as best they could their ill-starred dreams of wealth. But from the chronicles of the period, one concludes that at least one half of the migratory population of the Amazon fell victim to this dietary deficiency.

The causes of the epidemic, which cost so many lives and which became one of the principal reasons for the failure to consolidate the Amazon economy during the rubber boom, can be traced to very definite social and economic factors. The fundamental causes were, in fact, strictly economic. Following the discovery of the vulcanizing process, the price of rubber in world markets reached fabulous figures; and as the quotations continued to rise daily, the whole population of the Amazon, permanent as well as temporary, forgot everything else and concentrated its whole energy on harvesting the precious latex. Fishing was paralyzed, herds were abandoned and left to drown in the floods, agriculture came to a stop for lack of workers. This drying up of all the local sources of wealth led to a tremendous crisis in the regional diet, which came to be made up almost exclusively of dry foods and of canned goods imported from abroad. The diet of the rubber worker consisted of jerked meat, corned beef, dried beans (usually old or wormy), manioc meal, polished rice, canned preserves, sugar, chocolate, and alcoholic drinks imported from Europe.

With this improper diet, completely lacking in fresh foods and very similar to that of the old sailing ships on which beriberi took a heavy toll, it is no wonder that an outbreak of beriberi followed. Then, after doing its terrible work, seemingly indifferent to all the medical and hygienic resources mobilized against it, the epidemic suddenly, and for no apparent reason, ceased—at least for no reason that could be explained by the medical knowledge of the times, which considered it to be a contagious and infectious disease. At the very time that Brazil's rubber monopoly ended, when the cultivated plantations of the Far East forced the Amazon's native product off the market, when the price of rubber collapsed and depression closed in, forcing the dealers into bankruptcy and the regional economy into collapse, the beriberi, as though it had been nourished by this bonanza economy, also began to decline.

When the cycle finally came to an end, with rubber exports dropping to 1 percent of national export volume, beriberi disappeared completely from the rubber region. When there was no more money to burn, no more cash to buy expensive drinks and English corned beef, the man of the Amazon had to go back to what he had been doing before the boom—to his hunting and fishing, to his harvesting of roots and wild fruits, to his incipient agriculture. The farming was only rudimentary, but it was enough to supply a few fresh products: corn, green and string beans, and other vegetables which, along with the wild products, greatly improved the quality of his diet, overcame the vitamin deficiency, and put an end to the beriberi.

In this way the cycle of the terrible disease came to a close, recalling in many ways the epidemic of scurvy in Alaska during the gold rush. Scurvy was one of the symptoms of gold fever just as beriberi was a symptom of rubber fever. Today, only a few small foci of endemic beriberi remain in South America: in the delta of the Orinoco, in Venezuela, and in certain zones of sugar cane monoculture, where it is called "sugar disease" or "plantation sickness."

In the Brazilian corn belt pellagra is practically unknown because the cereal is always eaten with milk and a little meat. In Venezuela, on the other hand, and in the northeast of Argentina, pellagrous skin lesions are much more frequent. In Bolivia the diets of 90 percent of the population are deficient in vitamins, but in spite of this fact, Dr. R. Passmore, an expert of the International Children's Emergency Fund, examined hundreds of children without finding a single case offering clinical evidence of Vitamin A, B, or C deficiency.[38] The situation is different with the latent or hidden cases, the symptoms of which are lack of appetite, fatigue, anemia, and so forth. These are extremely common.

Both scurvy and rickets are rare on the South American continent. Children with clear signs of rickets are found only in Chile, with its cold and temperate climates, and in the Bolivian highlands. According to Dr. Passmore, rickets in Bolivia is limited to children less than a year old; they recover spontaneously as soon as they begin to walk and to expose their skins to the ultraviolet rays of the sun.

Such, in rapid strokes, are the principal characteristics of the eating habits and the state of nutrition of the human groups that inhabit this one geographical zone. Now let us take a look at conditions in the second South American area.

In area B—Uruguay, west-central and southern Brazil, parts of Paraguay and Argentina—nutritional conditions are definitely better than in the area of chronic hunger, but they are still far from perfect. This relative dietary superiority has many causes. In the first place, this is the richest part of the continent, where the greater part of its economic activity is concentrated. The sector of Brazil included in this area, although it represents only a third of the national territory, includes 80 percent of the nation's economic capacity and produces more than 50 percent of the food consumed in the country. The part of Argentina included in this area, the so-called humid pampas of the littoral, takes in only 21 percent of the land area of the nation but in it are concentrated 68 percent of the population, 82 percent of economic activities, and 85 percent of the agricultural production of the country.

The per capita production, buying power, and living standards of this area, which includes all three of the great industrial cities of South America—Buenos Aires, Rio de

Janeiro, and São Paulo, each with a population in the millions—are a great deal higher than in the sectors included in area A. Per capita production in southern Brazil, for example, is ten times higher than it is in the extreme north. This area includes the most developed transportation network of the continent, and the populations enjoy a higher educational level—both of which factors are of great importance in maintaining a rational diet. Then too, the soil and climate of this area are superior both for farming and for cattle-raising. The continent's great herds of cattle, sheep, and swine are concentrated here.

This complex of favorable factors rules out any quantitative deficiency in the regional diet. A study carried out in Rio de Janeiro before World War II established an average daily consumption of some 2,800 calories.[39] Pedro Escudero estimated the average consumption of Buenos Aires factory workers at 3,000 calories a day.[40]

Another aspect of relative superiority in the diet of this area is the much higher consumption of protective foods [those that contain adequate amounts of the elements that prevent the development of deficiency diseases]. Meat consumption varies from 154 pounds in the south of Brazil, 244 in Uruguay, 253 in eastern Paraguay, to 300 in Argentina. The average milk consumption is 143 quarts in the Plata countries, somewhat less in the Brazilian sector. The average consumption of fruits, on the other hand, is higher in the south of Brazil (143 pounds) and more moderate in Argentina (130 pounds), Uruguay (106 pounds), and Paraguay (66 pounds). It is easily seen from these figures that protein deficiencies must be exceptional in this area; they are limited to the more miserable inhabitants of the city slums, who are in fact a marginal population.

When it comes to the supply of minerals and vitamins, the situation is less favorable. In many sub-areas there are partial deficiencies of calcium, iron, and iodine, as well as of the A and B groups of vitamins. The existence of these is substantiated by a number of facts. In an investigation carried out in 1933-34, covering 50,000 schoolchildren in Buenos Aires province, it was observed that 81 percent suffered from dental caries. In 1939 Argentine Senator Alfredo Palacios revealed to his colleagues that 30,000 children in Buenos Aires were unable to attend school because of malnutrition.[41] In a study made in Uruguay by Dr. Bauza at about the same time, it was found that out of 5,000 children from 17 departments of the country, 21 percent showed unquestionable signs of undernourishment. And if rickets is exceptional in the tropical zone of the continent, it appears with great frequency in this temperate area. Thus in Uruguay, according to Carrano and Bazzano, 15 percent to 18 percent of the children admitted to hospitals in Montevideo showed signs of rickets.

The most spectacular deficiency to be observed in this sector is the lack of iodine. In all the territory of Brazil west of the Serra do Mar mountain range, endemic goiter occurs in high proportions. Alvaro Lobo observed an incidence of 44 percent among the schoolchildren of a municipality in Minas Gerais;[42] and in the neighborhood of the city of São Paulo, Arruda Sampaio found that the figure was 60 percent.[43]

It may seem from this outline that the alimentation in all parts of both South American areas is more or less seriously defective. This general nutritional deficiency is one of the reasons, beyond a doubt, for the physical inferiority of the populations that inhabit this continent. The high index of general mortality and of infant mortality, as well as the high index in these areas of certain infectious diseases such as tuberculosis, are in the final analysis indirect manifestations of chronic malnutrition. The general mortality indices of South America are twice as high on the average as those of North America. The figures on infant mortality are among the highest in the world: 277 per thousand in Bolivia, 335 in the northwest of Argentina. In South American countries during the 1940's tuberculosis almost always stood first among the causes of death, and in certain zones it reached a figure ten times as high as the average death rate from tuberculosis in North America.[44]

What is responsible for this alarming nutritional situation in South America? Is it possible that the land is overcrowded and the starvation due to overpopulation? Far from it. I really do not know on what William Vogt based his statements, when he asserted that all the South American countries, excepting only three or four, are overpopulated.[45] The truth of the matter is that South America has an extremely low demographic density. A population of only 90 million inhabitants* is scattered over an area of more than 7 million square miles. This, I believe, is a relative density of only 13 to the square mile†—among the lowest in the world.

If hunger is not due to excess of people, is it perhaps due to the absence of soils suitable for agricultural production? Again, no. It is true that South America is no Ukraine or American Midwest, spectacularly fertile, but neither is it a barren Sahara. The greater part of the South American continent is covered with soils tending to tropical laterite, and this limits their use to the cultivation of plants that produce carbohydrates: sugar cane, manioc, corn, and rice. It is true that the yield from tropical soils is almost always lower than that from land in temperate regions: an acre of land in Brazil produces an average of 890 pounds of corn and 1,340 pounds of rice, while a similar area in the United States yields 1,425 pounds of the one and 1,980 pounds of the other, and in Italy the figures are 1,420 pounds and 4,100 pounds respectively.[46] In addition, tropical soils are extremely subject to

* 280 million inhabitants.
† 40 to the square mile.

erosion, and this rapidly leads to a decline in productivity. The climate of South America, moreover, which has too much rain in areas such as the Amazon and too little or too irregular a rainfall in others—such as the semiarid Brazilian northeast, the coastal areas of Ecuador and Peru, and the region of the Atacama Desert in northern Chile—makes agriculture somewhat difficult in a large part of the continent.

But the limitations imposed by these natural factors are far from making necessary or justifiable the existence of undernourishment and hunger. There is not a single large expanse of land in the world that does not have its waste areas, so much so that in the world as a whole, less than half of the land can be put to use. Although they may be scattered and irregularly distributed, a great many areas of very good soil are to be found in South America. If these soils were cultivated, they would be capable of producing sufficient food for a population many times greater than South America has today.

It is estimated that at least 25 percent of South America could be cultivated for one purpose or another, but the land actually in use does not exceed 5 percent of the total area. The F.A.O. has found that in spite of its low demographic density, South America has only 1.5 acres in cultivation per person, as against 4 in the United States and 2 in the U.S.S.R.[47] It is clear that social factors, rather than natural factors, are responsible for the precarious and insufficient food supply of the continent.

The prevailing starvation in South America is a direct consequence of the continent's historical past. This history is one of colonial exploitation along mercantile lines. It developed through successive economic cycles the effect of which was to destroy, or at least upset, the economic integrity of the continent. These were the cycle of gold, the cycle of sugar, the cycle of precious stones, the cycle of coffee, the cycle of rubber, the cycle of oil. And during the course of each of these cycles, one finds a whole region giving itself up entirely to the monoculture, or mono-exploitation, of a single product—at the same time forgetting everything else and thus wasting natural wealth and neglecting the potentialities of regional food supply.

The one-crop culture of cane sugar in the Brazilian northeast is a good example. This area once had one of the few really fertile tropical soils. It had a climate favorable to agriculture, and it was originally covered with a forest growth extremely rich in fruit trees. Today, the all-absorbing, self-destructive sugar industry has stripped all the available land and covered it completely with sugar cane; as a result this is one of the starvation areas of the continent. The failure to grow fruits, greens, and vegetables or to raise cattle in the region has created an extremely difficult food problem in an area where diversified farming could produce an infinite variety of foods.

Another phenomenon intimately associated with the kind of colonial land exploitation that aims at the production of cash crops for export is the latifundium, or great estate. One-crop agriculture and the latifundia constitute the two greatest evils of the continent; they are terrible handicaps to its agricultural development and consequently to its food supply. A few statistics on landed property in some of the South American countries are sufficient to make the situation clear. In Buenos Aires province, with a population of 3.5 million, a handful of only 320 aristocratic families monopolizes about 40 percent of the land.[48] In another province of Argentina, Santa Fé, there are 189 great estates, each with an average of 62,000 acres. In the central valley of Chile, where the bulk of the country's agricultural production, as well as 80 percent of its population, is concentrated, the latifundia remain unshaken. In Curico province, 437 great plantations take up 83 percent of the land, leaving only 17 percent of the province for 5,937 small proprietors.

Brazil, with the same population as France and an area fifteen times as large, has only half as many individual properties (1.9 million in Brazil as against 4 million in France). There is a reason for the fact that only 2 percent of the territory of Brazil is under cultivation and only 1 percent of it is devoted to the production of food.

Since food production in each country is limited almost exclusively to a small area, there is a lack of regional balance. In conjunction with this, the problem of food supply in South America is greatly aggravated by the lack of means of communication between these separate economic islets. To these main causes may be added others, such as ignorance of the simplest nutritional hygiene on the part of the people, and the wave of inflation that followed World War II. All these factors help to preserve the deplorable nutritional situation that prevails in the region.

[The Brazilian Example:
The Conflict Between Industry and Agriculture

The growing popular consciousness of the problem of hunger has spurred a strong and widespread impatience to be free of the grip of misery. Social tension in some Latin American countries is therefore extreme, amounting to a state of latent revolt that could erupt at any moment, and in the face of this situation various Latin American governments are trying to promote basic reforms to improve the living conditions of the people. Unfortunately, these reforms are usually applied with such timidity that they fail to reach the roots of the problem. Efforts at industrialization do not always result in any real improvement in living standards, for victory in the struggle against hunger, ultimately a struggle against underdevelopment, can be achieved only through balanced economic development and emancipation from all forms of economic colonialism. This is no easy task, for though political colonialism is dying out, economic colonialism, the neoimperialism of the great powers, is on the increase.

Brazil, which in recent years has been changing from a basically agricultural country to a partially industrialized one, is a useful example of a Third World nation striving to break the shackles of underdevelopment, for while certain new social patterns have emerged, the country remains in the grip of hunger. All recent studies of the question bear witness to the astonishing persistence of hunger in Brazil, in spite of the spectacular progress made in many other areas. Despite its economic development, Brazil remains a country of scarcity, where two thirds of the population suffer the consequences of inadequate nutrition. Brazilian economic development, as it relates to the phenomenon of hunger, thus deserves more detailed analysis.

Brazil's hunger is first of all a consequence of its history of human struggle against the natural environment, a struggle sometimes occasioned by the environment's hostility but most often provoked by the ineptitude of a colonial element indifferent to anything that did not represent direct and immediate gain. The colonial experience unfolded in a succession of cycles that were economically destructive or, at their least harmful, led to economic imbalance. These stages were the "pau-brazil" (the black forest), the period of sugar cane, the hunting down of Indians, gold prospecting, "nomad coffee cultivation," the rubber boom, and, finally, an artificial industrialization based on the fiction of tariff barriers and inflation. The same exploitative spirit has provided the drive behind each of these stages and has corrupted any efforts to develop the country's real wealth. This "get rich quick" spirit has been powerfully portrayed by Sergio Buarque de Holanda in his book *Raizes do Brasil* (*The Roots of Brazil*). The national impatience for profit obsessed the pioneers, constantly provoking them to waste the wealth and potential of their own land.

The nation's hunger is also a consequence of the state's inability to arbitrate private and public interests and, even more damaging, its ineptitude in protecting national interests from exploitation by foreign monopolies. The foreign interests have always won out and have directed the country's economy toward the exploitation of the land and its raw materials. Thus Brazil developed a maritime trade, exporting its potential wealth—the products of both its soil and its labor—for ridiculous prices, leaving itself without sufficient resources to provide its people with consumer goods or to permit its own internal development.

For more than four hundred years—from its discovery by the Portuguese in 1500 until the world-wide crisis of 1929—Brazil lived under an economy of the classic colonial type, marked by the extensive exploitation of raw materials destined for export. The Portuguese *conquistadores* were at first content to extract certain natural products like wood, but before long they turned, in the northeastern section of the country, to the extensive cultivation of sugar cane. For more than a century the Portuguese retained a commercial monopoly on this tropical product. The establishment in this region of an economy based on sugar gave rise to a feudal agrarian system, traces of which still dominate the economic life of the area today. Both the system of latifundia and single-crop agriculture, which spread together across the country, drastically impeding its social and economic evolution, owe their origins to this type of Portuguese colonization.

The golden age of sugar lasted until the second half of the seventeenth century, when the production of the West Indies broke the Brazilian monopoly. The country then entered upon a new economic cycle as gold was discovered in abundance in the south-central region. In time Brazil was the principal source of the metal that was to give a strong impetus to European capitalism and accelerate the Industrial Revolution, especially in England. At the end of the seventeenth century, however, the amount of gold produced drastically diminished. The economy was then reoriented around the production of coffee in the southern provinces, now the states of São Paulo and Rio de Janeiro.

The coffee cycle, which indisputably played a major role in the expansion of the Brazilian economy, passed through periods of crisis. The first, which began in 1888, was directly connected with the abolition of slavery and the consequent disappearance of the cheap manpower that had, along with the abundance of fertile land, assured low-cost production. The attempt to keep the coffee economy going by encouraging the immigration of Europeans to work on the plantations brought into being a mass of agricultural wage-earners and, thus, the beginnings of a capitalist system. This created an economic chasm between the south of the country and the sugar-producing north—for the north, where the rural populations had been untouched by the gold cycle because of their lack of purchasing power, continued in a state of agrarian feudalism. The chasm grew ever deeper, eventually separating the two sections into different worlds, never to be unified into a single economic system.

The solvency of the government, and hence its stability, depended on foreign trade, which soon came to mean the export of coffee, for the coffee planters wasted no time in wresting power from the sugar barons.[49] The north entered upon a time of decadence while the south monopolized the country's decision-making centers. A protectionist policy, which worked to the detriment of every other economic activity, made possible a rapid increase in coffee production, and coffee soon enjoyed a clear lead over the few other products in the export market. But overproduction and a drop in the world price of coffee worked against the Brazilian economy, which soon suffered from a profoundly unfavorable balance of payments situation, to the point where the country was forced at the beginning of the twentieth century to restrict imports. This led to numerous attempts to find new avenues into the world market in order to re-establish the country's economic balance.

The discovery of the vulcanization process and the beginning of the automobile industry created a large-scale demand for rubber, and the Amazon was then the only producer. The tonnage of latex extracted from the Amazon jungle increased rapidly, until at the beginning of the century it represented 28 percent of total Brazilian exports.[50] But this expansion was brief, and the export of rubber brought only temporary relief, for the country's economy was simplistically extractive, incapable of responding to world demand. Brazil soon lost out in the world rubber market to the countries of southeast Asia, which organized the systematic production of rubber based on the cultivation of *hevea brasiliensis,* a species that, as its name indicates, comes from Brazil. The country then turned to other products—cacao, maté, and cotton—in an attempt to diversify its exports, but none ever attained the importance of coffee. The amount of increase they represented barely matched population growth. Their export was only a palliative and the country was obliged by force of circumstances to maintain the reign of coffee despite the insecurity involved.

Brazilian governments have almost always been incapable of impeding the greedy interference of foreign monopolies in the economy, for political authority has been unequal to coping with colonial adventurism or to directing the social organization of the nation. Historically, the reasons for this lay in the governments' frailty and weakness vis-à-vis powerful and independent landowners, who were little kings within their closed domains, indifferent to any government regulation or decision contrary to their interests. Recent years have seen a striking exaggeration in the opposite direction, an excessive centralization of power that has taken almost all income and rights away from the local jurisdictions and handed them over to a central government incapable of distributing benefits. The government has never possessed an adequate understanding of how to use political power in the administration of such a vast territory.

When central authority was weak, the colonial powers were able to maneuver the country's economy for their own ends, increasing the profits of a small number of landowners associated with the colonial enterprise without benefiting the population as a whole. As Gunnar Myrdal has made abundantly clear, the great powers, in their efforts at colonial exploitation, have always made use of "oligarchical groups who are themselves interested in the maintenance of the political and social status quo and, consequently, opposed to true and liberating development." On the other hand, the logical consequence of centralization and the republic's dishonest policies is the abandonment of the countryside and the drive toward urbanization that have been evident in Brazil since the end of the last century. Because no healthy society organized for efficient use of the soil existed in rural areas, urbanization alarmingly aggravated the nation's poor diet. This does not mean that urbanization is an evil in itself: it represents a necessary transitional stage between a purely agrarian economy and an agricultural-industrial economy. In the United States this sort of population movement assumed vast proportions without imbalancing the country's nutritional situation; on the contrary, it stimulated agriculture and the raising of livestock. The move toward industrialization and urbanization in the American east gave rise to intensive grain farming and meat production in the Middle West and made California, with its orchards and truck farms, the foremost farming state in the union. But in Brazil the imbalance accentuated evils that had been present since the first European adventurers, financed for the most part by international capital, introduced their "get rich quick" policy—which was for most of the population a policy of hunger.

This is the essential characteristic of colonial economic development. Throughout the world, colonialism promised progress, but only the sort of progress that served its own interests or, at best, those of a small number of privileged native citizens uninterested in the future of their nation or the political, social, and cultural aspirations of its masses. The result is abnormal and partial development, limited to those sectors of the economy most profitable to speculative capital and ignoring other economic areas that are indispensable for true social progress. As a consequence of this selfish conception of economic progress, several economically dependent countries came to possess what some sociologists have called a "dualist social structure": one well-developed social framework superimposed upon another that is economically stagnant. Even today some groups retain this colonial mentality, conceiving of economic progress in terms of short-term benefits or of a simple injection of dollars for the immediate exploitation of certain resources. The structural duality of Brazilian society—the two Brazils described by the writer Jacques Lambert—is the country's heritage, the legacy of political behavior imposed upon it by the European colonialists beginning in the sixteenth century, from which it is just beginning to free itself.

The pressure of anti-national policies allowed a small group to monopolize the country's wealth and to waste large areas of the soil cultivating products for export. Railroads were constructed exclusively to connect the centers where these products were grown to the ports of embarkation. Political adaptations were made to serve these economic manipulations. Behind the appearance of progress, there remained huge unproductive estates, a plantation system based on slavery, backwardness, ignorance, poverty, and hunger.

Another aspect of Brazilian development that has worked against improvements in the nutritional situation has been the relative neglect of the poorest regions of the country, where hunger still rages. Granted, that when the resources of a country seeking to develop itself primarily on its own are minimal, they must be distributed according to a rigorous system of priorities so that the potential for investment is not diluted by inefficiency and lack of productivity. But this should not mean concentrating all resources in the most developed areas, which already possess expanding productive centers, and ignoring vast regions that are potentially capable of participating in the economic process. That is what has happened, however. The Brazilian philosophy of development during recent years worked on the principle of developing further what was already developed, rather than integrating into the national economic system neglected areas such as the northeast and the Amazon.

The northeast is the more alarming case because one third of the Brazilian population is concentrated there, living, as previously described, under precarious economic conditions. Nevertheless, the whole Brazilian economic policy conspires against the real economic integration of this region of the country. Federal policy in the northeast is limited to some protection of the sugar economy, which will never by itself emancipate the area, and to "fraternal" aid during disastrous droughts—an aid that is largely ineffective because it benefits certain protected groups more than those who are the real disaster victims. The northeast is treated like a colony—quite the opposite of what it needs. It is this total economic dependence of the northeast and Amazon areas upon other regions of the country that prevents the eradication of hunger there. If the northeast—or rather, the entire north—were granted a price and credit policy that did not unjustly favor other regions of the country, its economy would develop much more rapidly than it can on the basis of the limited budgetary credits it receives—mere grains of sand in a sea of misery.

Writing of the relations between underdeveloped countries and the major powers, André Philip says that those underdeveloped countries who do not need financial aid or assistance to develop themselves desire above all that their economies be given respect rather than aid. Within Brazil the situation is the same. The wealthier areas, which have the lion's share of economic and political power, must come to respect the poorer regions and seek to cooperate in their emancipation for the benefit of the whole nation.

This is no mere jeremiad. I have no wish to partition Brazil with wailing walls. I do want to see it achieve a greater unity by melding its fragmented economy into an integrated system. To accomplish this, superannuated prejudices—such as the view that the poorest regions of the country are beyond recovery—must be overcome, for we know that these areas have failed to progress only because historical conditions have been unfavorable and the economic situation has not permitted the fulfillment of potential. The northeast is not irremediably condemned to poverty and its people to hunger because of some inexorable determinism but because, although economic changes have weakened the colonialist policy in the south, that policy still thrives in the "nordestina" region, which produces only raw materials and basic products. Sometimes I think that what the northeast needs most is a little more political strength and direction, so that it could demand, rather than beg for, its human rights. Basically, the politicians of the northeast have never made much effort to assert the area's rights to liberation and integration into the national economic system; on the contrary, they have prevented the people from doing so.

A good example of the discriminatory treatment imposed on the area's economy is the problem of return on exports. The exportation of the northeast's basic products—such as cacao, sugar, carnauba, cotton, oils, and certain minerals—accounts for a good part of the foreign currency entering Brazil. But this currency benefits the northeast only slightly; the largest portion is drained off by the state to equip the industry of the south and sometimes, even worse, to cover the importation of luxury products—the Cadillacs and perfumes underdeveloped countries believe will hide their wretchedness but that actually throw their backwardness into bolder relief. For this is exactly what underdevelopment means: drastic economic contrasts, gaps in terms of productivity, revenue, and consumption among the various levels of the population and the different regions. The promotion of real socioeconomic development would mean, first of all, an attempt to narrow these gaps by means of a better distribution of wealth and a fairer apportionment of investments in the different regions and in the different sectors of the economy. Although the economic development plans established by Juscelino Kubitschek's government aimed at promoting a faster pace of economic progress, they did not give sufficient attention to these basic needs and consequently did not contribute effectively to the diminution of hunger in many areas.

The government that took power on April 1, 1964, following a military coup d'état, declared as its policy:

1. Acceleration of the rate of national economic development, which had been halted during 1962-63.

2. Progressive control of inflation during 1964-65 in order to achieve a reasonable degree of price stability beginning in 1966.

3. Reduction of the economic gaps among various groups and regions and thus, thanks to an improvement in living standards, a lessening of social tensions.

4. Guaranteed employment for the large work force continually crowding the labor market, by means of a policy of investment.

5. Rectification of the balance of payments, whose uncontrollable tendency to a deficit threatened the continuity of the process of economic development by periodically reducing import capacity.[51]

In fact these aims have never been achieved and Brazil's economic situation is now more precarious than ever. The rate of economic development has been negligible and is today still below the level reached under the Kubitschek regime.

In its fight against inflation, the present government has made use of two methods that have a strong tendency to depress the economy: the drastic lowering of real salaries and the excessive restriction of credit. The lowering of wages is the result of the government practice of readjusting them on the basis of forecasts contained in its own plan for fighting inflation. The Brazilian economist Dias Leite correctly states:

The gap between reality and the forecasts of this plan is such that it can be imputed to the incertitude inherent in all economic forecasts. Beyond this, the government assigns two different weights and measures to the indices of inflation foreseen as 25 percent for 1965 and 10 percent for 1966. To defend its anti-inflation program it declares that these estimates must not be taken literally. But in the application of its wage policy it does not hesitate to make readjustments on the basis of these figures. This is still the case, as on January 13 [1966] the Budgetary Council decided to fix the inflationary residue for 1966 at 10 percent. The indices become working instruments whose direct consequences on the national economy bring about distortions in the social structure of the country.[52]

Because, as its critics had foreseen, this policy gave no consideration to the purchasing power of wages, it seriously worsened the living conditions of the working classes. The destruction of purchasing power occasioned a general stagnation of the Brazilian economy. Calculations made by the Planning and Development Commission show that in 1964-65 purchasing power diminished by 8 percent among those who earned the minimum wage, by 15 percent among bank employees, by 7 percent among textile workers, and by 15 percent among civil service employees. As a result, there was a drastic drop in sales throughout the country. Sales of textiles fell 40 percent in the state of Parana, 33 percent in Guanabara, 28 percent in São Paulo, and 18 percent in the state of Rio de Janeiro. A local correspondent for *Time* reported in the December 16, 1966, issue that Christmas sales were the lowest ever registered in Brazil. If, along with this shrinking market, one considers the restriction of credit imposed as a stabilizing measure, it is easy to understand the great number of bankruptcies that took place throughout the country during this period of crisis. A document prepared by the technicians of the National Industrial Confederation shows that in 1963-65, while the real product increased by 90 percent and industrial growth was 134 percent, the availability of credit increased by barely 40.5 percent. Furthermore, various privileges granted to attract foreign capital made the lot of national industry even harder, because it was forced to compete with foreign companies that had available, through internal credit, superior financial means.

Nevertheless, foreign capital has not entered in the proportions the government counted on to revive the economy. Foreign aid has had a greater impact in the forms of merchandise and services than in terms of currency, another strike against the present economic plan's chances of success.[53] Stagnation reigns. Small and medium-sized industries are disappearing, absorbed by large foreign companies that are able to grow without importing currency to meet their need for new capital.

This analysis need go no further into the details of the

present situation in Brazil to make it perfectly clear that the measures the government has taken since 1964 have not succeeded in freeing the country from economic stagnation and the resulting social tension. Inflation continues to rage, although at a lower rate, and the economy is paralyzed. Moreover, this situation could have been foreseen by anyone aware that inflation in Brazil is the fruit of underdevelopment and of the dangerously dependent economy. Inflation in such a case is no accident; it is integral to the structure of an underdeveloped country subject to monopolistic conditions in its markets.

As long as Brazil retains its semifeudal structure, attempts at stabilization will continue to fail, and each failure will further delay development. This will go on despite the capitalistic overlay on the feudal foundations that is represented by the industrial centers—for these centers have been, little by little, monopolized by foreign interests. The *Time* article cited above remarked: "The danger of Brazilian 'denationalization' is not purely imaginary." It is, indeed, a sad reality.

The economic and social crisis now gripping Brazil—once closer than any other tropical country to growing beyond its underdeveloped economy and attaining an autonomous and balanced development—carries a significant lesson for the Third World in its search for economic emancipation. Four centuries after being settled, a so-called "agricultural country" is using only about 2 percent of its developed land to raise essential products, and of this insignificant area only one third is given over to growing food. The natural result of such insufficient production is a per capita rate of consumption that ranks at the bottom of international tables, especially in terms of basic nutrients—meat, milk, cheese, butter, fruits, and vegetables. Per capita meat consumption is 117 pounds annually, while it is 228 pounds in Argentina, 235 in New Zealand, 183 in the United States, 140 in Great Britain, and 147 in Denmark. The consumption of milk is ridiculously low: 39 quarts per year, or about 100 grams a day. In Denmark it is 278 quarts; in the United States 223.5; in Australia 107; and in France 100. The rate is similarly low for other sources of protein such as cheese and eggs: 21 ounces of cheese, while in Denmark the figure is 11 pounds. In Brazil, butter is consumed in the same quantity as cheese—21 ounces—while in the United States, Great Britain, and Denmark the figures are, respectively, 40, 22, and 18 pounds. The consumption rates of other basic foods are analogous; they are the lowest in the world.

The picture these data present is not a portrait of the past but of present-day social conditions, with all their complexities and confusion; it fully justifies Roger Bastide's title, *Brésil: Pays de Contrastes.* The contrasts are indeed astonishing. For example, there is on the one hand the resplendent urban life of some of the great cities, and on the other the social mire and stagnation of rural life around these same cities. A high level of modern industry exists beside a feudal agriculture using the most conservative methods. This explains why, despite all the surprising economic successes in the areas of heavy industry, automobiles, the building of Brasilia, and other astonishing achievements, Brazil remains a country of hunger, one of the largest regions in the universal geography of hunger. While the spread and the intensity of the problem have been slightly reduced, the general picture remains more or less the same.

In recent years, awareness of the problem has grown. The government and the people are giving it their attention. Basic principles of nutritional hygiene are better known. Little has been accomplished, however, in the way of concrete improvements in the nutritional situation. In some places it even seems to have grown worse in the face of the industrial thrust that the country is experiencing. Those who guide the destiny of Brazil have not yet really grasped that a solution to the problem requires a courageous and decisive attack upon its roots. Even those governments most committed to the country's economic emancipation have had no success in this vital area. Let us take a closer look at the recent course of national economic development.

Economic development is a powerful concept today, capable of mobilizing the popular will. The Brazilian people want to participate actively in transforming the economy and are ready to cope with whatever results from this collective effort. The process of transformation began more than forty years ago. Starting in 1930 various segments of the economy were gradually brought together into a system capable of autonomous development, and the pace of expansion has been accelerating since World War II. An examination of certain economic signs makes it possible to evaluate the thrust of Brazilian development. One indication is that the country's rate of real production doubled between 1945 and 1960; but while industrial production increased by about 190 percent, agriculture grew by only 40 percent. Brazil is becoming industrialized and its productive capacity is increasing. But how effectively is this productive capacity being used? Such effectiveness is the best measure of a plan for economic development, for the rate at which an economic system expands depends largely on the validity of the criteria that direct its investments.

What has happened in Brazil? How intense is its economic growth and what restricts its productivity? If economic development is measured by average per capita income, there is no argument. But measured by real distribution of income among different social groups, it is clearly much less effective. And the truth is that social progress cannot be reckoned in terms of the overall volume of income or average per capita income—a statistical abstraction—but only in terms of real distribution of income. Instead of showing a tendency toward broader distribution, income in Brazil is more and more concentrated in particular areas and among particular groups. The government has lacked the courage to reform the basic structures responsible for this imbalance and to promote a process of development that would remedy the country's economic weaknesses.

Even as the Brazilian economy became industrialized, it continued to behave like a colonial economy, politically uninterested in the lot of the majority. The developers' sole preoccupations were developing what was already there and further enriching those already enriched by the existing system. Because of this imbalance Brazil's economic development has not been matched by the genuine social development desired by the masses.

There is still far to go. The policy of concentrating intensive industrialization in the south, which already possessed an economic system that combined the exportation of coffee and a nascent industry, has aggravated imbalances that already existed. The contrasts between the south and the north and northeast stem from the imbalance between industry and agriculture. The regional disequilibrium is, indeed, only the geographical reflection of the gap that separates the two economic systems. This imbalance between sectors is of the first importance, for it constitutes, in my judgment, the most serious distortion of the dynamics of the country's economic development and the principal stumbling block to industrialization, one of development's basic goals.

Every instance of directed development in an underdeveloped country automatically creates a series of imbalances that continually demand corrective measures. The sociologist Costa Pinto points out that "in the social structures of the less developed countries, the essential characteristic is not the absence of change but the fact that different parts of the structures change at different rates, causing distortions, contradictions, and resistance." As a result, it is impossible to import prefabricated development models and apply them locally, even insofar as the experience of other peoples can be validly transferred. Each expanding economic system must set its own course, in terms of its particular economic and geographical situation, though the results are always to some degree unpredictable.

In Brazil's case the most drastic distortion is the backwardness of agriculture in relation to the industrial sector. Some dispute this, arguing that Brazilian agriculture has developed at a faster rate than the population, at a ratio of three to two. But this is an extremely weak argument. It must be remembered that Brazil's nutritional level has always been the lowest in the world, both in overall underconsumption of calories and in specific underconsumption of many foods, including the most basic. Brazil's food production has never come close to meeting its actual needs, even limited as they are by the population's lack of purchasing power. Clearly, now that purchasing power is increasing because of industrial progress, the demand for foodstuffs is also rising sharply, requiring a much higher rate of agricultural production than has so far been achieved. Then, too, the agricultural sector of the economy furnishes 60 percent of the raw materials for Brazilian industry, the expansion of which therefore requires a parallel increase in the volume of these raw materials.

But the backwardness of Brazilian agriculture is demonstrated most clearly not by the volume of its production but by the rate of its productivity, which is the lowest in the world in terms of both the output of the farm workers and the yield of the land. Because of the Brazilian farmer's low rate of return on his labor, millions of workers are needed to cultivate only 50 million acres of land, while in the United States 8 million men can cultivate an area almost ten times as large. The low productivity of the land can also be demonstrated by some unfavorable comparisons: the average yield of sugar cane per acre is 94 tons in the northeast, against 173 in Puerto Rico; for cotton the figures are 1.7 tons in the northeast, 2.776 in São Paulo, and 3.22 in the United States;

for corn 1.67 in the northeast, 3.46 in the state of Minas Gerais in eastern Brazil, and 8.08 in the United States.

The weakness and backwardness of Brazil's agriculture sap the entire national economy and in various ways limit the country's rate of industrialization. Because of the scarcity of raw materials and the high cost of production, agriculture is indisputably one of the factors that stifle a large number of the processing industries. The short supply and high prices of food products necessitate salary levels for industrial workers that seriously add to the cost of industrial production, still without enabling the workers to obtain the sort of diet that would improve their productivity. This increases the difficulty of establishing large-scale industrial zones and in certain parts of the country makes supplying them one of the greatest headaches of planners and business leaders. The economic marginalism to which peasants, with their lack of purchasing power, are condemned rules out the existence of an internal market that could absorb the growing industrial output. The high rate of migration from the country to the cities chokes the urban centers with unproductive masses of humanity— economically dead cells that clog the social fiber—and vastly overburdens the public treasury with indispensable social services, the high cost of which necessarily absorbs a large part of the resources that should have been devoted to productive investments.

I have no doubt that the regrettable imbalance between the agricultural and industrial economies lies behind the slowdown in the rate of industrial expansion observable during the 1960's, just when the efforts and resources dedicated to the promotion of industrial development were at their peak. It is no longer any secret, nor a question of pure speculation on the part of economists, that several industrial sectors have reached the limits of the internal market and have begun to cut production, causing growing unemployment in certain urban centers.

This imbalance, which threatens every effort to unify the economic system by undermining its productive capacity, must be corrected. But it can be corrected only if public authorities respond more effectively to the most pressing needs of the agricultural economy. It is a grave risk to count on the gap's closing by itself, on the premise that industrial progress, when it reaches a certain level, automatically brings about rural progress. In terms of social reality this premise is false; it would be valid only in a world governed by the principles of liberal economics, in which the "invisible hand" invoked by Adam Smith would always ensure, through the action of free competition, the re-establishment of the "natural order." This kind of thinking denies the efficacy of economic planning and the possibilities now available for directing economic development toward defined objectives without taking commercial gambles. The Chinese economist Pei Kanh-chang is right when he states that industrial development by itself does not lead to reform of the agrarian economy. It is a necessary, but not a sufficient, condition for the transformation of rural economic life. But even if, for the sake of argument, we admit the point that when industrial development reaches a certain level the economic impact will move agriculture forward, two important questions remain: what is this level and what guarantees that it can be reached —when Brazil's development is blocked and stifled by the underproductivity and underemployment of the two thirds of its work force now existing apathetically in the agricultural sector?

The excessively slow growth rates of farm production and livestock-raising, far below those needed to match the economic expansion of the country, bear witness to the relative neglect of agriculture. If we take 100 as the base index and 1949 as the base year, we observe that for 1958 and 1966:

Year	Agricultural production	Industrial production	Gross domestic product
1958	141.3	213.2	160.7
1966	202.2	355.9	236.3

The increase in agricultural production is slight and, in any case, insufficient to compensate for the population increase. In addition, during years like 1958 such growth as there was reflected a higher production of export crops—principally coffee—rather than an increase in basic products for domestic consumption.

Obviously, this economic distortion weights heavily on the nutritional situation of the people by increasing inflation and thus raising food prices. A few figures will demonstrate inflation's crushing progress. During the years 1956, 1957, 1958, and 1959, the cost of living rose at the following rates: 20.8, 16, 14.9, and 39.1 percent. An increase of close to 40 percent, as in 1959, devours all the resources of the salaried classes, whose loss of purchasing power forces them onto a terribly restricted diet. That explains the veritable epidemic of protein deficiency—kwashiorkor—in the urban proletariat. The foods that combat this illness, notably milk, have become inaccessible and remain so, despite salary adjustments that always come too late and are always below the levels of inflationary increase.

In all these ways, the gap between industry and agriculture seriously hampers the progress of Brazil's development. What does it really mean? It is a normal crisis of national growth, although the risks of profound imbalance that it entails make it dangerous. Economic development is the only real solution for underdevelopment and its basic accompaniment of underemployment, underproductivity, and generalized poverty. The Brazilian people's growing understanding of their true situation has led them to a profound conviction that only real economic development will deliver them from the economic oppression and slavery that are now the lot of the majority. Today, the only possible attitude is to hope for and to cooperate in the rapid and balanced promotion of the country's economic development. To think otherwise is simply to serve the anti-national interests, to play into the hands of international trusts which desire to stifle progress in those areas with primitive economies that furnish raw materials to the great industrial centers. The policy of development represents a historic necessity, an imperative that cannot be escaped.

But questions, doubts, and disagreements as to this policy's implementation and the choice of methods remain. The Kubitschek government, anxious to promote rapid economic expansion and convinced that only intensive industrialization could emancipate the country economically, carried out its program in a manner that I found deeply disturbing. Priorities for the use of Brazil's insufficient economic resources were set according to a criterion that was far from ideal. It is my belief that industrial development must be hastened without unduly sacrificing investments in the agrarian economy. To concentrate all efforts in a single economic sector is to stimulate unbalanced development; the effects of the imbalance will soon appear and the rate of expansion will slow down. A planned development must act upon the whole economic system if it is to avoid imbalances that will eventually prove stifling. Brazil is now coming to recognize that the backwardness of its agriculture is choking its industrial economy as well. Industry will not be able to maintain its rate of expansion unless it fosters the development and consolidation of the agricultural economy. This point is so central to plans for Brazil's development that I must insist upon it, at the risk of my readers' patience with arguments that may seem repetitious. So long as the structure of the agrarian economy remains unchanged, it will be very difficult to obtain the raw materials necessary for industry to compete on the world market and to provide adequate food for the working masses in the large industrial centers. In addition, because a domestic market that would absorb the increasing industrial production is now lacking, measures must be taken to integrate into the economic system the great mass of the peasants—about 55 percent of the population—who today live practically without the bare minimum.

The relative neglect of the agricultural sector was formerly partly justified because in a precapitalist economy resources were scarce, and to concentrate them in the most productive enterprises seemed the best route to national emancipation. But it is now becoming clear that this course threatens the desire for emancipation as well as the mammoth effort toward national industrialization.

The existence of what some sociologists call "swollen" cities—Recife, for example, with 400,000 unproductive migrants from other areas—makes it perfectly clear that the imbalance between the cities and the countryside in Brazil has grown worse in recent years. Likewise, the contrast between the industrialized south and the predominantly agricultural north and northeast is growing more severe. The situation in the north constitutes Brazil's most serious problem, threatening not only the economy but also—and more importantly—national security.

In seeking to foster economic development, the government has made no clear decision between bread and steel: that is, whether to use its insufficient resources for the production of consumer goods or to concentrate them in intensive industrialization, while temporarily sacrificing the people's aspirations for social improvement. The predominant opinion among economists is that it is necessary to concentrate at the beginning on steel, that is, on industrialization, and that society must make sacrifices in the cause of national recovery. This is called paying the price of the progress that is indispensable for economic emancipation.

Social reality, however, is more complex than such an approach suggests. The proper choice is not bread *or* steel but bread *and* steel, in the proportions imposed by social circumstances and existing economic resources. Attempts to demand from any society a faster rate of progress than is acceptable to it will cause resentments and dangerous social tensions. It is my impression that the Brazilian people, imbued as they now are with the ideas of development and social progress, are ready to sacrifice so that the country may be developed and liberated economically. But they must be convinced that the sacrifices are shared equally by every national group and social class—and I am not at all sure that this is now the case. To make its economic development program succeed, the government will not only have to attend to the needs of groups within the agricultural sector; it will also have to promote better regional distribution of credit and investment so that the Brazilian giant does not become crippled or deformed. To aim at the development of only one part of the nation, sacrificing to this new Moloch other even more underdeveloped regions of the country, will warp the real economic thrust desired by the majority of Brazilians.

Measures must also be taken to counter the excessive concentration of economic power so that the sacrifices that must be made will be more justly distributed. Today they weigh almost exclusively on the less well-off classes, already crushed by the terrible increases in the cost of living. The government seems able to ignore the problem, but the people's bodies show the sad effects of the inflation that caused the purchasing power of Brazilian money to fall by 1959 to one thirty-fifth of its 1914 value. (In 1958 one American dollar was worth 100 cruzeiros. The devaluation of August 1968 fixed the price of the American dollar at 3,650 cruzeiros or 3.65 new cruzeiros.)

From this brief exposition we can conclude that since national economic development is imperative, the government and the people must unite, in trust and mutual interest, to see that this development goes steadily forward, that the shortcomings inevitable in any plan are rectified before they lead to economic disaster. There can be no doubt that Brazil is making a great leap forward. At all costs, it must avoid leaping into an abyss. The leap must be measured so that it does not exceed the nation's strength.

Such a leap is impossible for a hungry people, a people without the bare essentials of nourishment. This is where national progress must begin. The minimum acceptable standard of nourishment can be obtained only if profound changes are made in Brazil's basic structures, now too antiquated to create the conditions necessary for the full exercise of the country's productive powers. The most regressive element in the whole situation, the one most opposed to true social progress, is undoubtedly the country's agrarian structure. Hence, the necessity to attack it with determination.

Structural faults are the essential cause of the country's poor use of natural resources, its low agricultural productivity, and the inactivity of its peasants—in short, of the general backwardness of Brazilian agriculture. The archaic nature of the agrarian structures is obvious not only in the unequal distribution of property but also in the feudal methods of production—including sharecropping and unpaid labor.

In distinguishing three characteristics of rural society, Moacir Paixao eloquently describes the essentials of the Brazilian agrarian problem:

1. The domination of great expanses of land, often the best land, by a class of capitalist farmers and landowners who prevent a broader utilization of the soil and reduce its productivity.

2. The existence of an enormous heterogeneous mass of landless peasants who are generally poor; to gain access to the land, they must work as sharecroppers, tenants, or hired laborers on the stock-farms and plantations raising coffee, cotton, rice, sugar, wheat, tobacco, cacao, or corn.

3. Social frictions over land, which usually start from the opposition between the large landowners and the landless rural masses and then affect other rural social groups. Indeed, hundreds of thousands of poor people who own small plots come into conflict with the large landowners.

The shocking anomaly of this feudal agrarian regime in the late twentieth century can be demonstrated by a few eloquent statistics: Brazil, enormous in extent, possesses the same number of farms as France, which is only 6 percent of its size. It is as if the regime of the hereditary *capitanias* established in 1534 by John III of Portugal were still in force. Sixty percent of the farms in Brazil are more than 1,200 acres, 20 percent of these are more than 2,500 acres. The 1950 census revealed the existence of dozens of properties that are real feudal *capitanias*—holdings of more than 250,000 acres. Alongside this harmful tendency toward latifundia—in which technical backwardness and nonproductivity are inherent—we find the anti-economic pulverization of property, the minifundia. Five hundred thousand holdings —one fourth of the national total—occupy only 0.5 percent of the land surface used in agriculture.

The latifundia system is responsible for the tiny percentage of cultivated land (only 2 percent of the nation's territory), the primitive farming methods that yield little and quickly exhaust the soil, the absence of scientific land management and of any effort at the capitalization that is indispensable for rural progress. It also lies behind the feudal exploitation of the landless, who work the land of others as laborers or serfs. On the other hand, the minifundia entail anti-economic use of the land and the chronic wretchedness of subsistence farming that does not produce enough to nourish even one family. Every effort at modernizing and stimulating Brazil's agriculture runs up against the antiquated framework of the agricultural infrastructure, a veritable rampart blocking the country's economic and social progress.

The kind of reform needed is not the mere palliative that

expropriation and redistribution of land in response to the aspirations of the landless would represent. Such a simplistic approach would not really solve the problems of the agrarian economy. I conceive agrarian reform as a revision of the juridical and economic relationships between the owners of agricultural property and the rest of rural society. In that way agrarian reform can translate aspirations into laws that limit the exploitation of agrarian property, so that output will rise and, most importantly, will be better distributed for the benefit of the entire rural community. The new laws must be so written as to settle innumerable problems: the expropriation of land, leases, work contracts, and many other complementary facets of land ownership.

Certainly, such a reform will encounter many obstacles resulting from the natural law of inertia and the inevitable reaction against progress on the part of those who possess special rights and privileges. In fact, however, these obstacles grow less formidable every day. They used to be much greater because the Brazilian elite did not understand the necessity of promoting change in the agrarian structures to parallel the changes in the industrial economy. Rapid industrial progress, made possible by a combination of largely favorable circumstances resulting from World War II, cast a kind of shadow over the need for agricultural development. Today, however, when industry is beginning to encounter difficulties in marketing its products, the agrarian problem is assuming greater importance and the national consciousness is awakening to the need for a rational solution.

One hundred and seventy-eight bills concerned with problems relating to land have been introduced in the Brazilian Parliament. Almost all have been paralyzed by the influence of the extremely reactionary forces that until recently dominated the Parliament's thinking. But now this situation is clearly changing. The fact that not only the industrially productive classes but also Brazil's leading intellectuals have come out in favor of agrarian reform tends to create a climate favorable to the approval of these bills, or others that may progressively modify structures and work relationships in the area of agriculture.

The main obstacle in the reformers' path is undoubtedly the rigidity of Article 141, par. 6, of the Constitution, which insures the right of property and allows expropriation only on condition of advance payment at just value in currency. If "just value" is understood as the market price—as the courts traditionally interpret it—any agrarian reform is practically impossible because of the fabulous amounts of money that would be necessary to expropriate the great expanses of land. If, however—given the new social meaning that Article 145 attaches to the use of property—some other measure of "just value" can be agreed upon in the case of expropriation for social purposes (for example, the "historic cost" proposed by Seabra Fagundes, Carlos Medeiros da Silva, and Hermes Lima or the "tributary value" suggested by Pompeu Acióli Borges), then the limitations of Article 141 can be overcome.

The implementation of this national imperative demands the participation of all patriotic Brazilians. It will require psychological preparation, a campaign to make the public aware that this is not a measure that favors only those rural pariahs, the landless, but one that will benefit all classes and social groups with an interest in the balanced economic development of the country. The taboo of agrarian reform— now a forbidden, dangerous, indelicate subject—must be challenged with the same courage as the taboo of hunger. The question must be openly discussed to rid it of its forbidden nature. A vast information campaign must persuade people that agrarian reform is not a bogeyman, an evil dragon that will devour all the wealth of the landowners, as the uninformed think, but that, on the contrary, it will be extremely beneficial for all who have a stake in agriculture. Only through such a reform will it be possible to inject into the rural economy the seeds of progress and development—the scientific tools of production, financial resources, and the guarantee of a just return for agricultural work—freeing Brazilian agriculture from its colonial status and, indirectly, the nation's economic development from the main cause of its stagnation. Thus, finally, the people can be liberated from the crushing burden of hunger.

There are other obstacles to be overcome as well. Besides the outdated agrarian infrastructure, there is the distribution process for farm products, with its interminable network of middlemen, profiteers, monopolists, and exploiters of hunger. All this must be reshaped. But this is a book, not a government program; I shall therefore only indicate the points where the problem must be attacked.

What we learn from an examination in depth of the state of diet and nutrition in the different sectors of Brazil, plus an overall view of the country's present situation and an analysis of the circumstances that most directly affect its structure and their consequences, can be summed up as follows:

1. As an underdeveloped country in the process of independent development and industrialization, Brazil has not yet freed itself from the hunger and malnutrition that have for centuries marked its social evolution and slowed the progress of its people.

2. The principal cause of the survival of hunger in Brazil is the dualism of its civilization: the well-integrated and prosperous economic structure of the industrial sector and the archaic, semicolonial agrarian structure dominated by plantations given over to single-crop agriculture.

3. The single greatest obstacle to the adequate nourishment of the country is the feudal agrarian structure, with its inadequate organization of ownership, its socially outdated work relationships, and its underutilization of the potential wealth of the soil.

4. The basic factors that make the food supply precarious

and ill-adapted to the population's nutritional needs are: low rates of agricultural output resulting from the opportunistic and disorganized use of the land; insufficient production due to the small amount of land under cultivation relative to the vast expanse of virgin land; and insufficient means of transporting and storing food products.

5. Inflation, which causes a continual spiraling of food prices and thus vitiates the purchasing power of large sectors of the population, especially in the rural areas, aggravates the problems of nourishing a high proportion of the Brazilian people.

6. Despite programs of nutritional education and agricultural expansion that seek to disseminate fundamental and practical knowledge about nourishment, the people make poor use of their financial resources, thus intensifying the inadequacy of their diet.

7. In the absence of a parallel effort to increase agricultural production, the drive for industrial expansion aggravates the nutritional problem; the growing demand for food on the part of a population seeking to raise its living standards, especially in the cities, cannot be met.

8. Throughout the country, the Brazilian's diet is, as a general rule, incomplete and unbalanced, giving rise to a traditional regime of hunger that is national in scope. The hunger of some areas is endemic, quantitatively and qualitatively, as in the Amazon region and in the northeast; in others it is epidemic, as in the *Sertao* region with its periodic droughts; and in still others, like the central and southern regions, it takes the form of chronic malnutrition and less obvious deficiencies.

9. The general and specific hunger exhibited in the innumerable nutritional deficiencies of the Brazilian people is undoubtedly the principal cause of the slowness of the country's economic progress. From this terribly degrading biological condition—chronic undernourishment—come the grave

weaknesses of the Brazilian demographic situation. These weaknesses are a direct consequence of the high overall death rate, the alarming rates of infant mortality, the incidence of mortality due to mass diseases like tuberculosis, widespread morbidity and incapacity to work, and the low rates of longevity—all statistical reflections of the general state of undernourishment. Hunger presses its destructive effects even further; it eats away the soul of the race, the moral fiber of the pioneer settlers who once conquered a hostile environment; it robs them of all initiative, reducing them to apathy, conformism, or the disorganized explosion of unproductive rebellions that are really expressions of the nervous crises inevitable among a neurasthenic and undernourished people.

10. No development plan is valid unless it leads within a reasonable time to an improvement in nutritional conditions, so that freed from the crushing burden of hunger the people can produce on levels that lead to balanced economic development. The importance of the goal cannot be overestimated, for "food for the people" means "deliverance from hunger."

The dramatic nutritional plight I have outlined is both cause and effect of Brazil's development and of the economic contradictions that go with it. The situation imposes the inescapable need for a truly effective nutritional policy that will go beyond palliatives and aid programs designed to correct the most crying defects. The policy it demands is one that will accelerate the progress of development, break the strength of the reactionary forces that prevent enormous groups from taking part in the nation's economic life, and thus set in motion the measures indispensable for raising the standard of living. For there is no specific remedy for hunger, no panacea that can cure this evil as if it were a sickness with a clearly defined cause. Hunger will disappear only with the disappearance of economic underdevelopment and the generalized poverty that it causes. The public authorities must organize development and direct it toward well-defined goals: first of all, the nutritional emancipation of the people. Only when economic development is directed toward the well-being of the whole society can the country be liberated from all forms of servitude—servitude to the external economic forces that for years have sought to trammel social progress and internal servitude to the hunger and wretchedness that have always blocked the increase of its wealth.

The Brazil that has constructed the capital of the future needs to free the rest of the country from the mires of the past, from the precapitalist economic infrastructure that still dictates the living conditions of more than half the population. Victory over hunger is the challenge laid down for this generation—a symbol and sign of the people's complete victory over underdevelopment.]

The American Mediterranean

Because of its geographical position and strategic importance, Central America has been called the "American Mediterranean." But if we consider the living conditions of the people, "American Balkans" would be a more appropriate title. The Balkans have always had the lowest living standard in Europe, and on the New Continent this honor goes to Central America. Many natural and cultural factors, down through the ages, have conspired to make the nutritional problems of Central America more difficult than those of South America.

For the purposes of this study, Central America is taken to mean all of the lands between South America and the United States, including both the continental republics and the whole Caribbean archipelago that used to be known as the West Indies. A study of this Balkanized region from a dietary point of view throws a bright light on the obscure history of the conflicts, the revolutions, and social agitation that have kept it in turmoil and seriously retarded its progress.[54]

Though all these countries situated on the rim of the Caribbean have certain common characteristics that make it appropriate to include them in one geographical area, this unity does not stand up when they are looked at from a nutritional standpoint. In order not to force the facts and oversimplify, two definite subregions must be considered separately: the continental mainland and the area of the Antilles.

In the continental zone, which extends from Panama to Mexico, one finds an extremely deficient diet based upon corn. From prehistoric times, corn has been the principal dietary element of the native populations that inhabit this region. On the basis of this cereal certain autochthonous cultures, such as the Mayan and Aztec, rose to high stages of development; but the excessive, practically exclusive use of corn was the principal reason, according to certain authors, for their early decay.

Corn is not a plant that carries a curse condemning those who feed upon it to irremediable decadence, as Francisco Bulnes has said.[55] It does not contain a poison, as was thought for a long time, because the groups who eat it suffer so frequently from pellagra. Corn is a valuable food and surely constitutes one of America's most important contributions to civilization and to the world. Unfortunately, however, it is not a complete food and cannot supply the organism with all the essential nutritional elements. Its proteins are limited in quantity and quality. When consumed along with other protective elements corn is an excellent complementary food, but it cannot nourish the organism adequately when it is the only source of proteins, mineral salts, and vitamins.

And that has been just the trouble in Central America. The diet there is the most monotonous of the continent, consisting exclusively of corn, beans, rice, peppers, a few roots and tubers, coffee, and sugar.[56] There are some zones in which the monotony is even more deadly, where groups of natives eat corn almost exclusively, either as cakes (tortillas) or as gruel (atole). According to Dr. Francisco Miranda, former director of the Mexican Institute of Nutrition, the diet of the Mexican peasant in certain areas consists of three tortillas in the morning, three tortillas at noon, and three at night.[57]

This narrowness of diet has serious nutritional results. It is no wonder, therefore, that investigations made in this area have revealed a striking amount of the most varied kinds of deficiency. The worst and most widespread is probably protein deficiency, which results from the total, or almost total, absence of meat, milk, cheese, and eggs from the diet of Central American farmers and workers. Dr. Epaminondas Quintana, studying the dietary problems of the Caribbean, called attention to the fact that the peasant of Guatemala, even though he may keep a milk cow and a few chickens, invariably sells the milk and eggs so as to buy corn and whiskey.[58] The same thing happens in Mexico, according to the evidence of the anthropologist Ramos Espinosa: "The milk, chickens, or eggs are sold at a low price by the humble folk, who then spend the money so obtained on *pulque* or whiskey."[59]

Among the vitamin deficiency diseases, the most common are pellagra, beriberi, and the ophthalmias resulting from lack of Vitamin A. Deficiencies of iron and iodine are the most serious shortages of minerals, manifested respectively by the anemia so common in this area and by the endemic goiter that ravages entire populations in the mountainous parts of Central America. Calcium shortage is avoided by the traditional practice of softening corn for tortillas with lime and possibly also by the local excess of sunshine, especially on the high plateaus where the sun is particularly favorable to the production of Vitamin D. By the side of this healthful corn cookery, unfortunately, we find another habit that is extremely harmful, that is, the practice of boiling food in several waters and throwing out the water with its rich content of mineral elements. In this connection Dr. Quintana observed that "throwing out the *nixtamal* water, in which the corn is cooked, results in a lamentable loss of phosphorus."

In certain areas such as El Salvador, in addition to the specific deficiencies one finds a tremendous energy deficit, with populations living on an average of about 1,500 calories a day. This absolute starvation diet led Vogt to refer to the tragedy of the Salvadorean people as a "parabola of misery."

The incidence of dietary deficiencies in both children and adults is among the highest in the world. Thus in 1944, when Dr. Rigoberto Aguillar examined 10,000 poor children in a dispensary of Mexico City, he found 5,000 with clear signs of dietary deficiency. The same pediatrician noted that the height of the children was much below normal, the stunting of growth from starvation amounting in some cases to alimentary dwarfism.[60] Many children of ten or twelve appeared to be no more than four or five years old. When I visited Mexico in 1945, I had occasion to observe, in the company of this doctor, innumerable cases of vitamin deficiencies in children, and I was greatly impressed by the extreme frequency of pellagra. Dr. Aguillar explained to me that this results from the fact that the poorer mothers are so underfed, themselves that they have no breast milk for their babies; the children receive instead a gruel made of corn and beans, and this soon produces the terrible splotches of pellagra. Espinosa, studying the diet of adults in Mexico, showed that alimentary deficiencies were excessively frequent, and the agrologist Medieta y Nuñez states that starvation was endemic in various parts of the country.[61]

One of the most serious consequences of this chronic hunger of Central American peoples is their notorious apathy—their traditional indifference and lack of ambition.

This depressed psychological state has been considered by many to be a kind of racial melancholy, but one of its causes is surely the chronic starvation to which these human groups have been subjected since before the time of Columbus. This state of chronic hunger with its shortages of certain vitamins begins by dulling the appetite; and when the native no longer suffers physical hunger as a result of lack of food, he has lost the strongest stimulus in the struggle for life—the drive to eat.

There is no question but that these hungry populations no longer feel genuine appetite; they eat mechanically, as though eating were a duty. This point has been made by a great many different investigators, who have been shocked at how little food—a tortilla with chili and a swallow of *pulque*—will satisfy an individual in this starvation area. Even for so light a meal, the native must stimulate his diffident appetite artificially, using, or rather abusing, stimulants and appetizers.

The multideficient diet throughout Central America and the chronic starvation that results are in a sense an inheritance from the indigenous pre-Columbian culture, although the situation has since been aggravated in many respects by the shortsighted methods of colonial exploitation. When the Spanish invaders came into contact with the various native groups, a diet based on corn was already in use. Students of the subject, piecing together a picture of the habits of that period, consider this diet to have been obviously deficient in proteins and in other essential nutritive elements. The Indian cultivated his corn on *milpas,* or burned-over tracts in the forest, and as soon as the land had been worn out by rapid erosion, he moved to another tract. Some insist that such an agricultural system, based on stripping the soil, in regions generally mountainous and therefore subject to erosion, was the fundamental reason for the decline of the great American civilizations, such as the Mayan Empire.[62]

Others hold that the decadence resulted not from exhaustion of the soil, because the population at that time did not by any means occupy the whole highland region, but from the monotony of a diet permanently short of good proteins. The fact that the Indians of this area raised no animals whatever is a sign that it must have been practically impossible for them to get a sufficient supply of animal proteins. They could still hunt, to be sure, but a large part of the plateau was semiarid, and wild animals were never plentiful there; and besides, the needs of a relatively dense population can hardly be supplied by hunting alone. Human groups that live by the fortune of the hunt are always widely dispersed within their geographical area, as are the Eskimos and the Pygmies.

In order to survive on so precarious a basis, the Indians, led by instinct (or as we would now say, by a variety of specific hungers), turned to the oddest kinds of natural resources. But such resources were adequate only in some areas. A Mexican anthropologist has called attention to the singular fact that at the time of the discovery the only two really powerful kingdoms remaining in Mexico—the Aztec and the Tarascan—were both located on the shores of large lakes, the Texcoco and the Pátzcuaro. These lakes constituted great reserves of food of animal origin. The groups living on their banks were thus able to improve on the regional diet and to survive longer than other groups, such as the Mayas and Toltecs, who had been prey to progressive biological and economic decline.

In the works of classical Mexican historians on the early days of the Spanish conquest—such authors as Sahagún, Torquemada, Diego Durán, F. Clavijero—one can see the ingenuity of the Indians in wringing from the lakes the resources they did not know how to obtain from the land. Thus these historians relate that they ate all kinds of fishes, frogs, shellfish, insects, water birds, and other inhabitants of the waters. "They even ate the foam off the water," says Clavijero, referring to certain species of light blue algae that floated on the surface of the lagoons.[63] Clavijero also reports that the Mexicans ate large quantities of the eggs of a fly—*axayaatl*—which were deposited on the surface of the water like a gelatinous scum. This delicacy, known by the name of *anuauhtli,* was a kind of indigenous caviar. The Indians also ate the flies themselves, reduced to a paste and cooked on leaves of corn. It is evident that such aquatic foods, though seemingly repugnant, would nevertheless be good sources of proteins, as well as of mineral salts and vitamins.

Consequently, we must recognize that the prehistoric Mexican diet was not so deficient as it seems at first glance. This supposition is supported by the facts that Mexican chili pepper is an excellent source of Vitamin C and that *pulque,* though it may be harmful on account of its high alcoholic content, furnishes appreciable quantities of the Vitamin B complex. It may be assumed, then, that some Indian groups at least succeeded in maintaining a balanced diet by means of food habits experience had taught them. Contact with the white colonizers, rather than improving the situation, made the regional diet a great deal worse.

Although Spanish colonization in Central America was not so dramatically destructive for the native as it was in the Antilles, nor so inhuman as British colonization in this same area, it had a terribly upsetting effect on the economic integrity of the region. The first exploitation was strictly destructive; it was aimed primarily at minerals and pushed all other productive activity into the background. The discovery of the mines had an evil effect on the incipient colonial economy, not only of the continent but throughout the Caribbean area. In the Antilles, where a promising beginning in agriculture had been made, practically all the white colonists abandoned their fields and rushed off to the mines. The historian Gonzalo de Reparaz has said: "Once the American mesas were discovered and their great mineral wealth brought to light, the Antilles were depopulated of Spaniards, and the native races began to disappear. Thus, half a century after the arrival of the white man in the tropics, his efforts at colonization could be said to have miscarried."[64]

The cultural shock involved in contacts with some of the more advanced groups also tended to depress the agrarian economy and to worsen living conditions in the region. Following the royal instructions of the Emperor Charles V, his Spanish agents first put the Indians in chains and then forced them to work under conditions of practical slavery in the mines and sugar mills and on the indigo and coffee plantations. But the Indians were in constant rebellion against this bondage; they often abandoned their lands and thus disrupted the whole regional economy.

The food supply was also greatly upset in this area by the diversion of the land of primitive Indian communities to huge tracts or latifundia, which were conferred upon individual colonists and then allowed, for the most part, to stand idle. Another factor that helped in definitively ruining the native populations was the one-track exploitation to which almost every region was dedicated: some were given over to mining, others to coffee planting, some to tobacco, and others to cacao. This specialization brought on the deformed economy that is still found in such countries as El Salvador, which produces practically nothing but coffee, and Honduras, which exports nothing but bananas. In this unilateral exploitation of the earth's resources, the great plantation owners concentrated all the available labor on their own monopoly activities. The result was an exaggerated ecological imbalance that destroyed the soil of the region as well as its living complement and led to the decline of the original inhabitants.

Thus the disruptive aspects of injudicious colonialism, rather than excess population, exhausted the sources of regional food supply. The Central American republics, taken as a whole, are far from having an excess of population that would in any way justify the precarious nutritional situation to be found there. Their population density is about 30 individuals to the square mile. This is higher than that of South America but is still far sparser than the world's really overpopulated areas, or even those of median density. It is only in El Salvador, with its limited territory and its concentration of 140 inhabitants per square mile, that the theorists of neo-Malthusianism can find some basis on which to argue that the misery of the people is due to a supposed excess of population. In the rest of the area the problem is not excess but shortage of people, particularly of healthy people capable of the organized and rational development of the region's potential wealth. In a country like Costa Rica with 10 million acres of arable soil, most of it volcanic in origin and extremely fertile, only 10 percent of the land is currently under cultivation, and of this, a third is devoted exclusively to coffee.[65]

George Soule, David Efron, and N. T. Ness state that a monopolistic system of control of the land and its natural resources is still in force today in the great majority of Central American countries.[66] Mexico alone, thanks to its revolutionary leaders, has succeeded in carrying out radical agrarian reform. Here, under a system known as the *ejido,* which is very similar to the primitive Indian community, the latifundia were broken up and the land returned to the peasants.

The *ejido* was undoubtedly a step forward for Mexico in the struggle against hunger, but unfortunately the results fell short of expectation. The Mexican revolutionists were idealists rather than technicians, and they forgot that a mere redistribution of the land is not enough. In order to cultivate it adequately, technical and financial resources are also necessary. The result was that the Indians, who were generally unprepared, disoriented, and without adequate technical knowledge, were unable to make proper use of the plots they received.

Agrarian reform did not lead to the increase in production or to the indispensable diversification of crops which was needed to raise the national living standard. As proof of this, one may cite the fact that Mexico imports appreciable quantities of its basic food element—corn—and still does not have adequate supplies of many protective foods. The report sent by Dr. Calvo de la Torre, of the Mexican Institute of Nutrition, to the first Latin American Conference on Nutrition at Montevideo in 1948 offers documentary proof that Mexican land reform did not lead to the expected improvement in the nutrition of the people: "The peasants were confused and upset by the change of regime. Their number has increased, but the land produces no more food than it did some years ago. The diet becomes ever more slender, and the people continue in poverty."[67]

Certain measures have been taken that tend toward a wider dissemination of technical knowledge among the Indian masses and toward a large-scale use of irrigation in the semi-arid zones. It is very possible that such steps—including the introduction of certain sanitary, economic, and educational measures, all linked to the plan of rural recovery—may result in an appreciable increase in production and an equal improvement in the living standards of the native population.

Central America is still in the grip of extreme social unrest, struggling to free itself from the pitiless yoke of malnutrition and hunger and from the unfortunate economic factors that are responsible for it. Attempting to explain this situation, Vogt states—and this time he is absolutely right—that "the Spanish tradition imposed upon the Indian tradition and reinforced by the modern competitive system, has resulted in one of the most vampirish, extractive economies existing anywhere in the world today."[68]

The Emerald Necklace of the Antilles

Even worse than the living conditions in the continental part of Central America are those that prevail on the long chain of islands that stretches across 1,500 miles of ocean, from the tip of Florida to the coast of Venezuela. In this subarea of the Antilles are found some of the hungriest, most underfed masses in the whole Western Hemisphere. This is surprising if one recalls that these islands, when they were discovered in the fifteenth and sixteenth centuries by Columbus and other navigators, dazzled the eyes like precious gems and gave promise of incalculable riches. And indeed it is no wonder that these islands with their luxuriant tropical vegetation, the priceless "Emerald Necklace of the Antilles," mounted like dark green stones in the blue immensity of the ocean, should have remained for more than two centuries, to quote from *Lands and Peoples*, "the constant lure and inspiration of sailor adventurers from almost every European port ... the fame of the rich islands attracting fortune hunters of all kinds."[69]

Four centuries after their discovery, these promised lands lie plundered and despoiled: a large part of their soil is exhausted, much of their forest is destroyed, and their people are underfed and debilitated. To the eyes of contemporary sociologists, the jewels of the Antilles look more like paste—their brilliance dulled and their mounts tarnished.

The fundamental causes of this rapid plunder of the Antilles were the same as those observed in other zones of tropical America. The only difference is that the destructive process is more obvious here. A rapid review of the colonial history of the islands reveals clearly enough the secret of their economic degradation. The Antilles were discovered by Spaniards, but their possession was soon disputed by other European peoples, including the French, English, Dutch, and Danes, and they became a storm center of colonial struggle and unrestrained plunder by the pirates and freebooters of the time. Agricultural colonization was begun on some of the islands, with diversified subsistence farming, but the discovery of gold and silver on the mesas of the continent led to the abandonment of such routine economic activity in favor of the eager and adventurous search for sudden wealth in the mines.

One very important element in the impoverishment of the area was the European colonizer's almost total destruction of the native population. Although we still do not have sufficient data to estimate with any accuracy the population of the islands at the time of discovery, there is no doubt that they were heavily populated. Padre Bartolomé de las Casas estimated the early population of Hispaniola (Haiti and the Dominican Republic) at 3 million,[70] while Baron Humboldt thought the population of Cuba to be about 1 million.[71] The historian Lopez de Velasco relates that sixty years after the discovery, these indigenous populations had been practically wiped out, and nothing remained but a few scattered tribes lost in the depths of the jungle.[72] By the end of the sixteenth century, the millions of original natives had been reduced to about 15,000.

To take the place of the Indians, who were quite uncooperative and even went so far as to prefer death to slavery, the colonizers proceeded to import African blacks, by which means they repopulated the islands and carried on their agricultural exploitation. "One Negro can do as much work as four Indians," said the colonizers of the period, and so Africa, the great reservoir of slaves, became the source of supply for colonial laborers.

Thus the plantation system was set up, based on great estates and slave labor, and after a short and fleeting period of dubious splendor it dragged much of the region down to ruin. There are those who attribute the greater part of the social ills of the area to the importation of slaves and to the type of culture that went with it. The use of slaves, however, was not a cause, but an inevitable result of the kind of colonial exploitation that was undertaken. One of the chief prerequisites of the plantation system was a cheap and abundant supply of labor. Since the Indian declined the role, the only alternatives were to import laborers from other parts of the world or to give up the colonial system itself, which would have meant abandoning an adventure that might well bring the colonizer all sorts of wealth and honors.

This colonial system of soil utilization and land tenure contains the germ of the defective economic organization that has brought the human groups of the area to their present precarious situation. The product chosen as the basis of the economic exploitation of the region—sugar cane—also had a decisive effect on the future of these people. C. K. Meek is undoubtedly right when he states that the type of product often determines the character of the tenure: "Some forms of cultivation can best be carried out on a plantation basis with the assistance of outside capital."[73] Now it happens that sugar cane is the sort of product that most encourages exclusive monoculture, great plantations, and even the practice of absenteeism—in which capitalists merely finance the monopolist enterprise, without ever appearing on the scene. Such an economic situation soon developed in most of the Antilles, which were devoted almost exclusively to the cultivation of this plant, with its evil individualism and its almost morbid hostility to other vegetable species. It is an extremely demanding plant; it forces soil and human beings into slavery, because only in a regime of total slavery can the sugar cane economy show a profit. The Portuguese, Spanish, French, and English, without exception, bowed to the demands of sugar cane and received the guerdon of their servitude. For colonial sugar was worth more to Portugal than the spices of the Orient, more to Spain than the gold of Peru, and worth as much to the English as the profitable traffic in African slaves.

American sugar, then, was a goodly inheritance for the

colonizing countries; but the countries that were colonized received only undernourishment and starvation as their share. One-crop sugar farming is responsible, in spite of a relatively fertile soil and a climate favorable to agriculture, for the chronic starvation of the peoples of the West Indies.

The subsistence problem is extremely serious and difficult of solution today because of the high population density of the area. This is the only subarea in Latin America, in fact, where one can speak of the danger of overpopulation. The average density, for instance, is some 157 people to the square mile, while in certain islands the figures are truly alarming. In Puerto Rico there are 546 individuals to the square mile, and in Barbados 1,192.[74] This subarea also has the highest index of population growth—about 3 percent annually (the rest of Central America reaches only 2.5 percent, and South America 2.4).* It is clear that this high demographic concentration is, on the one hand, largely a product of sugar cane monoculture with its labor demands and, on the other, of chronic starvation acting as a factor favoring population growth.

In studying the problem of alimentation and hunger in the Antilles, we should not lose sight of the fact that some of these islands were colonized and held by Latin peoples and others by Anglo-Saxons. For the moment, therefore, I will treat only the islands colonized by Latins—the Spanish and French—and leave the others for separate study in a section dealing with hunger areas in British America.

The people of the Latin American Antilles, whether in independent countries like Haiti and the Dominican Republic or in colonies such as Martinique and Guadeloupe, exist on a predominantly vegetable diet, based upon starchy tubers, beans, rice, plantains, and sugar cane derivatives, including

* 4 percent annually in Puerto Rico, 3.2 percent in Central America, and 2.8 percent in South America.

alcohol. This is clearly a defective diet; there is an excess of carbohydrates in the manioc, yams, and sweet potatoes—all basic foods of the region—and a deficiency of protective elements. Such foods as meat, milk, eggs, greens, and vegetables have always been a rarity on the table of the peasant.[75] Only occasionally does he get a piece of dry meat—*tasajo*—or some fruit. And this happens only in one period of the year, during the sugar harvest, when work is to be had and when there is some money for expensive foods. In the slack period, the so-called *tiempo muerto*,[76] consumption is reduced to little more than tubers and a certain amount of cereal or, in some areas of absolute monoculture, to what Soule, Efron, and Ness have termed "a diet of sweet potatoes and cane juice."[77]

The same types of deficiency we have discovered in other areas of America occur here among both urban and rural populations, and there are, in addition, certain deficiencies, diseases such as "tropical sprue," which are characteristic of this zone. The country people suffer most, because they usually sell all the products of the land in order to get a little money. It is a notable fact that though the peasant eats hardly any fruit, a great abundance of tropical fruits may be seen in the markets of big cities. They come in all shapes and colors, giving the impression of an area of optimum nutrition. But these fruits, unfortunately, are consumed by only the tiny minority that is able to buy them. These appetizing and succulent fruits piled up in the markets are both evidence and denunciation of those factors that lead to widespread starvation in a zone so well constituted by nature to feed its inhabitants abundantly.

[The Cuban Explosion

Cuba's situation in the years since Fidel Castro's revolution requires more detailed analysis, especially because the bitter and frightful hunger of half the country's rural population who lived on the giant jungle plantations was a determining factor in bringing the revolution about. Few countries in the world possess climate and soil conditions as favorable as Cuba's to a varied agriculture capable of feeding the population well. Rainfall is regular and relatively abundant between May and October. Droughts are the exception. Deep, fertile red clay covers the vast plains that take up three quarters of the island and are a magnificent agricultural resource. Shamefully, this superb land was misused and wasted under the "vampire" exploitation of the sugar monopoly. The multicrop subsistence agriculture of the early colonial period was soon stifled by the huge stock farms established on the *mercedes*—lands granted by the Spanish crown to the courtiers who came to exploit the island. The result was extremely low nutritional standards that were further depressed when the best land was taken over for the growing of sugar cane at the beginning of the eighteenth century. Two great systems of latifundia were thus established on the island—one for cattle and the other for sugar cane—and insufficient land was reserved for growing other produce. Cuba was obliged to import food. During the nineteenth century, Spain exploited the sugar industry for its own exclusive gain and left the Cuban people in complete wretchedness, tormented by hunger and endemic diseases. By the middle of the century, the United States was replacing Spain as the country of primary commercial importance to Cuba. The American government even offered to buy the island from Spain for $100 million, so important did it seem to them. But the sugar business was so profitable that Spain rejected the offer and Cuba remained under its colonial domination. Politically and economically, however, the island moved ever closer to the United States. This trend was so obvious even before the middle of the century that John Quincy Adams remarked that Cuba would sooner or later fall into the arms of the United States by the law of political gravitation.

Cuban colonial revolts and, finally, the Spanish-American War provided the long-sought pretext to transform Cuba from a Spanish colony into an American one.[78] Driven to desperation by the inhuman exploitation of its wealth and by Spain's indifference to its misery, the Cuban people rose in armed rebellion in 1868; after ten years of fierce fighting, the revolution was totally crushed. In 1895 there was a second uprising, this time with American support. But while invoking the humanitarian and anticolonial sentiments of the Monroe Doctrine in favor of political independence for Cuba, the United States was in reality defending American capital investments, which at the time amounted to $50 million in sugar refineries and in mining. Using as a pretext the explosion of the *Maine* the United States intervened in the Cuban-Spanish war and established Cuba's independence. On January 1, 1899, when Spanish troops evacuated the island, the Americans occupied it to protect it from "foreign ambition." Thus, Cuba ceased to be a political colony and became an economic one. Giving in to the persuasive pressure of the American occupation forces, the Cuban parliament approved the Platt Amendment, under the terms of which the United States could intervene in Cuba whenever it believed the island's independence or internal security was threatened.

Cuban independence was a fiction. The country was simply an American protectorate, its government supervised from the U.S. military bases established on the island. The national economy, manipulated by Wall Street, operated against the interests of the Cuban people. The sugar industry was greatly expanded by fresh investments of American capital. United Fruit, for example, acquired about 175,000 acres in 1901 and built two great sugar refineries. In 1896 American capital owned 10 percent of the total sugar industry. The figure reached 35 percent by 1914 and rose to 66 percent by 1926. This represented a virtual takeover of the Cuban economy, for in other areas as well—tobacco production and processing, the hotel industry, and thus tourism— almost everything belonged to American investors.

With the establishment in the United States of import quotas for Cuban sugar, the island's economy became completely subject to the will of the American market, especially because the United States paid Cuba more than the world market price for its sugar. Through this maneuver, which on the one hand served to protect the uneconomical American sugar industry and on the other obliged Cuba to produce only sugar, the economic independence of the island was completely destroyed. Under the illusion of prosperity Cuba came to resemble a diabetic, gorged exclusively on sugar. By increasing or decreasing import quotas (depending on how acceptable it found the decisions of the Cuban governments), the United States could make Cuba prosperous or bring it to the edge of bankruptcy. Successive governments were forced to obey American orders. Though it received a relatively high price for its sugar, Cuba was obliged to import everything it needed to live from the United States, so the Cuban people derived no economic nourishment from the sugar they produced. Cuban imports of food produce alone had risen to about $140 million annually in the years before Fidel Castro's revolution. And this was for beans, rice, and other farm products that could have been grown in sufficient quantities to export. Smothered by single-crop farming and the plantation system, and strangled by American imperialism, the Cuban people went hungry. Unemployment increased enormously. Even during the harvest season it remained around 25 percent, and at other times of the year it reached twice that. It should be noted, moreover, that the other 50 percent were underemployed, producing at ridiculously low rates and living on starvation wages.

A 1939 study revealed an extreme nutritive poverty among Cuban workers; families of five lived on a daily calorie total scarcely sufficient for one.[79] Dr. Fernando Milanez, in a report presented to the First National Food Conference of Cuba in 1943, wrote that "more than a third of the population lacked the purchasing power to provide themselves with a normal diet," and he added that in consequence the island suffered frequent outbreaks of the most varied kinds of nutritional deficiencies. Another specialist, Dr. Antonio Clerch, Cuban delegate to the first Latin American Conference on Nutrition in 1948, presented that assembly with a report that ended: "In the hospitals it is common to discover various types of nutritional deficiency, especially protein insufficiencies with their symptomatic parade of edema and other signs of deterioration due to states of hypoproteinemia, deficiencies of vitamins A, B-1, B-2, C, D, rickets, osteomyelitis, macrocytic anemia, endemic goiter, dental disintegration, and other diseases."[80]

On top of this state of chronic malnutrition, the Cuban people suffered from innumerable endemic diseases, which gravely lowered their productive capacity. Widespread illiteracy and a total lack of technical know-how served to keep it low and locked them into the vicious circle of hunger. Thus, of the 6.5 million Cubans who inhabited the island's 44,127 square miles, about two thirds led marginal lives; they lived in straw huts called *bohios*, eating only part of the year, and then badly. Their diet consisted of beans with rice and only rarely a piece of dry meat. In contrast to the misery of the rural areas and small urban centers, Havana became one of the most beautiful cities of Latin America. There a privileged minority lived intoxicated on what was called "the dance of the millions": the millions of dollars the sugar industry poured into the pockets of a tiny group associated with the international sugar trust. Conscious of this fact and of the true causes of their wretchedness, the Cuban people once again approached the point of rebellion against the inhuman colonial exploitation to which they were subjected. This condition of latent revolt created a collective consciousness and a violent desire for economic emancipation. Castro's revolution was the crystallization of this drive. It was a mass rebellion of the Cuban people against the corrupt Batista regime and the international trusts that controlled it. With Batista's expulsion from power on January 1, 1959, Cuba's era of economic colonialism ended, exactly sixty years after the island's political emancipation from Spain. The colonialist economic system that maintained misery in the midst of abundance provided the revolution's principal explosive fuse. In spite of the smallness of the country, the revolution was one of the most significant in history, for it embodied the spirit of revolt felt by all the hungry peoples of Latin America who wish to escape from their misery,[81] and who know that emancipation can come only through social upheavals that will free the forces of production from the archaic feudal plantation system that prevails over most of the continent. The Cuban revolution has a great attraction for Latin America for, as Walter Lippmann has pointed out, it is an authentic revolution that has created a new social order. It produced a series of basic structural reforms that attacked the whole colonial economic organization of the country.

In the beginning, the most important reform in terms of the nutritional situation was agrarian reform, which aimed not only to give land to the landless but to make it productive for those who worked it. This is not the place to analyze the reform's strengths and weaknesses, but it must be pointed out that the results significantly altered the panorama of hunger that had prevailed in Cuba.[82] On the eve of the revolution, twelve American companies owned about 2.5

million acres, of which 617,500 belonged to the Cuban Atlantic Company alone. After the revolution, the great plantations were broken up and turned into farming cooperatives that started the process of diversifying agriculture, and the nutritional situation began to change. The cultivation of beans, rice, potatoes, and other products rapidly reduced the need to import food and raised the rate of consumption. Today, the peasant no longer sends the entire produce of his fields, orchards, and vegetable gardens—the eggs, milk, vegetables, and fruits that were formerly luxury foods—to the city, keeping only beans and rice for his own meager nourishment. Now he consumes a good part of these products, and this has, of course, raised his nutritional level.

Unfortunately, the overall volume of agricultural production has not greatly increased, and Cuba remains a one-product economy, dependent on sugar for more than 80 percent of its income. The regime believed that the development of sugar production would put it in a more favorable position to trade with Communist countries. Six million tons were produced in 1967, and the quota for 1970 was set at 10 million, though real production fell about 2 million short of that goal. The Ministry of Sugar, the *Minaz,* is a permanent institution, and Cuba is not yet liberated from its single-crop economy.

Castro himself, in a speech delivered in May 1970, acknowledged that the obsession with meeting the year's sugar quota of 10 million tons was seriously harming the economy, especially in the vital areas of agriculture and food production. Attempts to reach that objective had drained off manpower from other agricultural endeavors, the productivity of which was suffering accordingly. Castro stated that, in his estimation, the cutting and transporting of sugar cane would have to be totally mechanized if Cuba were to increase its sugar production without damaging other sectors of the national economy.

It must be recognized that the Castro government has made great efforts to improve irrigation, seed selection, cattle-breeding, fruit production, and fishing techniques, all of which are reflected in the diet of the Cuban people. Though a great variety of foods is still unavailable in Cuba, widespread hunger has been practically stamped out. Certain deficiencies, especially of proteins, still exist but periods of famine and the chronic hunger of the majority of the population are things of the past.

But although foreign experts who have visited Cuba and analyzed its revolution with open minds stress its successes in the area of nutrition and elsewhere, they also recognize that grave errors were committed in the implementation of agrarian reform—notably in land distribution, organized utilization of various types of soil for different crops, and insufficient diversification of agricultural production. This is indeed the case. In the years immediately after the revolution, the Castro government had at its disposal only a small group of qualified technicians, and the execution of its agricultural policies reflected this lack. Now the professional cadres are much more numerous and include qualified people who have studied in various foreign countries, especially in Eastern Europe and the U.S.S.R.

In a discerning book, René Dumont describes some of the worst errors of the early days, which involved a great expenditure for very small return.[83] He points to the negative effects of an overly bureaucratic and costly administration, but he concludes that "this is of little moment, for Cuba has received an important stimulus." This stimulus is moving the country toward a new social system in which balanced economic development will benefit the whole population, rather than a privileged minority allied with foreign interests. This is what really counts. Despite the errors of the handful of young idealists who governed the country in the period just after the revolution and despite the difficulties created by the blockade imposed by the United States and its closest allies, the positive side of the ledger speaks eloquently. Providing work for all has raised both purchasing power and productivity. Cuba's misery was the direct result of chronic unemployment, of the forced idleness of the majority of its manpower. Once the workers were mobilized, the principal stumbling block to economic development was removed and the wisdom of the policy of full employment prescribed by the economist Gunnar Myrdal for underdeveloped and underfed countries was confirmed in practice.[84] For Myrdal, the essential step in such a country is putting the population to work, and this depends principally on organization.[85] He stresses that fundamentally a country is poor when its work force is not utilized. Mobilization of the work force creates the capital that an underdeveloped country needs. This is what the Cuban revolution has accomplished.]

Conditions more or less similar [to those of pre-revolutionary Cuba] prevail on the other islands of the Caribbean sea. Some are a little better off; in Hispaniola, for example, the abolition of the latifundia in Haiti and the relative tendency to polyculture in the Dominican Republic help to relieve the situation. Some, such as the French possessions of Guadeloupe and Martinique, are in a worse state.

The Antilles suffered greatly from the plantation system during the colonial period, but after certain of the islands gained their independence another factor appeared, which helped to prolong an economic regime unfavorable to the biological interests of the population. This factor was the economic influence of the United States or, as it was called at the beginning of the century, "dollar diplomacy."[86] Because of the weakness of the Central American countries, there was thought to be a danger to the United States if one of them were to fall under the domination of another great power. The United States, therefore, attempted to maintain absolute control in this area and even went to the extreme lengths of using force and of resorting to military occupation in order to protect the interests, or to impose the will, of Washington. The United States looked upon the tropical lands of Central America as a kind of necessary complement to its temperate zones, and for a long time it pursued a policy in this area almost identical with that of the British in Africa. It was a policy exclusively aimed at the strategic and economic defense of empire interests. The United States policy, imposed by force, of support to the great landowners held back the social evolution of many of these countries to a marked degree and thus contributed toward keeping them in a state of poverty.

[The influence of the United Fruit Company has been the cause of several American military interventions in this region. Coups d'état arranged by Washington to get rid of governments that oppose the imperialist domination of this banana empire are a fact of life, underlining the harm massive capitalist imperialism has done to these little Central American republics. The relationship between these exercises of force and the giant company is easy to grasp, given that United Fruit does an annual business of $300 million, that it owns 1,000 miles of railroad track, radio and telegraph stations, and a fleet of about fifty ships (more than half of which do not sail under the American flag), and that its plantations extend over 395,000 acres, a third of them in banana production.

Since United Fruit constantly does business with governments, it naturally becomes intimately involved in their political crises. The best-known example of such involvement took place in Guatemala during the administration of Jacob Arbenz. Under an agrarian reform program in 1952, Arbenz expropriated the noncultivated lands belonging to United Fruit, the largest landowner in the country. The United States Department of State joined in a suit claiming an indemnification twenty-six times that offered by the government: $15,854,849 instead of $609,572.

The claim was all the more outrageous since United Fruit was exempt from taxes in Guatemala and owned half the country's railroads, the profits of which were taxed at 38.5 percent by the United States government but not at all by Guatemala. Under these conditions, United Fruit succeeded in having the Arbenz government overthrown and the constitution that it deemed unfavorable abolished.[87]]

It is easy to see why the Central Americans have developed a spirit of suspicion with regard to the gringo which has added greatly to the difficulty of genuine collaboration in the interest of the two Americas. American technical proficiency, which could have done so much to improve the food supply of Central America, has always been checked by political and economic interests and as a result has contributed little or nothing.

The Hunger Spots of British America

The parts of the American continent that were colonized principally by the British are the United States, Canada, Newfoundland and Labrador, British Guiana, British Honduras, and a series of islands in the Caribbean—Jamaica, Trinidad, Tobago, Barbados, and lesser islands. Most of these places are somewhat better off, nutritionally, than the areas settled by Latins, but that is by no means true of all of them. In certain spots of British America, dietary conditions are extremely precarious; in fact, some of the British West Indies "lead" the whole American continent in human malnutrition.

Even the inhabitants of the better-fed areas, such as the United States and Canada, are a long way from escaping completely the effects of nutritional deficiencies. Although no masses of human beings in these regions of more balanced economy are exposed to outright starvation, we must nevertheless record the existence of certain specific deficiencies which have an unfavorable effect on the health of these peoples. On close analysis it is found that hunger, open or concealed, extends throughout the enormous land mass that stretches from Alaska to Tierra del Fuego.

A few cases will suffice to prove that no nation or geographic area on the American continent is entirely free from the perils of hunger and malnutrition. In such great cities of the United States as New York and Chicago, there is a great deal of rickets among children, the result of a relative deficiency of Vitamin D and of certain mineral salts. A series of surveys carried out in various Canadian cities in the 1940's showed that a large part of the population did not receive the minimum nutritional elements dietary specialists consider indispensable. Thus, a survey made at the beginning of World War II in Halifax revealed that a third of the families checked suffered from deficiency of proteins and iron. Further, half of them were not getting enough phosphorus and Vitamin A, and more than half were not receiving enough Vitamins B-1 and C.[88] In Quebec, too, the diet was shown to be somewhat deficient, particularly in the A, B, and C groups of vitamins, and the B-1 deficit was truly alarming.[89] A report from Toronto, finally, came to the following conclusions: "There is a widespread deficiency of vitamin B-1, and the quantities of vitamin C available cannot be regarded as adequate. Marked deficiencies of calcium and iron were found in the food consumption of women and of calcium among teen-age girls."[90]

In another British dominion—Newfoundland—nutritional conditions are a great deal more difficult, and the deficiencies appear as definite clinical symptoms. A survey made there in 1944 and repeated in 1948 by a group of outstanding experts in nutrition revealed multiple dietary deficiencies among the population of this island.[91] Deficiencies in the Vitamin A and B groups had diminished in the interval between the surveys, illustrating the success of certain measures taken by the government, but the second survey showed that deficiencies of Vitamin C had at the same time grown much more serious and widespread. Typical scurvy may no longer be seen in Newfoundland as it was in the past, but a high percentage (41 percent in 1944 and 54 percent in 1948) of the individuals examined revealed definite Vitamin C deficiency by a reddening and swelling of the gums.

These people are inadequately fed, but they are not grossly starved. There are, however, two regions of British America where whole populations suffer real starvation. These typical areas of intensive, mass hunger are the British West Indies and the old plantation region in the South of the United States.

"British Failures in the West Indies"

"British Failures in the West Indies" is the title of a chapter from the great work by Grenfell Price, *White Settlers in the Tropics,* in which this outstanding geographer analyzes the progress of British decadence in the Antilles. In describing the disintegration and degradation of the colonial populations, he assigns a decisive role to improper nutrition. The dietary regimes of these islands have been extremely inadequate throughout their history. They are much like those of the Spanish Antilles; they result from the same soil and natural environment and from the same type of preponderant economic exploitation—the one-crop culture of sugar cane.

They are all predominantly vegetable diets, with an excess of starchy foods in the form of cereals, roots, and tubers. Such foods as meat and milk have practically no part in the alimentation of the people. Within this framework, each island has its own characteristic local variations. Thus in Jamaica the staple foods are yams, sweet potatoes, cassava, and breadfruit, while in Trinidad the principal foods consumed are polished rice, dry peas, and coconut products. In

Barbados, where the food situation is truly alarming, the normal diet is rice, sweet potatoes, yams, onions, tea, and sugar. Sometimes a little codfish or salt pork may be included. The menu of this island never includes milk, eggs, or fresh vegetables. British nutritionists report that babies are weaned at three months and fed from then on with tea and corn-meal gruel thickened with rice or potatoes.[92]

The notorious defects of this sort of diet are greatly aggravated by a custom that is general among the local populations—the habitual use of alcohol in excess.[93] Many years ago, William Ripley wrote that a Sunday of rest killed more people on these tropical islands than a whole week of backbreaking labor on the plantations because Sunday was a day of drunkenness that undermined the health of whole populations.[94] Grenfell Price described the effects of excessive use of alcohol in this area: "Drunkenness was prevalent and gambling a consuming vice. Many a young West Indian immigrant of good family drank himself to death. Friends notified his parents he had died of 'fever' and that good old whipping horse, the tropical climate, took the blame."[95] The association of an extremely defective diet with the abuse of alcoholic drinks persists today, and this is a combination of terrible potency in the degradation of colonial peoples.

It is not surprising that health conditions are wretched on these islands and nutritional diseases very frequent. The heavy rate of infant mortality and the high incidence of dental caries, tuberculosis, and infectious diseases in general are signs of a lack of organic resistance on the part of these populations. Pellagra, beriberi, and the xerophthalmias are often encountered on one or another of the islands. In Jamaica, cirrhosis of the liver in children is of a frequency unheard of in other parts of the world. There, too, is a great deal of the fatty liver disease so thoroughly studied by Dr. J. C. Waterlow, who considered this illness an unquestionable sign of undernourishment.[96]

The shortage of food and the deplorable nutritional conditions in the British West Indies are direct results of the defective system of colonial exploitation developed by the British in this area. The system rested on the one-crop culture of sugar cane with an exclusive and monopolistic concentration without parallel in the monoculture of any other crop and even without parallel in the culture of sugar cane by any other colonists. The story of this area is the most vivid example in economic history of how a group of human beings, moved by greed for immediate profits, can destroy the natural wealth of a highly endowed region and reduce its people to misery and starvation.

Nowhere else in the world did the sugar economy evolve with such velocity, quickly reaching its peak of splendor and passing immediately into hopeless decadence.[97] V. T. Harlow, in his excellent book *A History of Barbados,* made clear the process of socioeconomic decline on that island[98]—a decay that because of the distinctness of its phases, provides a good illustration of the course of British colonial policy in the Antilles.

Harlow's data and documentation indicate that at the beginning the settlers of Barbados relied on polyculture; the land was divided into small holdings and devoted to cotton, tobacco, citrus fruits, cattle and hogs, and other subsistence products. During this first phase of the island's history, between 1625 and 1645, the English population grew rapidly, as the following figures show:

Year	White Population
1628	1,400
1638	6,000
1643	37,000

But with the development of cane growing, in the middle of the seventeenth century, diversified agriculture was gradually strangled, the small properties were swallowed up by the plantations, the island's food reserves became progressively more scanty and the life of the colonists more difficult. This retrograde economic revolution led to a general exodus of the whites, and the demographic curve started downward:

Year	White Population
1667	20,000
1786	16,000
1807	15,500

The white population remains at about 15,000 today.

As sugar cane culture developed, slaves took the place of the whites in agricultural labor. The slave-owning plantation economy grew, rose to a transitory splendor that lasted from 1650 to 1685, and fell into decadence. By this time the island was already worn out. Forests, once so dense that it had been hard to find an open space in which to build the first settlement, were completely razed;[99] subsistence culture had come to a halt, and sugar itself was economically ruined because it could no longer be produced at prices to meet the sharp international competition. Such is the fleeting history of sugar in Barbados, as told by Harlow and confirmed in general outline by other responsible historians.

What happened in Barbados was repeated in the other islands. Jamaica, Trinidad, Tobago arrived by the same steps at the same dénouement, only not quite so quickly. Just a few years after the beginning of English settlement in the Caribbean (which started on St. Kitts, in 1623), the colonists had begun the process of monopolizing the land, setting up plantations and organizing the planter caste, a "cruel planter aristocracy tyrannizing over a poverty-stricken mass of enslaved white servants," said Price.[100] In order to carry out their plans of large-scale production, this sugar aristocracy was forced to import black slaves, since the white population soon starved to death or fled the country.

Thus the typical slaveholding plantation regime was established. As living conditions became more difficult under the pressure of this economic system, the income from sugar declined to such a degree that the British Parliament, considering this trade the most important element of overseas commerce at the time, decided in 1737 to investigate conditions in the colonies and to try to remedy the situation. When the Special Commission made its report to Parliament, it emphasized the significance of inadequate diet in the decadence of the islands. The report read, in part: "The feeding and treatment of the slaves (418,000 Negroes as against 82,000 whites) and as a result, their working capacity, leaves a great deal to be desired. Only 25 shillings a year is spent on feeding a slave with an estimated value of 50 pounds."[101]

The report was correct. The planters were interested in the slave only as a machine, and they consequently limited his alimentation to the bulk fuel necessary to keep him going. These bulk calories could be supplied by the cheapest foods: manioc meal, sweet potatoes, yams, and rice. Of this kind of food, and of this kind only, the blacks enjoyed a certain abundance. The planters imagined that by filling the bellies of the blacks with starchy, high-energy foods they were feeding the sugar industry itself and, by means of the black labor machine, transforming low-cost foods into sugar that was worth its weight in gold. Neither the report to Parliament, nor the complaints and revolts of the slaves, resulted in measures adequate to improve the situation in the islands. On the contrary, living conditions grew worse and worse.

With the revolt in 1776 of the North American colonies, from which the British Antilles were accustomed to receiving the greater part of their food supply, the situation became absolutely desperate. Where there had been chronic hunger there now appeared outright starvation—famine itself. It is said that on the island of Jamaica alone, between 1770 and 1777, at least 15,000 blacks starved to death. When this widespread distress, including the danger of mass starvation of black slaves and the consequent loss of the capital tied up in them, began to threaten the interests of the dominant class directly, the British Empire for the first time took steps to improve the food supply.

Among the measures adopted one in particular, because of the strange adventure it led to, has become a part of world history and legend. By order of His Britannic Majesty, the good ship *Bounty* set out for Polynesia in December 1787. Its mission was to get breadfruit seedlings from Tahiti for introduction in the West Indies. This plan for Caribbean relief grew out of the stories circulating in England about the providential Polynesian tree which Captain Cook had discovered on his various voyages to the South Seas.

The *Bounty*, under the command of Captain Bligh, remained at Tahiti until April 1789, at which time, having filled its hold with breadfruit seedlings, it sailed off across the southern seas for Jamaica. Then came the mutiny and the subsequent abandonment of Bligh, with eighteen men, in a lifeboat. The mutinous crew proceeded to establish themselves on deserted Pitcairn Island, which they populated with a race of English-Tahitian half-breeds; Captain Bligh and those who had remained faithful to him, after 3,618 miles of wandering, were saved and returned to England. In spite of the disastrous results of the first expedition, the project seemed so important to England that a new expedition was organized and entrusted to the same Captain Bligh, who succeeded this time in introducing breadfruit into the British West Indies.[102]

Anything so simple as the introduction of a new plant was a long way from remedying the situation in the islands. Breadfruit perhaps improved the food supply somewhat in times of famine, but it could not correct any of the permanent nutritional deficiencies. Captain Cook had reported that by planting a few of these trees a whole family would have food enough for the rest of their lives, but the truth is that the breadfruit tree alone was not responsible for the Tahitians' magnificent physiques, which made such an impression on the first European navigators who put in at these paradisaical islands. The health and resistance of the Tahitians were the result of a diversified diet, abundant in fish, innumerable fruits, and green vegetables, and of clothing and shelter intelligently adapted to the climate in which they lived.[103] Although Captain Bligh succeeded at last and the black slaves of the West Indies began to have breadfruit alongside their potatoes and yams, still they lacked protective foods, and they still died of malnutrition.

Emancipation of the slaves was approved by the British Parliament in 1833. It was thought in some quarters that the freedmen might return to diversified, subsistence farming in the African tradition and that their living conditions might improve. But nothing of the sort happened. The great landowners felt the foundations of their plantation system crumbling, and they erected a thousand obstacles to keep the free black from growing his own food. They carried their obstructionism to the point of putting prohibitive taxes on lands devoted to food production, and thus they managed to shackle the slaves anew and force them to continue working on the sugar plantations for starvation wages. In order to keep wages down, the planters proceeded to import laborers from the poorest areas of the Far East, and in a short time East Indians were replacing blacks on all sorts of jobs. Their diet was made up almost exclusively of rice, their needs were few, and thus they were admirably suited to the demands of the sugar oligarchy, whose interest in cheap and abundant labor accounts for the fact that much of the present population of British colonies in the American tropics is of Indian origin. There are 168,000 East Indians in British Guiana, out of a total population of 380,000; and in Trinidad, 200,000 individuals out of 560,000 are Hindus.

In Jamaica, this system of disguised slavery brought about a sharp reaction. The blacks took possession of abandoned lands in the interior of the island and set up autonomous societies based on subsistence agriculture. This movement resulted in a definite improvement in the local food situation, and even today, Jamaica has better dietary conditions than the other British colonies of the Caribbean. Although the children suffer from deficiencies which I have mentioned, the adults enjoy better health than the blacks of the other islands. In the report published in 1939 by the Committee on Nutrition in the British Colonial Empire we find that "the generally strong physique, good humour, contentment, and patience of the Jamaican negro labourer are regarded by some as evidence that the nutritional conditions are not seriously at fault." [104]

If the Negroes had been able to exert as great an influence on the economic regime and dietary habits of other American regions as they did in Jamaica, it is very possible that conditions of alimentation in this continent would not be so defective as they are today. But their influence was slight, and the nutritional situation of the Antilles continues to be one of the worst in the world, with hunger stalking the slums, urban and rural, of these ravished lands.

Puerto Rico, America's Hong Kong

There is one small island in the great reaches of the Antilles that deserves special attention. It boasts, according to a team of outstanding American experts—Soule, Efron, and Ness—the worst and the most dangerous nutritional conditions of the whole Caribbean area. [105] This is Puerto Rico, a very black spot on the map of universal hunger.

Within approximately 3,400 square miles Puerto Rico contains a population estimated at 2 million.* And on this

* In the 1960's, the population was estimated at 2.7 million, with a growth rate 50 percent higher than that of the United States.

crowded little island one of the most dismal dramas of hunger ever seen in the Western Hemisphere has been stated. The fate of Puerto Rico was unlike that of the rest of the Antilles; its tragedy did not develop through the errors of the old colonial system of the great European powers. It was due, instead, to the utter failure of modern methods of commercial exploitation.

When the United States took possession of Puerto Rico in 1898, following the victory over Spain, it found a population which, if not exactly swimming in wealth and abundance, was far from the misery and hunger that it suffers in our times. The ensuing catastrophe is worth analyzing in detail.

Puerto Rico, to the Spanish, had not looked very promising in terms of sugar raising. It is an extremely mountainous island, with a comparatively irregular surface. The only level land is a narrow strip along the coasts. Its first impression on the Spaniards who discovered it in 1493 is indicated by a passage in Columbus's memoirs, in which he tells of reporting his discovery to Queen Isabella. She asked what the island was like, and Columbus crumpled a piece of paper in his hand. Laying it on the table, he said, "Your Majesty, it is like that."

The Spaniards quickly brought sugar cane culture to this crumpled countryside, but the industry developed neither the size nor the intensity that characterized the colonial exploitation of islands with soil better adapted to the cane plant. Large-scale monoculture, with its typical regime of great landholdings and slavery, did not exist during the Spanish tenure of Puerto Rico.

Because of this agricultural difference, Puerto Rico never lost its white colonists. The British Antilles came to be almost exclusively inhabited by blacks but in Puerto Rico there were large contingents of Spanish settlers, principally from Galicia and the Asturias, to balance the black population.

Nor, until the end of the last century, was the land monopolized by great plantations. Until the time of the United States occupation, 75 percent of the arable land of the island was broken up into small lots containing an average of 12 acres, devoted in the main to subsistence crops. The United States Military Census Commission reported in 1899, immediately after the occupation, that "this general ownership of farms has unquestionably had a great influence in producing the contented condition of the people of this island, as contrasted with the restlessness of Cuba, where a large proportion of the cultivated area was in the hands of comparatively few landlords."[106]

It is true that the sugar industry flourished, at the expense of the black, on the lowlands along the coast; but in the central areas, large numbers of small farmers carried on subsistence agriculture. When the United States took over, there were 250 small, farm-sized sugar factories on the island and 20 centralized mills.

Profound changes were soon brought about. Small growers were swallowed up by great plantations, with their centralized production, and practically disappeared. Through the agency of United States capital, the sugar industry fell under the monopolistic control of a small but powerful group of absentee owners. At the same time, it expanded enormously and came to be the axis of Puerto Rico's whole economic life.

In the period between the two world wars, sugar cane plantations occupied 40 percent of all the cultivated land of Puerto Rico. Cane sugar accounted for some 60 percent of the island's total exports.[107] Great aggregations of capital owned tracts of 40,000 to 50,000 acres, and these took up the most fertile zones of the country. Before the last war, four of the largest organizations produced half of all the sugar of Puerto Rico.

The commercial exploitation of the territory, however,

was not limited to sugar production. On the lands not adapted to sugar-raising, American capital undertook to raise tobacco and coffee, both export products. Thus nearly all the island was converted to supplying the United States. Ellsworth Huntington presents the following figures concerning land use in Puerto Rico in the years before Second World War II: "240,000 acres are devoted to sugar, 190,000 to coffee, and over 50,000 to tobacco, but only about 160,000 to corn, beans, and sweet potatoes or yams, the three main subsistence crops. Taking all the land into account, the Puerto Rican crops raised primarily for export occupy between three and four times as large an area as those devoted to food for home consumption."[108]

It is no wonder, then, that in order to feed the population, and to feed them badly at that, Puerto Rico has had to import great quantities of food, at prices above the purchasing power of the bulk of the inhabitants. The blame for this critical situation belongs in great part to the United States. As the American geographer Preston James very properly emphasized, "Far from showing the way to a stabilized economy, the United States has provided an unhappy example of commercial exploitation of land and labor by absentee owners."[109]

The United States points with pride to what it has accomplished in a material way for an ancient and poverty-stricken Spanish possession. And indeed, since Puerto Rico has been under the protection of the Star-Spangled Banner, there have been considerable accomplishments, such as the building of good roads, beautiful palaces like the Capitol at San Juan, and a model university. But these mean little, in the balance of colonial accomplishment, in comparison with the misery in which the Puerto Rican people are forced to live—stark misery that led the investigator Eric W. Zimmermann to state that they constitute "probably the largest single group of destitute people under the American flag."[110]

[It must be stressed that Puerto Ricans, though American citizens, do not have the right to vote. They are drafted into the American armed forces but they have no voting representatives in Congress. I recall the case of Sixto Alvelo, a young objector who was sentenced to prison—like many other young Puerto Ricans—for refusing in January 1965 to serve in the United States Army. Since the Cuban revolution, furthermore, successive American administrations have viewed the island as a replacement for Cuba, both as a strategic base and as a paradise for investors. The American military is the island's leading "landowner," occupying 100,000 acres or 13 percent of the arable land—an enormous amount considering the nutritional situation of the Puerto Ricans.[111]]

Prevented from producing the food it needs and forced by customs restrictions to import it from the most expensive source in the world (60 percent of food imports are from the United States), Puerto Rico has been dragged into the labyrinth of a dead-end economy. Preston James expresses this untenable situation very well: "In no small part the poverty of the majority of the people is due to the fact that Puerto Rico is included behind the tariff wall of the United States. For while this economic position of Puerto Rico makes possible the profitable production of such commodities as sugar, tobacco, and fruit in competition with places outside of the United States, it also makes it necessary for the Puerto Ricans to purchase whatever they do not produce for themselves in the world's most expensive market. Not only must the Puerto Ricans help to maintain the relatively high standards of living achieved by industrial labor in the United States, but also they must support the higher wage scale of American seamen, since the goods are brought to the island in ships which fly the flag of the United States. The tariff increases the distinctions between the prosperity of the producers and the poverty of the rest of the people."[112]

The economic policy of the United States has been based on the protection of an insignificant minority at the cost of bitter sacrifice by the majority of the native population. This state of striking economic imbalance led an American nutritionist, H. C. Sherman, who was assigned to study the island's dietary situation in 1930, to state that he had never seen any place in the world "where the profits of a rich land go into so few pockets (largely those of absentees) and the people who work the land are not only kept so poor in money, but also so inadequately fed and housed. . . ."[113]

Living conditions in Puerto Rico have been growing progressively worse, as the Zimmermann report showed, partly because of the concentration of human beings that has developed. The demographic density is currently calculated at 574 individuals per square mile of surface, which corresponds to about 1,500 persons per square mile of cultivated land*— an agricultural density among the highest in the world. However, although this density of population may aggravate certain aspects of the food problem and make it more difficult to solve, it cannot be considered the cause of the existing chronic starvation.

Actually, the undernourishment and overpopulation are symptoms or consequences of economic disorganization—of the defective economic setup and of the unrelieved commercial exploitation. It was the sugar industry that determined the high demographic concentration, just as it did in all the other areas of sugar monoculture. We have proof all over the world—in Java, in Barbados, in Louisiana—that sugar culture can only develop and prosper on the basis of a dense rural population. Even in Brazil, where the demographic density is low, the area of sugar cane monoculture in the northeastern states is one of the most heavily populated zones of the country.

---

* 713 in the early 1970's, corresponding to 1,825 persons per square mile.

In Puerto Rico the hunger of the cane fields for human hands, plus the chronic hunger of the laborers, gave rise to an impetuous increase in the population of the island. In spite of a shocking mortality index, particularly as regards infants, the population has doubled since the United States occupation.

Food conditions in Puerto Rico reached an extremely perilous state during World War II when imports became exceedingly hard to get. The country was carried to the brink of famine. E. B. Hill and J. R. Noguera reported that when the war broke out, Puerto Rico "depended entirely on outside sources for fats and oils, cereals, and preparations and imported 89 percent of the fish and 60 percent of the legumes it consumed."[114] With imports paralyzed, there followed a veritable panic among the population; the situation became so bad in 1944 that some 40 percent of the inhabitants were registered for relief.

The habitual diet of the island is composed of beans and rice, starchy vegetables, and codfish. The lower classes, however, cannot afford codfish, and on the other hand the higher classes use meat and eggs. But among all classes the basic diet is monotonously the same—beans and rice, rice and beans. An analysis of the usual diet of this people reveals serious deficiencies of proteins, mineral salts, and vitamins.[115] The low nutritional level is immediately manifest in the underdevelopment of the children, who are always greatly inferior to the growth standards of the United States. Xerophthalmia, scurvy, tropical sprue, and pellagra are seen everywhere among the poorer people. In short, practically all the signs of malnutrition, with the exception of widespread dental failure, can be observed in the island. For some reason still not understood by nutritional science, the children and even adults of Puerto Rico, who drink hardly any milk and do not eat cheese or other rich sources of calcium, possess admirable teeth, the envy of well-fed visitors from the mainland. Good teeth, exhibited in broad, Latin American smiles, are the only sign of health left to the primitive Puerto Rican population.

On all other counts, the population has been reduced to inferiority. It is not extreme, indeed, to compare the island of Puerto Rico, so far as the living conditions of its people are concerned, to the island of Hong Kong in the China seas. The British established themselves on Hong Kong by the Treaty of Nanking, in 1842, but they have done nothing to improve the living conditions of the Chinese who subsist there, bound in mire and misery like the natives of this other "island slum," as Vogt called the territory of Puerto Rico. [Because of changes in the island's political status, energetic steps were taken to improve its diet in the years following World War II. But nonetheless, Puerto Rico's nutritional situation is still far from good.

The United States has too often regarded the island only as an important strategic base and has ignored the nutritional needs of its inhabitants. In addition, Puerto Rico has been fair game for American investors, who have dominated it economically and have made disproportionately high and tax-free returns on their investments. No wonder that the United States government has been unable to impress many Latin American countries with this "model for Latin American development."

The recent increase in per capita income is almost entirely a reflection of luxury investments in hotels and apartment houses in San Juan, a city that, as Manuel Maldonado-Denis points out, has replaced Havana as a center of corruption, bad taste, and vulgarity. The living standards of the island's inhabitants remain low: in 1940 per capita income in Mississippi—the poorest state in the Union—was 80 percent higher than in Puerto Rico. In 1960 it was 81 percent higher, and it was still 62 percent higher in 1971! Sixty percent of the families on the island do not eat properly. The economy retains all the characteristics of a colonial system. Puerto

Ricans are obliged to import what they consume and cannot consume what they themselves produce. Eighty percent of the companies on the island are controlled by American capital, which profits from an array of fiscal incentives and a supply of cheap manpower.

Manuel Maldonado-Denis's call to revolt is understandable: "The United States owns Puerto Rico; it is destroying its culture and its personality."[116] If the United States does not soon adopt a policy of integration for its Caribbean "possession," Puerto Rico will continue to be the Hong Kong of the Americas.]

The Old South, a Landscape of Contrasts

No doubt it will come as something of a shock, particularly to American readers, to find a large region of the United States included among the great hunger areas of the world. And it does seem paradoxical that hunger should exist in a land of abundance like the United States, where agriculture has always had to contend with surpluses and where productive capacity during World War II was sufficient to help feed half the world.

But the existence of hunger right in the world's supply house is an undeniable fact. It is not a matter of a small plot but of a geographical region large enough to include whole countries. This hunger area in the United States is the South, a region with about 500,000 square miles of surface and a population of some 30 million people.*

[Mass hunger exists outside the South, notably among the subproletariat of such large cities as New York, Chicago, San Francisco, and Los Angeles. The majority of these people are blacks, Puerto Ricans, and Mexicans who endure on the

* 50 million in 1970.

fringes of the country's major industrial centers, hoping to discover some way to achieve an average living standard in this consumer society. But let us first examine the South, which has always been a region marked by hunger, like the Caribbean or northeast Brazil.]

In the colonial period, the South was represented by the five English colonies of Maryland, Virginia, the Carolinas, and Georgia. Today it is a hard task for the geographer to set precise limits to the region, but for the purposes of this study I will consider the South, somewhat mechanically, to be the area corresponding to the old, agrarian, slave-holding South, including the following eleven states: Virginia, North Carolina, South Carolina, Kentucky, Tennessee, Georgia, Florida, Alabama, Mississippi, Louisiana, and Arkansas.

There is no doubt that the Old South has always been a hunger zone. Its habitual condition is demonstrated by certain figures published by the National Research Council, which examined nutritional conditions in the country during World War II. In a bulletin issued in 1943, the special committee set up to study this question reported that in the South, only 27 percent of the population made use of an adequate diet.[117] That is to say, more than two thirds—73 percent—of the inhabitants of the South received an improper diet and consequently suffered from one kind of hunger or another [in the same proportion one finds in Latin America.]

Such a situation is shocking to the layman but even more so to those who have a detailed knowledge of the geographical background of the region. A study of the roots or causes of starvation in the southern United States reveals another typical example of hunger as a man-made plague, since the region is eminently suited by nature to the production of adequate food supplies. Few regions of the world have such a high potential agricultural yield, such abundant natural resources lying ready to the hand of man. Few regions of the world have been so ruthlessly sacked and plundered, so wasted by ill-conceived use and by permanent maladjustment between man and his environment.

Howard W. Odum, who is considered one of the greatest living authorities on the geographical and social problems of the South, has made an admirable summary of the impressive natural wealth of the region, which he pictures as a veritable kingdom of abundance:

> This superabundance of well-nigh limitless sources of natural wealth is measured also by great range and variety: rainfall and rivers; climate and growing seasons; land and forests; minerals from the land undug; sticks and stones of fabulous quality and quantity for the fabrication of great buildings and for the construction of roads and bridges; energy and power, and tidal power; iodine and phosphorus and nitrogen wealth; chemical resources from pine and vegetable, cotton and corn; parks and playgrounds, mountains and seashore, summer and winter resorts, play places of a nation; nature reserves and sanctuaries for wild life; flora extraordinary, grasses and cultivated plants to feed man and animal and land; fauna of the woods and fields, millions of game, for commerce and recreation; domesticated animals on farm and grazing lands, race horses and work mules, makers of a culture; and many other tangibles and intangibles of geography's situation, relief, and area.

> If the enumeration of the superabundance of natural resources begins with oceans and rivers and rainfall, and if to abundant waters be added long, frostless growing seasons and soil of variety and richness, there will be projected boldly the basic vein of natural resources stretching across and through this Southeastern Region of eleven states no one of which is outside the range of superior advantage. In the measure of its rainfall, the whole of the Southeast lies within the bounds of that magic area which measures more than forty inches average annual precipitation. Of the 27 percent of the nation's area in which a frostless growing season of six months or more is available, the Southeast itself has nearly a third, while the Southeast and the Southwest together aggregate more than two-thirds of the total.[118]

Two fundamental traits which Odum has mentioned warrant, for the purposes of our study, a more detailed analysis: the soil of the region and the climate, both of which are extremely well suited to agriculture. The greater part of the land is yellow and red podsol. This may not be so fertile as the black soil, or chernozen, of the northern and central United States, but it is far superior to the tropical soils that cover most of the other regions of the hemisphere that we have studied so far. And in addition to the podsol in the South, there are great stretches of still more fertile soil, such as the black lands of Alabama—the Black Belt—so called not because some 87 percent of its population is black but on account of the dark coloration of a soil rich in organic matter. Strips of fertile alluvial soil cut across the South in various directions—the James River Valley in Virginia, the cradle of Southern culture; and the Mississippi Valley, which extends, 80 miles wide on the average, for a distance of 500 miles from the mouth of the Ohio to the delta. This alluvial strip, according to Emory Hawk and other authors, has proved "as fertile as the famous Nile Valley."[119] Although the climate of the South shows considerable local variation, it is on the whole very favorable to agriculture. It has an abundance of rain and sun and well-defined seasons, with mild winters little subject to snow or freezing.

The natural advantages were of no avail to keep starvation away in the face of colonial economic policy. In the economic history of the South may be found the whole explanation of its tragedy, of "the dramatic struggle of a large and powerful segment of the American people for mastery over an environment capable of producing a superior civilization," as Odum said.[120] The present "landscape of contrasts," as he has called it, with hunger as one of its outstanding features, is a cultural heritage of the pioneering epoch, of colonial conditions and of slavery. It has been further impoverished in modern times by the activities of land speculators.

The first settlers of the southern colonies attempted to set up on the soil of Virginia a diversified agriculture based on the same plants they were accustomed to growing in England. Opening clearings in the forests around Jamestown, they sowed wheat and fruits and vegetables which they had brought from the Old World. The fruit trees developed well, but the wheat was another story. "They soon discovered," Hawk relates, ". . . that, while the plant shot up to an amazing height in the extraordinary soil, the kernels unfortunately would not harden into grain."[121] So the colonists gave up the idea of growing wheat; and learning from the Indians, they undertook to grow native plants such as corn, beans, sweet potato, squash, melon, and strawberries. Some European products were gradually introduced, and the colonies began to develop toward a subsistence culture which promised to become self-sufficient.

Unfortunately, this line of development was not looked on with favor in the England of that day, whose colonial system was based on mercantilism. Colonies were considered simply as sources of raw materials not produced in the mother country and as new markets for manufactured products.[122] The London Company, which had obtained the rights to exploit the South from James I in 1606, considered that the most urgent problem for the economic success of the enterprise was to discover an exportable product that could be produced on a large scale. It should not be forgotten that the company was made up of "knights, gentlemen, merchants, and other adventurers" from London and other places, all of them interested in one objective—large profits, and quick, from their colonial investment.

The first staple export crop that the directors of the company attempted to produce was silk. The attempt failed. Grapes were then tried, and this crop too failed to come up to expectations. The company was on the verge of bankruptcy when the profitable export commodity was finally discovered—a native agricultural product, tobacco. A system of great plantations rapidly sprang up, and the culture of tobacco soon spread to the greater part of the cultivable land of Virginia, Maryland, and the Carolinas. Further west, particularly in the Mississippi Valley, cotton established itself first on an experimental basis and later as absolute king, while sugar cane later took possession of the coastal areas of Louisiana.

Thus three products—cotton, tobacco, and sugar, with cotton in the lead—took over the South and enslaved both man and soil to the caprices of speculative fortunes. The cultivation of these commercial products transformed the regional economy completely. Land tenure, which began as a system of small holdings, soon reached extremes of concentration. The size of the average farm was as much as 160 acres in 1626 and had risen to 446 acres in 1650 and to 670 acres by 1700. At the beginning of the eighteenth century the government, in an attempt to limit the concentration of landholding, limited land patents to 4,000 acres. But the great landlords were by then absolute sovereigns of their domains, making and breaking laws at will, and they chose to ignore the federal legislation.

The great plantations continued to grow, so that by the middle of the eighteenth century there were southern aristocrats with properties of 150,000 acres.[123] In order to work these huge tracts of land, black slaves were introduced into the southern colonies in 1619 and from that moment the typical system of monoculture began to develop, with all its train of melancholy consequences: insufficient food, wearing-out and erosion of the soil, slavery or forced labor, periodical economic crises, and a low biological and cultural level of the population.

The process by which the plantation system brought starvation to the regional population was the same, in general outline, as that in other one-crop areas of the world. Food shortages appeared at once, the logical result of the fact that slave labor was directed exclusively toward the planting of crops for export, while subsistence culture was reduced to a minimum. The consequence was the most inadequate kind of diet, a hunger diet that killed off the blacks in a short time. But under this economic system it was cheaper to replace the dead slaves than it was to permit them a normal lifespan, with proper nutrition and fewer hours of work.

After the Civil War and the emancipation of the slaves, southern agriculture relied on the labor of tenants and share-croppers, who made up the bulk of the rural population. As an indication of the predominance of such workers in the labor system of the region, Odum pointed out that of the 2 million families living in the cotton belt in 1936 more than half owned no land. They lived as tenants, at the mercy of the price fluctuations of their speculative commodity. And in certain sub-areas, the number of tenants approached the total number of inhabitants: in the Black Belt, 73 percent; in the Red River bottoms, 80 percent; and in the Delta region, 90 percent.[124]

The sharecropping system, which is a hangover of European feudalism and of the slave system of colonial times, has permitted the survival of a kind of semislavery, which limits the freedom of the laborer, forcing him to do a certain kind of work and to accept only a part of the product in payment. The percentage is calculated in such a way that it ordinarily fails to provide enough to eat. The majority of American sociologists who have given thorough study to this system consider it one of the "public scandals of America." Gunnar Myrdal, the renowned Swedish sociologist, sees in the system one of the most tenacious links in that vicious circle of misery—monoculture, tenancy, soil exhaustion, and erosion. This system brings with it "poverty for most, economic insecurity for all, widespread ignorance, low health standards, relative lack of an enterprising spirit, high birth rates, and large families."[125] In these words we can read the step-by-step development of this area, beginning with the improper ownership and exploitation of the land and bringing human beings to inevitable poverty, hunger, and overpopulation.

Even where the plantation system fell into decadence, through parceling out the land in certain places after the Civil War, living conditions remained precarious, because wages in the South were kept to the lowest levels in the country. King Cotton imposed these levels in order to compete in world markets with the product of other countries where living standards are low. And substandard wages were endured because the rural population had no other work to turn to.

On the one hand, the raising of cash crops for export degrades human labor; on the other hand, it exhausts the soil. Cotton and tobacco were planted in the early period without any fertilizer and without crop rotation, and this soon led to the depletion of the best regional soils. These soils were so thoroughly stripped of their humus and mineral salts that huge and continuous quantities of fertilizers are now necessary in order to keep them in production. This constitutes a heavy burden on southern agriculture.

Thanks to the exhausting monoculture practiced in the South, the greatest stripping of topsoil ever seen anywhere in the world has taken place there, and enormous areas have been rendered sterile by erosion. In a study carried out in 1933 by specialists in the subject, it was demonstrated that a third of all the land in the South is eroded and that at least half of all the eroded land in the United States is found in the South. The figures, which told of hundreds of millions of acres become useless, particularly on the slopes of the Piedmont—great gullies showing red at the bottom like bloody gashes in the body of the earth—produced a state of national alarm. And the result was a rash of narrow theories which attributed all the misery and hunger of the South exclusively to soil erosion.[126]

In truth, the alarmists had the effect of producing a certain confusion in the interpretation of the facts. Erosion is not the cause of the decadence and hunger in the South. All of these things, erosion and hunger and misery, are effects of a single cause: improper economic development of the region. Soil erosion, as well as erosion of the human potential, is the disastrous result of a single factor: the plantation system. The eminent American expert, Charles Kellogg, was quite right in saying that "soil erosion is an important symptom of bad relationships between people and soil, just as a headache is often a symptom of some more fundamental illness. Civilizations can hardly be said to have declined from soil exhaustion—soil exhaustion is more a result of the decay of the people, of the civilization."[127] Caught in this net of negative factors—inadequate production, worn-out soils, and low salaries—the human beings of the region necessarily suffer from improper diet, a diet both insufficient and incomplete.

It is a well-known fact that the bulk of the people "live on the three M's: meat, meal, and molasses." The meat is salt pork, practically all fat; the meal is corn meal; and molasses is cane syrup. To these basic foods, rice, beans, or sweet potatoes may be added in certain areas. But they do little to improve the diet, which is tremendously defective on the face of it, lacking protective elements such as meat, milk, eggs, and fresh vegetables.

In a notable study of the relationship between economic factors and nutritional conditions in the South, Joseph Goldberger and Edgar Sydenstricker showed how the lack of protective foods is a result of the one-crop system, and of nothing else.[128] These scientists pointed out that there have never been enough milk and meat in the South because the great landowners always discouraged cattle-raising. Pastures would divert land from their cotton fields, and tenants would give the cattle hay that was needed for the mules and horses used in growing cotton and sugar cane. In the same way, the big planters never encouraged the planting of gardens and orchards. They would take up space and would absorb labor that could not be spared, even for a moment, from the fields devoted to cash crops. And although from 60 to 70 percent of the tenants keep chickens, they are generally few in number, and eggs come into the diet only occasionally.

The restrictions imposed on slaves, and later on tenants, against using the land for raising fruits and vegetables have broken not only the will of the people to raise such foods but also the habit of using them. The result is that today, when the South is tending to diversify its agriculture and produce appreciable quantities of fruits and vegetables, the farm families, through force of habit, still stick to their dangerous and monotonous diet of corn, sowbelly, and molasses.

It is clear that the continued use of such a diet must have serious physical consequences. And indeed, ever since colonial times, both blacks and "poor whites" have exhibited a series of complaints that were surely due to faulty nutrition, although they have been attributed to such causes as bad climate, poor working conditions, or even to some sort of racial atavism.

Of the deficiency diseases common to the zone, one stands out for its alarming frequency: pellagra. Although Babcock believes that it has been widespread in the southern states since 1828, medical men began to call attention to the disease only at the beginning of our own century. They pointed out also that it seemed to be increasing at a shocking rate throughout the area. An alarmingly high incidence of pellagra in all the southern states was recognized in 1909, and in a few years the number of cases of the terrible illness reached 100,000, with an annual death toll of some 4,000 persons.[129]

As we have seen, pellagra represents a complex of dietary deficiencies, centered in a lack of nicotinic acid. It is the characteristic disease of poverty and misery, and its increase in a region always reveals an intensification of distress and wretchedness. There are some who would explain the increase in the number of pellagra cases in the South, between the end of the past century and the beginning of World War II, simply by the greater skill of doctors in diagnosing the disease. Others, however, see the phenomenon as a reflex of the economic evolution that has taken place during these years. And the latter would appear to be right.

Pellagra takes such a toll in the South that in certain localities it affects 25 percent of the rural population. In 1938, Sydenstricker and William H. Sebrell arrived at independent estimates of 100,000 as the number of cases of pellagra in the United States at that time, with mortality, in 1940, reaching 2,123 cases.[130]

An analysis of the incidence of pellagra by years reveals a close correlation with the movements of the cotton market. The number of cases increases in years of economic depression, diminishes following periods of prosperity. Thus, in 1916, following the 1914-15 depression in the cotton exchange, pellagra reached alarming proportions, even becoming in South Carolina the second most frequent cause of death. There was another epidemic of pellagra in 1927, following the low cotton prices of the previous year and the great Mississippi flood which destroyed a good many plantations in Tennessee, Arkansas, Mississippi, and Louisiana. After the 1929 crash, the line of pellagra incidence rises again. And in spite of improvements in dietary conditions accomplished during and after World War II, pellagra continues rampant, although on a more limited scale, in both its typical and its milder forms.

Besides pellagra, many other vitamin and mineral deficiencies have been registered in the area. Anemias due to iron deficiency, generally aggravated by worms, are extremely common, especially among children. Vitamin A deficiencies have been noted in proportions that reach 50 percent of the rural population of Tennessee.[131]

Vitamin B-1 deficiencies, which formerly took a heavy toll in Louisiana in the form of beriberi, still continue, particularly in partial form. The absence of other elements of the Vitamin B complex is troublesome locally; riboflavin deficiency, according to T. D. Spies, Wm. Bennett Beans, and others, is the commonest of all the dietary deficiencies of the South. Food conditions are so bad in some areas that along with specific deficiencies, one finds quantitative hunger or semistarvation as the result of insufficient calories. A study made in Tennessee by J. B. Youmans and others demonstrated that all sections of the population, except children from one to six, received less than the recommended number of calories daily. In certain groups, the deficiency represented 45 percent of the total energy required.[132]

It is no wonder that under such conditions of quantitative and qualitative starvation, many individuals are, through lack of energy and initiative, incapable of working.

Internal Colonization

Although small landholdings have increased in the South since 1900, so that latifundia are now less common there than in other parts of the United States, the same period has seen an increase in the number of absentee owners. Although 64 percent of southern farms were operated by their owners in 1880, this figure fell to 53 percent in 1900, to 44 percent in 1930 [and to 25 percent in 1970]. This increase in absentee ownership represents the purchase of run-down southern farms by bankers and financial groups of the North.

These same financial groups also turned toward the industrial exploitation of the South. But this industrialization—which has expanded greatly in the last decades—became, in certain cases, a cause of pauperism rather than enrichment of the local populations. The reason was that many northern factories moved South in search of cheap labor and succeeded in maintaining wages at extremely low levels. [Thus an economic neocolonialism was established in the South. It was national, rather than international, in form but nonetheless the North exploited the South like a colony.]

Absentee ownership has greatly aggravated the economic plight of the South. With absentee capital in the saddle, living conditions in the area became worse than ever, and the nutritional situation during this period was worse than that of the slaves in colonial times. It was perhaps this new form of colonization of the South by great insurance and banking houses that led to a large-scale migration of the southern rural population to other parts of the country.

The economic disorganization caused by capitalist land exploitation, mechanized farming, and cheap-labor industries resulted in the expulsion of large numbers of tenants and sharecroppers. Many of these set out in the 1930's for the West, forming the strangest and most paradoxical caravan of all time. The poor victims, ragged and starving, traveled mainly in automobiles—the symbol of prosperity in a technological civilization. It is true of course that the cars they used were old and secondhand, pieces of junk that burned up their worn-out motors and fell apart along the way, swelling the junk cemeteries by the side of the road in competition with their owners, who also populated the cemeteries of the West with their old and worn-out remains. As portrayed by John Steinbeck in *The Grapes of Wrath,* these travelers, with their ruined cars but without a nickel to buy bread for their starving children, are a perfect symbol of misery in the midst of plenty, a characteristic condition of the Old South.

In recent years this dark picture of hunger has been somewhat improved thanks to measures taken by various governmental agencies. The impact of World War II drew some attention to the production and distribution of food and had a very beneficial effect on dietary conditions in the South. In a report entitled "Our Food Front" issued in November

1943, Dr. Russell Wilder commented that "there is reason to believe we have less hunger in America than we had before the war."[133]

Federal projects such as the Tennessee Valley Authority, which benefited 4.5 million people in seven states through rational control of land, water, and all the various resources of the region, necessarily brought with them a relative improvement in local living conditions. Within ten years, for instance, the T.V.A. effected an increase in the regional individual income of about 75 percent, as compared with an increase in national income for the same period of 56 percent.[134] This rise in the economic standard is naturally reflected in all aspects of life in the region, including diet.

Nevertheless, nutritional conditions in the South leave much to be desired. In spite of improvements, many types of nutritional deficiencies still remain, especially in their milder forms. For a long time the dilemma of hunger in the South will challenge the best efforts of the economic planners and technicians of the United States, and the dark blotches of hunger will continue to mark the "rural slums of the South."[135]

[Destroying the Hunger Taboo

The panorama of hunger in the southern United States remains basically as I described it in the first edition of this book in 1952. The additional details drawn from recent reports serve only to confirm the sad truth. Nothing essential has changed. Nonetheless, until recently the ruling classes in the United States refused to recognize the reality; on the contrary, they were determined to deny that hunger existed in the land of prosperity and abundance. The authorities concerned with hygiene and social welfare tried to make light of the situation, admitting that although some nutritional deficiencies could still be found among the unemployed, mass hunger had long ago been wiped out. When my book appeared, denouncing this hoax on the part of officials, it was considered suspect in certain influential circles, and I was accused of denigrating American society for political motives.

In the past few years, however, the truth has come to light; the wretchedness in the midst of abundance has been exposed and has created a major scandal. Finally, the authorities have been forced to recognize that the United States is still a long way from solving the problem of hunger for a large part of its population. The publication of John Kenneth Galbraith's *The Affluent Society* in 1958 and, four years later, Michael Harrington's still harsher and franker *The Other America* contributed greatly in the attack on the castle of illusions into which American society had shut itself to avoid seeing the negative aspects of the "American way of life." Rising protests from the ghettos and the campuses finally captured the castle and forced all the windows of the Establishment, so that today no American can be unaware of the tragic presence of hunger in that country. The time of denial and camouflage is over. Major political leaders now speak the same language as this book, and the information and statistics presented in official documents solidly support my statements.

In a famous speech in 1963 President Kennedy declared that "every night more than ten million Americans go to bed without eating." In 1967 President Johnson pointed out that "nine million American children under six years old live in families that cannot feed and house them decently." Finally on December 2, 1969, President Nixon, addressing the opening of the Conference on Nutrition and Health called by the federal government, confessed that the United States had "a long way to go before resolving the problem of hunger in the country." These remarks were made as if they were sensational revelations. All these leaders were trying to convince the public that they were terribly surprised and shocked by the existence of mass hunger in their country.

Such an attitude points up the collective alienation of the ruling groups in America. They are deeply astonished by a situation that has, in fact, been a constant in the economic structure of the United States. Senator Jacob Javits's description of his own recent discovery of hunger among the American people offers a striking proof of this alienation of American political leadership. He said:

I first came face to face with the hidden shame of hunger in America when I visited Mississippi in the spring of 1967. I was one of four members of the Senate Subcommittee on Employment, Manpower, and Poverty, and we traveled to Jackson to "examine the War on Poverty." We went to Mississippi because we were anxious to see how much such federal programs as Head Start and the one-dollar-per-hour minimum wage for farm workers were faring in the poorest state in the nation.

It frankly never occurred to me nor, I believe, to the other Senators on that trip—the late Senator Robert F. Kennedy and Senators Joseph Clark and George Murphy—that the ravages of American poverty could produce conditions of malnutrition and hunger that were thought to exist only in parts of India, Africa, and Asia.

Looking back now to that trip made just two and a half years ago, I still find it difficult to understand how we Senators—and the nation at large—could not have been more aware that poverty breeds malnutrition just as surely as poverty breeds unemployment, bad housing, crime, and illiteracy.

What has happened in the United States since the shock that these terrible revelations provoked? Nothing significant, nothing that could alter this pitiful situation. All the initiatives taken so far have been palliatives or paternalistic gestures. In 1963 President Kennedy, alerted to the true situation by the intellectuals who surrounded him, instructed his economic adviser Walter Heller to work with Michael

Harrington and the economists Leon Keyserling and Robert Lampman to design a plan to fight hunger and misery on a national scale. Later that year Heller presented a plan to Kennedy and, three days before his death, the President gave him the go-ahead to launch the War on Poverty. President Johnson reaffirmed the government's desire to attack vigorously in the fight against poverty and named the head of the Peace Corps, Sargent Shriver, to direct the Office of Economic Opportunity. The official policy was to apply domestically the sort of tactics employed abroad to help Third World countries escape their underdevelopment and misery. Johnson promised to lower military expenditures and use some of those funds for the struggle against poverty. The *New York Times* commented on this policy in an editorial published on February 26, 1964, entitled "Poverty and Disarmament." It included the following passage:

> By a decision now that a large part of the funds released from defense will be earmarked for schools, housing, health, and public works, the movement away from military war could be coupled with a movement forward in the war against poverty. By this example, a powerful spur would simultaneously be applied to other governments to make similar commitments for reallocation of their resources to peaceful programs. The campaign against poverty could eventually be turned into the worldwide undertaking it must be for true security and the abolition of want.

The program never became a reality, however. The escalation of the Vietnam war involved enormous costs that rose continuously until, in 1971, they reached a figure of $60 billion, and the desire for prestige persuaded the United States to fund the series of Apollo moonshots, meanwhile abandoning the crusade against poverty to token funding. The war on hunger never took place, for the O.E.O. never had an opportunity to deploy its forces. President Johnson surrendered in advance.

Poverty therefore remained at the same level, and the situation grew more explosive every day. The urban riots that broke out across the country expressed the frustration of the marginal populations of the major cities—islands of poverty, in Galbraith's phrase, surrounded by seas of abundance.[136] On these islands, as Galbraith stressed, almost everyone lives in poverty, a phenomenon that cannot be explained in terms of individual lack of ability. Its causes lie in the social context that creates these islands.

To damp down the explosive situation, a plan for nutritional assistance was established: the food stamp program. This plan was simply one more paternalistic policy conceived on the level of public charity.

As scientific studies show, the nutritional situation in the United States today is a true public calamity. A national survey conducted by Dr. Harold Schaefer of the Department of Health revealed that diseases resulting from hunger are extremely widespread and of many varieties. His investigation showed that in certain urban areas 92 percent of the children suffer from a nutritionally rooted anemia and that goiter, rickets, pellagra, and several other vitamin deficiencies have a high incidence throughout the country. Dr. Schaefer, who had spent many years investigating the nutritional levels of underdeveloped countries in Asia, Africa, and Latin America, confessed that he was shocked by the unexpected revelations of the investigation carried out in the United States. Testifying before a Senate committee, he said: "The malnutrition that we found was much more serious than could have been expected in a country described as the best fed in the world." And he added that, having worked in this area in thirty-three countries, he was in a position to say that the inadequate nutrition in the United States was as serious as that found recently in the six Central American countries of Guatemala, Puerto Rico, Panama, Honduras, Nicaragua, and El Salvador. Responding to one of the committee members—Senator

Javits—who asked if he thought there was a correlation between serious malnutrition and low wage levels, Dr. Schaefer answered, "Not at this point." In other words, he was unwilling to label the true causes of hunger in the United States.

But the roots of this distress are examined in other readily available sources: "Poverty U.S.A.," *Newsweek*'s issue of February 17, 1974; *Hunger U.S.A.*, Report by the Citizen Board of Inquiry into Hunger and Malnutrition in the United States, published in 1960; Michael Harrington's *Toward a Democratic Left*, 1968; *Prelude to Riot: A View of Urban America from the Bottom*, by Paul Jacobs, 1966; Jeanne Lowe's *Cities in a Race with Time*, 1967; and *Poverty: Views from the Left*, by Jeremy Larner and Irving Howe, 1968. Hunger in the United States is rooted deep in the country's social and economic structures, many aspects of which are founded on social injustice and an inhuman exploitation of certain groups.

The situation preoccupied President Nixon who, in November 1969, convoked the Conference on Nutrition and Health in order to define some directions for concerted and effective action. The results of the conference were not very encouraging. The President's speech to the delegates showed he had nothing to add to the paternalistic plans of his predecessors and avoided any reference to the real causes of the scourge. When he had finished speaking, the nonwhite delegates—blacks, Indians, Puerto Ricans, and Mexican Americans—demonstrated in protest and returned their food stamps, stating that the President had offered only "empty words" that would lead to no worthwhile action.

Thus the scandal of hunger in the United States continues to worsen, and the world learns how different is the Other America from the America of moon landings. Official estimates state that 50 million persons—almost a fourth of the population—are inadequately nourished and that 20 million are literally starving, both qualitatively and quantitatively, since they have neither a balanced diet nor enough food to fill their stomachs.[137] In the United States today the civilization of abundance lives side by side with the civilization of wretchedness. The presence of the starving in the richest country in the world, a country that presents itself as a model worthy of imitation, justifies the world-wide opposition to the civilization of technology that is called the post-industrial society—a society that constantly creates new, increasingly artificial needs through advertising at the behest of the manufacturers. Despite the unbelievable waste for which this superindustrialized nation is noted, the indispensable nutritional needs of certain classes of its population are not being satisfied.

More than twenty years ago I denounced the scandal of hunger in America—to no avail. The scandal's persistence into the 1970's dramatically calls into question the almost universal belief that the United States is a truly well-developed country and gives lie to those apologists of the civilization of weapons and machines who assert that the country of the dollar, which has made technology its ethic, is without doubt the best developed country in the world.[138]]

4
Hunger in Ancient Asia

Asia, more than any other continent, is the land of man and the land of hunger. Nowhere else has man carved the evidences of his presence so deeply into the earth and nowhere else has hunger left such profound marks on the structure of human society. The oldest human fossil, that of *Sinanthropus pekinensis,* was found in Asia, and from Asia came the tales of the first famines to ravage the human species.

It was, then, in Asia, whose name means "Land of the Rising Sun," that man first arose, and along with man, hunger. Every day that the sun rises above the waters of the Great Ocean and lights the Asian countryside with all its contrasts, it throws into violent relief the visible evidences of man's age-old struggle against starvation. For Asia is the most humanized of the continents; men have lived there longest and, in our time, in the greatest concentration. When one examines the religious doctrines, the moral codes, the community customs, and the living habits of its people, one sees that throughout the centuries the most decisive influence on all these cultural manifestations has been the state of nutritional poverty to which these human groups have been subject. No other social factor anywhere has molded human conduct with such despotic control as has collective hunger in the Far East.

Three quarters of all these peoples' activities are devoted to grubbing in the reluctant soil for their slender subsistence. Consequently, all their impulses, thoughts, gestures, and actions are forever directed toward that vital objective. This is life in ancient Asia, that mysterious cradle of the human race, where more human beings have been born and have died than in any other region on our planet.

Asia makes up only a third of the land surface of the globe, but in it are concentrated two thirds of the world's population. The continent thus has a demographic density of 72 inhabitants per square mile, as compared with 26 for the rest of the world.* It is undoubtedly this enormous reserve of humanity, this compact human coating, more dense and varied than in any other part of the world, that gives the continent its peculiar geographical personality. Beneath the feet of those pullulating Oriental multitudes, there stretches a landscape which is enormously varied in form and characteristics. The immense continental mass may be divided into at least five great natural regions: the Far East, including China and Japan; southeast Asia, consisting of the peninsula of Indochina; the subcontinent of India; the Near East; and, finally, the immense expanse of continent in the extreme north, which makes up part of the Soviet Union. In this chapter the first four regions of Asia will be treated as a unit, leaving aside the Soviet Union. The Soviet Union cannot be considered as entirely Asiatic, just as it is not entirely European. It is, in fact, a sort of bridge between the two continents and the two cultures. As the Iberian Peninsula has always been a bridge between Europe and Africa, Russia, even before the advent of Soviet socialism, has served as a transition zone between the cultures of Europe and of Asia.

* 80 inhabitants, as compared with 30.

"Farmers of Forty Centuries"

Agriculture has been practiced on Chinese soil for more than forty centuries, since the first farmers took root around the banks of the Yellow River. These were the people who expanded their dominions and spread their culture, customs, and traditions over the enormous area that makes up Greater China, the second largest country in the world in area—exceeded only by the Soviet Union—[and the first in terms of population. Until the revolution of 1949, this huge country was the quintessential region of hunger. To view China's present nutritional situation in perspective requires an acquaintance with the history of hunger in its pre-revolutionary civilization. For that reason the following pages present an overall view of the problem of hunger in the old China.*]

China's typically agrarian civilization covers an area of 3.5 million square miles. At least 400 million of the 500 million individuals† who inhabit this giant among nations live in intimate contact with the soil or with rural activities. China has the densest concentration of rural population in the world, and the character of Chinese life is predominantly rural. Where 23 percent of the residents of the United States live on farms, the proportion in China is upwards of 80 percent.[1] In spite of such devoted and all-absorbing agricultural activity or, indeed, as a result of it, China has always lived in a shocking state of nutritional poverty, and its people, more than any others in the world, have suffered the painful consequences of hunger. Nowhere has hunger been

---

* These conditions still obtained when I was working on the first edition of this book, and to avoid confusion the present tense has been maintained. Most figures are based on data from the period between World War II and the revolution of 1949.
† 500 million of the 600 million.

such an overwhelming problem as it has in this civilization based almost exclusively on subsistence agriculture. Alimentation is so urgent a question that colloquial peasant speech employs more metaphors referring to food than to any other aspect of life. Walter Mallory points out that the polite salutation between friends is, "Have you eaten?"[2]

Although the country is essentially agricultural, farming goes on, practically speaking, only in the third of it that lies nearest the coast. Two thirds of China, including the central area, is almost entirely desert or mountain territory, unadapted to agriculture. This situation is reflected in the distribution of the population, which is closely concentrated in the more easterly part of the country. If the map of China is divided by a north-and-south line running through the center of Yunnan province, the population of the western part, which takes in 2 million square miles, is 17 million, while 450 million people are jammed into the 1.5 million square miles of the eastern section. The population of China piles up in regions where the soil can furnish at least a minimum subsistence—in the great river valleys, particularly in the alluvial deposits of the deltas, and on the broad northern plains where the winds, plundering the great central deserts of Asia, have deposited a fertile layer of loess.

The uneven distribution of human beings shows how strictly the Chinese are dependent on the soil and climate of their country. Yet these are far from optimum for farming. John Lessing Buck, whose study of rural life in China is objective, says that the agriculture of no other country faces so many natural obstacles, especially climatic hazards.[3] The exceptional heroism of the Chinese farmer's struggle against fickle nature has been well described in F. H. King's *Farmers of Forty Centuries.*

The first difficulty of Chinese agriculture is the relative scarcity of tillable soil; great areas, as the geographer G. B. Cressey points out, are too cold or too dry, too mountainous or too sterile, to make farming worthwhile. Thus in spite of the pressure of an extremely dense population, only a small part—10 to 15 percent—of the national soil is cultivated. According to the estimate of Dr. Gerald Winfield, China has only 217 million acres of land under cultivation to provide for 500 million inhabitants, whereas the United States tills 365 million acres for a population less than a third as large.[4] China's disproportion between population and cultivated land has two results: regional overpopulation and an extreme subdivision of the land, far beyond the limits of reasonable economic exploitation.

The concentration of humanity on the land reaches absurd extremes in the alluvial plains of the great rivers. On the Yangtze delta near Shanghai and on the delta of the West River at Canton, density rises to the imposing figure of 4,000 individuals per square mile. In these superpopulated zones the subdivision of the land is carried so far that Cressey, forcing the metaphor a bit, speaks of "microscopic" plots.[5] Seen from an airplane, these areas actually do suggest a cross section of tissue under the microscope, with its thousands of cells of various sizes and types, alike and yet slightly different, crowded against each other. Each cell is a farm and a whole family depends on it for subsistence.

The veritable mincing of the soil of China creates the problem of microfundia, a threat as serious to the agricultural potential of the region as the opposite extreme—latifundia—is to Africa and Latin America. The average size of a Chinese farm is 4 acres, compared to 14 in Holland, 39 in Denmark, 63 in England, and 157 in the United States. This is the average size; there are a great many properties much smaller. According to Buck's researches in several parts of China, some 23 percent of the farms were only one and a half acres, and there, without other income, lived an average of 4.4 persons! The Chinese peasant, isolated and without commercial exchange, absolutely dependent on local food resources, preserves an economy very similar to that of feudal times.

China's economic organization forces the farmer to root himself to the ground as tightly as a tree and to set up such an intimate relationship with his environment that China functions, in the felicitous phrase of Gerald Winfield, like a balanced aquarium, where plants and animals are mutually and indissolubly adjusted to each other in order to maintain the cycle of life. Just as in an aquarium, everything in Chinese agrarian economy is fixed in its relationships and governed by hard-and-fast rules, so as to avoid the imbalance that would spell disaster for the human groups concerned. This precarious ecological equilibrium, which is continually threatened by adverse natural conditions, has forced the Chinese farmer to utilize only the most favorable soil and to concentrate on the cultivation only of those plants that give a high yield in his particular locality. The result is a limitation of the cultivated area as well as a limitation of the number of crops grown on any appreciable scale.

[The aptness of the aquarium image as a metaphor for the relation between the Chinese and their economic system became clear to me one day when I was visiting the huge aquarium in New York. I was looking through a glass wall at a collection of fish in a big tank. The oxygen that aerated the water entered through tubes at the base of two corners of the tank and was therefore most abundant at these points. While I was watching, I noticed that almost all the fish gathered there to satisfy their hunger for oxygen, and although one of the fish would on occasion venture away into another part of the tank, it soon eagerly returned to one of the privileged breathing zones. It seemed to me that these two points in that watery world corresponded to the fertile river deltas, breathing zones for the Chinese people within their strict aquarium economy.]

Buck, trying to describe the agricultural organization of

China in detail, has divided the country into eight zones, but in terms of food production many of these zones are practically alike. There are significant differences only between two great areas, the north and the south. The natural and cultural features of these regions are so different that in the thirteenth century Marco Polo, who was one of the first Westerners to explore the East, described two separate Chinas: the north, which he called Cathay, and the southern kingdom of Manji.

The warm and humid south, with its heavy rains and its mountainous soil traversed by fertile valleys, is the great rice bowl of China. Above the Yangtze River and the Chinling Shan lie the broad and semiarid plains of the north. Here there is hardly any rice; it is the land of wheat, millet, sorghum, or kaoliang—the land of the soybean.

Agriculture in both of these great areas is intensive; in the wheat country as in the rice country the farmer strains his hardest for the largest possible yield. It is surprising to find that the Chinese, ignorant of scientific agriculture, working with his antiquated methods a soil that has been cropped for more than four thousand years, can still take out a harvest that, acre for acre, is larger than those achieved in the United States. Dr. Winfield points out that average rice production in the United States is forty-seven bushels to the acre while in South China it is 67 and that the wheat production figure of 14 for the United States is exceeded by North China's 16. To get this yield, the Chinese peasant devotes himself body and soul to the cultivation of the soil, paying the land back in full for all it gives him. This intimate mutual dependency of man and the good earth has created the Oriental philosophy of life, and it underlies the mystical conception of an unbreakable bond between the everlasting land and the everlasting blood—the union of the soil with the soul of the race.

So that their meager earth will let the Chinese people go on living, the maximum number of arms are set to tame it, and the maximum number of hands nurse the plants that grow in it. The typical plant of Oriental culture—rice—is so petted and caressed throughout the year by Oriental hands, planting it, transplanting it, weeding it, irrigating it, that one geographer has remarked that Chinese rice grows half the time in the soil and the other half in the palm of the farmer's hand. The excess of living care the Chinese lavishes upon his rice has made the plant, like a spoiled child, exacting in its demands for attention. As a natural consequence of so much hand labor, the production, although relatively high per acre, is extremely low *per capita*. According to Winfield, a Chinese farmer harvests only 3,000 pounds of grain from a whole year's work, while the American farmer produces 44,000 pounds, fourteen times as much.

Meager Is the Table of the Poor

Asia has been called the land of contrasts, and these contrasts are even more violent in the human than in the geographical sense. The distance that separates a pariah of the lowest caste—untouchable, dispossessed of all human and property rights—from a maharajah in his indescribable wealth and power is far greater than that between the Himalayan peaks and the deepest point in the Pacific Ocean. There is an equally striking difference between the menu of a high Chinese dignitary's feast-day banquet and the daily diet of a simple peasant.

Illustrious travelers have described Oriental banquets, with interminable courses of esoteric dishes; surveys made in rural China paint a picture of millions upon millions of people who, throughout their whole lives, day after day, year after year, eat one food, morning, noon, and night—rice. B. S. Platt tells us that in the south a newborn baby begins to be fed a thin paste of slightly sweetened rice flour on his second day and that the adult depends on rice for 80 to 95 percent of his energy ration.[6] In the north, the farmer bases his diet on wheat bread and sorghum. In both sections, the diet has three fundamental characteristics: it is almost exclusively vegetable in origin, it is scanty in quantity, and it is extremely monotonous. The Chinese does not limit himself to this sober menu because he enjoys it. On the contrary, it represents a kind of sacrifice for him, since on feast days he changes his habits and stuffs himself with a variety of food, animal as well as vegetable. This happens on the great occasions, once or twice a year. The habitual vegetarian diet, meager and monotonous, is a necessary evil for those who must practice the strictest economy in order to have food to eat the year around.

Vegetable foods are so predominant in the diet that only 2 or 3 percent of the total calories are of animal origin, compared to 39 percent in the United States. The Chinese cannot afford to waste his limited soil in the raising of animals and he knows it; animals yield much less nutritional energy per acre than do plants. The Chinese knows that a vegetable eaten directly by man furnishes infinitely more energy than the same product indirectly utilized in raising livestock. Unfortunately, the task of obtaining enough energy for his basic, vital functions has always been the immediate and burning problem. By giving himself almost entirely to agriculture and planting only high-energy foods such as rice, wheat, and millet, the Chinese farmer still falls short of a ration of 2,250 calories daily. Where would he be if he indulged in the luxury of converting vegetable calories into animal calories? In this conversion, the scientists have found, a very small part of the energy consumed by the animal is recovered. Fifteen percent is recovered in producing milk, 7 percent in eggs, and only 4 percent in beef. Biological determinism keeps the Chinese from raising animals to eat. In the United States 90 percent of the domestic animals are raised for food; in China, only 25 percent. Most of them serve merely to assist man in growing plants.

The only domestic animal of real importance to the Chinese dietary economy is the pig, because the pig fits better than any other into the restricted relationships of the balanced aquarium. First, the pig recovers more energy from his food than other animals, averaging a recovery of 20 percent of the energy expended in feeding him. Second, a pig in the Far East is a sort of scavenger whose job is to clean up all the scraps and leftovers of the household. As Winfield puts it: "In a balanced aquarium there must be some snails—scavengers to eat up and break down waste and to prevent the collection of debris. The pig is the snail in the China aquarium."[7]

By tossing the household leftovers into the "pig latrine" against the side of the house, the Chinese obtains an extra quantum of energy from materials otherwise of no further use to man. Winfield writes what he calls the biography of the Chinese pig, showing its various functions as an important link in the nutritional life-and-death cycle. As evidence of the lengths to which the Chinese go in economizing food energy, it is interesting to note that the pig is never driven to market on foot, as is done in certain parts of the West; it is carried, by one or two peasants, so as not to walk off any weight on the way. The energy expended by two men who walk for miles with a live hog strung to a pole across their skinny shoulders seems less important than the energy embodied in the pig, even though it is a product of human waste.

In certain areas of the West where agricultural production exceeds local consumption, as is the case in the American corn belt, the excess grain is used to fatten hogs, this being the most economical way to market the corn—sacked, that is, in pigskin. In China, on the other hand, there is never any question of excess, and the pig's hide holds only what could not be used in any other way. Then too, the pig contributes to the delicate balance of the China aquarium by producing a regular supply of manure, which is mixed with the human product and saved to fertilize the fields.

The scantiness and the monotony of the Chinese diet exist because of an economic structure that can only result in a production both insufficient in quantity and limited in variety. This insufficient and incomplete diet gives rise to chronic starvation in various forms. The Chinese suffer, first of all, from quantitative hunger—the lack of enough energy to cover the needs of living and working. Almost everyone in this part of the world is skinny, because there is no margin, no surplus in the ration that might be used to accumulate a reserve of fat. The rhythm and the yield of labor in China, among the slowest and lowest in the world, reflect in part this lack of the fuel required for muscular labor.

Far more serious than this quantitative hunger are the qualitative hungers, the specific hungers to which these people are permanently subjected: hungers for proteins, mineral salts, and vitamins. Protein hunger is practically universal, since the sources of complete proteins—meat, eggs and milk—are almost entirely absent from the diet. The pig is the only domestic meat animal in China, and the consumption of pork, in proportion to the population, is quite insignificant. Pork products are used more as appetizers or as seasoning than as basic food elements. They merely serve to improve the flavor and aroma of rice or of soybean soup.

Religious prescriptions, both Buddhist and Brahmanist, help keep down the consumption of animal protein. The Buddhist belief in metempsychosis, the transmigration of souls, forbids the slaughter of animals for fear of killing a relative or an ancestor reincarnated in the animal. Fortunately these prohibitions, in the majority of sects, do not apply to fish. Fish may be eaten in some areas because, not having warm blood, they are not among the true animals of transmigration; in other areas it is felt that fish may be eaten without killing them, since if they are caught and removed from the water, they die tranquilly by themselves. These religious prohibitions, of course, simply work a magical sublimation of a hard economic and geographic reality: the scarcity of meat in the region. As the population outgrew the supply of animal products, the religious code sought to relax the tension by setting limits to the consumption of meat—a good example of the hidden connections between the economic and religious life of a people.

Protein deficiency is more serious in the south, among the rice eaters, than it is among the wheat eaters of the north. Wheat is richer in proteins than rice, and the soybeans of the north supply proteins of high biological value. Protein hunger shows itself in various ways. The primary sign of its presence is the retarded growth and reduced stature of the average Chinese. The majority are short people and the more deficient their diet in protein, the shorter they are. The average height of the Chinese people increases from south to north as the protein in the diet increases.

Another serious result of protein deficiency is the appearance of liver lesions, which are the basis of the hepatic cirrhosis so common in the Far East.[8] It was discovered only after World War II that these liver conditions are due to a deficiency of certain indispensable amino acids which are constituents of proteins. According to a commission set up by the Food and Agriculture Organization to study nutritional conditions in the Far East, this is "the most common of all food deficiency states in the tropics and in the East."

The effects of protein deficiency on the general health, in the broadest sense, are shown in a definite lessening of the body's resistance to infection. This lowered resistance has its disastrous reflection in health indices and vital statistics. Protein hunger has a significant effect on the conduct of human groups; in the *Chinese Yearbook* some Chinese authorities consider this grave nutritional deficiency to be one of the basic reasons for the "lethargy, inefficiency, [and] indecision" of their own people.[9]

A second serious and widespread specific hunger among the Chinese is that caused by a deficiency of calcium in the diet. It has been experimentally demonstrated, as the physiologist Maynard emphasizes, that it is rather difficult to supply all the calcium needs of a population without using dairy products. Yet milk is almost never used in China; even children consume ridiculously small amounts. The alternative, though less efficient, source of calcium is the leafy vegetables, but these hardly enter into the Chinese diet. Thus there is no compensation for the calcium deficit and no way of avoiding its usual results: tooth decay, rickets, and softening of the bones.

Rickets attacks the children in zones where there is little sunshine and consequently little Vitamin D. Softening of the bones is common among women, particularly after repeated pregnancies when their bones have been robbed of calcium to build up the babies' bony structures and to supply them with milk. In Shansi province, where there is a vicious custom of feeding mothers nothing but rice gruel for a month after delivery, a shocking number of women are crippled by softening of the bones;[10] while in parts of Tibet where pregnant women are customarily given pork ribs cooked in vinegar sauce (which attacks the bone and dissolves out the calcium), the disease is a rarity.

Iron deficiency is another specific hunger with grave results for the Chinese people, some of the most anemic in the world. Their nutritional anemia is greatly aggravated by worm infestation, particularly by the hookworm disease which is so extraordinarily widespread in China. The worms responsible for this disease, operating in the intestine, rob the body of an appreciable amount of blood, as much as half a pint a day in cases of severe infestation. Since the body has neither proteins nor iron available for the manufacture of blood corpuscles to replace this loss, the result is anemia, very often fatal anemia.

Parasites are an aggravating factor in mineral deficiencies; on the other hand, the high incidence of worms and such other intestinal parasites as the agents of amebic and bacillary dysentery is mainly the result, although indirect, of nutritional poverty. It is indeed a vicious circle, as Dr. Winfield has pointed out in the profound study of these filth or fecal-borne diseases which he made during his long stay at Tsinan's Cheeloo University. The prevalence of these diseases, which affect 90 percent of the rural inhabitants of China, has several causes, but the principal one is the use of human wastes as fertilizer. Completely lacking chemical fertilizers, and lacking sufficient quantities of animal manure, the Chinese use the only means available to restore nitrogen to the soil; human wastes are recovered in both city and country and returned to nourish a soil weary with forty centuries of fruitfulness. The forced use of human excreta is one of the most tragic examples of the circulation of matter in this land of starvation. Everything that comes from the soil must be returned, so that the soil and the human life and civilization based on it will not perish. Everything belongs to the soil and man lives on loans, made out of the supposed generosity of that earth which religion orders him to venerate as the altar of his ancestors. If a people's food comes entirely from the soil, then they must return all their waste to the soil and when they die be buried there, making restitution to the last particle of the organic matter they have borrowed. If for hygenic reasons the Chinese ended their unwholesome practice of using human feces for fertilizer, the production of their fields would decline and the periods between the famines that they dread grow shorter. Yet, as a result of fertilizing the fields with human waste, several million people die every year—perhaps about the same number that would die of hunger if the fields were not so fertilized! Everything comes back to a tragic balance in this aquarium of starvation.

Human wastes are always a powerful factor in the dissemination of filth diseases, whether the feces are diluted and used in liquid form, as is done in the south, or dried and mixed with ashes from the kitchen and manure from the stable as is the northern custom. A few eggs and pathogenic germs may be killed during the storing and curing of the fertilizer, but "millions of worm eggs, billions of protozoan cysts, and trillions of pathogenic bacteria survive and are transported to the fields," where they quickly infect the Chinese either through their laborious hands, always in such intimate contact with the soil, or by way of their mouths, always avid for the products of this polluted soil. Dr. Winfield calculates that some 4 million people die in China every year as a result of this contamination by human excrement; this is almost a third of the total deaths and double the losses in the bloodiest years of the Sino-Japanese War.

The specific hunger for iodine is common in the mountainous central provinces, Yunnan, Sinkiang, and Tibet. According to Dr. James Claude Thompson of the University of Nanking, more than 25 percent of the local inhabitants suffer from goiter.[11]

Vitamin deficiencies are very frequent, although in view of the scanty and monotonous Chinese diet, they are not so common as one would at first expect. The Chinese have always used small quantities of some products—leaves, oil, seeds, and roots—that supply these essential elements to a certain extent, particularly since the foods are prepared by a quick cookery that tends to preserve the vitamins.

The most common of the typical diseases caused by vitamin shortages is undoubtedly beriberi; it is most common in the south where the rice is milled and polished and thus robbed of its Vitamin B-1. There are no reliable statistics as to the incidence of beriberi, but Dr. T. P. Kuo notes that in 1937, out of all the patients admitted to hospitals in the great cities of China, between 3 and 4 percent were suffering from beriberi, and that this percentage rose to 15 during the Sino-Japanese War. Xerophthalmia and pellagra abound in China too, but there are no available figures.

These are the principal specific manifestations of the starvation that regularly ravishes this part of the world. There are many indirect consequences of nutritional poverty in this immense human mass. Hunger is in large part responsible for the shocking figures on overall mortality, on infant mortality, and on life expectancy. China's death rate of some 30 per thousand is the highest among the larger nations, and her infant mortality of about 160 per thousand is among the highest in the world. The life expectancy in China is only 34 years, compared to 68 in the United States, according to actuarial tables, and 65 in New Zealand. The only country with a lower life expectancy figure than China's is India, where the average lifespan is only 26 years.

As if this lurking tragedy of chronic hunger, with its continuous degradation of Chinese life, were not enough, there come from time to time great natural disasters which throw this long-suffering people into the clutches of famine. No country in the world boasts of so many natural agencies for the affliction of man as does China. Droughts, floods, locust plagues, earthquakes, cyclones—these are the habitual instruments with which nature periodically eliminates some millions of the Chinese population. Since the Chinese people live continually on the verge of falling below their minimum needs for subsistence, with never an opportunity to accumulate reserves, every natural cataclysm that breaks over the land brings immediate black starvation, mass killing, and mass exodus from the afflicted area.

The most terrible famines in China, according to the historical record, have resulted from the great droughts. A statistical tally of these disasters has been compiled by Alexandre Hosie; out of the thousand years from 620 to

1620, 610 were drought years in one province or another and 203 of these were years of serious famine. In at least fifteen of these famines the Chinese gave in to the pressure of hunger and used human flesh for food. Droughts occur most often in the broad, semiarid plain of the central and northern part of the country.

Next in frequency as a cause of famine in the Celestial Empire are the floods, which are a problem principally where the great meandering rivers flow through broad alluvial plains. The floods also do tremendous damage in the deltas which they themselves have produced and where the fertility of the soil has brought about a concentration of the great human anthills of the Orient. The rivers have built up these coastal plains by depositing large quantities of silt floated down from the interior and the process continues today. The old earthen dikes intended to keep the rivers within bounds have to be built higher every year as the stream beds rise with new deposits of silt. There are a number of rivers in China whose beds are now well above the level of the surrounding plains; as L. H. Dudley Buxton aptly puts it, "The rivers are on the plain, not in it." Even so, the rivers break or overflow the dikes from time to time, flooding the fields and villages, destroying the crops, killing humans and animals—and fertilizing the soil, so that when the waters go down the survivors can draw dividends in the form of abundant harvests. That is the Chinese earth, where the Lord giveth and the Lord taketh away, in keeping with the whims of nature and the powerful gods concerned.

Locusts are a third natural cause of famines in China. When the dense swarms of insects descend on a region they destroy absolutely all vegetable life, leaving green and blossoming fields as bare as deserts. Certain provinces suffer more than others but all China is subject to these plagues. Walter Mallory reports that out of 162 famines on record in the province of Shensi, 20 were due wholly or in part to locusts.

When the Chinese peasant is faced with the desperate prospect of having his fields completely despoiled and his whole crop eaten by the insatiable grasshoppers, he does the only thing left to keep from starving—he begins to eat the grasshoppers. Thus the Chinese demonstrates again his ability to bow to the inevitable and to find an escape valve for threatening pressure in his aquarium of hunger.

Although somewhat less destructive of food resources than locusts, floods, and droughts, the earthquakes and typhoons that regularly devastate the coastal regions of China are well capable of causing famine or of aggravating famines originally due to other causes. Impelled by one or another of these natural forces, or by several of them at once, stark hunger comes on and reduces these people to the extremity of physical misery. Fearful descriptions, details more macabre than any facets of famine in the Americas, are the stock in trade of writers who deal in the tragedy of Chinese life. That life is one of utter human degradation, moral as well as physical. Vandalism, invasion of private property, mass murder for a handful of beans and rice—these are commonplaces in China when human senses are lacerated by the sharp needles of hunger. Even cannibalism puts in its hideous appearance. The people dwindle to a mass of living specters, who lie down to die with that ancient resignation of the Chinese or else abandon the famine-stricken region in search of places the plague may not have reached.

Departure comes about only after a painful struggle with conscience and after begging forgiveness of the ancestors for abandoning their tombs. The aged father of Wang Lung, hero of Pearl Buck's *The Good Earth*, although he sees his family starving, practically reduced to eating grass and bark, still exclaims, "There have been worse days—there have been worse days. Once I saw men and women eating children." This dismal idea frightens Wang Lung so that he thinks of leaving. But when speculators from the city, taking advantage of the situation, offer him next to nothing for the soil he loves so much, where his ancestors are buried and his children have starved to death, he revolts. He cries out against the brute forces united to break his ties with the sacred earth: "I shall never sell the land! Bit by bit I will dig up the fields and feed the earth itself to the children and when they die I will bury them in the land, and I and my wife and my old father, even he, we will die on the land that has given us birth!" As his children starve before his eyes, however, the fear of death becomes the final argument. Wang Lung abandons all and sets out with his family, so that the name of his ancestors may survive.

When one tries to find out the causes of the constant and imperative hunger that rules China, one is forced to conclude that they are of several types. Although they act and interact, generally speaking, in the most intricate manner, these causes can be systematically divided into two broad groups, the natural and the social. An analysis of the problem of hunger as a whole makes clear at once that the so-called natural causes are only the immediate factors and are themselves the result of social causes in the background, of factors inherent in the structure of the Chinese economy. It is the tragic and absurd economic organization of the country that leads to its state of permanent nutritional poverty and exposes it to periodic crises of hunger.

When a natural cataclysm breaks over a certain region and brings starvation with it, study of the mechanism involved will show that the catastrophe is so thorough only because the social environment is especially favorable to the spread of calamity. In the case of the great famines that sweep the northern provinces in the wake of droughts, destruction is widespread because most of the people live continuously at the margin of subsistence, without organic or financial reserves or even local stocks of food with which to meet any temporary scarcity that may result from drought. And since food surpluses are hardly ever available in other provinces, and transportation is extremely dubious anyway, crises cannot be resolved by outside help.

Similarly it can be seen that the fundamental reasons for the frequency of floods in China are such social factors as the destruction of forests and the neglect of dikes and embankments. If floods were due to natural causes alone, they would be a hundred times more common in the Netherlands, with its concave soil below sea level, than they are in China; floods are rare in the Netherlands because society controls the menace of nature. If the floods, droughts, locusts, and other calamities of nature that produce famines in China could not be completely eliminated by the intelligent intervention of man, their unbridled excesses could at least be moderated, and, more important, their effects could be mitigated by means of social organization and the application of human technique. This process may be observed in various parts of the world. Many of the lands that bloom today as a result of the Tennessee Valley Authority were formerly ravaged by calamities like China's. The greater part of California is actually much more arid than the plains of Shantung, Honan, and Hopei in north China, but aridity has not prevented California from applying technical measures that have made it the leading agricultural state in the United States.

The peoples of China, far from organizing to combat the violence of their environment, seem almost to have allied themselves with it in such a way as to stimulate and encourage its very excesses. There is no other way to describe the stripping of the forest from the whole country or the arbitrary utilization of the rivers, in one part or another of their courses, with no regard for the good of the river system as a whole. The abusive deforestation of the Chinese soil is one reason for the fury of the great rivers which, feeling their margins shorn of trees, begin to swallow up the loose and unprotected soil of the valleys and to take revenge by overflowing their banks. The destruction of the forests cuts down the reserves of humidity in the soil and even, according to some authorities, reduces regional rainfall, thus cooperating to intensify the droughts. The Chinese have busily destroyed their timber down through the centuries to the point where only 8 percent of the national territory has forest covering. Thus they have greatly increased the likelihood of droughts and floods and aggravated their effects.[12]

China's supposed overpopulation is without doubt the most notable of its strictly social characteristics and the one that apparently contributes most toward keeping the country in a state of starvation.[13] The excess of people in China seems, on its face, so striking and obvious, it appears to exert such terrific pressure on the land, that superficial observers attribute not only hunger but all of China's difficulties to this one source.[14] More thoroughgoing students, too, have been so impressed by the phenomenon that they have considered it, if not the only factor, at least the most important factor of the chronic starvation and undernourishment of the Chinese people. Dr. Walter Mallory, who worked in the years following World War I on the China International Famine Relief Commission, ended his impressive and well-documented book *China, Land of Famine* with this statement: "In the writer's opinion it is overpopulation that constitutes the fundamental reason for the recent famines in China."

It seems to me rash to assert that hunger in China is primarily due to overpopulation when the demographers have not yet been able to fix a clear definition of overpopulation. The experts do not even agree about what an ideal population, an optimum number for individual and collective well-being in any given area, would be. China, moreover, even in the light of the somewhat indefinite principles of current demographic science, turns out to be far from one of the most densely populated countries in the world. In the nation as a whole, there are about 104 people per square mile, whereas the Netherlands and Belgium, which are practically free of hunger in peacetime, have 725 and 686 inhabitants respectively for every square mile. The critical factor in China is not the density but the irrational distribution of the population. On the one hand there are enormous empty spaces and on the other, limited areas of shocking concentration, like the section of a northern province where Mallory found an average of 6,880 persons to the square mile.

Obviously, the peculiar distribution of the Chinese population is caused not by its numbers but rather by the lack of opportunities for employment in the greater part of the country. The imbalance between the number of individuals and the number of available jobs gives the impression that there are too many people, so that some parts of China seem like human anthills. New York with its 7 million inhabitants seems deserted in comparison with Shanghai, where there are only some 3 million. The difference is that in the Oriental city there are hundreds of competitors for every little bit of work. When the foreigner, outside his hotel, calls a coolie to deliver a message or a package, he is besieged by a regular swarm of applicants in avid competition for the modest task. The truth is that the strange distribution of the population, which gives the country the appearance of being over-crowded, is the direct result of its elementary economic organization. China is limited to virtually one type of economic exploitation—agriculture—and even this is confined to certain areas only and restricted by primitive methods. Thus when we examine the functional demographic density in China, the index turns dangerously upward; according to John Buck, there are 1,541 individuals for every square mile of cultivated soil.

It might be expected that there are natural causes for this concentration in limited areas while the rest of the country is deserted. Scientists and students of the Chinese problem, however, find that this is not the case. In the greater part of

China there are rich and varied natural resources which, if they were developed, could make possible a better distribution of the population and put an end to all symptoms of overpopulation.

China's agricultural resources, which have been very slightly utilized up to the present time, are an outstanding example of undeveloped possibilities. Dr. O. E. Baker, of the United States Department of Agriculture, stated in an article published in 1928 that there are 700 million acres of land in China fit for agricultural cultivation but that of these reserves only 180 million were then in use.[15] If the cultivated area of China is now estimated at 217 million acres,[16] more than two thirds of the natural reserves still remain unused and undeveloped. I shall explain later how it is that a people living in chronic starvation fails to exploit these precious agricultural resources.

Besides land for farming, China has many other natural resources. If properly developed, these resources could expand the country's economic frontiers, which now take in about a third of the country, to make them coincide with its geographic borders. China's wealth in coal and other minerals and its enormous potential water power could well support an extensive industrialization. One of the elements necessary to such an economic revolution is a labor supply large enough to mobilize the riches which have slept for thousands of years in the soil and subsoil. Considering that the geographic picture shows a country which needs above all to be exploited and economically mobilized by human labor, it seems a bit precipitate to speak categorically of overpopulation and to insist on the necessity of limiting natural population growth by all possible means. Furthermore, as I have said before, there is no way of limiting the growth of the Chinese population without first changing the whole economic and social structure of the country. I shall try to prove this with objective facts.

China's high demographic potential is a feature of her cultural organization, and it cannot be eliminated independently of the other features that go to make up the face, the individual expression, of that culture. Any attempt to prescribe neo-Malthusian measures as a means of alleviating Chinese hunger will be lacking not only in scientific justification but in social effect, since it will not awaken the slightest response in the Chinese masses. In this closed economic system, with the interdependence of a balanced aquarium, no one dares break a single link of the natural chain for fear of terrible consequences. In such a system, everything must be changed at once, or nothing at all. This applies not only to moral commandments, beliefs, and popular customs but to material progress as well. It is impossible to end the misery and poverty of China by applying isolated measures. Any such attempt would either have no effect at all or would make the situation worse by upsetting the delicate balance of the aquarium.

Human life in this part of the world is so directly dependent on natural phenomena and ancient custom that nothing can be changed without a compensatory change in all the other links of the chain. For example, there is the question of improving the country's health conditions by eliminating the principal carrier of fecal-borne diseases—that is, the human excrement used as fertilizer. In his *China, the Land and the People,* Dr. Winfield shows how indissolubly this method of fertilizing is connected with the economic structure of the country and how difficult it would be to alter the custom without altering the whole structure of national life. As things are now in China, there are no other fertilizers available to the farmer in any quantity and he simply cannot get along without the use of human feces.

The dependence of the Chinese people on human wastes is so complete that along the roads in certain remote parts of the country the traveler finds special pavilions where suggestive, poetical inscriptions invite him to rest awhile and leave his small, personal contribution of organic matter in the receptacle provided, for the sake of the regional soil. The same traveler may be amazed as he approaches the cities to see the belts of greenery that girdle them. This wealth of vegetation is owing to the abundance of fertilizer in the cities; the sale of this material is actually one of their chief sources of income. In the 1920's, the International Settlement in Shanghai collected $31,000 in gold every year from its monopoly of the garbage collection, which amounted to 78,000 tons of waste from the sewers for sale to the surrounding farms.[17]

Since human excretions are so tremendously important as manure, some way ought to be found to destroy the dangerous parasites and bacteria they contain without injuring their value as fertilizer. Unfortunately, all the methods that have so far succeeded in sterilizing the product also free a good part of its nitrogen, thereby reducing its value considerably. After long experiments, the American technicians Stanley Wilson and Gerald Winfield came to the conclusion that if human feces were treated by composting, mixing suitable quantities of "night soil," animal manure, and vegetable matter, the pathogenic organisms would be killed and the product rendered harmless. To use this method, however, 20 percent of vegetable matter must be added to the human excrement, and this is more vegetable matter than the country has available. Vegetable materials are used up either in feeding draft animals or as fuel for the kitchen; the shortage of wood in China and the low coal production, which amounts to one sixtieth of the production per capita in the United States, make plant wastes valuable as fuel. Crop residues, leaves, and grass cannot merely be thrown on compost heaps.[18] Winfield judges that in order to bring the compost method into general use it would be necessary to increase the country's vegetable resources; this could be done only by reforestation and the expansion of coal mining, with parallel improvement in transportation so as to keep prices down. Thus a minor change in the method of fertilizing the soil would require profound, nationwide alterations in agriculture, industry, and transportation.

What is true in the case of fertilizer holds true for all the other elements that make up the economic and social life of China. It would be futile to try to control reproduction by means of propaganda when biological, psychological, and economic patterns all work to make the population bigger and bigger. The uselessness of such an approach is especially apparent if its sponsors hope in this way to put an end to starvation. It cannot be denied that population growth and starvation are intimately related to each other, but not in the cause-and-effect relationship artificially established by the proponents of the theories of Malthus. There is no evidence whatever that hunger results from China's presumptive overpopulation. The biological and social facts point clearly in the opposite direction: it is rather hunger that is the cause and overpopulation the result. The enormous human masses that characterize certain parts of China are only the by-products of starvation.

"Fertile Is the Bed of Misery"

Growth of population is determined, in the final analysis, by the play between two basic factors: fertility and mortality.[19] Everything that affects the trend of a population does so by means of one or the other of these elements. Since starvation undeniably raises the death rate, it has always been thought that it operated, like wars and plagues, to retard the growth of population. It seems highly paradoxical, then, to say that hunger, far from leading to *de*population, tends to bring about *over*population.

My statement, however, is based on a series of fully demonstrated facts. First, it is a matter of common observation that following periods of calamity, famine, and pestilence, populations always increase their rate of growth. It is also clearly observable that the countries on the lowest nutritional level, where millions of people regularly and "normally" starve to death, are also the areas of most violent increase in population: China, India, Egypt, and various Latin American countries. On the other hand, the countries at the highest nutritional level show unmistakable evidence of early population decline, with births barely equaling deaths. That is the case in Australia, New Zealand, and the United States.

That paradox is explained by the fact that while hunger as a social phenomenon increases the death rate, it increases the birth rate even more, so that the net effect is to speed up the rate of population increase. It is commonly noted that the undernourished classes are the most fertile; the ancient Romans had a word for those who, on a starvation diet, had many offspring or *proles*—"proletarians." There is a popular saying in Latin America that "the table of the poor is meager, but fertile is the bed of misery. . . ."

In spite of these significant commonplaces, however, speculation on the question of population growth has generally followed the line that food scarcity is associated with population decline or reduced rate of growth, while abundance of food has been held to determine more rapid growth. That has been the established opinion, although toward the middle of the last century there lived one philosopher and demographer who thought otherwise. Thomas Doubleday, reacting against scientific conservatism, undertook a systematic description of the manner in which lack of sufficient food increases the rate of population growth. In an essay which has been completely forgotten, "The True Law of Population Shewn to Be Connected with the Food of the People," he wrote, in 1853, these prophetic words:

The GREAT GENERAL LAW then, which, as it seems, really regulates the increase or decrease both of vegetable and of animal life, is this, that whenever a *species* or *genus* is *endangered*, a corresponding effort is invariably made by nature for its preservation and continuance, by an increase of fecundity or fertility; and that this especially takes place whenever such danger arises from a diminution of proper nourishment or food, so that consequently the state of depletion, or the deplethoric state, is favorable to fertility; and on the other hand, the plethoric state, or state of repletion, is unfavorable to fertility, in the ratio of intensity of each state, and this probably throughout nature universally, in the vegetable as well as in the animal world; further, that as applied to mankind this law produces the following consequences, and acts thus:

There is in all societies a constant increase going on amongst that portion of it which is the worst supplied with food; in short, amongst the poorest.

Amongst those in the state of affluence, and well supplied with food and luxuries, a constant decrease goes on.[20]

Doubleday's theories, unfortunately, did not become widely known. Official circles rejected them for various reasons, of which the most powerful was, according to the canny observation of Raymond Pearl, that "he offended the sentimental susceptibilities and moral judgments of the early-Victorian middle and upper classes."[21] And since Doubleday could not muster enough facts to prove his intuitive assertions, his whole theory was forgotten. This was another striking victory for the taboo that has made hunger a forbidden subject!

Today, however, the supporting facts are at hand and we can risk a collision with Victorian prejudices and neo-Malthusian theories. It is high time to challenge a point of view which, inspired by economic or political interest, regards as a natural human condition what is in fact the result of social factors.

In the chapter analyzing the various disguises under which

hunger ravages mankind, it has been pointed out that a certain type of specific hunger, the hunger for proteins, can cause a high fertility index in both man and animal and that liberal doses of protein rapidly bring that index down. The table, arranged by countries, showed the correlation between daily protein intake and fertility and indicated the general rule: the lower the protein in the diet, the higher the fertility. In a country like pre-revolutionary China, where protein consumption, particularly consumption of animal proteins, was extremely slight, this specific hunger constituted a biological factor of high fertility, with a consequent permanent tendency toward overpopulation.

The notion that lack of proteins stimulates fertility is not merely a hypothesis that happens to be borne out by the facts. Enough is known about protein metabolism so that we can trace the actual mechanism by which protein deficiency leads to increased fertility, while an abundance of protein has the opposite effect. A detailed explanation of this process is beyond the scope of this book, but I should like to outline its fundamental points in order to clarify the scientific basis of certain of my assertions.

Biologically, fertility depends on the functioning of organs whose action is regulated, in large part, by hormones, which are the secretions of certain ductless glands. Fecundation in women is closely related to the functioning of the ovaries, to the production of their hormones, particularly the estrogens, and to the quantity of these substances present in the blood and internal organs.

It is known that there is a direct connection between the functioning of the liver and the ovaries, the role of the liver being to inactivate the excess estrogens that the ovaries throw into the bloodstream. Fatty degeneration of the liver and the tendency to cirrhosis are, as we have previously seen, among the characteristic results of protein deficiency and are very common in the Far East and in certain tropical areas of other continents.[22] When degeneration of the liver occurs it begins to operate less efficiently and is less effective at its job of inactivating excess estrogens. The result is a marked increase in the woman's reproductive capacity.

The total reproductive capacity of an organism—its fertility—is the result of a series of physiological processes. In viviparous animals such as man, it depends on the production of the ovum by the ovary, on its fertilization and its development *in utero*. These processes, ovulation, fertilization, and fetal development, are highly dependent on the functioning of the estrogenic hormones. Sexual appetite, the libido itself, which Raymond Pearl includes among the factors determining the level of fertility, depends on the percentage of this hormone within the body.

It is no longer necessary, then, to imagine that by some obscure and mysterious process Mother Nature speeds up reproduction when the species seems threatened with extinction. [There is nothing supernatural about teleonomy, the mechanism whose purpose it is to defend the survival of the species. It is a natural mechanism, for] animal metabolism maintains functional equilibrium, complex but not at all mysterious: protein deficiency leads to deficiency in the functions of the liver; this results in a reduction or loss of the liver's ability to inactivate estrogens; the excess of estrogens increases the woman's fertility. Then too, we have examined the psychological mechanism by which chronic hunger intensifies the sexual appetite at the same time that it lowers the appetite for food and the assistance this process gives in maintaining a high birth rate among the hungry peoples of the world.

Parallel with these biological mechanisms, there is a complex social mechanism through which chronic hunger works powerfully toward speeding up population growth. In prerevolutionary China, the most vivid effect of hunger on the economic and social structure was the sharp limitation it imposed on individual production. Constant chronic starvation so incapacitated the Chinese people that the farmer felt himself unable, through his own labor, to make the soil produce enough food to nourish him. John Buck's estimate that the Chinese farmer produced only a fourteenth as much as the American farmer has been previously cited. Poor health, limited muscular energy, and, above all, rapid tiring due to nervous fatigue, held labor productivity down in the Far East. All these were the results of hunger. No matter how tiny his scrap of soil, the Chinese felt that the starved muscles of his arms could not force the land to produce its utmost. His inadequacy became a pressing problem in his economy: first, he had to get hold of some land on which to raise food to keep from dying of starvation; then, he had to arrange for additional workers to help him. An urgent and permanent need for help lay at the bottom of the ardent Chinese aspiration to have many sons—new hands to help in the struggle against starvation.

When Chinese religion and philosophy, Buddha and Confucius, glorified the large, patriarchal family closely linked to the land, they were sublimating and giving moral justification to an economic necessity.[23] The economy of hunger to which the Chinese people were subjected had more bearing than might at first be supposed on the underlying structure of their religious beliefs and moral codes. "Religion and philosophy could not exist," wrote a disciple of Marx, "if economic situations did not make it possible for them to appear." Even those who are not historical materialists are obliged to recognize the force of economic necessity in the structure and evolution of religious doctrines. Roger Bastide is entirely right in reminding us that "a man is not only spirit; he also has a body and biological necessities that must be satisfied" and that "religion is often no more than a stratagem of the instincts in search of satisfaction."[24]

The doctrines of Confucius would not have penetrated and taken such deep root in the soul of the Chinese people if his precepts of love for one's family and worship of one's ancestors had not coincided with the people's economic interests and satisfied so fully their most intimate aspirations.[25] The religious principles prescribed large families to worship and carry on the family name and then tied them to the ancestral soil, thus serving the needs of a family head wonderfully well, guaranteeing him a supply of labor to work his soil and attend to his needs. The open preference for sons is evidence that what was wanted was a labor force. Sons were really welcomed; daughters were merely tolerated as a hazard of nature. Sons alone were responsible for the duties and rites of ancestor worship. Preference went to such extremes that female children were often neglected and more girls consequently died in infancy than did boys. Statistics gathered by the China Rehabilitation Commission showed a clear excess of men over women in the adult population.

The idea that a large family of sons was the indispensable base for broadening production led the Chinese, otherwise so spiritual, ascetic, and moralistic in their habits, to tolerate and even prescribe early marriages and the practice of keeping concubines. A number of women were established in the house of one patriarchal chief to further his desire for a big family.

The nutritional poverty in which the Chinese lived allowed no accumulation of reserves for rainy days or for old age, and there was consequently a common wish for many children as a kind of insurance against future want. Mallory wrote that a large family with many sons constituted "the old-age insurance policy of the Chinese." Western law compels the payment of an insurance policy at the proper time; religion in the East required the sons to repay the debt they incurred when their father did them the service of begetting them. Rarely did they fail to fulfill this duty, putting the interests of their parents ahead of their own and those of their children.

Thus, the need for hands to grow food, to fend off the

chronic hunger, and the need for hands to help in the terrible hours of famine, built up a whole complex social structure favorable to a high birth rate. Hunger led to a very high death rate; half the children died before they were adult, and death was always watching for a chance for mass attacks. The death rate, too, explained the tormented desire of the Chinese for a large family. He had to have an ample excess of sons, so that after most had been cut down by disease, plague, famine, and war, there would still be one or two left to work the soil and worship the name of his ancestors.

Those are the underlying reasons, biological and economic, that made the Chinese one of the most prolific peoples in the world and that, taken in conjunction with economic conditions, led to relative overpopulation. Admittedly, these deep reasons might well seem absurd and paradoxical to people outside the "aquarium," breathing a different air, on a different soil, under a different sky. To them, the love of the Chinese for his children and his veneration for fertile motherhood must have seemed as absurd as another Chinese weakness—that of raising dogs, when there wasn't enough food to go around for human beings. Mallory said that there was probably not a "leaner, fiercer, more pitifully neglected collection of dogs" in the whole world than were raised in the rural zones of China,[26] but they too had their excuse for existence in the aquarium of hunger. Here is how the Chinese put it: "The dogs always find something to eat, and when we can't find anything else to eat, we can eat the dogs."

In view of these motives, the popular notion that hunger in China was due to overpopulation clearly puts the cart before the horse. The Chinese were not hungry because there were too many people, but because there was too little production. John Buck's studies led him to conclude that Chinese agricultural production was low because the farms were exceedingly small. I think, however, that we have to look further for original causes. The farms were small because the

Chinese farmer, even with the help of his family, was incapable of cultivating a larger area. An insignificant scrap of earth drained all his available energy.

Chinese agriculture began as an oasis culture, the cultivation of small areas of high fertility. And so it continued. Chinese farming communities developed in isolation from each other, each group concerned only with the intensive exploitation of its own oasis. When the population of these centers grew beyond a certain point, a healthy social structure would have led to the adoption of other methods—extensive rather than intensive—but instead, the Chinese went on following the primitive routine, and paid the biological penalty. They insisted on continuing a type of cultivation more like gardening than farming and left great areas unoccupied because they could only be worked by a different system. These areas were not even used for other economic purposes, for raising stock or forests. Perhaps this lack of initiative, or excessive conservatism, of the Chinese was itself just another result of hunger, another sign of the low vitality of a race perpetually starved.

The Rebellion of General Hunger

The primitive structure of the Chinese economy was an ideal vehicle for famine in the first place; contacts with the West and the increase in Western influence, rather than improving the situation, made it worse. For [more than a century before the revolution,] China had been the stage for tremendous underground struggles between the great imperialist powers from whom hegemony in the region was at stake.[27] When the Treaty of Nanking brought the so-called Opium War with Great Britain to an end in 1842, China was forced to open its doors to Western influences [and to colonial opposition]. The American geographer G. T. Trewartha put it very well when he said: "While China has not been a colony of any single power, it was nevertheless exploited by several and was not master of its own house. Like other colonial regions of exploitation, the ambition of the white masters was to obtain large profits; the welfare and development of the native populations was of secondary importance."[28]

In keeping with this policy of colonial exploitation, the great Western powers, joined in 1895 by imperialist Japan, worked to keep China in a state of semifeudal, agrarian backwardness favorable to their colonial designs. Throughout the century before the revolution the imperialist powers continually placed obstacles in the way of the agrarian reform that would have increased food production and opposed the industrialization that would have modernized the Chinese economy. By using their influence to disorganize the traditional forms of economic life, without introducing industry to take their place, the Western powers increased the pressure on the soil and the fragmentation of the land. They thereby strengthened the hand of starvation.

It was always said in the Occident that the decadence of China was due principally to the lack of national unity. But the fundamental fact was always left out: the fact that this national disorganization had been encouraged and lovingly tended by the imperialists. Every time the country tried to rise out of its chaos of misery it ran into insuperable obstacles in the form of Western interests, for whom the "monsoon realm" was, according to E. R. Hughes, "the most important focus of profitable, exploited colonial empire anywhere on the earth."[29] It is true that the Western countries had "aided" the Chinese with religious missions and exported scientific missions which tried to improve Chinese health—which tried, at least, to keep the Chinese from sinking altogether out of sight so that this magnificent potential market of 500 million customers for Western industry would not wholly disappear.

The same self-interest, on the part of each of the great powers separately, saved China from being completely swallowed up by any one of them; every time one opened its mouth the others bristled and bared their fangs. But the quarrel was all in the family, after all, and a division of the prey could be worked out among gentlemen. The Treaty of Versailles was such a gentlemen's agreement. China was represented at Versailles but refused to put its name to the dismemberment of Chinese territory in favor of Japan. A similar case was the Washington Conference, called by President Harding in 1921 for the purpose of buttressing the status quo in the Pacific, including the foreign concessions and the Open Door policy that subjected China to Western mercantilism. To maintain the status quo, it was obviously necessary to maintain the status of starvation in the young Chinese Republic, which had just been established under Sun Yat-sen by a revolution with the idealistic aim of abolishing misery and hunger. This was the issue that brought a split between the leaders of the new China and the governments of the Western powers. Sun Yat-sen and his Kuomintang appealed to the great Western nations for support in promoting Chinese economic recuperation, but, according to the documented study of three American historians—F. P. Chambers, C. P. Grant, and C. C. Bayley—"unfortunately these Powers were not too inclined to give them sympathy and help."[30]

Abandoned by the capitalist countries, Sun Yat-sen turned to Soviet Russia, which was thus able to increase its influence in the Far East. So began the bitter struggle of the Kuomintang against the imperialism, feudalism, and militarism that were smothering the Chinese economy. The only possible strength for such a struggle would have to come through agrarian reform, replacing the wooden plow, the bamboo rake, and the water wheel with modern machinery and scientific agriculture. This kind of progress required capital and technicians that the Nationalists did not have.

They needed help. When Chiang Kai-shek first rose to power after the death of Dr. Sun in 1925, he followed the existing policy, trying, in more or less close collaboration with the Soviet Union, to develop an effective program for raising the living standards of the Chinese people.

This was the phase of the Nationalist politics when four-year plans of economic recuperation were drawn up. The statement of purpose of the first of these plans, prepared in 1933 by the then Minister of Industry, Chen Pung-po, is quoted in Maurice Lachin's book *La Chine Capitaliste:*

> From a territorial and racial viewpoint, China is a single people, but the same cannot be said of its economic and political structure. A nation may be unified by military, political, or economic forces. My experience leads me to think that genuine unification should be sought through economic factors. It is not my position to judge whether feudal hangovers still exist in China, but there is no doubt but that the economic configuration of the nation is deformed by economic elements of a feudal type. And only by the destruction of that feudalism can China become a modern state.[31]

Chen Pung-po's plan called for the agricultural and industrial development of the Yangtze Valley, which was then to serve as a model for the economic reconstruction of the whole country. There were many good reasons for the choice of this area, the principal consideration being that the Yangtze, 3,200 miles long, passed through six of the most fertile provinces of China, where half of the country's population was concentrated. The Western powers, however, were frightened by the possibility of Soviet collaboration and proposed to furnish all the aid necessary for the economic reconstruction of China. Under their pressure, Chiang Kai-shek sought to turn the Kuomintang toward an alliance with the Occident.

It soon became apparent, however, that the promised aid would never reach the rural areas, where the forgotten farmer continued to starve as usual. The Western loans were expended on military installations, strategic roads, and fortifications to keep the Nationalists in power much more than they were used to stimulate production. As a result, the Communist opposition gained in strength, and the country was again divided in two as it had been during the first years after the 1911 revolution. The Communists won prestige during the war with Japan [and finally gained control in China], modifying the economic structure of Asia and thus the economic balance of the entire world.

Some people seem to think that Soviet infiltration and material aid were the principal explanation for the victories of the Communists over Chiang Kai-shek's troops. It is my impression that there was a more profound reason. The Communist revolution won in China because, although Chiang Kai-shek had a powerful ally in the United States, the followers of Mao Tse-tung had a stronger ally. That ally was hunger. For a long time the Western powers thought that starvation was *their* ally, because it regularly killed off some millions of Chinese and thus held the Yellow Peril in check. It now becomes clear that they were wrong. The forces of Chiang Kai-shek collapsed because he allied himself with the interests of the United States and against those of his own people, while Mao Tse-tung led his people in a struggle to end starvation. The fear of famine was the great recruiting agent of Mao's armies, and the decisive factor in the Chinese civil war was the strategy of starvation.

The success of the Chinese revolution resulted, in my opinion, from the fact that, on practical grounds, Communist objectives were at one with the people's deepest desire: they promised freedom from the threat of starvation. Starvation is in turn a result of imperialist exploitation of man and the soil. No one can deny that this Chinese hope was a natural one and that its frustration had been nothing less than inhuman.

American observers in Communist China reported that Mao Tse-tung's most enthusiastic partisans in the beginning were the 50 million peasants to whom he distributed land. These people were former sharecroppers. Before the 1949 revolution, the large property-owners—the rich farmers who made up only 5 percent of the farming population—owned roughly 70 percent of the cultivated land. They rented it to poor peasants for between 50 and 80 percent of their gross annual production.

Everything I have described to this point applies to classic China, before the victory of Mao Tse-tung. Such was China: an economic colony of the great powers, dominated and torn apart by international interest groups. Let us now look at the new China—the China produced by the 1949 revolution which brought about radical changes in the country's social structure and established a new system of government and economic organization.

[The New China Awakens

Twenty years ago, a group of progressive British legislators (headed by Sir Richard Acland and Ted Castle) who wished to draw attention to the urgent need for change in Britain's colonial policy, published a pamphlet called *It's Time to Wake Up*. Their point was that the colonial powers must awaken because the colonial peoples had already done so and had embarked upon a vigorous struggle to liberate themselves from the colonial nightmare. No country awakened with a more profound desire for liberation or a more intense appetite for social renewal than the old China, which had long seemed unable to rouse itself from its opium-induced dreams.

Socioeconomic developments since 1949 justify the belief that the new China's struggle against hunger can be victorious, that it will be able to banish forever the thousand-year-old specter of starvation.[32] It is still too early to make any categorical predictions or to measure the price the Chinese people will have to pay in toil and sacrifice to free themselves from the yoke of hunger. But already the somber panorama of Chinese wretchedness has obviously brightened in many ways, and this favorable development deserves consideration in an analysis of the phenomenon of hunger and its social correlates. So, leaving aside the purely political, which is beyond the framework of this book, we will examine the major changes in the living conditions of the Chinese since the fall of the Kuomintang and the establishment of the People's Republic.

By producing profound alterations in the balance of social forces, the new political regime brought about drastic changes in the economic structure and rapidly ameliorated the wretchedness, hunger, and stagnation described in the preceding pages. The first result of the liquidation of the Kuomintang was the pacification of China. Guerrillas who for hundreds of years had ravaged the country, supported by the war lords, were dispersed in 1949. With them disappeared one of the causes of the periodic bloodbaths suffered by the Chinese population.

The second immediate result was the abolition of the semicolonial treaties that the Western powers had imposed on successive Chinese governments since the Treaty of Nanking. The revocation of these treaties had many consequences: to begin with, it abolished the extraterritorial concessions that allowed foreign companies to direct China's overseas trade for their own imperialistic ends and permitted the infamous opium traffic to prosper. Once it was attacked at the root, this destructive vice, a cause of much hunger, sickness, and traditional apathy among the Chinese, was quickly stamped out. The smoking dens were closed; those addicts capable of recovery were rehabilitated and the incurable were isolated.

Another consequence of the revocation of the treaties was

the repudiation of foreign debts contracted by preceding governments. Though this measure aroused violent resentment among foreign creditors, especially Americans, it had extremely favorable repercussions on the economy of the Chinese aquarium, making it possible to lower the taxes that had inhibited local commercial and agricultural activities.

Finally, China was able to replace the old semicolonial treaties with new ones, which it signed on an equal footing with the Soviet Union, Korea, Great Britain, India, and others. These treaties enabled China, for the first time, to negotiate important commercial exchanges with the highly developed industrial nations, an opportunity it seized upon to make massive investments in the machinery and factories that were needed to industrialize the country. This in turn broadened work prospects for the urban industrial labor force and improved the economic balance in the rural areas.

The third result of the fall of the Kuomintang was reform of the property system. In the countryside, the great estates were abolished and land was distributed to the poor peasants. In the cities, state-owned heavy industry was established and support was given to cooperatives and municipalities engaged in medium-sized industry and in commerce.

The overall import of these achievements becomes clear when data concerning the old China are compared with current statistics. Infant mortality had stabilized by 1935 at a rate of 99 per one thousand births. During the Japanese invasion it rose alarmingly to 190 per thousand. In 1950 it dropped to 77 per thousand, in 1951 to 74, and the following year to 53. By 1965 the figure was down to 30 per thousand and by 1970 to 25. Deaths in childbirth, which had reached 15 percent during the war years, sank to less than 1 percent in 1953. This remarkable achievement—the almost complete elimination of one of China's most terrible scourges—was brought about by widely fostered campaigns of hygiene and asepsis. Between 1949 and 1952, according to official statistics, 240 million inoculations against plague, cholera, typhoid fever, and diphtheria were administered, and these diseases diminished dramatically. For example, although about 3,000 cases of plague had been officially recorded each year, in 1952 there were only a few sporadic outbreaks and by 1953 plague had completely disappeared. In 1952, more than 500 million smallpox vaccinations were administered; for the first time in China's history, the entire population was vaccinated against the disease.

The problem of internal parasites was far more complicated. The most serious were those of fecal origin, historically a major cause of death in the countryside, as we have seen. To break the growth cycle of these organisms, it was necessary to introduce radical changes in the people's living habits. The complex program and complete sanitary campaign required was accomplished with the help of a voluntary organization—the Patriotic Hygiene Movement—which instructed practically the entire Chinese population in methods of prophylaxis. The peasants learned how to purge themselves, which eliminated most of the parasites, and how to dispose of human excrement safely; they were also taught to avoid touching the earth with their bare hands and other exposed parts of the body, since it was such direct contact that caused worm contamination. Several million wells were dug or reconstructed; 57,000 marshes were drained; 74 million tons of ordure piled up around villages were eliminated. Domestic production of DDT and other insecticides made possible the extermination of many of the carriers of endemic diseases.

Along with these direct and urgent health measures, the state began a systematic struggle against the causes of hunger and undernourishment. It was fought out primarily in the economic arena.

After the triumph of the revolution and the establishment of the People's Republic, the government realized that the first step was to increase agricultural production so that the people's perennial hunger could be satisfied. At that time, grain production in China had fallen to an extremely low level, about 110 million tons. The Sino-Japanese War and the decadence of the Kuomintang regime were to blame for the drastic reduction, for before the war output had averaged about 150 million tons. As a result of the new government's energetic measures, production began to recover: in 1952 it was 163 million tons; in 1956, 180 million and in 1957, 200 million. In the space of seven years, China almost doubled its grain yield, averaging an annual increase of about 8 percent that astonished the entire world, since elsewhere the growth of agricultural production does not exceed 3 percent a year. This tremendous increase in production and the lower costs that resulted from rising rates of productivity improved the standards of diet and freed the Chinese people from the clutch of famine.

When I visited China in 1957, I had the opportunity to ascertain that the population bore almost none of the classic signs of hunger, signs that I was used to encountering in the other underdeveloped regions of the world. The whole range of hunger symptoms, formerly so common among Chinese children as to suggest racial traits—retarded growth, emaciation, paleness, aphtha, eye inflammations, the doleful cast of features, dull skin, bleeding gums, and bone malformations—are now so rare that only a determined search can uncover them. The whole physiognomy of a chronically hungry people has been transformed into that of a well-nourished one. I am not suggesting that the Chinese people have completely solved their nutritional problems and that no sort of hunger now exists in this ancient home of famine. Undoubtedly there are still forms of specific hunger, particular deficiencies that are not immediately apparent but still indicate the presence of hunger, though at a reduced level. But hunger of that sort is easier to bear than the tragic endemic hunger caused by the chronic lack of several kinds of nourishment, and certainly easier than the hunger of famine, the total starvation in times of disaster.

What persists in China is partial protein deficiency due to a shortage of animal products—meat, milk, and eggs, which are in short supply because the country was until recently almost exclusively agricultural. Before the revolution, 90 percent of the farmland was reserved for the growing of food and only 1 percent for pastures and livestock-raising. As a result, animal products were a rarity in the diet. China was a vegetarian civilization. In north China during the winter Vitamin C deficiencies that cause scurvy persist because of the lack of fresh fruit and vegetables. But according to the report of the Polish pomologist, Professor Pieniazec, who visited China in 1958, the country was beginning to make great strides in the cultivation of fruit trees—a task that should not prove too difficult for a population that has always tended its vegetable gardens and orchards even more carefully than its fields. Total fruit production is about 6 million tons a year, or 22 pounds per capita, which is still low. But there is every chance of increasing it now that innovative methods of grain farming have raised the yield per acre to the point where land can be opened up for planting fruit trees and even for raising livestock. Formerly, all the land available was still not enough to raise the amount of grain the population needed.

More telling than my own direct observations are those made by Professor Li Chiang-han, a great nutrition expert. Mine lack a point of comparison since I did not know China before the revolution but Professor Li conducted inquiries in Chinese villages both before and after. His testimony does not appear suspect because he was initially opposed to the revolution. For many years he lived in the United States, where he was called Franklin Lee, and he later worked for the F.A.O. outside China. Strong factual evidence, which he discussed with me and later published in the journal *People's*

China, convinced him of the correctness of what the government was doing to improve the lot of the people and he was won over.

Professor Li made studies in 1957 in a number of villages around Peking and was impressed by the extraordinary change in the peasants' diet. Before the revolution the basic food was hard grains like millet, sorghum, or *kaoliang;* these represented 95 percent of the usual diet, while rice accounted only for 5 percent. In winter the diet included only potatoes and tea, though many families could not even afford tea and drank hot water with their meals. Vegetables were a luxury and meat a rarity, eaten only on national holidays like the days of Spring, Mid-autumn, and the Dragon. Today the diet is not only noticeably greater in volume, but 60 percent of it is composed of such choice grains as wheat and rice, and only 40 percent of hard grains. Whereas formerly the only vegetables were onions and peppers, more than twenty varieties are now available, ending the monotony once so striking to outsiders. Pork and eggs are staples. Sugar, which used to be considered a pharmaceutical product—as it was in Europe before the Renaissance—is today consumed by the peasants. This radical change of diet, Professor Li concludes, had a "noticeable influence not only on the level of health and well-being of the population but also on its productivity."

It would be false to attribute this spectacular victory to any particular measure or to dramatic technical innovations. It is the result of a whole group of measures that turned the Chinese economy into an organized system, and first and foremost of the mobilization of the enormous human mass whose productive capacity had been restricted by inertia of every sort. Richard Crossman, a Member of Parliament in England, wrote in *The New Statesman* after a visit to China that the Chinese regime "is by far the greatest and most impressive mass movement in the entire history of humanity."

A good part of the "miracle" is due to the leadership of this mass movement, for the government's initiatives needed the support of the collective consciousness that had been awakened. As soon as the new regime was inaugurated the government began to act in terms of well-defined objectives; it did not merely improvise. Taking the country's history into account, it avoided the violence and social disruption that would have hindered the establishment of revolutionary production procedures in a society long stamped with the marks of feudalism. Thus at the beginning it eschewed radical agrarian reform, which might have restricted the expansion of agricultural production, and merely put into effect some measures to limit unbridled exploitation and the landowners' thirst for profit. For example, farm rentals and interest on loans to farmers were reduced. But on the initiative of the peasants themselves, a certain number of properties were expropriated and divided and the government did not interfere, being anxious not to come into conflict with the widespread yearning of the peasant masses for their own land.

The agrarian reform law, approved in June 1950, was a response to this aspiration. Its goal was "to abolish the property system based on feudal exploitation by the class of large landowners and to establish a system of peasant holdings aimed at liberating the productive forces of the rural regions and at developing farm production to open the way for the industrialization of the new China."

With considerable tact and little violence, the different categories of peasants were classified and the partition of the land began. The division was not egalitarian. Instead of matching the needs of the peasant family or giving land to peasants who had none, the grants were made on the basis of potential. The government opened the way for cooperatives organized by activists or rural leaders, to collective working methods, and to a system of mutual-assistance teams. These mutual-assistance teams—initially established on a temporary basis and later made permanent—met with an extremely favorable response, for they revived an ancient custom of association known in all central Asia as *Jashar,* that is, fraternal assistance in the achievement of major projects. These developments led in 1952 to the establishment of quasi-socialist cooperatives, in which work was done in common but each property-holder retained rights over his own land, receiving a portion of the total income and having the power to withdraw from the cooperative if he so desired. It was a simple step from there to the total collectivization of the land, a step for which Mao Tse-tung provided the impetus when conditions were considered favorable for a consolidation of socialist progress.

I shall not cite statistics on the numerical growth of cooperatives and their fusion into large units. The important thing to bear in mind is that all land in China is now collectivized. Little by little, resistance was overcome and increasing numbers of landowners were persuaded to give up their property titles in exchange for the advantages of collectivist production. All the psychological factors that could promote the success of agrarian reform in China were utilized at one stage or another, from the discontent and rebelliousness of the landless peasants vis-à-vis the large landowners in the first phase of the process to the rivalry among cooperatives during the great battle for liberation that involved the entire nation. This galvanization and emotional energizing of the masses was accomplished with a skill and effectiveness that I have never seen equaled in any other country. Each citizen was transformed into a spontaneous propagandist for the reigning theories and an enthusiastic collaborator in their implementation. Prepared by the government's ideological campaign, the people willingly accepted their share of the sacrifice—the demanding work necessary for the progress of which they are so proud.

The government has taken an equally wise approach to the

problem of how best to invest the meager financial resources of an underdeveloped, and consequently undercapitalized, country. At issue was a choice between bread and steel, a choice faced by all developing countries that must concentrate their resources either in industrial growth or in meeting their people's increasing need for consumer goods.

While conceding that only industrialization can emancipate the country economically, China has not allowed itself to become entirely absorbed in organizing its industry. It has not neglected agriculture—contrary to what occurred in many other countries, including the U.S.S.R., where for a time the imbalance between the two threatened the very structure of the economy. The Chinese development plans did not give exaggerated priority to either bread or steel; they fixed reasonable proportions for both necessary industrialization and satisfying the needs of a people anxious to raise its level of social well-being. The government of the new China did not subscribe to the belief that the expansion of industry automatically stimulates agricultural growth. (That theory is very dangerous, for when the agricultural structure is neglected in favor of economic development, it automatically begins to stifle industry and restrain its productivity. A safer course is to liquidate the existing agrarian structure, thereby freeing the workers, while admitting that industrial development cannot by itself bring about agrarian reform; it is undoubtedly a necessary factor but alone it is not enough.) Instead, the Chinese leaders considered the situation from quite another angle. "The industrialization of China must be based on the vast market of rural China. Consequently, without a radical agrarian reform, the new China cannot be industrialized," declared Liu Shao-ch'i in 1950, while listing the justifications for the agrarian reform law.

An analysis of the Chinese five-year plans shows that the proportion of agricultural investment called for has always been higher relative to industry than that of the Soviet plans.

The Chinese government, though eager to industrialize, knows and respects the people's impatience to appease their hunger. Its plans have demonstrated the realization that solid industrial development is possible only on the basis of an equally solid agriculture—an agriculture that can lead to creation of a large-scale internal market among the rural population and also furnish the raw materials needed for industrialization. This policy has brought about a rapid increase in the purchasing power of the peasants and in the consumption levels of the rural regions. Thus, according to a report by Tao Shen-lin, consumption of shoes and textiles tripled in the rural areas between 1950 and 1956 and fuel consumption increased twelvefold.

New farming techniques have been introduced gradually. The government is developing the use of fertilizers and insecticides, but the amount produced is still insignificant in terms of national needs. Agriculture is not yet mechanized; the land is still worked with the primitive tools the Chinese farmer has always used.

Mao Tse-tung's government has held that the system of cooperatives must precede the mechanization of agriculture in a country poor in capital and rich in manpower. Through collective effort and the adequate employment of its work force—or by concealing unemployment—the government has been able to overcome the forces of inertia and achieve impressive success. Mobilization of the labor force has made possible the construction or repair of millions of miles of dikes along the banks of the great rivers to prevent the flooding of cultivated land. Millions of miles of irrigation canals have been dug, making modern China the possessor of the largest irrigated area of any country in the world. By these measures China has considerably increased its cultivated areas and has destroyed the myth that it does not have enough land to feed its constantly growing population.

Its principal success, however, is not the increased amount

of cultivated land but the rise in the land's productivity. Since China is poor in fertile land and rich in manpower, it seems logical to concentrate the efforts of huge numbers of workers in attempting to increase output. But despite the existence of an enormous human potential, such an effort had not previously been made. It seemed contrary to the classic economical law of diminishing returns: that it is useless to develop investments of capital and labor beyond a certain point because the additional returns progressively diminish and the enterprise becomes uneconomical. The truth is, however, that this law operates only when production techniques do not change. If the techniques improve, the return on labor increases. What China has accomplished during the last few years by using extremely intensive methods of cultivation demonstrates that the law of diminishing returns is a myth in the area of agriculture, for the Chinese are now achieving rates of productivity that were previously inconceivable. The average productivity of the soil rose during 1957-58 from 100 to 239 for cotton, from 100 to 171 for grain, from 100 to 182 for rice, and so on. In certain selected areas known as "sputniks," productivity increased even more sharply: it doubled and even tripled during a single year of experimentation with new methods.

These methods involve neither miracle fertilizers nor automation. They come simply from a carefully worked out combination of traditional methods of Chinese farming and new techniques that make for a greater and more specialized division of labor. Everything is planned and scheduled; nothing is left to the mercy of circumstance. These new methods—already applied to 300 million *mou* (a *mou* is slightly more than one seventh of an acre) or nearly 20 percent of the area planted to grain—are disciplined irrigation, the reasonable use of organic fertilizers, intensive labor, concentrated sowing, and careful seed selection. Any one of these measures by itself could render impressive results; for example, the new concentrated method of sowing grain and rice is sufficient to double productivity. Their combined use in one area, along with an increase in the number of working days, brings about fantastic results in the "sputnik" zones, where the yield has often reached ten times the traditional level.

Through organized and effective political action, the new China within ten years solved its greatest problem: the feeding of its 700 million inhabitants—or at least this was the impression I carried away from my 1958 visit. It is true that starting in 1959 this extraordinary agricultural expansion slowed down, and in 1960 and 1971 China had to import great quantities of grain to meet the needs of its rapidly growing population. In some Western countries the press went so far as to say that hunger had returned to China and that its reappearance was caused by the establishment of the communes. The Chinese government pointed out, however, that during 1960 and 1961 China underwent a series of exceptionally severe droughts, floods, and other natural disasters and that this combination of violent climatic changes completely defeated all efforts to organize agricultural planning. Even under the burden of these natural calamities, it added, the population did not go hungry; there was only a relative shortage of certain products, and that was made up without delay by importation. Thus the Chinese government viewed the nutritional situation during those difficult years as a credit to itself and stressed that formerly such climatic disasters would have caused a famine that left millions dead. No such catastrophe occurred because the state was able to control the situation by moving food reserves from one province to another and importing grain to cover the deficit— proof of the country's present economic strength. An important witness to these facts was Marshal Montgomery, who made a long visit to China during 1961. In an interview with the *Times* of London he stated that he had seen no hunger in

China, that the population seemed well nourished, and that only certain products were rationed as a result of an exceptionally bad year for agriculture.

An objective analysis does lead to the conclusion, however, that the fundamental factor in this setback (it took three years to recover the lost ground) may well have been the premature establishment of the system of communes, aimed at bringing about a drastic acceleration in the country's rate of economic growth. Until 1958 all new measures had been tested experimentally, at the regional level, and the Chinese revolution had been distinguished for its prudence. But at that time the political leaders decided to risk putting a whole group of radical innovations into effect on a national scale. These innovations—what Mao's political technicians called "the great leap forward"—were applied in the social domain before the technical reforms essential to their success had been determined. The leaders attempted to integrate all the forces of agricultural and industrial production into a single system, the people's communes, which absorbed the agricultural cooperatives. By the end of 1958, 700,000 cooperatives had been fused to form 24,000 communes. Within each of these new economic units all the huge masses of workers were engaged in building up the economy of the country: constructing dams, irrigation canals, and agro-industrial combines and producing steel both in small family kilns and in huge collectivized factories. The Confucian tradition of family life was forced to disappear, with mothers freed from the care of their households and children entrusted to giant nurseries. Immense refectories furnished the meals for the masses of humanity committed to perpetual and intensive labor.

Unfortunately, this plan, though spectacular in theory, turned out to be impractical. The Chinese peasant felt rudely uprooted from his land and lost in this new world, foreign and even hostile to some of his deepest principles and desires.

He therefore reacted negatively. Far from inspiring the workers, the commune system drove the peasants to the rebellion, sabotage, and grave disorders that broke out in the Chinese countryside during 1960-61, causing a drastic drop in the country's agricultural production.

The government soon understood that this rash leap, too ambitious relative to the nation's actual abilities, was a political error and it quickly retreated a step, putting forward the program called "readjustment," which was approved at the Communist Party Congress of Lushan. The policy of people's communes was to be pursued, but the existing communes were broken up into units of more human dimensions, and within them production brigades were created, comparable in importance to the agricultural cooperatives that had existed before the great leap forward.

With this adjustment of policy, China avoided the abyss and resumed its social progress, more slowly, but more surely. Industry reduced its rate of expansion and gave priority to the agricultural sector, a corrective that enabled the country to regain the economic balance the adventure of the great leap forward had threatened.

Since 1962, despite a population increase of about 2 percent a year, agriculture has expanded at an annual rate of 4 percent, and has been able to keep pace well enough to banish the specter of famine completely. Actually raising the nutritional level of the population, however, would require a growth rate of at least 6 percent, which has not yet been achieved, and the Chinese government is obliged to import great quantities of grain from Western countries to cover the difference. But the government is proud to be able to import and pay for what it buys in hard currency, instead of having to appeal for international aid. That China has sufficient credit at its disposal—because of the export of minerals, especially thousands of tons of gold—is, in the government's eyes, proof of its prosperity. Thus China today is able to provide a balanced diet, sober but sufficient, for the human masses who had formerly seemed condemned to live in hunger.]

Before closing this discussion of China, I would like to deal in broader terms with the sudden change of national policy after 1958.* Because for a time this change threatened the new-born stability and prosperity of the People's Republic, it has frequently been regarded as a serious political error on the part of the revolutionary leaders. Was the profound upheaval, which resulted in the cultural revolution that shook the entire country, really a political error, or was it rather a tactical withdrawal, inevitable and necessary in terms of the interplay of forces within the revolutionary process? This is a crucial question in China's modern history, and we must try to find an interpretation. In the above analysis of the repercussions that the Great Leap Forward had in the area of nutrition, I called the policy rash and a political error. This statement needs to be clarified and put into perspective. I consider the policy a failure insofar as it concerned nutrition, because it represented a turning away from the nutritional policy of 1949-58, which had been a brilliant success. My negative judgment does not apply to the other aspects of the policy's overall strategy of socioeconomic development.

Beyond that, another facet of the situation should be stressed. Considering its purely nutritional results, the Great Leap Forward can be viewed as a short-term failure—for example, in terms of the limitations placed on agricultural production. In the long run, however, it may prove to have been a political action of great wisdom.

The first imperative is to understand the factors that conditioned this spectacular socioeconomic change. Let us look more closely—and as much as possible from a perspec-

* This section was not included in the 1973 French edition and appears here for the first time.

tive *within* the revolutionary process—at what occurred in China during this period of profound transformation.

As soon as the Communists attained political victory, China developed a vast plan for the expansion of its economy and the social integration of a population that until then had been almost entirely marginal to the country's economic and social life. But an underdeveloped and famished nation, torn to pieces by long years of war, could not succeed in such a gigantic undertaking without a good deal of outside assistance. This was provided by the Soviet Union. During the ten years that followed the Communist victory, the U.S.S.R. granted credits estimated at $2 billion to answer China's material needs. In addition, it furnished 7,000 technicians who helped in setting up different types of industry, especially heavy industry, with enormous effects on the national economy. More than 12,000 Chinese studied at Soviet technological centers.

All this technical and financial assistance enabled China to make rapid advances, but it was not enough to free it from foreign economic influence, and it continued dependent. This was the conclusion of those responsible for national economic development when they evaluated the results of the first Chinese five-year plan, which ended in 1957. Certain sectors showed very satisfactory results: agricultural production and industry, which had grown by 80 percent during this first plan. But for China to reach a level of self-development that would free it from its backward state, the effort had to be redoubled, investment intensified, and new techniques created. The Chinese leaders' hopes of seeing Soviet aid increased and strengthened found no support in the U.S.S.R. The Socialist alliance between the two countries had already been shaken when the Twentieth Soviet Communist Party Congress called for de-Stalinization in 1956. From that point on, ideological differences, superimposed on already divergent interests in the area of international politics, had caused a progressive parting of the ways. China showed its irritation with Moscow's policy of coexistence with American imperialism and energetically denounced the dangers inherent in revisionism and in making concessions to the West. That 700 million younger comrades in Asia voiced dissatisfaction with the behavior of the elder, thirty years more experienced in the struggle for practical socialism, considerably cooled Soviet enthusiasm for helping the new socialist power in the Far East. Instead of an increase in Soviet aid, cooperation, and technical assistance, there was a noticeable decrease. The Chinese leaders quickly realized that they could count only on their own resources to defend their economy, culture, and national existence and that as a result of this dramatic political turn they were obliged to move rapidly to make certain innovations. Moreover—and this is crucial—they came to realize that Soviet development techniques, especially those the U.S.S.R. had learned from the West, were not entirely appropriate to their country, that they might indeed destroy its cultural fabric, the very essence of the Chinese people's philosophy of life.[33] It had become necessary to react to this threatening domination of foreign technology, to erect cultural barriers against its assaults. The whole Chinese people had to prepare for the herculean effort involved in building a new Great Wall, not out of stone but out of the materials of the spirit: certain moral principles derived from their Confucian heritage and certain values stemming from both their traditional culture and their first-hand experience in the struggle against colonialism. This was essential if China was not to be crushed by an insidious foreign technology that, by imbuing the national structure with a culture different from the one that had formed it, would rupture its social fabric and might in the end completely destroy it. This does not imply that the Chinese were hostile to the introduction of technological elements that were necessary tools of the development. Nevertheless, they felt that their technology could not be foreign to their culture; it must be a creation or an outgrowth of their own cultural life. An autonomous technology was the indispensable instrument for the maintenance and expansion of both China's economy and its culture, which were viewed as two aspects of a single reality, the "face" of the country. China had to create its own technological instruments, within its own cultural ambit, and not simply receive them from without, in a process that would surely be more rape than cultural development. Any other course would have relegated Chinese culture to a secondary status, making it the servant of technological advance rather than the master.

It was in response to this paradoxical situation, in which the opportunity for accelerated modernization had to be grasped without destroying the social and moral values that give meaning and character to Chinese culture, that the second five-year plan was conceived in 1958. This plan was in no way inspired by the Soviet model of a centralized economy. China formulated a program designed to create a new society integrated into large autonomous groups—the people's communes—which were to be charged with managing all their own closely related activities. The key to the new society's success lay in the formation of a new kind of human being, who would be identified body and soul with the task of creating a new world, and the shaping of human lives thus became the predominant preoccupation. Henceforth China was to attempt, by means of basic education and technological and managerial training, to direct human development at all levels, forming humans united by a profound ideological consciousness. This was the ruling consideration of the whole educational system. The technicians who were to use the peculiarly national technology must themselves have a critical awareness of the subordinate value of technique in relation to the supreme objective of collective well-being: they must remain conscious of the true goals of the country's socioeconomic development. The investment of human wills united in a common cause became more important than the investment of capital. The aim was not merely to acquire a larger quantity of material goods, as in Western development; it included the achievement of other goals and values for which the Chinese revolutionaries had fought tenaciously because they considered them indispensable to the process of integral human development. The society that China is trying to form, from which the phenomenon of hunger will be eliminated, concentrates its developmental strategy not on the "maximization" of revenues but rather on that of the mental energies that will most quickly enrich human life and bring greater happiness.

Such is my impression—formed on the basis of what I saw for myself and heard from other travelers and also from what I have read in books by authors of various persuasions—of this immense country whose features will decisively influence that of all humanity.*

Old Mother India

The overpopulated subcontinent of India, with 20 percent of the world's population concentrated on only 3 percent of the world's surface, appears at first to be a living argument in favor of neo-Malthusian theories. The fact that its 450 million inhabitants† live in a state of chronic malnutrition, besides being subject to periodic famines; the still more alarming fact that this tremendous mass of people has been expanding at the rate of 40 million per decade‡ while food production has remained more or less stationary—these seem

* End of new material.
† 560 million.
‡ 80 million.

to be obvious signs that the country is marching toward inevitable catastrophe. Total annihilation would appear to be the only solution to India's tragic and irreconcilable dichotomy between Malthus's two factors of alimentation and population.

Yet even here, in the very region picked by the neo-Malthusians as a demonstration area for their doctrines, they are right only in appearance, before all the facts are in. When population and production are considered separately, as though they were independent variables, there is no way to avoid the conclusion that Malthus was right. But if we analyze the Hindu nation as a socioeconomic whole, as a living organism whose functions are interdependent, as is actually the case, we find no natural or inevitable justification for the misery in which these people live or the state of hunger in which they die. The desperate situation in India can be explained neither by the shortage of land nor by the excess of people. The reign of starvation in India is upheld by elements disguised and hidden in the complexity of this people's socioeconomic life. Reasons are to be found that explain the situation more satisfactorily than the neo-Malthusian theory.

In order to understand the background of India's socioeconomic structure, with its grave deficiencies, it is necessary to have a clear idea of certain geographical factors. In many respects, India can be considered a continent in the same sense that Europe is. It is larger than Europe and shut off from the rest of Asia by the wall of the Himalayas, which make a much more definite boundary than the indefinite eastern frontiers of Europe. The races and languages of India are fully as various as those of Europe. Continent, subcontinent, or mere peninsula, India constitutes a cultural world of unmistakable individuality, isolated as it was for dozens of centuries by the natural frontiers of impassable mountains and mighty oceans.

Within its area of about 1.8 million square miles, India includes three geographical regions that are well differentiated and that have very different economic possibilites. In the north is the great Himalayan Mountain chain; in the southern point is the Deccan plateau, crossed by low mountains; and in between are the vast fertile basins of the Ganges, the Indus, and the Brahmaputra.

The region of the Himalayas, mostly covered by dense forests, is unfit for agriculture and is only thinly populated by primitive peoples who live by harvesting the products of the jungle. Although the soils are poor in the Deccan plateau, agriculture is possible in the valleys and on the gentler mountain slopes, where terracing and irrigation from artificial reservoirs are used. However, this type of farming, which depends on the domestication of water, has not attracted a large population.

In the geologically recent alluvial plains of the central part of the country, where the soil is rich and rain frequent or irrigation easy, the great masses of India's population are concentrated. More than half of the inhabitants of India are settled on these alluvial belts of the north, which occupy only a fifth of the total area of the country. There is also a high population density in the low and humid lands to the east and to the west of the Deccan plateau. In contrast with these swarming centers, which reach a density of more than 1,000 persons per square mile in the Ganges Valley, India has extensive areas, such as the Thar Desert and the Naypur plateau, that are practically unpopulated.

Variations of climate as well as of soil produce India's irregular distribution of population. Lester Trueblood, the geographer, says that in no other part of the world is there such a pure type of monsoon climate and that nowhere else are people so dependent on climatic conditions.[34] The rain pattern is determined principally by the winds, which come in in from the oceans laden with moisture. Their paths and their

intensity are of fundamental significance to this predominantly agrarian people. The distribution of rain is extremely
irregular in the Indian peninsula; there is a mean annual
rainfall of 451 inches at Cherrapunji, in Assam, making it one
of the rainiest places in the world (drier only than Mt.
Waialeale, in Hawaii, with 460 inches), while in certain parts
of the Thar Desert it hardly rains at all.

More than three fourths of the population is engaged in
agriculture. The Hindus, whose religion prohibits the use of
meat, particularly beef, as food, have developed a type of
diet which is overwhelmingly vegetable in origin. Rice is the
basic food, although it is cultivated on only 25 percent of the
total tilled land. Sorghum, millet, wheat, and lentils, although
consumed in various parts of the country, are considered to
be complementary foods. Rice is the largest crop, yielding
annually some 40 million metric tons, but India also imports
quantities of this cereal.

In the greater part of the country rice is eaten with
vegetables and with small quantities of vegetable oils and fish.
A favorite rice dish is mulligatawny, a kind of rice soup
cooked with onions and seasoned with good doses of pepper
and garlic. Rice with curry sauce, which gets its hot taste
from various seeds and leaves, is another habitual dish. Meat
consumption in India is extremely low and practically confined to the Mohammedans. Consumption of milk and its
derivatives is equally low; India is estimated to contain half
the world's cattle, but they are so badly fed that they
produce hardly any milk.

On their scanty and monotonous vegetable diet, the Indian
people are not surprisingly among the world's most undernourished. They show symptoms of the most varied kinds of
deficiencies and specific hungers.

The biological structure of the Indians is most seriously
undermined by their extreme shortage of high-value proteins;
this deficiency sets in motion a series of evils that leads to a

shocking decline and degradation of the race. We have noted that the differences in height and physical resistance between the Sikhs of the northern Punjab and the populations of the south are a result, as Robert McCarrison proved experimentally, of the greater proportion of protein in the Punjab diet. The Punjab diet includes whole wheat bread, milk, milk products, and meat, in contrast to the rice-and-vegetable menu of the south. The almost universal absence of good proteins contributes to the Indian's low stature, to his low energy quotient, and his susceptibility to disease.

Protein deficiency also bears relation to the frequency of specific diseases. Doctors have long been aware that cirrhosis of the liver is very common among the poorer classes of India, and they have attributed it to malaria and other pathogenic agents which are active in the region. Only comparatively recently was it suspected that the condition might be related to nutritional deficiencies. In 1937 Dr. Aykroyd wrote prophetically: "Portal cirrhosis, not associated with malaria or alcoholism, is a common cause of death among middle-aged Indians of the very poorest classes, and it may well be that this condition follows the consumption throughout life of a grossly defective diet."[35] His suggestion has been wholly confirmed. It has become clear through research that the lack of certain elements contained in proteins causes the cirrhosis conditions that carry off so many lives in the Far East.

One further effect of poverty in proteins is a lowering of appetite. The Indians have tried to compensate for this by an exaggerated use of seasonings. Curry, one function of which is to make foods sharp and appetizing, is so widely used that it has come to be called the "salt of the Orient."

Certain vitamin deficiencies are also very common in India. In Orissa province, where N. Singh conducted a nutritional investigation in 1939, it appeared that children in particular suffered from a whole series of vitamin shortages. Colonel

R. E. Wright, a doctor who was for many years superintendent of the Madras Eye Hospital, has said that disorders of vision due to Vitamin B deficiency are more common and more serious in this area than anywhere else in the world. Beriberi also exacts a heavy toll from this rice-eating population. One of its most unpleasant forms is the acute beriberi which strikes suddenly and violently; in the Madras state, according to a report of the Food and Agriculture Organization's experts, this malady is responsible for a "high mortality among infants," especially between the second and fourth months. It is unnecessary to describe in detail the many other deficiency conditions that exist in India; they are the same as those in all the other starving areas of the world.

Chronic hunger in India is without doubt one fundamental cause of the high death rate. In the late 1940's, official statistics set the death rate for all India at about 24 per 1,000, but S. Chandrasekhar, the demographer, considers this figure to be far short of the truth. His estimate for the same period was 30 deaths per 1,000 inhabitants.[36] By that reckoning, more than 10 million people* died in India every year.

The great tragedy for the national economy is not so much the number of people who die but the age at which they die. Infant mortality as of the 1940's was higher even than in pre-revolutionary China. A quarter of the babies born died in their first year; 40 percent died before they were five, and only half survived to the age of twenty. In that way the pitiful conditions of Indian life eliminated half the human beings that the country produced before they became adult. The effects of this situation on the economy are disastrous; it is as though half the individuals born were defective, having mouths to fill but no hands to work. Half the Indian children are born merely to consume a starvation diet and to die before they are old enough to produce. The Indian's life

* 20 million.

expectancy of twenty-six years*—less than half that of the American or Englishman—is one striking aspect of this terrible waste of human potentialities.[37]

[One of the principal obstacles to social progress in this huge country is that India is essentially a land of orphans, young people who never had a chance to know their parents well, for the parents died prematurely, before they could pass on their life experiences. This is one of India's tragedies, a strange and frightful result of its hunger. The cultural discontinuity, which forces each generation to learn for itself many things that would normally have been transmitted to it by its elders, explains to some degree the slow pace of the country's evolution and the strength of the forces of tradition. Most of the knowledge that each generation acquires is lost before it can take root and modify the cultural heritage —which, as a result, is all but static.]

Hunger and undernourishment alone do not effect this massive slaughter of the Indian people; there is obviously a whole complex of unfavorable health conditions. Yet there is no doubt that undernourishment lowers the resistance of the organism and prepares the ground for other enemies, especially infectious diseases, to do their deadly work. The people's susceptibility to disease was amply demonstrated in the 1918 influenza epidemic which took more lives in India than in all the rest of the world—between 15 million and 20 million. Then too, there were 100 million to 200 million Indians in the 1940's who suffered from malaria; 1 million died of it every year. Poorly nourished people are easy prey to malaria. Geddes, to emphasize the influence of diet on this disease, has shown that the meat-eating Mohammedans are much less subject to malaria than are the Hindus with their very faulty vegetable diet.

Tuberculosis, cholera, dysentery, worms—all the great

* 32 years.

killers have their work immensely simplified here by starvation. And every once in a while hunger becomes more than an assistant and itself strikes down human beings on such a scale that it piles up the greatest death rates in the world. That happens in the times of famine, when mortality figures climb as high as 60 out of 1,000.

Famines have apparently always existed in India, but they grew much more serious with the unfortunate intervention of the British in the Indian economy during the nineteenth century. The famines of the early 1800's killed off half the inhabitants of Madras, Mysore, and Hyderabad.[38] Toward the end of the century more than 20 million people starved to death, 4 million of them in the one terrible year of 1877.[39] Famines have become somewhat less severe in our own century, but they are far from vanishing. In the winter of 1942-43, the bodies of the famished littered the streets of Calcutta so profusely that their mere removal became impossible.[40]

Love-making the National Pastime

What are the causes of this permanent state of hunger in India? In two centuries of domination the British did not succeed in alleviating the situation but in fact aggravated it. Apologists for British policy have attempted to justify the resounding failure of their colonial administration by citing "natural causes" in the face of which man is helpless. The leading causes thus presented (backed with a great deal of expert testimony) were the exaggerated demographic pressure and the hopeless wearing-out of the land. Many of the experts have categorically stated that hunger and misery in India are entirely the results of nature's stinginess and of the uncontrolled reproductive appetites of the Indian people. For them India is a living example of the gloomy predictions of Malthus. In their view, India, with its excess populations and its land stripped of natural resources, might just as well abandon the problem as insoluble.

Fairfield Osborn expressed such a view when he asserted that the internal enemy of India is "too many people for the land to support. India's land has long ago been depleted, yet her population continues to increase." So did C. C. Furnas when he said the population of India had reached its "saturation point,"[41] and so did the Indian scientist, S. Chandrasekhar, when he treated as a major disaster India's population growth of nearly 4 million per year* in the face of insufficient resources to absorb this increase.

The pessimistic Vogt, enthusiastically adopting Chandrasekhar's point of view, makes the egregious statement that "sex play is the national sport." What sport does he suggest for these people whose energies are spent and whose economic resources are scanty? Does he want them to reduce still further their tiny plots of land by setting aside a rectangle of packed earth for an energetic game of tennis, Anglo-Saxon style? Would he suggest a violent game of English soccer—or, perhaps, that other English sport of confiscating foreign lands and carrying imperialist rule to the ends of the earth? No, such exertions are too strenuous for this undernourished, peaceful, and moderate people. The Hindus have never distinguished themselves by physical or even political strength—only by cultural strength. The strength of a culture that for three thousand years has resisted the attacks of a whole series of other cultures that have tried to crush it commands respect. By concentrating on the "sport" of reproduction, which is so looked down on by the neo-Malthusians, Indian civilization has outlived the Greeks and their Olympiads. It has outlived the Romans with their passion for the sport of war, and it may yet outlive other modern civilizations with their love of sport for sport's sake.

* 10 million per year.

But to know the true importance to India's social and economic structure of these natural factors that are cited as the cause of its decadence, one must look at the facts. When India's population of 450 million* is compared with its land area, which is about two thirds that of the United States, it can be seen that its average relative density of 250 per square mile,† though not low, is not among the highest in the world. It is exceeded by a dozen countries, including the relatively prosperous nations of Belgium, the Netherlands, and England. What differentiates India's demographic character from those of densely settled European countries is its rural nature; 87 percent of the people of India live in tiny villages, of which there are close to 1 million.[42] This rural population collects, as has been noted, in the fertile valleys and on the alluvial plains and cultivates some 330 million acres of land, 50 million of them by irrigation. Farming only the more fertile and easily watered zones, the Indians have so far left uncultivated an area estimated at 150 million acres, all of it arable land. It can thus be said that in spite of tremendous pressure on certain areas—the valley of the Ganges, the Bengal delta, the Orissa, and Cochin regions—a third of India's land resources remain unexploited.

It is not strictly true, then, that India has exhausted its natural resources. Beyond its agricultural opportunities, moreover, there are its very considerable mineral reserves. India's oil is estimated to constitute 3 percent of the world's potential supply. Its potential water power is assessed at 27 million h.p., which is a higher figure than the 20 h.p. granted China and Canada, and almost equal to the 28 h.p. given the United States. These resources, far from being exhausted, are virtually untouched. The surface has not even been scratched. Certainly there is no demonstrable excess of people in India in relation to the potential resources of the country.

* 560 million.
† 280 per square mile.

Starvation in India is not due to an absolute excess of people, nor is it the result of too rapid growth. As P. K. Wattal has pointed out, the population growth of India as a whole has been relatively slow and irregular, because of a high death rate.[43] India's fertility index is not among the highest, although it is sometimes erroneously thought to be so. Its rate of 33 per thousand* is well below the birth rates of the majority of Latin American, African, and Oriental countries. Factors such as protein deficiencies, universal marriage, and child marriage (nearly all girls marry before the age of fifteen) tend to bring about a high birth rate, but certain other factors operate to keep it within reasonable limits. There is a high mortality of girls too young to reproduce; there is a stupidly vast number of deaths in childbirth (the estimate is 200,000 such deaths annually); and there is a religious prohibition against the remarriage of widows. The population increase of some 4 million per year amounts to about 1 percent, a figure not very different from the European rate since 1900.†

Misery exists in India neither because the nation is overrun with people nor because the soil is saturated. The true causes have to do with inadequate exploitation of resources both natural and human, longstanding tendencies that were gravely aggravated by the economics of British colonialism.

Although most of the country's productive energy goes to agriculture, India cultivates only two thirds of the arable land. And while this limited area undergoes intensive cultivation, it yields much less than the average for the rest of the world. Italy and Germany, containing more people in proportion to their land, extract an annual return of food from the soil amounting to 1 million and 2 million calories respectively for each inhabitant. In India, the individual's yearly share of

---

* 21 per thousand as of 1967.
† 10 million per year or 2.5 percent, a rate lower than that of some Latin American countries.

home-grown calories is only 800,000, an amount utterly insufficient for minimum needs.

The precarious state of Indian agriculture is apparent from the figures on specific crop production. [India raises 870 pounds of rice per acre while China produces 1,605, the United States 2,230, Japan 2,765, and Italy 3,210.] India's low return from rice cultivation has been attributed to the poverty of a soil situated almost entirely in the tropical zone, but that argument does not stand up against the following facts. First, equally tropical countries have achieved a much larger yield; Egypt, Surinam, and Guyana all produce three times as much as India. Second, much of India's soil, particularly that of all the alluvial plains of Hindustan where most of the farming is concentrated, is made up of materials brought down by the rivers from nontropical latitudes. Thus, although the climate of the Ganges and Indus deltas is tropical, the soil there is composed of elements carried from the temperate zones where the rivers originate.

Low farm income in India is primarily due to primitive methods of cultivation. Techniques are rudimentary. Agriculture is carried on at the mercy of the capricious monsoons, without seed selection or pest control, with crude tools and inadequate fertilizer (mainly cow dung). India's immense herds of cattle, estimated at 2 million head,* would seem likely to provide a fairly good supply of manure, but the rural population are too poor to use it all for fertilizer. Instead, because wood is scarce and expensive on the tillable plains, the farmers are forced to use cow droppings for fuel. The dung is molded into blocks and left to dry on rocks or in the backyard. In some areas, fuel is as difficult to procure as food itself. People thus enslaved by their environment find manure the only answer to their fuel problem.[44]

Aldous Huxley tells of a scene which epitomizes the role

---

* 3 million head.

of manure in the domestic life of the poorest Indians. The novelist was traveling by elephant in the Jaipur region. As he left the palace of a feudal lord his mount stopped in the street and relieved itself on an elephantine scale. Hardly had the beast finished when an old woman dashed out of a nearby shack and hurled herself joyfully on the enormous pyramid of dung. As the elephant moved off she gave infinite thanks to the "Salaam Maharaja" for the princely gift he had left her—it would keep her cook fire going for a week!

Elephants being rare, and such monumental contributions quite unusual, the farmer must get along with his modest bovine briquettes. He burns up 65 million tons of manure, roughly 40 percent of the total annual production estimated to be 160 million tons dry weight. About 20 percent of the supply is lost because it is not collected, and only 40 percent of it is left to be used for fertilizing the soil.

Another cause of low farm income is a set of property relationships that make rational use of the soil impossible. In colonial times, about 48 percent of the cultivated lands belonged to large-scale landlords; the great latifundia were owned by some 6 million or 8 million of these feudal lords, while hundreds of millions of sharecroppers occupied the land. The great proprietors were businessmen rather than farmers and took no interest in agriculture except as a source of their superprofits. They left the sharecroppers to their fate and appeared only at harvest time, to collect their shares of 40 to 60 percent of the crop. Since the government took out another 10 percent, the worker had very little left to show for his toil. Perhaps this economic situation is a partial explanation of the Indian's lack of enthusiasm, or even distaste, for work, for no matter how hard he works he receives almost nothing.

The feudal regime also lay at the root of the large number of famines which occurred when there was in fact no real crisis in food production. The farmers could not use their own harvests to keep alive, and they were simply unable to buy back the products of their own sweat. It used to be common practice in India for food exports to continue while great numbers of people starved to death. Richard Temple tells us that throughout the famine of 1877, when 4 million people died of hunger, exportation of cereals through the port of Calcutta never stopped for a moment. André Philip accurately observes that "famine is not always the result of an insufficient harvest but rather of an insufficiency remaining to the farmer after the tax collector, the landlord, and the usurer have taken their share."[45]

In addition to the system of great landed properties, called *zamindari*, there is a system of small individual holdings known as *riotwari*. In *riotwari* areas some millions of small farmers work their tiny scraps of soil and pay the land tax directly to the government. These farmers were free, even in colonial days, of the terrible exploitation of the landlords, but other evils prevented them from gaining economic freedom. First, the state collected a higher tax on this type of farm, taking about 25 percent of the farmer's net income. The government exacted this tribute rain or shine, good year or bad, and the farmer often had to borrow, thus falling slave to the extortionate rates of the usurers.

A second evil of the *riotwari* areas is the extreme subdivision of the land. Among both Moslems and Hindus, the land has been divided by inheritance generation after generation until the average Indian farm is only five acres. These miniature parcels, each occupied by a whole family, produce an individual agricultural income even lower than incomes in old China and Japan.

The work capacity of the Indian peasant is extremely slight, and his low energy limits his utilization of what land he has. The most obvious reasons for this incapacity are chronic undernourishment and low levels of health and hygiene. Careful inquiries have shown that the Indian farmer loses a month each year through attacks of malaria and that at least a quarter of the rural population work throughout the year in a state of fever. Malaria is not the only disease which sucks these people's blood; worm infestation and dysentery are everywhere.

Such then, are the dark outlines of the defective social structure which holds down the living conditions of the Indian people. The picture is filled in with the castes, which separate the population into two or three thousand closed compartments, each with its special codes, rights, customs, and interests. Religious fanaticism is added to the scene. And then there is illiteracy, still the condition of 88 percent of the populace.*

Famine as a Heritage of the Middle Ages

The modern situation in India can be regarded as a natural evolutionary outcome of the country's primitive social organization, which grew during the Indian Middle Ages into a despotic tyranny of the Brahmans over other castes. By the time the British arrived in India the inequalities of Indian life were well developed, but the British must accept a heavy responsibility for their preservation. The British administered India just as the Indian landlords managed their lands, interested strictly in maximum profits and without romantic preoccupations about the native life.

The Spanish and Portuguese came to tropical regions and took root in the soil, to lay foundations for new nations and new kinds of society; British colonists went to the Orient to establish trading posts through which to exploit native labor. It is no longer denied that British colonization in the tropics

* 80 percent.

was always merely a matter of administration, but it is still debated whether Britain's extreme mercantilism was ever of any benefit to the people under its dominion. Impartial analysis indicates that colonization resulted in much more evil and suffering for the Indians than it did in advantages.

The first British colonists arrived in 1753 to find a relatively prosperous country, with a population of 100 million farmers and artisans. India had long since ceased to be a purely agricultural country; it was an important manufacturing center, exporting finely worked merchandise to Europe, Arabia, Egypt, and China. Delicate silks, muslins, laces, embroidery, jewelry, and rugs were sent abroad. Père Vath, in his history, says that India was rising out of its Middle Ages and its relative prosperity was the product of a transitional economy, moving from a closed medieval system into a nascent factory capitalism.[46] Rural artisans were coming to the cities to work in factories and laying the foundations for an industrial development which could raise the national income and living standards ever higher. There were still occasional famines, a heritage of the medieval period, just as there were in Europe. But famine was on the way out, and it certainly would have disappeared with the development of industrialism just as it did in western Europe. It was the intervention of the British with their insatiably greedy traders that violently cut short India's economic revolution and forced the country back to a medieval economy and into permanent starvation.

From the very beginning of their occupation, the handful of military and civilian Englishmen who were in charge of dominating and administering the monster colony formed their policy exclusively in favor of British mercantile interests. The activities of Robert Clive, who is considered the true founder of the British Empire in India, were typical of this economic exploitation. Clive indulged in such excesses of oppression and brutality that the English had an attack of conscience and called him home to answer for his behavior. He won a vote of censure from Parliament and put a bullet through his head, but his successor, Warren Hastings, continued his tradition. Hastings sold, for instance, two Indian provinces which did not belong to the British. He sold them to the Great Mogul for 25 million rupees. He then rented out, for 10 million, the services of a British brigade to "persuade" the local governments to recognize the illegal sale. Hastings' administrative acts finally resulted, like Clive's, in a Parliamentary summons, but by this time India had proved so profitable that Parliament, according to a document cited by the historian Gonzalo de Reparaz, acknowledged that he had "acted criminally" but absolved him because "his crimes had been advantageous to England. . . ."[47]

Indian manufactured goods interested the English very much at first. As R. C. Dutt points out in his *Economic History of India,* these goods could be very profitably sold in London for half the price of English products, in spite of transportation costs. The traders soon grew discontented, however, with their considerable profits. They managed, through the East India Company, to monopolize the buying of the most important products and began to force the artisans to sell at prices so low that they "brought on the complete ruin of Indian industry and commerce." Meanwhile the English government, to protect its growing native industries, started in the early nineteenth century to levy prohibitive duties on Indian imports. These import taxes, which amounted to 60 or 70 percent of a product's value, were a deathblow to Indian manufacture. While British merchandise circulated freely in India, Indian wares were taxed out of the English market—until England had cornered the markets of the world and no longer feared Indian competition.

Dutt said about this competition: "The fabrics and silks of India, until 1813, were sold in British markets at prices 50 or 60 percent lower than the products of British industry, and therefore it was necessary to protect the latter with duties of 70 to 89 percent *ad valorem*. If this had not been done, the factories of Manchester would have come to a halt at their birth, and it would have been extremely difficult to rebuild them later. Thus English industry was born from the sacrifice of Indian industry."[48]

[England's behavior in this case is characteristic of the colonial system of economic exploitation. It was, in fact, the key point of the colonial compact that no colony could, in any way whatever, compete with the domestic products of the colonizing country. In the view of the defenders of the theory that each people has its own economic calling, the duty, the task, and even the interest of the colonies was to provide low-priced raw materials to speed up the economic expansion of the industrial imperialist countries. It was the role of the latter to compete for privileged positions in a world market regulated by the law of supply and demand, an economic dogma to liberals where international trade was concerned. On the basis of what they called the natural order, the apostles of laissez-faire stated that this type of trade would automatically bring prosperity to all the peoples of the world. Viewed from such a perspective, colonialism seemed a very generous policy. "The invisible hand," in Adam Smith's phrase, was supposed to redistribute throughout the world the wealth that the pioneer spirit of the great colonial ventures had generated, and every nation would thus have a share of the profits. Unfortunately, the "invisible hand" never showed any favor to the peoples oppressed by the colonial system, in India or anywhere else. For this reason, India was never able to free itself from Great Britain's economic domination, and all its production efforts served only to enrich the industrial mother country, while the colony sank further into wretchedness. The heavy hand of monopoly has always proved more active than the "invisible hand" of colonialism's spurious liberalism.]

When Indian industry was stifled, the class of artisans was completely ruined, and the country's economic strength shattered. Destruction of the artisans' livelihood had particularly dire effects on the Indian economy since it forced these people to take refuge in agriculture. The rural proletariat thus created increased the pressure on the soil and led to a gradual reduction in the size of rural properties. The proportion of artisans in India fell, during the nineteenth century, from 25 percent of the population to 10 percent, while the proportion of agriculturalists rose from 60 to 75 percent. Hunger took possession of the whole country; the nineteenth was the century of India's most terrible famines.

Throughout the whole history of British domination, the only genuine plan for Indian industrialization ever developed was put forth during World War I, when imperial survival seemed temporarily more urgent than the lust for profit. Yet it is clear that a well-considered industrial program would have been the decisive remedy for India's misery. India's economic plight is shocking; the average annual income for each individual is 19 dollars.* That is 5 cents a day.

The English could perhaps have been expected to bring benefit to Indian agriculture, but they never did. It is true that they developed a really magnificent plan for expansion and brought a desert estimated at 20 million acres under cultivation, by means of irrigation. British-built engineering projects—dams and irrigation canals—are as big and as valuable as any British works in India. A single dam in the lower Indus Valley waters an area larger than all the cultivated land of Egypt; the 80,000 miles of modern irrigation canals in India are more than exist in all the rest of the Third World. There is only one thing to be said against this vast agricultural program—it did not affect the food of the people. Its benefits went almost exclusively to cash crops for export.

* About $100 dollars annually.

So far as subsistence products—crops for domestic consumption—are concerned, the area tilled and the quantity yielded have remained more or less constant for the last half century, while the population has increased by dozens of millions. Sir Azizul Huque, a member of the Indian government, had this to say to the Legislative Assembly in 1943:

> The food problem [in India] today is much deeper than it appears on the surface. If statistics are correct, rice production in India during 1911-12 to 1942-43 has remained nearly constant between the figures of 25 million tons and 27 million tons. . . . As compared with the three pre-war years the combined acreage for our basic food crops, rice and wheat, is almost constant, viz., 107.5 to 109 million acres. . . . In the meantime, the population has increased from about 311 million in 1910-11 to 388 million in 1941, with the corresponding increase in rice-eating population. The main food grains production of India has remained almost constant between 50 and 51 million tons with small variations from year to year. . . .[49]

It does not appear that the British colonial government made any very great efforts to improve the techniques of Indian agriculture. The first step in that direction would have been to raise the educational level of the rural populations, but that was never tried. On the contrary, the English in 1830 decreed their own language to be the only one permissible in schools. Far from promoting a diffusion of culture, this language requirement succeeded in restricting it to an insignificant number of privileged students. One result of that simple British dictum was an enormous reduction in the actual number of schools, for lack of English-speaking teachers to teach in them.

Barring the masses from education was of course in the interest of the colonizing power. By means of an antidemocratic education they created a small caste of trained Indians that was enough to help administer the rest of the country, thus adding still another caste to the thousands in existence. Until the dense, rural masses are raised from the obscure mental climate where they live among their prejudices and their fantasies, it will be indeed difficult to introduce rational agricultural methods to the soil of India.

[The Illusions of Independence

As the preceding analysis indicates, the dominant characteristics of India's nutritional problems took form during the colonial period, which ended in 1947. Very little has altered in the twenty-odd years since I first described the situation in the period between 1947 and 1949. Nonetheless, we must briefly examine what has occurred since 1947, when, after a long and stubborn struggle, the Indians won their political independence.

Three serious problems faced the leaders of the new nation, all requiring solutions if independence was to be not just a holiday for the Indian people but a genuine new stage in their history. These problems dictated the new government's essential objectives: first, national unity, so that India could truly take its place as a free nation; second, peace, so that the people could dedicate all their efforts to solving their internal problems; and third, the rapid development of this great mass of humanity that had until then existed in an inert, almost drugged state, stagnant both socially and economically.

In my view the third objective—freeing the people from the web of underdevelopment, tightly enmeshed with the constant hunger and misery that were both cause and effect of economic backwardness—was the greatest challenge. The new leaders came to power with the hope that independence would bring about rapid overall changes and that all manner of obstacles would be overcome without great difficulty. This hope was quickly dissipated. In India—as in many other colonial regions—political independence did not mean the country's economic liberation from the great Western powers. The poverty of the nation rules out the miracle that alone could have rescued the economy from its state of dependence, since it was still primitive, weak, and without the levers necessary to make possible autonomous development. The grave racial conflicts with the Pakistanis, the permanent war of nerves over the establishment of frontiers with China, political dissensions and partisan quarrels, all further blackened the picture of long-standing wretchedness. The threat of death continued to loom.

A whole series of adverse factors thus stood in the way of the necessary structural reforms. Together they prevented the country from shedding its feudal shell and colonial skin, from ridding itself of the evils of the caste divisions. Since no structural reform of any dimension was achieved, India continued in practice to be a colony. Its production resources remained at the service of the great colonial powers, its land and capital continued to be monopolized by external and internal colonial interests, to the profit of a few privileged groups. These privileged few were completely unconcerned with the lot of the masses, who remained divided into hundreds of totally powerless inferior castes, deprived of all opportunity to participate in the social, economic, and political life of the country.

Given the stagnation of India's productive forces and its absurd social structure, it is easy to understand why the nutritional situation remained precarious and hunger continued to be one of the country's unalterable features. In reality, everyone had an interest in maintaining these structures: the oppressors derived great profit from the surplus of marginal manpower and the absence of political consciousness; the oppressed strove to escape their oppression by fleeing from reality into a traditionalism that represented a naive form of security, grounded in the solidarity of all victims of colonial exploitation.

It is difficult to distinguish to what degree the Indian people's resistance to technical innovation is an idiosyncracy of their traditionalist society, hostile to the very idea of progress, and to what degree this resistance is a weapon against those who would crush them even further by extending an economic system whose advantages have been systematically denied them. The latter may have been the source of the widespread feeling that they were happier, or at least less unhappy, in their culture of wretchedness than they would be in the oppressive new order that they saw rising around and above them. These feelings, which were in good part justified, made it difficult for the Indian leaders to defend the process of national development and to motivate the people toward it. Thus originated the agonizing doubts and the lack of a firm political orientation that marked Nehru's administration from its early days. Nehru was a great defender of the people's rights, but he was torn by inner conflict. He would have liked to transform his country's archaic structures—both material and mental—but he was afraid to recommend implanting other structures that he knew the people thought of not as instruments of liberation but as those of subjugation.

Convalescence from the sickness of colonialism was slow, with after-effects lasting more than a generation. During the same period in which China nearly eliminated hunger, India continued to suffer its consequences almost to the same degree that it had done before independence. Understanding that hunger is ultimately only the biological expression of an economic phenomenon—underdevelopment—the Indian government decided to initiate a program aimed at fighting the economic sickness, and thus in 1951 it established the first five-year development plan. But although the government recognized its famished population's urgent need for nutritional resources, investment priority was assigned to the industrial sector.

During the 1950's industrialization was regarded as a panacea that could single-handedly resolve all the economic problems of Third World countries and release them from their underdeveloped state. In the case of countries such as India or Brazil, with extensive land areas and also large populations that seemed to promise potentially vast markets, industrialization was viewed as the only real solution. Like Brazil and several other developing countries, India took this course without achieving results that measured up to expectations.

The Indian planners' preference for the industrial sector was obvious in their budget. For example, until the end of the third five-year plan in 1966, the amount devoted to farm equipment did not exceed 9 percent of total anticipated expenditures, while industry was allotted more than 20 percent. The portion assigned to irrigation projects, indispensable for Indian agriculture, fell, between 1960 and 1966, from 9.2 to 6.5 percent.[50]

The prime place accorded industry did not mean that agriculture was completely forgotten. Indeed, at the time of the first plan there was even some talk of granting it priority, and some efforts were made in the area of agricultural production. In 1952, an agrarian reform law was enacted to dismantle the abusive system of *zamindariat*. Most of the huge estates were broken up, but either demagogy or ignorance of techniques led to the opposite extreme, and land holdings were pulverized into units too small to be economically viable. Gilbert Etienne estimates that in 1966 about 82 percent of the families, with less than 5 acres apiece (30 million with just over 1 acre), occupied a total of 26 percent of the cultivated land.[51] But these minifarms could not be exploited rationally, for they made impossible the use of certain modern techniques (especially those involving tools and machines) that are profitable only on larger farms. Furthermore, while the destruction of the land monopoly broke the despotic power of the feudal masters who had been an overwhelming economic burden to the peasants, it likewise turned private capital away from rural areas at the very time that public investment was being channeled into industry. Thus agriculture fell into a state of financial neglect that prevented it from improving its methods, using fertilizers in adequate quantities, carrying out irrigation projects, and even selecting quality seeds.

Part of the nutritional problem was met by international aid. During the twenty years following independence, the United States alone provided India with loans and grants amounting to $9 billion, two thirds of the total that all Europe received under the Marshall Plan. Half of this so-called aid, however, consisted of surplus agricultural products that the United States did not know what to do with. India received $4.5 billion under the terms of PL-480, which regulated the disposition of food surpluses. Although this food partly relieved the country's hunger, especially in the crucial years of 1965-66 when famine threatened to wipe out 110 million people, it did not help agriculture develop. On the contrary, it served to delay its expansion, a situation that led the opposition parties to violently attack this kind of assistance, which they considered negative and suspect. Basically, the opposition thought that India was helping the United States dispose of its burdensome surpluses, while the United States was not helping India in its efforts to surmount hunger. It is a fact that the nutritional situation was worsening: while the average daily caloric consumption was 2,000 in 1960, the figure fell to 1,900 in 1963 and 1,600 in 1965. Animal proteins played no part to speak of; the diet was almost exclusively vegetarian. India's enormous cattle population suffered from the general scarcity of food, and milk production, inadequate to begin with, fell to practically nothing. Only shipments of powdered milk from abroad saved from kwashiorkor some of the 50 million children whom lack of proteins threatened with death.

During this agonizing period, there were efforts to put a

gradual end to the sacredness of cattle. The government recommended that aged and ill animals be sacrificed, both to make their meat available and to reduce the herds to a size that would permit proper feeding so that they could give more milk. But this attempt to touch a sacred tradition provoked serious trouble. Popular uprisings led to the resignation of several ministers and the precipitous adoption of a law strictly forbidding the slaughter of cattle. This example shows how difficult it is, even under pressure of drastic necessity, to erase one isolated characteristic from the sociological context of a culture. Cows remain sacred just as the castes continue to exist, despite all the laws approved by Parliament intended to suppress them constitutionally.

These cultural and historic factors, along with the droughts of 1965-66, served to keep India's food situation at a level so alarmingly low that various specialists on the subject predicted apocalyptic famines for 1970-75—famines that even the most ambitious and generous aid programs would be unable to remedy.[52] This frightening and seemingly inescapable situation, particularly explosive in view of the country's demographic expansion (the population was then increasing by 2.5 percent a year), led the Indian leaders to conceive a new, overall strategy for the fight against hunger.

As René Delécluse aptly observed: "Years of half successes and partial failures secreted a precious fluid: experience. Agricultural research—especially in high return seeds—moved from the laboratory to the field. Pilot farms and demonstration fields became more numerous. Trends toward an increase in production appeared in various places. The droughts and scarcity of 1965-66 added two final catalyzing elements: the stimulus of the threat of famine and the increase in the price of grains that was to make agriculture a profitable activity."[53]

The primary objective of this change in the country's economic strategy, which dates from 1965, was to free India from the humiliation of being dependent on world charity, especially American charity, for food. Because there were no large amounts of land available to add to the area already cultivated, this goal could be attained only by a substantial increase in the productivity of the soil. Every piece of land in India that could yield a reasonable return had been worked for centuries in such primitive manner that its productivity was almost nil. The land produced food as the cow produced milk; both were practically unproductive because both were sacred and badly treated. Accordingly, treating the land well, cultivating it scientifically, had to be the first step in the struggle against century-old hunger. This policy took form in what was called the "program of intensive agriculture" or the package program, carried out partially with the cooperation of the Ford Foundation.]

[The Program of Intensive Agriculture

The first measure called for in the new program was a substantial increase in the financial resources invested in the agricultural sector, which meant giving agriculture priority, indeed, super-priority, instead of continuing to relegate it to the second rank. The second measure consisted in concentrating these resources in limited areas possessed of all the natural conditions favorable to agricultural exploitation. Previously, the meager funds available to the public treasure had been distributed according to essentially political criteria, throughout thousands of communities in the seventeen states of the union. The new policy, which concentrated the benefits of federal aid on a small number of privileged districts and left the majority of the communities in relative neglect, aroused a wave of protests, especially in Parliament where the representatives of the bypassed regions spoke out vigorously. The political problem was difficult to resolve but the government firmly maintained its decision to concentrate its re-sources instead of scattering them fruitlessly throughout the Indian subcontinent. It committed itself, however, to estab-lishing at least one center of intensive development in each state.

The program strove to bring together all the elements that could help to ensure increased productivity: fertile soil, abun-dant water, fertilizers, selected seeds, pesticides, improved storage and transport installations, easy credit, and profitable prices. Such coordination is no easy task in an under-developed country in which separatism, political antago-nisms, and immense distances all conspire to defeat any project of even moderate complexity. It demands detailed planning, incentives of all kinds, and, above all, a high degree of patience and determination on the part of the authorities. For the first time in the history of India all these human qualities came into play in a project of social improvement—proving the insubstantiality of the fatalistic view that holds underdeveloped peoples of traditional culture to be incurably inefficient and irresponsible. What these peoples need to demonstrate their capability and awareness of their respon-sibilities are convincing motivations and circumstances favor-able enough so that the efforts they put forth may be rewarded. This is what happened in India.

Another weak point of Indian agriculture was the lack of necessary fertilizers. The soil had been worn out by centuries of destructive cultivation methods: first, by those of primi-tive subsistence agriculture, and subsequently, by the exhaust-ing single-crop system employed for colonial products, which did even greater violence to the land. But India, which has little organic fertilizer, has no synthetic fertilizer either. Before independence, nitrate fertilizers were practically un-known to Indian farmers, and even in 1962 the amount used was ridiculously small (some 200,000 tons). By 1968, how-ever, this figure had risen to 1.2 million tons, half of which were produced in Indian factories. Several projects in progress make it seem likely that production will soon be three times the present level and will meet about one third of the country's needs, estimated at 3.5 million tons.

An important role was played by communities known as "rural development blocs" that were formed by uniting from 80 to 100 villages. These blocs are directed by rural leaders who act in close cooperation with the village councils, the *panchayats*. The village communities, or *gramdan*, in which all resources and workers are mobilized to reach a common objective, function rather like a kind of kibbutz. Vinoba Bhave, who created seven thousand of these communities and is the theoretician of their philosophy of action, rightly stated that no authentic revolution could succeed in India without starting from the bottom, without being based on the vitality of decentralized and freely organized units. René Dumont has sharply criticized these communities for the number of their officials and for a certain level of luxury in their equipment, though Pierre Marchand and Maurice Guernier believe that these criticisms are not well-founded.[54] The large number of officials reflects the desire that everyone in these densely populated communities contributes, and the apparent luxury corresponds to a certain need for ritual proper to a traditionalist society in which every act, even a revolutionary act, is always a rite. A radical change in the rhythm of life from one day to the next simply because of the creation of these communities is not to be expected. Roger Livet explains this with considerable lucidity: "These changes were worked out slowly, according to Hindu methods that reject any appeal to authoritarian procedures, constraints, and more or less disguised pressures. Thus they gain in democratic character what they lose in efficiency."[55]

The increasing use of several varieties of high quality seeds—among them the famous Mexican hybrid corn and Taiwanese and Filipino rice—is another weapon in the campaign to mobilize Indian agriculture.

Because of technical and organizational measures, India's

nutritional situation, until 1966 among the worst in the world, began to show signs of reaching a turning point. During the past two years farm production has increased at a rate of 8 percent, which is a real miracle—provided that it is not merely a coincidence due to exceptionally good climatic conditions during this period. Sufficient time has not yet passed to permit definitive conclusions. For this reason I am not completely able to share the extreme optimism of Jagji-van Ram, Minister of Agriculture. In light of the magnificent grain harvest of 95 million tons estimated for 1968 (in 1965 it had been only 72 million and in 1966, 78 million), he stated that India would soon be free from hunger and able to export wheat. This ambitious goal is still far off. It will be remarkable enough if India can satisfy the minimal nutritional needs of its population during the 1970's. The optimism of the Ministry of Agriculture is not shared by all, for the government is concentrating enormous efforts on its birth control plan, in an attempt to restrain the rapid population growth. The terms in which S. Chandrasekhar, Minister of Family Planning, refers to this program indicate that the authorities are counting more on that method of combatting hunger than on any other. They seem more enthusiastic about the idea of reducing the number of stomachs to be filled than about the prospect of producing enough food to fill them. Thus, to show how significant the birth control program is in his eyes, Chandrasekhar declared: "Moral or immoral, possible or impossible, the birth control program is necessary."[56]

Leaving aside the moral aspect and looking only at possibility and necessity, let us consider whether it is possible in India to achieve a birth control program that can effectively check the demographic explosion. The government is ardently dedicated to this objective and annually allots it about $100 million out of a total budget approaching $3 billion. On top of this $100 million, massive financial aid is furnished by American groups interested in the birth control problem.

Results to date show the program to be largely ineffective. The population is increasing at an annual rate of 2.5 percent, which means 13 million new mouths to feed each year. The Indian government is making more effort than any other nation in the world to lower the rate of demographic growth. Its aim is 1.5 percent a year. In absolute terms, the amount of contraception of all kinds is truly impressive but, in relation to the country's population, it is deceptive.[57] In 1966, some 700,000 sterilizations were performed, but this is relatively few.[58] Even if this effort were multiplied several times over, it would still be ineffective for two reasons. First, while the mortality rate is still relatively high, it should show a tendency to diminish over the next few years because of scientific progress. Second, efforts over the last twenty years to lower the infant mortality rate have been so successful that an extremely high proportion of youth are now reaching the age of reproduction. In the face of these facts, one writer estimated that India's rate of demographic increase will rise to 3 percent before it can begin to diminish.[59]

When the cultural values that come into play are also taken into consideration, the program's chances of success appear even slimmer. It is almost impossible to introduce a new and totally foreign element into a cultural complex without a prolonged and convincing process of justification. A culture so violated always reacts. The forced regulation of births in India appears to me for the moment to be destined to the same failure as the desanctification of cattle and the abolition of castes—the more so because the need for it is much less pressing than the need for the abundance of animal proteins that meat and milk would provide or the need to level the absurd barriers erected by the caste system that impede true collective progress. Indeed, the very need for birth control is arguable: it is beginning to be realized, even in India, that it is possible to substantially increase the amount of food produced and that, by diversifying its production, the country could have sufficient resources available to import the food it lacks, as China now does. Why concentrate enormous sums on a plan of such arguable effectiveness? There is still another argument: rising standards of living and education, further bolstered by the enormous amounts now spent on birth control, will cause the birth rate to fall automatically; this will re-establish the country's demographic balance, which is now upset not in relation to the nation's real potential but because of the massive failure to utilize its natural and human resources.

This overall examination of the lines along which India is currently working to resolve its Malthusian dilemma—the relation between its nutritional needs and its resources—leads to the conclusion that while, on the one hand, the country is far from having resolved this problem, on the other, the prophecies of catastrophic famine during the 1970's are even further from reality. At the present time the facts contradict the macabre assertions of the prophets of the Apocalypse. The demonstration that agricultural production can be increased four times faster than the population is growing is all the more significant because certainly what is now being achieved in India is far less than what will be possible both technically and politically in the years to come. In 1965 a serious and scientific consideration of the question—no longer as a problem of charity or assistance but as one of national security—was enough to generate effective remedies for this reputedly incurable evil. Now those remedies must be applied unsparingly on the national level in order to work the fastest possible radical transformation in the country's archaic economic structure—the seedbed of hunger that everyone wishes to stamp out.]

Hunger as a Weapon of War

Hunger is a social force capable of leading human societies down strange paths. They blindly rush toward an unknown destination, lured on by the beckoning hope that in some way, somehow, their desperate and torturing instinct to eat may be satisfied.

In the great monsoon realm of the Far East live a singular people, the Japanese, who were driven forward with dizzying speed under the biting lash of hunger and so skipped over several whole stages in their social evolution. Prolonged and repeated exposure to bitter starvation led them to burst savagely out of the economic swamp in which, less than two hundred years ago, they were sunk in feudal stagnation and sent them plunging into the most frenzied capitalism, into aggressive imperialism and dangerous adventures for economic and territorial expansion. But the significant thing is that all the bold economic experiments into which Japan threw itself so avidly were nothing but doomed and desperate attempts to break its age-old siege of hunger.

On four large volcanic islands surrounded by a cloud of 4,000 tiny islets, in a total area of barely 150,000 square miles, the Japanese people have lived for countless generations. In the sixth century China extended its cultural influence across Korea and into these semibarbarian islands, implanting Buddhism, and the basic pattern of Chinese civilization. While accepting the benefits of this cultural influence, Japan soon freed itself from it by taking advantage of the decadence of China at the end of the T'ang Dynasty. Then began a long period of isolation.

Hermetically sealed in its island territory, Japan developed a characteristic type of agrarian feudalism. For seven centuries, in the name of an Emperor descended from God Himself, the daimyos, or great feudal lords, ruled with a rod of iron. As representatives of the Emperor they owned both the land and the people—the soil to be cultivated and the peasants to wring the necessary subsistence from it. Each feudal state was a closed world, with its army to keep order and enforce the will of the daimyos, and its serfs permanently attached to the land. Each estate was a sealed compartment, an economic autarchy, depending on its own serfs for the whole of its needs.

Since three quarters of Japan is excessively mountainous, only the easily farmed plains areas, which make up about a quarter of the national territory, were occupied.[60] Dietary essentials were obtained by the intensive cultivation of rice in the river valleys and coastal plains and by fishing, an activity that had been characteristic of the Japanese from the earliest times. Rice was always the basic food; in fact, rice was so basic an element that for a long time it was used as money. Even today, sacrificial offerings of rice to the gods are an indispensable part of all traditional rites and religious ceremonies.

On their diet of rice, supplemented by a little oats, sorghum, millet, and fish, the Japanese people were able to maintain a relatively balanced diet in normal times. It was a meager regime but without obvious deficiencies. However, let some unforeseen eventuality—abnormal rainfall, earthquake, or civil war—reduce the harvest of one of these feudal domains, and the closed compartment would immediately be drained of food. The result was famine, of the spasmodic type so greatly aggravated by lack of trade and communication.

As in the closed aquarium of China, life in this aquarium had to be rigidly regulated. But many of the moral principles of the Chinese proved inappropriate to local conditions in Japan. Consequently, a new and different moral code had to be created—one which anticipated and went beyond Malthus in its determination to limit, by all possible means, the growth of the population. The leaders of the nation were afraid that an increase beyond certain limits in the number of inhabitants would inevitably lead either to a change in the economic system or to forced emigration, two dangers that the shoguns, or military chiefs, were anxious to avoid. The daimyos were living quite comfortably in their fine medieval castles. They were amply protected by their armies of samurais and had a sufficient number of vassals to work their lands and pay them a fat tribute. They saw no reason, therefore, to let the plebeians become too numerous. Growing hunger might lead to growing restlessness, and the tumult and the shouting might even shake those high seigniorial walls. The Japanese policy of population restriction was fundamentally a result of the desire on the part of the feudal lords to preserve the existing setup—the comfort and privilege of 260 individuals based on the slavery of 26 million.

In spite of the high fertility of the people, it was possible by rigid control and by a shockingly high death rate—principally due to periodic famines, internal wars, and epidemics—to keep the Japanese population practically static for four centuries. Among the measures recommended—and widely practiced—from the fifteenth to the nineteenth century were: abortion, infanticide (especially of female children), the abandonment to death of aged parents, and the application of the death penalty for almost any crime. A Japanese writer asserts that during this epoch the people thought no more of doing away with extra children than of thinning out a row of beans. In some provinces two out of every five babies were killed, and in others, all beyond three per family. In Hyuga province, the first-born alone escaped. It was by such wholesale slaughter that the Japanese feudal regime kept its power stable and avoided the universal starvation that was always just around the corner. For two centuries, from the middle 1600's to the middle 1800's, the population fluctuated between 25 million and 27 million.

Such was the social and economic organization of Japan,

isolated from the world in a bitter struggle for subsistence, when one memorable morning in June 1853 Commodore Perry of the United States Navy breached the inviolable Imperial waters by forcing entrance into Uraga Bay. He carried a letter from the United States government requesting the opening of Japanese ports and negotiation of a commercial treaty. These "requests" were accompanied by persuasive arguments in the form of 10 warships armed with excellent cannon and carrying 2,000 fully equipped soldiers. The Japanese recognized the reasonableness of the requests, and on February 13, 1854, signed a treaty that for the first time opened their ports to the Occident—to Western technique and to Western business appetite. Soon similar treaties were signed with England, France, Russia, and Holland, and Western ideas began to invade Japan.

As a result of their first contacts with the industrial civilization of the Occident, the Japanese discovered that there were less inhuman means of escaping the pressure of hunger than the mass assassination of their newborn children and aged parents. The problem might rather be solved by the application of Western technical efficiency. This discovery aroused such enthusiasm in the Japanese that they now thought of little else, and they rushed to take advantage of these new methods regardless of cost.

What followed was the concentration of the will of a whole hungry people on one objective: obtaining food. This polarization, according to P. A. Sorokin, absorbs the individual so completely in a frenzy of activity that he is no longer sensible of sacrifice or fatigue.[61] The Japanese people adopted Western methods of fighting hunger so quickly and so thoroughly that just six years after the coming of the white men, in 1860, a revolution broke out that abolished feudalism and set up the economic principles and technical methods of the West.

With the death of the old Emperor Komei in 1867,

Japanese feudalism came to an end; and with the accession of the young Emperor Mutsuhito, the Meiji Era, that was to create modern Japan, began. The first step toward modernization was agrarian reform, which involved the division of the daimyo holdings among the masses of peasants and the introduction of scientific agriculture. Although it was asserted at the time that not an inch of Japanese soil that could be cultivated was left, the tilled area has been noticeably increased since then. A century of rational agrarian policy increased the area of cultivated land by about one third, and it was estimated that another 3.7 million acres might still be brought under cultivation.

[The splitting up of the feudal domains led to an extreme fragmentation of agricultural property. Before World War II, less than 25 percent of the farms in Japan were larger than two and a half acres. Despite this, however, the great majority of rural people continued to farm soil that did not belong to them. In 1935, according to the International Labor Organization, nearly three quarters of all Japanese farmers were tenants or hired workers. But even though they were working parcels of land too small to be economical, the Japanese peasants managed to obtain the most startling increase in production ever recorded.] In the feudal Japan of 1860 an acre planted to rice gave an average return of 1,430 pounds. This figure rose to 1,785 in 1890, 2,140 in 1910, and 2,500 in 1930—the production of the prescientific period was almost doubled.[62] By adequate selection of seed, and by rational irrigation and fertilization, the Japanese achieved an average productivity among the highest in the world. They were exceeded only by Spain, Italy, and Egypt. It must be remembered that the Japanese plant their rice in all sorts of soil, but these countries raise only limited amounts of rice and concentrate production in certain small areas of extremely fertile land.

It was also a striking victory for Japanese agricultural

technique that they accomplished this increased production without exhausting their soil. Western technicians state that Japan has reduced losses from erosion more effectively than any other agricultural country. Two American experts, G. V. Jacks and R. O. Whyte, go so far as to assert that, for all practical purposes, there is no such thing as erosion in Japan.[63]

In order to obtain these remarkable results, Japan put into practice all the agricultural techniques it could learn from the West and adapted them to the traditional processes of Chinese and Japanese farming. But though these people have always been under pressure to produce more food, they have never robbed and abused their soil or worked it out in a few years as has been done in various parts of the Occident. In spite of the tremendous pressure of population, great tracts of land have been set aside as insurance against erosion. Foreign specialists have wondered why Japan, with its shortage of food and particularly of proteins, never took up cattle-raising. It could have been done just as well there as in New Zealand, where the topography is very similar to that of the Japanese islands, by taking the same advantage of mountainous lands unsuitable for agriculture. The reason lies in Japan's wise policy of soil conservation, a technique that this country was the first in the world to adopt. Once the forests had been sacrificed to pasture, waters pouring off the slopes with nothing to stop them might well have done tremendous damage to the soil of agricultural areas. For this reason Japan still has a forest reserve of 5.2 million acres, an area almost as large as that given over to cultivation.

Fertilizers are used on a large scale and in the most varied combinations. Natural manures have been in use since primitive times. The farmers also employ all sorts of vegetable residues to enrich the soil: cereal straw and the leaves of leguminous plants, ashes from the kitchen, and, in keeping with the old Chinese custom, human waste itself. More modern methods involve fertilization with soybean cakes, which are extremely rich in nitrogenous materials, and with ground residues of cottonseed hulls, corn stalks, coco, and pig nuts. The extreme importance attached by the Japanese to the fertilization of their soils is shown by the fact that a significantly large part of the product of their fishing indus-try—45 percent—is sacrificed to the manufacture of fish meal for fertilizer.[64] For example, about half a million tons of fresh fish went into fertilizer in 1950.

There is no doubt that, long before World War II, these technical advances, in combination with parallel improvements in transportation, distribution, and internal commerce, put an end to the famines that periodically decimated the population and left the survivors with lifelong signs of physical degeneration. But there was almost no change in the chronic hunger of the people. The increase in production did not permit an increase in individual consumption, nor did it provide a more varied diet. Nothing was done to relieve the specific nutritional deficiencies, particularly the protein deficiency. To a certain extent, in fact, this desperate but controlled race to increase production, by doing away with certain sources of food supply, made the national diet more monotonous than ever. Great quantities of vegetable proteins from soybeans and animal proteins from fish were sacrificed to fertilize the soil and produce more rice.

How can one explain the fact that the techniques imported from the West and applied with such enthusiasm and discipline did not abolish starvation in Japan? Unfortunately, along with the techniques, the Japanese imported new problems that only served to make life more difficult. While Japan was absorbing this miraculous technique, which momentarily took the sharp edge off its hunger, it was finding out that to survive in this world, a country must do more than simply increase its food production enough to satisfy its own needs. It must also become sufficiently strong to resist the economic greed of rival countries. The lesson of China—divided up among foreign interests and forcibly prevented from achieving national unity and economic independence—served as an example to Japan. The country realized very early that it must be ready to fight to keep from becoming a colony of the Western powers and that the first need was to develop its human potential to the maximum. Japan too must become a power.

Whereupon the population policy of Japan was reversed. Severe laws were passed against abortion and infanticide. The birth rate rose sharply. (The increase from 25 per thousand in 1872 to 34 in 1926, a rise unique in history, can be explained in large part by the starvation regime to which the industrial populations were subjected during this period of imperialist industrial expansion.) At the same time the death rate fell as a result of the elimination of the great plagues of feudal times—the civil wars, famines, and epidemics. The Japanese population began to increase at an astonishing rate, as the following table shows:[65]

Year	Inhabitants
1875	34 million
1900	43 million
1915	52 million
1930	64 million
1945	78 million

Thus the iron circle of hunger, which seemed for a while to be loosening, closed about the nation more tightly than ever. With this tremendous human pressure on the soil, represented by the world's highest density of population in relation to cultivated area (more than 2,500 inhabitants per square mile), Japan, even after every possible expansion of area and improvement in technique, was unable to support itself by agriculture alone. That is the reason why Japan, from the

beginning of its modern period, has thrown itself unre-
servedly into large-scale industrialization. It was the only way
to make use of the human potential and to feed the growing
population.

Japanese industrialization came up against serious obstacles, particularly the lack of fuel and the domestic shortages of raw materials. The fact is, as G. T. Trewartha insists,
that "nature did not cut the resource pattern of Japan on a
scale befitting a great power."[66] In the face of these heavy
handicaps, and hampered by a late arrival on the scene, how
was Japan to compete successfully and find a market for its
products, so it could increase and stabilize its production?

The first thing necessary was a control of industrial policy
that would guarantee a rigorous economic balance. Consequently, the incipient Japanese capitalism diverged right at
the start from Western capitalism; it did not establish absolute control by interested individuals or groups but became a
capitalism directed and co-ordinated by the Imperial Power.
By means of this controlled capitalism, Japan attained such a
degree of efficiency that the Western peoples, amazed at the
prodigious capacity for expansion of its industry and commerce, sent technical delegations to study the country's
organizational methods.[67] These missions came to the unanimous conclusion that the secret of Japan's success in competition for the world's markets lay in the fact that it had
available, in unlimited quantities and at a negligible cost, one
of the most necessary raw materials—that is, the human crop
from which Japanese industry got its workers. The cheap
labor provided by a constant increase in population furnished
the basis for Japan's great economic expansion.

In order to meet foreign competition, Japanese industry
had to set up a labor system that was little short of slavery
and that resembled the semislavery of feudal times. Factory
workers were housed in ill-constructed barracks and fed
hardly more than a handful of inferior rice. Thus hunger was

responsible for the slavery of the Japanese people, while this slavery became in turn the solid foundation of Japanese industry. This is the thesis William Brown offered in his famous book announcing the "yellow peril."

The Western nations outdid themselves in furnishing the necessary tools. And in these most modern factories in the world, fitted out with machinery representing the last word in German, English, and American inventive genius, worked men and women still bound by feudal relations and by the traditional unquestioning obedience to their ancient masters —the daimyos and medieval barons. But the daimyos of the industrial era became monopoly capitalists making up the financial oligarchy of the country, the controlling figures of Japanese supercapitalism, organized in great cartels including almost all the economic activities of the nation. A handful of these oligarchies, literally supertrusts controlling the whole economic life of Japan, put into effect the great national plans for industrialization. Their names became familiar throughout the world: Mitsui, Mitsubishi, Sumitomo, Yasuda, and Furukawa.

These were the "big five" of Japanese industry. An examination of the various prewar activities of one of them, the Mitsubishi, shows how such groups exercised absolute control over the country's business. Its operations included coal, iron, steel, shipyards, airplane and automobile factories, oil, aluminum, electrical goods, chemicals, textiles, sugar, flour, and ocean shipping. In some of these fields, E. M. Hadley asserts, it accounted for one third to one half of the entire national production.[68] This example makes it abundantly clear how the Japanese combines could gain relatively more economic power than the large American trusts.

These new daimyos protected their interests by means that perpetuated the starvation and unemployment that furnished a cheap and abundant labor supply. In big industry, about 70 percent of the workers were women, subject to the most tyrannical working conditions. It must not be forgotten that the country had only recently emerged from feudalism. A woman had no rights, and was, as William Brown said so well, "the slave of a slave."

Thus the industry that was prescribed by the Western advisers (who were interested in selling their machines) as a panacea to save the people from the siege of hunger, preserved or even increased the existing starvation and created a new class of chronic starvelings—the industrial workers. As an example of how lack of adequate nourishment affected the workers' mortality rate, Tadasu Saiki recorded the following eloquent figures on a definitive experiment carried out by the Imperial Institute of Nutrition in Tokyo in 1935.[69] In a factory of that city where the death rate from tuberculosis was extremely high, the introduction of an adequate diet reduced the incidence of this disease some 78 percent.

The effect of this outburst of industrialization on the country's agrarian economy was also bad. Controlled capitalism, supported and protected by the state, followed a policy of assistance to industry by setting up tremendous taxes on agricultural production. Until the Sino-Japanese War, the peasant paid three times as much in taxes as the city dweller. It is true that the government gave the peasant technical aid and taught him the best methods of fertilization and irrigation, but it never gave him enough financial assistance. The industrialists fixed the prices of fertilizer and farm machinery as high as possible, while holding the price of farm products down to a point just high enough to keep the country's agriculture from going bankrupt.

The country's ruling financial clique—the *zaibatsu*—went on treating the rural population in accordance with the old Japanese saying that "farmers should neither live nor die." The farmer could not raise his living standard by increasing production because of progressive increases in taxes, rent, and the cost of agricultural machinery.

A good example of the cold inhumanity with which this industrial economy looked upon the Japanese farmer is the ruin of the natural silk industry following the 1929 stock-market crash in the United States. Up until then the greater part of Japanese natural silk production was absorbed by the United States, and about a million and a half Japanese families had a chance to improve their living standards by raising silkworms. But financial breakdown came, a poverty-stricken world could no longer afford to use large quantities of silk; economic artificial silk appeared on the world market, and Japan was forced to stand by and see her silk industry ruined.

Immediately, however, the state reacted. The raising of silkworms was thrown overboard along with the looms and an artificial-silk industry set up—even though this gave employment to no more than 200,000 families. More than 1 million families were sacrificed—but it was considered the only way to save this important branch of the national economy. A great many people died of hunger as a result of this desperate maneuver, but in a few years Japan became the world's number one producer of artificial silk.

When the industrial powers of the West woke up to the fact that Japan was flooding the world with a torrent of cheap and shoddy merchandise at prices with which it was impossible to compete, they reacted at once. The customs barriers that they erected were a deathblow to Japan's industrial and economic structure. And it must be said that Japan had at first tried to achieve an economic and social equilibrium by pacific means, through simple commercial maneuvers. The following words are those of William Vogt: "In all fairness to Japan it should be recognized that for decades she made vigorous efforts to secure more raw material and food by purely economic means. These were denied her finally largely through American tariffs. We were eager to sell to Japan but quite unwilling to buy her coolie-made goods."[70]

Blood and Hunger

In spite of Japan's vigorous industrialization, its farm population was still 50 percent of the total as late as 1930 and 40 percent as late as 1945. The misery in which the agricultural population was forced to live furnished the principal driving force of Japanese aggression. This depressed rural population made up the bulk of the Japanese army, which interpreted popular sentiment and represented a search for better living conditions for the people. It was a search for social justice, even though the method was force, military conquest, and expansion.

For many years, two distinct political tendencies struggled for supremacy in Japan. They were both nationalist and imperialist, but they preached different means to the same end. The party directed by the leaders of industry advocated simple economic expansion, without wars of conquest; the militarists, on the other hand, called for a solution to the economic problem by force of arms. The industrialists opposed open conquest because they feared the inevitable complications with the Western powers, with whom they had reached a certain diplomatic understanding through their interests in the great international cartels. This antiwar party also feared that the conquest of new territories would relieve population pressure in Japan and create new opportunities for the surplus population, thus forcing wages up and reducing industrial profits.

For these reasons, the political groups controlled by the Mitsui and Mitsubishi called simply for an extension of the sphere of Japanese economic influence over foreign territory, and their expansionist policy was disguised as a program of fraternal cooperation with the other countries of Asia. Taking advantage of the hostility felt by Asiatic peoples toward Western colonial exploitation, Japan coined the celebrated phrase, "the Greater Eastern Asia Co-prosperity Sphere."

This policy was not successful, primarily because the other nations of Asia did not trust Japan. It had a way of showing its claws from time to time in predatory raids on neighboring countries. In the second place, the Western powers opposed any such unification of interests as altogether too favorable to their formidable Oriental rival. In the face of this breakdown, and of the continued hunger and misery goading the Japanese people, the pro-war expansionists began to gain the upper hand in national politics. The influence of the army grew stronger and stronger, until the militarists were able to drag the country into the adventure with China and then into the great war against its two century-old enemies, Great Britain and the United States.

In order to carry out these dangerous adventures, the Japanese militarists saturated the country with propaganda to the effect that the farmer's hunger and the city worker's extreme poverty—all the miseries of the nation—were exclusively the result of the white man's undying hatred of the Japanese. It was the white man's hatred that would not let Japan get its head above water, that refused it raw materials for its industry, that denied it markets for its products and even prohibited it from relieving the congestion of its lands by emigration.

Japanese hatred and desire for revenge flourished in conditions of hunger as if in a culture medium and helped greatly in building up a stubborn and fanatical army. The prevailing mood was that the Western powers hated Japan and wanted to keep it in hunger and misery and that the army was justified in undertaking the violent conquest of National Liberation. In its desperation to break out of the iron circle of hunger, Japan adopted the barbarous methods of aggressive imperialism and threw overboard all respect for the rights of others. When it succeeded, with its first impetus, in humiliating the great powers of the West, it felt that it had merely got even for a long and systematic persecution. Analyzing those terrible war years, when Japanese fascism, expelling the Western overlords, won control of a great part of Asia, Frederick Schuman writes as follows: "That the youngest of the great powers should have taken the initiative in bringing the oldest of the great powers to the brink of ruin was perhaps the penalty which age must ever pay to youth when age teaches youth not virtue but vice."[71]

The peoples of the West must bear a large part of the blame for the fact that Japan fell into the hands of fascists and militarists and for the fact that by following the sickly star of aggressive imperialism it brought about the terrible evils of the war in the Far East. The error was not a question of race hatred, for that is something that really does not exist. The peoples of the West never exhibited a national sentiment of hatred for the Japanese or for any other people. In moments of suffering, on the contrary, Japan's sorrows always found a sympathetic echo in Western hearts. After the 1923 earthquake, which almost leveled Japan, the people of the United States hastened to organize an extensive relief campaign and sent enormous aid to the devastated country.

The sin of the Western peoples lay in letting interested imperialist groups block the just aspirations of the Japanese people for a better life and in letting the Japanese capitalists preserve a regime of medieval semislavery in a country that was, in terms of technical development, Westernized. If it had been possible for Japan to stabilize industry by selling products to the same areas of the East from which it got its raw materials, and if the Japanese government had established more humane living conditions for the peasants and factory workers, the birth rate would have fallen just as it fell in the 1920's, after the years of prosperity that World War I brought to Japan. And with internal economic equilibrium the aggressive sentiments would have cooled off; the war propaganda expressed in documents like the memorable writings of General Araki and the famous Tanaka memorial would no longer have found an echo in public opinion.

But nothing, or almost nothing, was done in this direction.

If anyone spoke of the misery of the Japanese people, or the chronic state of famine in which they lived, the leaders of the West replied that these people were not like other human beings. They had abnormal powers of resistance to suffering and had no objection to going hungry. But the hunger of the Japanese people, which seemed so remote and unimportant to the West, built up a permanent spirit of revolt and led the Japanese into one of the greatest bloodbaths of history, which was only stanched by recourse to atomic terror.

Imperialism, however, brought no improvement in Japanese living conditions either. When war was declared on China in 1937, the Japanese government took energetic measures to improve the nation's food supply by stimulating agriculture. They arranged for subsidies to farmers, for crop insurance, and special courts for agricultural disputes. These measures had little effect, and beginning with the attack on Pearl Harbor in December 1941, food production, instead of increasing, suffered a decline. It is true that the occupation of extensive new territories brought new food resources under Japanese control, but many of these lands were devastated to the point where it became a problem to feed the local inhabitants. The food needs of an ever-expanding army did not permit a liberal ration for the civilian population; and as the war went on and Japan suffered mounting reverses, the situation grew progressively worse. When Japan sued for peace, the average ration of the civil population was about 1,000 calories per person per day—absolutely a famine regime.

In an investigation carried out just after the end of the war, the Medical Division of the Bombing Survey revealed that in Kyoto, a city that had not even been bombed, the whole adult civilian population had lost an average of 10 pounds apiece; 65 percent of the population had lost 20 pounds. When Prince Fumimaro Konoye advised the Emperor Hirohito to surrender he suggested, according to Jerome B.

Cohen, that a Communist revolution might result from the desperate living conditions of the Japanese people.[72]

When they set up their military occupation of Japanese territory, the Allied powers faced a grave problem of food supply in a country of more than 70 million inhabitants with its food stocks practically exhausted. A careful study of the problem made it immediately clear that the situation was really serious at the moment and that it would certainly be worse the following year. They foresaw that the spring of 1946 would bring an acute food crisis and that the famine would be accompanied by inflation and, consequently, social unrest. The Supreme Command of the Allied Powers (SCAP), in order to meet this crisis and its unpredictable consequences, immediately put an emergency plan into effect, which included food rationing, the urgent importation of certain basic foods, and control of distribution.

Along with this emergency plan, a long-range plan was put into operation, based on a reconstruction of the national economy along democratic lines. Basic to this plan were agrarian reform and a new industrial policy. In the field of agriculture, SCAP acted with great foresight and obtained relatively promising results. Under its auspices the Japanese government passed the law of October 21, 1946, calling for the transfer of the ownership of land to those who actually cultivated it. In order to carry out this measure, the government was to buy up 70 to 80 percent of the land cultivated by tenants and resell it to them. The tenants were to pay for it over a period of twenty-four years by means of annual installments proportional to, and never more than a third of, their farm income. This project in agrarian economy on a grand scale was to involve nearly 5 million acres, or roughly a third of the nation's cultivated area. The plan was efficiently executed; three years after the occupation the government had already acquired about 80 percent of the lands to be distributed.

Measures to stimulate the farm cooperative movement were put into effect by legislative decree, and this too gave a certain impetus to agriculture, with the result that food production in Japan proper soon returned to prewar levels. But the loss of other sources of supply—Formosa, Korea, and Manchuria—which formerly contributed a quarter of the home islands' needs, resulted in a tremendous dietary deficit. Two years after the beginning of the Allied occupation, the daily individual ration had been increased to only 1,240 calories, in contrast with the minimum diet necessary for health of 2,160 calories. The estimated deficit for 1950 was 4 million metric tones of rice, that is, 24 percent of the Japanese people's total needs.

Undoubtedly, the food problem was greatly aggravated and the benefits of increased production canceled out by the tremendous increase in population that took place during the years of the Allied occupation. A SCAP report of 1949 stated that from 1945 to September 1949, the population of Japan proper increased by about 10 million, reaching the total figure of 82.5 million inhabitants.[73] This terrific population increase resulted, in part, from the repatriation of some 5 million Japanese who were scattered in various overseas areas at the end of the war. The balance, about 5.1 million, was an extraordinary natural increase resulting from the excess of births over deaths. This natural increase of 5 million individuals in four years had no precedent in the demographic history of Japan and can only be explained as the surge of biological recuperation that occurs in the vital history of societies following the shocks and losses of war, famine, or pestilence. In the various five-year census periods between 1920 and 1945, the increase of Japanese population was 3.6, 4.4, 4.6, 4.1, and 3.9 million persons respectively.[74] The figure of 5 million, registered in the postwar period of 1945-49, never once was reached, and I take this as a confirmation of my theory that hunger is a factor in regional overpopulation [and that the mechanism of teleonomy comes into play to defend a threatened people].

With such a volume of population, it was patently impossible to raise Japanese dietary standards by stimulating agricultural production alone. A SCAP report made it perfectly clear that food and raw materials sufficient to meet Japan's needs could only be obtained through foreign trade. Any hope of a solution, therefore, lay in recuperation of the country's industry, which would then serve as a basis for commerce abroad. In its early stages this industrial recovery was unsatisfactory. The intervention of the United States in this field was not nearly so happy as in the field of agricultural activity. The principal point of SCAP industrial policy was the destruction of the great combines and the liquidation of the gigantic trusts that had monopolized Japanese industry. Under the inspiration of this policy, the Japanese government passed special legislation aimed at "elimination of excessive concentration of economic power." This legislation, which proposed a housecleaning of the national economy, was opposed head-on by the tremendous underground forces of the interests it sought to control, and it never succeeded in breaking the power of the *zaibatsu*, the old financial oligarchy of Japan.

Although industry was cut loose from its totalitarian relationships, it was not reorganized on any other basis. The Allied intervention succeeded in demolishing the monstrous totalitarian economy that had kept the country in misery, but it was incapable of setting up any other type of industrial economy in its place. It is for this reason that Japanese theorists stated that the new industrial policy inspired by the Americans, by completely destroying the leadership, the best brains, and the technicians of the Japanese industrial organization, put an end to its creative potentialities. These apologists of the *zaibatsu* called the new economic policy one of "atomizing" Japanese industry, implying that Japanese industry was annihilated by a force as destructive as the atomic bomb.[75]

And until 1950 industry, in fact, showed little sign of recovery, remaining below 50 percent of the prewar level. The effects of industrial stagnation were disastrous for the economic equilibrium of the nation. One result is that Japanese foreign trade was less than 30 percent of its 1930-34 level. About 90 percent of Japanese imports came from the United States, but the United States took in return only about 10 percent of Japan's exports. Another result of the breakdown of Allied industrial policy was the terrible inflation, which brought about shocking increases in the cost of living. During the first two years of Allied occupation, the cost of living in Tokyo rose (according to the *Times Review of Industry*) 2,000 percent and food prices reached a point 65 times higher than in 1937. This serious economic situation kept the Japanese people in a state of chronic undernourishment and misery and constituted a critical impasse for the Allies.

[In 1950, however, with the coming of the Korean War, relations between Japan and the United States completely altered. At that point the United States realized that it could no longer continue to treat Japan as a conquered enemy but had to see it as a political ally in the face of the growing power of the new China. Japan skillfully profited from this situation and immediately began to re-equip its industry at an impressive rate that has today made it the third ranking industrial power in the world. Freed from the factor that choked its economy and from the American occupation (which ended in 1953), Japan began to develop industrially at a rate unprecedented in history, in some years achieving an increase of more than 13 percent in its gross national product.[76]

The real implementation of the principles of agrarian reform established by General MacArthur during the occupation and the re-establishment of a rigid policy of birth control, which basically served to restore old family and national traditions, greatly contributed to the improvement of the Japanese diet. It must be stressed that in Japan, as Roger Livet correctly points out, the policy of birth control "had no sociological or religious barrier to overcome; its success required only an appeal to long-standing popular traditions."[77] Sterilization and abortion had been legalized in 1948; in 1954 a vast program advocating the application of contraceptive methods began. These efforts, accompanied by a remarkable rise in living standards, resulted in a drop in the population growth rate from 2 percent in 1946 to 1 percent in 1960. Furthermore, economic expansion annually creates two million new jobs, a decisive contribution to national prosperity. An increase in farm production of 3.3 percent a year is another element in the economic upsurge.

Diet has improved notably: the average daily consumption of calories, 2,400 in 1968, may still be below the optimum, but it represents an immense increase over the figure of ten years before, which was only 1,800. Qualitatively, the diet is more varied and better balanced, including less grain and more animal products, mainly because of the large amount of sea food consumed (over 60 pounds a year, higher than the average for either Norway or Sweden). The consumption of meat and milk, which played practically no part in the classic Japanese diet, has further improved nutritional standards. The sea also annually yields half a million tons of seaweed for the nourishment of the Japanese. Intensive breeding of carefully selected cattle enables the Japanese farmer today to obtain an average annual milk production of 9,300 pounds per head, one of the highest in the world. Most of the stock are raised in special mountain pastures, where conditions are controlled for them, and also receive artificial feeds of high nutritional value.

Thus, through the relatively well-balanced development of

both agriculture and industry, Japan has freed itself from its perennial hunger. Certainly, some types of nutritional deficiencies and some islands of misery still exist, especially on the outskirts of such great cities as Tokyo, Osaka, and Yokohama, but the most dramatic aspects of hunger have been virtually stamped out. Though rice continues to be the basic food of the 100 million Japanese, it is no longer their sole, or practically sole, source of nourishment as in the past, for various other products greatly augment the quality of the national diet.]

5
Hunger
in the Dark Continent

One of the world's oldest authentic documents on hunger is the "Stele of Famine," which was found over a granite tomb at the first cataract of the Nile. This famous gravestone is inscribed with the report of a terrible famine that ravaged Egypt during the reign of Tosorthrus, some 2,000 years before the time of Abraham. The king's own lamentations have been preserved for us in hieroglyphics which read as follows:

> "I am mourning on my high throne for the vast misfortune, because the Nile flood in my time has not come for seven years. Light is the grain; there is lack of crops and of all kinds of food. Each man has become a thief to his neighbor. They desire to hasten and cannot walk. The child cries, and the youth creeps along, and the old man; their souls are bowed down, their legs are bent together and drag along the ground, and their hands rest in their bosoms. The counsel of the great ones of the court is but emptiness. Torn open are the chests of provisions, but instead of contents there is air. Everything is exhausted."[1]

Documentary evidence as to incursions of famine in the African continent has been accumulating since remote antiquity. And famine remains in power there to this day, ruling the destinies of the African peoples in one form or another. Sometimes it is the pitiless yoke of starvation, periodically taking possession of the semiarid steppe lands of the north,[2] and at others it is chronic hunger permanently oppressing the populations of equatorial forest and tropical savanna. Among the continents, only Asia has provided an equally broad stage for the drama of universal hunger.

No corner or scrap of land in Africa has escaped hunger. This is a continent of the starving, all of it. And in hunger and chronic malnutrition may be found one of the most decisive reasons for the backwardness of Africa, for the relative stagnation and lassitude of the greater part of its peoples.

Strategic Africa

Africa is the second largest continent in the world and one of the least heavily populated. Within 11.5 million square miles (four times the area of the United States) live only 180 million people.* Yet with this vast territory, making up the most compact of the continents, at its disposal, the scant population has been unable to escape the siege of hunger.

As happens in other hungry lands, there are in Africa a whole series of factors conspiring against the liberation of man from the pressure of his anguished search for food. Some are natural factors, resulting from the geographical conditions of the continent itself. Others are cultural, inseparable from the economic conditions of life of the African populations, most of whom are now subject to the pressure of [economic neocolonialism, following a long period of political subjection to the developed countries of Europe].

Nobody can say that Africa as a whole is the promised land, flowing with milk and honey like the land of Canaan. Far from it. At first sight the continent seems well adapted to human habitation, situated as it is between Europe and Asia, in the center of the world's great land mass. It possesses great expanses of level lands, a large part of them watered by the

* 250 million.

greatest rivers in the world—the Nile, the Congo, the Niger, the Zambezi—and it has great mineral wealth and a high potential hydraulic power.[3] But these advantages are offset by other features extremely unfavorable to man in his struggle with his environment.

Africa, with practically the whole of its great triangle of land falling within the Torrid Zone, is the most tropical of the continents. The African climate is, of course, not an absolute barrier to human occupation, especially with modern technical methods that permit the effective adjustment of man to tropical climates, but nevertheless it is a serious obstacle. The difficulty is not so much the direct action of the climate, asphyxiating and annihilating human beings, as the hasty generalizations of certain followers of climatic theories of civilization would have it.[4] Rather, it is an indirect effect of the types of soil and vegetation that such climates produce. More than half of the African continent is made up of two kinds of country quite unfavorable to human habitation —tropical desert and equatorial jungle.

The outstanding trait of the physical geography of Africa is a broad band of desert extending from 15° to 30° north latitude and stretching more than 1,000 miles from the Atlantic to the Red Sea. This is the Sahara, the great desert, which divides the continent into two distinct cultural worlds —White or Mediterranean Africa, and Black or equatorial Africa. In the desert, the great obstacle to the production of food is a permanent shortage of water. In the jungle, it is the relative poverty of the soil. As we have seen with reference to Latin America, equatorial soils are generally poor and are rapidly exhausted when submitted to continuous cultivation. On the savannas and steppes, which are transition zones between forest and desert, the soil is somewhat better, but the irregular and unpredictable rainfall is a serious hazard to productive agriculture. There remain only a few fertile and well-watered spots—oases—where production is undeniably high.

That is the somewhat deceptive picture of the physical geography of the dark continent which led Vogt to make the extreme statement: "Nearly all of Africa is marginal for agriculture."[5] I would not go so far. As I shall point out later, a great deal of African land has proved suitable for the cultivation of many different plants. But such cultivation depends upon special measures, without which it is doomed to failure.

Africa's unfavorable natural factors could have been overcome or at least minimized by rational human conduct. Adequate technical methods could have been supplemented by the experience of natives who have lived there since prehistoric times. But on the contrary, Africa's difficulties were greatly aggravated by the ill-conceived practices of European settlers. This continent was one of the greatest hunting grounds for colonial piracy, which committed all its usual exaggerations, illegalities, and crimes against defenseless populations.

The negative effect of European colonization on natural resources made itself felt through the whole series of social and economic pressures which constitute the very essence of colonial exploitation in all ages. The first of these was that mercantilism which, motivated by greed for quick and easy profits, has been the moving force of colonial adventure since earliest times. The colonist concentrates all his attention on easy profit, with complete indifference to the ecological balance of the regions to be exploited. Ever since the days of Rome, when the empire expanded into all Africa north of the Sahara and forced the region into a Mediterranean type of culture, the technique of colonization has practically always been one of systematic looting of natural riches. *Delenda est Carthago* is a good symbol, a watchword that expresses the European conqueror's code of conduct toward the people of other continents.

The Romans found fine fields of cereals and great olive orchards planted on the slopes of the Atlas Mountains and in the coastal valleys along the Mediterranean, but in a short time they transformed the region into desolate steppes and desert. The soil was overworked to produce the grain demanded by the mother country, and the Atlas forests were destroyed to supply wood for the Caesars' armadas and luxurious trimmings for Roman palaces. The result was the rapid downfall of Roman colonies in the north of Africa. It is true that the Romans built great aqueducts, dams, and pompous cities in North Africa. But with the economic decadence of Rome all this came tumbling down and was covered by the sand of the desert, which began to advance across a landscape denuded of its original coat of natural vegetation.[6]

As an example of the destructive fury with which Europeans treat colonial wealth, E. F. Gauthier cites the case of the disappearance of elephants from the Atlas Mountains during the Roman occupation. It was here that Rome procured the elephants for its army, but by the end of the empire all the pachyderms were gone, "annihilated by the demands of the Roman ivory trade, and by the destructive fury characteristic of the European throughout the ages."[7]

Modern colonization in Africa also began under the flag of mercantilism. The first Europeans to reach the west coast of the Dark Continent in the fifteenth century had no other thought than profitable trade—how most easily to get hold of merchandise that could be negotiated for good prices in the various European countries. The Portuguese, pioneers of colonial expansion in the modern world, were soon to prove themselves the most capable of all peoples in putting down colonial roots in the tropics. But at first they merely established trading posts along the coasts for their overseas commerce and took no interest in occupying African territory. Here there comes into the story a geographical factor that cannot be ignored—the natural resistance of the African coast to penetration. A shore line largely lacking in natural ports and a continental tableland rising abruptly from the shore and difficult to scale make Africa the most impenetrable of the continents. It is even difficult to ascend the rivers, because successive falls and rapids make them unnavigable from the mouth upward.

Whether on account of this geographic barrier, or because of the dominant spirit of the epoch, the Portuguese, and after them the Spanish, French, English, and other peoples interested in economic expansion on other continents, were not concerned with Africa except as a supplier of merchandise. It soon became clear that the most profitable merchandise was the black himself, to be sold as a slave in other colonial countries. Consequently, the slave trade was established, which, according to Grenfell Price, was the principal cause of the failure of British colonization in the Antilles and the principal reason for the failure of all European colonization in Africa.[8] It is clear that even today, the suspiciousness of the native, and his unwillingness to collaborate with Europeans in the development of Africa, are results of the fear and distrust Western conduct has built up in the spirit of the African.

After the great European explorers of the last century opened up the continent, colonial exploitation was no longer limited to the slave trade and the purchase of ivory and spices through the coastal trading posts, but there was still no improvement in the treatment of the natives by the European colonizers. Penetrating and occupying the most fertile valleys, the whites systematically drove the blacks before them, forcing them up the slopes and to the cultivation of soils that were rapidly exhausted by erosion.

The establishment of plantation colonies, originated by the English and afterwards imitated by the other imperialist countries, had a grossly disturbing effect on the African nutritional economy. The plantation system is based on great landholdings, or latifundia, organized for the large-scale production of cash crops. It implies the destruction of natural wealth—regional fauna and flora—as well as the suppression of local subsistence agriculture. We have already seen how this system devastated entire populations and great expanses of land on the American continent, and here I merely wish to insist on its inhuman quality, so well brought out in the words of that great student of colonial questions, Paul Leroy-Beaulieu:

> The plantation colonies became regular factories, whose only purpose was the production of sugar, coffee, and other high-priced merchandise; subsistence agriculture vanished, and the land was exploited in season and out with only one product in view. There was in fact no colonial society. The absenteeism of the proprietors, the absence of a middle class, the oppression of a multitude of men who had no rights but were considered mere tools recruited for the traffic, all these anti-social factors gave European establishments in the tropics a sad and pitiful character, quite contrary to the generous principles of our civilization.[9]

In Africa, as a result of excessive stripping of the soil, the harmful dislocation of workers, and the stagnation of agriculture for food production, this system was disastrous to the population of various areas. The plantation system, and later the exploitation in mines and factories, created a new social class in Africa—the proletarians, uprooted from the soil, cut off from their tribal organizations, and living, as Gilles de Pelichy has pointed out, lives of intense misery.[10] Today two societies exist side by side in Africa. There is the traditional society organized in family groups, living by primitive agriculture, stock-raising, hunting and fishing, all within a certain ecological balance, and the society of agricultural and industrial wage-workers, who represent the lowest nutritional level of the continent and perhaps, according to F.A.O. experts, "the lowest in the world."[11] It is estimated that a fifth of the population of Africa has become a part of this black society on the way to proletarianization.

An idea of how European influence upset the African food

economy emerges most clearly through a regional analysis, taking into account the peculiarities of each of the great divisions that make up the mosaic of the African landscape. This analysis will give separate consideration to the two Africas—White Africa, lying to the north of the Tropic of Cancer, and Black Africa, to the south.

Famine in White Africa

White Africa, so called, includes the lowlands along the Mediterranean, the high steppes of the Atlas Mountains, and the immense Sahara Desert, where the only signs of life are the scattered oases lost in the tremendous desolation of rock and sand. This is the part of Africa, peopled by Semitic and Hamitic racial stocks, that has been longest known to the Western world. Politically it takes in Egypt, Tunisia, Algeria, Morocco, and Libya.

With the exception of Egypt, where nutritional conditions have always been precarious, this area typically affords a diet which, though not at all abundant, results in fewer and less grave deficiencies than occur in Black Africa. The most serious nutritional problem of the whole region is in Egypt. Although this country has 380,000 square miles of territory, it is practically all desert. The only usable land lies in the oasis of the Nile, which, including valley and delta, amounts to only 13,600 square miles. In this limited strip of fertile soil, irrigated by the Nile, are concentrated practically all of the country's estimated 19 million inhabitants.*

About 62 percent of these are the *fellahin*, Nile peasants living in the most absolute dependence on the products of their irrigated fields. For innumerable centuries the *fellahin* have cultivated these lands, whose harvest was contingent on

---

* 30 million inhabitants.

the periodic overflow of the Nile. The cultivation of cereals and other food plants in the valley of this fabulous river supported the splendor of ancient Egyptian civilization. With the vegetable products of their soil, supplemented by animal products acquired by trade with the stock-raising nomads of the neighboring steppes, the Egyptians managed a more or less balanced diet. It is true that they suffered from the irregularity of the floods—the mysterious and omnipotent will of the divine river. The Nile often failed to overflow and left the land thirsty and the whole region famished. According to an old Egyptian saying, "when the land is thirsty, the *fellah* is hungry." But aside from these calamitous periods of drought and of famine, the *fellah* was reasonably well fed; he had whole-grain cereals (wheat and barley), legumes, olive oil, and fruits.

English intervention in the economy of Egypt upset this precarious balance. Today, with the Nile harnessed by Western technique, the *fellah* has been freed from his periodic famines but in exchange has been condemned to a regime of chronic hunger. His diet is not only insufficient and monotonous but deficient in many nutritive essentials. The construction of the famous Aswan Dam in 1902 put an end to the dependence of the *fellah* on the floods of the Nile but marked the beginning of his dependence on a complex of British commercial interests that were to alter his way of life completely. The replacing of flood-time irrigation by year-round irrigation led to a sharp reduction in the fertility of the soil, which by and large ceased to receive the precious gift of mud, carried down periodically from the heart of Africa to revitalize the age-old farm lands of Egypt. The year-round cultivation made possible by the new irrigation methods also helped to hasten the progressive exhaustion of the soil.

The proletarianization of the rural population, combined with the elimination of famines and the beginning of chronic starvation, soon produced the amazing population growth that has been registered in the first half of the twentieth century—from 8 million to 19 million inhabitants. Such a growth of population in so limited an area has tremendously increased the demographic pressure on the soil, which has reached an extreme limit of almost 2,000 individuals per square mile of cultivated land. Moreover, a large part of the irrigated land was reserved to produce cash export crops of interest to the British Empire—particularly cotton and sugar—which further aggravated the nutritional poverty of the *fellah.* "In such an overpopulated country, the reduction of food crops in the interest of industrial crops becomes a real danger," says Gauthier, one of the best-informed students of this region of Africa.[12]

[The immense effort to acquire modern armaments that international circumstances forced upon Egypt and the grave economic consequences of the Arab-Israeli wars in 1956 and 1967 have weighed heavily on the country and considerably aggravated its nutrition problems. On the other hand, the new Aswan Dam, completion of which will permit an increase of 25 percent in the amount of arable land, is cause for hope that Egypt will, in the years to come, be able to bring about some improvement in its food situation.]

The *fellah* today has no food surplus available for exchange with other zones and must satisfy all his biological necessities with a little wheat or rice alone. These he cultivates on tiny scraps of land which average only five feddan (one feddan is equal to 1.038 acres). Such a situation leads to an extremely inadequate diet; the most serious deficiency is the small amount of animal proteins—about 12 grams a day. Vitamin deficiencies also must necessarily be general in this area, as is demonstrated by the high pellagra rate. This disease, as we know, results from many different deficiencies and is characterized by many different symptoms.

The alimentation of the North African Berber population is much more varied and better balanced. It is made up of cereals—hard wheat, barley, and sorghum in the form of *galetas* or *couscous*—olive oil, milk, cheese, dates, and figs.[13] Meat consumption is very low, but the use of goat, sheep, and camel milk answers perfectly well the needs of the organism for high-grade animal proteins. Europeans have long been intrigued by the excellent physiques and remarkable resistance of these people. This is particularly true of the nomads who live along the edges of the desert, Berber peoples of characteristic Bedouin type whom Paul Harrison described as "the lean, indefatigable nomad, with the eyes of a falcon, but proud, hungry and indescribably dirty."[14]

The Arabs succeeded the Romans in this region and by overgrazing the land contributed greatly to the decline of native vegetation. But although this region has suffered the destructive impact of various civilizations, it retains, even today, a good reserve of sheep and goats which helps to hold up the quality of the regional diet. Unfortunately, the great drawback of the region is the inconstancy of its climate. Rainfall is extremely irregular, and the traditional Mediterranean type of diet, frugal and healthy, cannot always be maintained.

The food intake of this pastoral and agricultural people depends absolutely on the amount of rainfall. North Africa is the typical land of Biblical fat and lean years—times of plenty and times of need. Whenever the rains fail or grow scarce, most of the fields wilt, and the stock begins to die of hunger and disease. So far, it has been impossible to save the local population from the recurring famines that follow periods of drought. It is mostly the natives, subsistence farmers, and stock-raisers of the steppe regions who suffer the brunt of these climatic shocks. The European population, estimated at about 2 million, is concentrated along the more humid coast and makes greater use of irrigation. For this reason they are better able to defend themselves, even without their additional economic advantage of superior buying power, which makes it possible for them to pay extortionate prices for imported food during difficult periods. Meanwhile, the improvident native populations, saturated with Mohammedan fatalism, are forced into extreme poverty and want. They have no recourse but to sell their lands, abandon their communities, and emigrate to the cities of the littoral, where they swell such terrible African slums as the notorious eastern section of Algiers, the Casbah.

Periodic famines, then, are a serious cause of social and economic disintegration in the region, leading to the progressive disappearance of small property and the growth of a rebellious and unemployed urban proletariat. Jacques Nouvel, in his interesting study of famines in Morocco, showed that the principal social victims of the catastrophe are the small farmer and cattle-raiser:

> When his reserves are used up, the small proprietor is forced to sell his land. The rich farmer with grain in his silo, as well as the city merchant with cash resources, hasten to buy up such land. In keeping with the ancient custom of the country, they buy on installments, and the result is that they hardly ever finish paying the amount stipulated or the agreed-upon quantity of grain. Or when they do pay, it is after so many delays that the grain or money has already lost its value. So it is that the "big fellows" gobble up the crumbs, the holdings of the "little fellows."[15]

This monopolizing of the land by capitalists and bankers had reached such a point that the Moroccan government, in 1945, was moved to pass a law making family property, fixed at a maximum of five hectares (about 12.3 acres), inalienable except on express official authorization. Students of the social problem in this area, however, say that this legal provision completely failed to prevent abuses, and that through its loopholes small landholders continued to be robbed of the scraps of land that represented their only means of subsistence. This increasing movement of the land from the hands of the native into those of the European explains why in Algeria before independence, although of its 7 million inhabitants only 1 million were Europeans, a third of the cultivated area (about 12,350,000 acres) belonged to the latter.

The Colonial Impact on Black Africa

From the southern edge of the Sahara to the Cape of Good Hope extends so-called Black Africa, where the Negroid populations of the continent vegetate. There are the Negroes proper, Sudanese and Bantu, and the Negrillos, the Hottentots and the Bushmen. In this immense area covered by the most varied types of vegetation, as against a native population of more than 100 million* there are only 3 million Europeans, two thirds of whom† are concentrated in the subtropical country of South Africa. In the humid and tropical equatorial belt, which constitutes the real heartland of Africa, the white man is a rarity, an exotic touch in the primitive landscape. Even in the cities—created by the white man and representative of his Western culture—the majority of the population is black rather than European. Léopoldville [now Kinshasa] in the former Belgian Congo has 5,000 whites as compared to 114,000 blacks; and Brazzaville in the former French Congo has some 2,250 whites as against a native population of more than 50,000.[16]‡

The Europeans never attempted real colonization here; they never undertook to put down roots and populate these areas. They merely set up a skeleton administration designed

* 200 million as of 1971.
† 4 million and seven eighths.
‡ Kinshasa has over a million blacks; Brazzaville has a native population of 150,000.

to exploit the productive capacity of native labor. A handful of colonists lost in the immensity of the jungle handled all the administrative work of the colonial enterprises.

The nutritional situation in Black Africa varies enormously in the different geographic regions, in keeping with the natural resources of each zone and the life of the people in relation to them. To facilitate our study, we can distinguish the following great natural regions of equatorial Africa: the tropical rain forest, the savanna region, the semiarid steppes, the desert and, finally, the subtropical regions of the South African plateau.

The broad belt of tropical rain forest extends on both sides of the equator. Next to the Amazon basin, it is the largest, thickest, and most impenetrable mass of vegetation in the world. It covers some 900,000 square miles, and half of it lies in the enormous basin of the Congo. Two sharply distinct racial groups live there: the Negrillos and the Bantus. The Negrillos, living in complete cultural isolation, occupy the practically impenetrable depths of the jungle between 6° north and 6° south latitude. Their economic regime, limited to hunting, fishing in the rivers and lakes, and gathering wild plants, is completely primitive. As a result of the lack of organized agriculture, their alimentation is extremely precarious. It is both insufficient and incomplete—quantitatively deficient in calories and qualitatively lacking in proteins, mineral salts, and vitamins. Hunting and fishing alone do not provide these groups with nearly enough animal proteins; and as fruits are not so abundant in the equatorial forest as might be supposed, the supply of vitamins also leaves much to be desired. So it is no wonder that this human group shows the anthropological characteristics of extreme malnutrition. They are Pygmies; their height varies between 51 and 57 inches, and they show marked prognathism, achondroplasia, and other deformations of the bones.

So far as the blacks proper are concerned, two separate

situations must be considered. On the one hand there are the populations who live in their natural surroundings, scattered through the forest or grouped together in native villages, and on the other, the populations influenced by contact with the Europeans. These make up the black proletariat, who live in towns and draw wages from the white man. Of the two groups, the better fed is certainly the primitive society, which still keeps up its tribal organization and its original tradition of diversified farming.

By burning over small areas in the midst of the forest, the blacks open clearings and set up their subsistence agriculture. This means principally the cultivation of manioc or cassava, bananas and plantains, potatoes and yams, supplemented by cereals such as corn, millet, sorghum, and rice. On the basis of these crops, plus certain oleaginous fruits and other products of the forest, the black organizes his predominantly vegetarian diet. The staple food of this diet is manioc, which is grown on more than half of the land cultivated. The diet may not be overly abundant but qualitatively it is a long way from any specific defects that might lead to true states of deficiency. It is true that cattle are not raised in this area, both on account of the absence of pastures and because of serious regional infestation by insects that transmit epizootic diseases, particularly trypanosomes, and this suggests an inadequate supply of good proteins. But the black does what he can to make up for this shortage by turning to the virgin forest, where he hunts and eats everything indiscriminately, from hippopotamus and crocodile to rats, snakes, locusts, and ants. Although manioc, consumed as flour, is extremely short in vitamins and salts, this is not true when the African black uses it as a raw salad, eating the tender shoots of the plant along with the tubers. And good supplies of vitamins are furnished by sauces prepared from jungle plants and by the palm oil that plays such a large part in the nutrition of this area.

This primitive economy, because it tends to exhaust the soils that are used, comes nowhere near guaranteeing a regular and adequate supply of food, year in and year out. But as the forest is immense, and the population reaches no great demographic density, this precarious equilibrium held up satisfactorily until it was upset by the coming of the white colonist. In fact, investigators who have studied the nutritional conditions of these primitive groups are unanimous in stating that they show no clinical signs of dietary deficiency. One of the most striking indications of the superiority of this primitive diet is the magnificent condition of the teeth of these native populations. Dr. Weston A. Price, for example, reported that among six tribes using the primitive diet in Kenya, he could not find a single case of tooth decay nor a single deformation of the dental arch.[17] In many other tribes too, this investigator observed an almost complete absence of caries. Among thirteen primitive tribes studied, he found not a single irregularity in the position of the teeth. But when these same tribes were transplanted and put on a civilized diet, their teeth began to decay at once.

E. J. Bigwood and G. Trolli, who studied food conditions in the Belgian Congo, came to the conclusion that although the diet was deficient in energy materials, it showed no deficit of protective elements. They attributed this to the use of "fruits and green vegetables, which seem more familiar to the average inhabitant of the Congo than they do in European countries." And they went on to say that "other typically colonial foods, apparently rich in protective elements, are no doubt also effective in defending the Negro against symptoms of deficiencies. Such is the case with edible insects, from which it follows that it is wise not to try to change these food customs, which have been confirmed by favorable natural selection."[18]

Unfortunately, contact with the Europeans brought a change in these primitive customs that had serious consequences for the health of the natives. The first European innovation that worked to upset native food customs was the large-scale production of cash crops for export, such as cacao, coffee, sugar, and peanuts. We already know how the plantation system works, but this instance provides some concrete evidence of its evil effects. A good example is that of the former British colony of Gambia in West Africa, where the culture of food crops for local consumption was completely abandoned in order to concentrate on the production of peanuts. As a result of this monoculture, rice and most other foods had to be imported, and the nutritional situation of the colony could hardly have been worse. In an inquiry carried out in the area in 1939 by the Committee on Nutrition in the Colonial Empire, the experts came to the following conclusions:

> In general, the diet is excessive in carbohydrate and deficient in the protective food substances, animal fat and protein, mineral salts and vitamins. . . . The high infant mortality (369 per thousand), the marked prevalence of dental caries, and the frequent manifestations of vitamin A and D deficiency are clear evidence of dietary inadequacy. Beriberi is comparatively rare, but mild cases of neuritis are not uncommon. A characteristic is the physical and mental lethargy of the native farmer which is undoubtedly due, in part at least, to lack of proper food.[19]

Wherever the black's contact with the European was prolonged, one finds a notably deficient type of diet. In various parts of Africa, for instance, a children's disease is found, almost always fatal, known as kwashiorkor, or malignant malnutrition. This is a typical manifestation of inadequate diet, characterized by cessation of growth, edemas, fatty diarrhea, fatty degeneration of the liver, and sometimes bleaching of the skin and hair. Although the disease cannot be traced to any one deficiency, it certainly represents a shortage of many elements, including proteins of good quality. In the opinion of Dr. H. C. Trawell, who studied the disease for twenty years in Uganda and Kenya, this last deficiency is the prime factor.

It is not only by reducing regional food production that the money-crop system is harmful to the native. It also ruins his soils by inviting erosion. This is the case with the cacao plantations of the Gold Coast [now Ghana] and the peanut culture of Senegal. According to P. Gourou, in the 1940's the forests of the Gold Coast were on the way to extinction, and the soils of Senegal were being destroyed in the most shocking manner.

> The soils of northern Senegal, in the Louga region, are already ruined, and those of Cayor, in central Senegal, are going the same way. The damage done by peanuts, in fact, goes beyond the borders of Senegal. The fields are cultivated, in part, by seasonal agricultural workers who come from the Sudan to make a little cash money. But the result is that there are not enough hands, during the rainy season, for the work in the Sudan. The widespread culture of peanuts represents false riches, because it compromises the agricultural future of Senegal and unbalances the economy of the Sudan.[20]

Gourou was right in calling attention to the problem of the native worker as one of the aggravating factors in the chronic starvation of Equatorial Africa. This was in fact one of the most difficult problems of colonial policy and still has profound meaning for the future of the African territory. Colonial land exploitation, based on cheap and abundant labor, ran into insuperable difficulties in these remote regions. The black was hostile in general to activity of the sort required, and he was besides not healthy enough to do a satisfactory amount of work. In order to overcome these difficulties, a colonial structure was set up that forced the native into wage labor and increased his productive capacity to a certain extent.

The policy of increasing the black's labor capacity would

have been truly beneficial if it had been carried out scientifically and not as it was usually done. Some colonial administrators soon realized that a profitable exploitation of colonial territory required, first of all, the strengthening and fortifying of the native population, something that had been entirely neglected at first. In the Belgian Congo, for example, at the end of World War I, the native population had declined by about a fourth. The Governor General of the colony, M. Lippens, wrote in 1920 that "the Congo has seen its native population disappear with incredible rapidity, because we neglected salads in favor of rubber and ivory."

Since he needed the black worker as an essential cog in the colonial machine, the smart administrator undertook to defend and protect the black laborer. This is the policy picturesquely expressed by a French colonial governor as: "It's necessary, first of all, to make the Negro." That is, blacks had to be produced in sufficient quantity for the labor needs of the colony, and toward this end the same governor declared that it was absolutely essential to have a "full-belly policy."[21] But when it came to carrying out the policy, any good intentions which may have existed broke down. The native worker at the mine, mill, or plantation may have received a stomach full of rice, or corn, or manioc meal. But this sort of stuffing, rather than improving his overall state of nutrition, had the effect of greatly aggravating any specific deficiencies he may have had.

The European colonizer, when he offered the black a larger quantity of food than was normally available in the native village, was merely trying to attract workers and to provide them with a quantity of energy which he expected to get back in the form of productive work. What he was really providing was not better nutrition but merely an abundance of fuel. The same thing happened in Africa that happened in tropical America in connection with the feeding of black slaves. The slave owners, anxious to get as much production as possible, always took care to provide them with reasonable quantities of beans, corn, manioc, and bacon. It was a diet that kept the slaves in apparent good health and made possible the hard agricultural labor demanded of them. This policy of the plantation owners of Brazil and the Antilles was erroneously interpreted by a certain Brazilian sociologist unfamiliar with the complexities of such biological problems; he was led to the mistaken conclusion that slaves were one of the best-fed groups in the colonial population. This was never true. The slave's diet was bulky, but it was always bad.

The so-called full-belly policy greatly worsened the nutritional situation of the black in Equatorial Africa. Bigwood and Trolli observed that the native showed much more frequent signs of dietary deficiency—particularly beriberi in both its dry and its dropsical forms—after entering the service of the colonizers than he had before. Innumerable cases of rickets, beriberi, and scurvy were noted in the colony of Tanganyika. The nutritional situation was especially precarious in the mining districts, where fresh foods were practically unknown. In fact, pellagra was observed in Nigeria and the Gold Coast.

Two other practices aimed at securing native laborers do not speak at all well for colonial policy. One is to limit sharply the land available to the natives, and the other is to make taxes payable only in money. The first, or land reserve system, consists of restricting the native population to areas insufficient to provide for their needs, which forces them to leave the reservation in search of work. A good example of this system, found in the territory of Kenya, has been described by Pierre Gourou. In 1939, 3 million natives of this colony were restricted to reservations of less than 62,500 square miles, whereas 21,000 whites (1,600 of them owners) enjoyed an area of over 25,000. In Southern Rhodesia, 60,000 Europeans have the use of more than 115,500 square miles while 1.5 million blacks are crowded into an area of some 72,000. The compulsory payment of high taxes in cash also limits the black's freedom of choice and forces him into colonial wage labor.

If these methods did not produce the desired results, the colonizers in some areas went even further. They set up a feudal labor system that had many of the characteristics of slavery itself. As late as 1945, according to Gourou, the administration of the Ivory Coast recruited labor by military draft and the workers were "badly paid and badly treated."

In the savanna region, nutrition is generally a little better than in the forest. This is the area of coarse grasses and scattered trees, where in addition to unproductive laterite there are scattered strips of alluvial soil and highly productive swampland. The two well-defined seasons offer favorable conditions for the development of agriculture and make this area much better adapted to farming than the jungle. Thus the savanna, midway between hostile jungle and hostile desert—one too west and the other too dry—represents a kind of oasis within tropical Africa. In its enormous area of almost a million and a half square miles lives a population devoted primarily to agriculture and cattle-raising. An abundance of fruits and animal products reinforces the protective elements of the regional diet. In certain zones where cattle-raising is relatively intensive, the nutritional level is among the best in the world, comparing favorably with that of some of the Berbers of the Sahara. The pastoral Masai tribe studied by John Boyd-Orr and Patrick Gilks and certain pastoral peoples of the Somali Republic offer examples of this well-balanced diet, rich in animal proteins. These Somali tribes, who live in a steppe zone transitional between savanna and desert, use a diet based upon milk—camel, cow, sheep, or goat—which they consume at a rate of five quarts a day per person. Meat, ghee, dates, and rice round out a diet that makes the Somali gaunt but tall and gives him magnificent physical resistance. Though they do not eat fruit, which is exceptionally rare in this semiarid zone, the Somalis never show signs of vitamin deficiency.

But though the peoples of the Sahara border regions enjoy good physical health, those who live on the fringes of another African desert in the Southern Hemisphere, the Kalahari, do not. These are, in fact, one of the most decadent strains on the continent, the disappearing race of Bushmen. They are nomadic tribes living exclusively on game and the few wild products of the region. Everything about the Bushmen, beginning with their stunted growth—they average less than five feet in height—bears witness to their precarious health and living conditions.[22]

Climate, the Old Whipping Horse

Nutrition is generally bad in the Black African tropics. One should not jump to the conclusion, however, that climate alone, by making human labor difficult and by creating infertile, quickly exhausted soils, is the reason for the miserable food situation of the continent. There are human groups outside the Torrid Zone with diets just as bad, or even worse, than those of tropical, equatorial Africa. This is the case in South Africa and in the former British South African territories of Basutoland, Bechuanaland, and Swaziland.

Except for a little piece of the Transvaal, South Africa lies entirely below the Tropic of Capricorn; and since the average altitude is 3,000 feet, the country enjoys a typical temperate climate. Nevertheless, in this fine climate to which some 2 million Europeans have adapted themselves, there are still great masses of human beings who are undernourished and starving. These are not entirely natives. Many of them are of European origin—the notorious "poor whites" who constitute such a serious social problem for the country.

It cannot be denied that food conditions have definitely

improved in recent years, along with the rise in living standards provoked by World War II. This improvement is shown
by the fact that South Africa used to export considerable
quantities of corn, butter, and fruit to England, but since the
war these products have been used up within the country and
still more imported. Various investigations have found that
increased wages of both Europeans and natives, resulting
from industrialization and the prosperity brought by the war,
have resulted in what the *Economist* termed "a definite increase in food consumption."[23]

Improved living conditions, however, do not extend to the
marginal populations, who continue undernourished. In
1932, when a scientific mission of the Carnegie Foundation
studied the problem of the poor whites in South Africa, their
number was estimated at about 220,000 individuals, or more
than 10 percent of the total white population. According to
the experts' report, the principal reason for the decadence of
these white populations is their deficient diet: "Conditions of
poverty and ignorance lead to lack of food and to wrong diet.
This weakens the resistance of the poor white to disease,
reduces his working power, and so makes the problem more
acute."[24] I have no more current figures on the number of
poor whites, but I know that the Welfare Department is continuing its policy of economic aid to these groups throughout
all the provinces.

As to the Bantu or Kaffir populations, estimated at some 7
million individuals, the greater part are restricted to an extremely deficient diet. When the Dutch settlers first appeared
in this area, they found native tribes of strong, healthy
people who lived by raising cattle, growing corn, and hunting
wild game. But the natives' long years of struggle with the
invader, ending in loss of their lands and segregation of half
the population on reservations, disorganized the native economy completely. Today the diet is almost exclusively corn.

In Transkei, the Inspector of Schools, J. H. Dugard, reported that out of 11,000 children observed, 84 percent had only one meal a day; 14.9 percent had two; and no more than 0.6 percent received three meals a day. In all cases, the meals were made up of corn in one form or another. Drs. Joseph and Theodore Gillman have written that only 40 percent of the children received milk during even a small part of the year and 8 percent consumed green vegetables.[25] With this almost exclusive corn diet, it is no wonder that nutritional conditions among the Bantus are precarious and deficiency diseases frequent.

Nutritional conditions in the former British colonies of the extreme south are even worse than those in South Africa itself. In Basutoland [Lesotho, since 1966], for instance, where the climate is subtropical and the average altitude 7,000 feet, the agrarian population subsists on a diet very short of protective elements. The following statement is from the report of the Committee on Nutrition in the Colonial Empire: "A high carbohydrate diet and serious lack of protein, fat, and vitamins prevails throughout the whole country." With such a diet, the population is naturally in poor health and reveals typical deficiency diseases such as pellagra, scurvy, beriberi, and so on.

The worst part of it is that malnutrition and hunger have grown more acute. The Committee's official report said that:

> According to residents of long standing, the physique and health of the Basuto today is not what it used to be. Malnutrition is seen in every village, dispensary, school, and recruiting office. Mild scurvy and subscorbutic conditions are not infrequent; pellagra is becoming more and more frequent and lower resistance to disease increasingly apparent. It is becoming generally accepted, too, that the occurrence of leprosy is associated with faulty diet.

It is interesting that the population of Basutoland doubled between 1910 and 1950, making it one of the fastest growing populations in Africa. This gives further support to my theory that hunger is a factor leading to overpopulation.

The former protectorate of Bechuanaland [independent since 1966] is a pastoral area, devoted almost exclusively to the cattle-raising and dairy industries; but in spite of this, its nutritional situation is very precarious. What happens is that the products of these industries, instead of being consumed locally, are exported, principally to South Africa. As a result, populations of the territory are found to be living "on a very poorly balanced diet and suffering from a serious lack of vitamins, which may show itself in frank manifestations of nutritional disease or as a lack of resistance to other diseases."

As compared to the other two former British territories in South Africa, food conditions in Swaziland [which became independent in 1968] may be said to be a little less black. Children alone, and not adults, show signs of dietary deficiency. The absence of vitamin diseases in the mature population is believed by nutritionists to be due to the habitual use of certain native plants which upon analysis reveal a high vitamin potential.

However sketchy, this panorama of nutrition and food supply in the lands of Africa shows the Dark Continent to be beyond question one of the blackest spots on the world's map of malnutrition and hunger. There is hope, though, that this horrible blot may soon begin to lighten.

[Since World War II, of course, Africa has experienced many changes, especially in its political structure. For years, national liberation movements, motivated by hunger for both liberty and food, had carried on intensive political action aimed at freeing their peoples from the yoke of colonialism. Historical circumstances were unfavorable, however, and the great European powers firmly maintained their domination. It was World War II that began to break up these empires and allowed the liberation movements to gain ground against adversaries physically and economically drained by the slaughter of 1939-45. During the years immediately after the war, the African struggle for emancipation became steadily more determined. In 1955, the first conference of peoples involved in the struggle against colonialism met at Bandung with twenty-seven Asian and African countries participating. Only six African delegations represented sovereign nations, for most of the continent was still under European domination. This essentially political conference put a match to the powder. The war of emancipation spread and in the following ten years more than thirty countries achieved political independence. Most reached it during 1960-62, a period that, historically, is considered pivotal for Africa.

What happened afterwards? The flags of many new nations waved and the many revolutionary leaders who had battled stubbornly to gain sovereignty for their peoples were fired with enthusiasm. But on a deeper level, little change took place. Unfortunately, political independence was not followed by economic independence. Indeed, the economy of these countries is still based on the export of raw materials and colonial methods of exploiting resources. Europe began by subdividing Africa to prevent the existence of large territorial units that might have allowed true development. Today the economy of the African countries is characterized by neocolonialism, a system of nominal independence that actually maintains the old economic, social, cultural, and political structures. This is nothing but a process of recolonizing the former colonies, which naively believed they had reached independence but in reality won only the illusion of it. In the final analysis, each new state has been transformed into a "client" state, in strict vassalage to the ruling economic system. Africa has been pulverized into a multitude of small weak nations, individually defenseless before the power of the neocolonial octopus. These small nations, with neither strength nor experience, are not difficult to trap with a "lump of sugar" policy, the bait being loans and preferential prices for some of their exported products. Bilateral aid is so organized around these procedures that the client country is overwhelmingly bound to and dependent upon the market that protects its economy. The proper symbol for this tragedy is that of the disabled mountain climber desperately seeking help. A rope is thrown to him and the victim is hoisted from the depths of the abyss but, from then on, he is at the mercy of whoever is holding the rope at the top of the precipice. Suspended over nothingness he is obliged to dance at the end of the rope to whatever music is played him, so as not to displease his rescuer.

René Dumont states that Africa "has gotten off to a bad start";[26] there are Africans who would answer him that Africa has not gotten off to any start at all. Why? First, because of the relative inexperience of these young nations, struggling against countries much better versed in the game of world politics. Gabriel D'Arboussier points out that, with the exception of Ethiopia, one of the oldest nations in the world, almost all the nations in Africa today won their sovereignty only very recently: "Almost all these states are apprentice states."[27] They are still searching for the paths that will lead to true human development.

As a result, it is not surprising that Africa has yet made no dramatic progress in solving the complex problem of nourishing its population. The continent as a whole, in the view of the F.A.O., is in a critical situation because for years its agricultural production has not even managed to keep pace with its demographic expansion.[28] The daily average of calories remains below 2,000, a level considered insufficient, and many countries suffer severe deficiencies, especially of proteins. To be sure, the continent does not present a uniform picture; there are important variations from one region to another. If, to choose an extreme example, nothing had been done in the Portuguese colonies (or "overseas provinces"), at the other extreme, in Algeria, for example, praiseworthy efforts have been made in terms of drafting a project for agrarian reform and setting up a very active agricultural self-management program that is raising the nutritional level of the people, both quantitatively and qualitatively.

But I shall not go into the details of regional situations, since the overall picture remains very much as it has been described in the preceding pages. It is true that the politics of cooperation that replaced the politics of occupation by the European powers has to some degree given Africa an impetus toward economic and social development. But the movement is not always in the desired direction, that is, in the interest of the masses, who are still for the most part excluded from collective benefits. Even the advantages enjoyed by the eighteen African states associated with the countries of the European Economic Community are highly arguable. The African states know very well that the aid of the E.E.C. is not a disinterested gift, that it exerts constraints upon various aspects of their aspirations for economic independence. They also realize that by belonging to the European Common Market system they are dividing the Third World and—to use radical terminology—playing the game of neoimperialism against those Asian and Latin American countries whose economies are also dependent.

Undeniably, however, the governments of the majority of African countries are concerned with the nutritional problem of their populations. Several inquiries carried out in different regions have yielded statistical information on the most serious defects in the various diets. Roger Livet, in a recent work entitled *Géographie de l'alimentation,* has brought together important material on this question and presents detailed analyses of the nutritional situation in certain countries and regions of the continent.[29]

To show how far Africa remains from solving its nutritional problem, one need only cite what D'Arboussier wrote in 1967: "The portion of food production necessary for subsistence has been sacrificed and we have the paradox of a continent that could be almost self-sufficient but today depends on foreign imports for nearly 80 percent of its sustenance."[30] The figure is more eloquent than any arguments or speculations on the question could be.

In conclusion, it must be pointed out that the ruling elites of Africa generally seek to deny that hunger still persists after the triumph of their revolutions. Two explanations suggest themselves: first, it is possible that, during the new countries' honeymoon period with independence, patriotic enthusiasm gives the leaders the impression that all ills disappeared when the colonial power was crushed; second, it is also possible that these patriotic men realize the bleak truth, but hesitate to confess their relative inability to solve the most important problem of their new nations.

In time, the hunger that most official documents now ignore will come to the surface, as has happened in Latin America after a hundred years of political independence. In Africa it will reappear much more rapidly, for even now a host of young scientists, trained in the climate that followed independence, are striving to gain a deeper understanding of their fundamental problems and are beginning to realize that hunger is a constant in the constellation of national ills. This more profound knowledge of the true nature of Africa's difficulties will probably make possible new political and economic strategies, capable of ending hunger once and for all in this rich continent where resources have been squandered for so many years.]

6
Starving Europe

Montesquieu, in the middle of the eighteenth century, stated that "Europe is nothing but several nations in one." The celebrated French philosopher was too optimistic. Social and political events of the last two centuries have failed completely to bear out his theory of European political unity.

Far from presenting the unity and economic structure of a nation, Europe, on the contrary, reflects a world of conflicting interests. In the face of current reality, we would have to paraphrase Montesquieu somewhat as follows: "Europe is nothing but several worlds in one"—or two at least: the capitalist West and the Soviet East. For through the very heart of Europe, cutting across the area that the English geographer Halford Mackinder christened so expressively the "world heartland,"[1] passes the line of demarcation dividing the earth into two areas of different outlook and social aspirations. This division into two cultural worlds is the prime characteristic of Europe's economic and social life and constitutes the first obstacle to a study of the region as a unit.

Even before the so-called "iron curtain" separated Europe into two great watertight compartments, the continent was a meeting ground for several cultures: the Atlantic, the Slavic, and the Mediterranean.[2] These differing worlds marked European civilization, in varying shades and degrees, with their multiple influences. And, further complicating European life, no other region on earth has lived in such continuous and absolute economic dependence on the rest of the globe.

It is obviously difficult, therefore, to study hunger and malnutrition on a continental scale where there are such well-marked local differences and such paradoxical and confusing contrasts. But I shall try to overcome the obstacles and to sketch a portrait of the continent that will reveal the signature of hunger on the face of the land and on the faces of the people who inhabit this many-sided and turbulent European world.

First of all, in keeping with our geographic method, we must accurately establish the limits of the area to be studied. The United Nations is the best source of information on the region, and in accordance with its viewpoint, we take Europe to be the more westerly portion of the Eurasian land mass, including all countries lying west of the U.S.S.R.[3] In a strictly geographic sense, there is no question that part of the U.S.S.R. is European, though it is customary nowadays to consider the Soviet Union as a whole, economically separate from Europe.

Within the limits thus established, Europe has an area of some 2.2 million square miles (4 percent of the surface of the globe) and a population of about 420 million* (20 percent of the world's inhabitants). Against the varied scenery of this narrow stage, human beings have, from the earliest times, been acting out the interminable drama of hunger.

One climax in this drama was reached during the Middle Ages, when devastating famines swept tremendous areas of Europe. The feudal system, with its huge and unproductive landholdings, reached its peak during this period. The closed seigniorial domains were almost completely independent of each other, and whenever some accidental factor caused a

* 500 million.

decline in local food production, the result was general starvation.

The territory of Europe was at that time divided into huge estates averaging, according to Henri Pirenne, 1,600 acres, with most of the land unused and "covered with woods, marshes, and swamps."[4] There was no external market for local products and therefore no reason to expand production. The feudal lords produced only enough for the basic needs of their serfs—subsistence items for immediate consumption. This limited production was the cause of the successive scourges of hunger during that dark period of history, when the human masses of Europe alternated, as F. Cruschmann put it, between "a stupid and hopeless apathy, or an intense mystic fervor."[5] Their hunger, sublimated in fanaticism, found an outlet in bloody religious wars.

Between the tenth century and the Renaissance, according to the historians, some 400 widespread famines racked the countries of the continent and the British Isles.[6] Cornelius Walford, in his famous study of the world's famines, lists 22 major ones, with their tragic train of miseries, in thirteenth-century Europe alone.[7] During many of these periods of acute hunger, cannibalism was practiced and there was traffic in human flesh. In a study of the scarcity of food in medieval England, William Farr states that there were twenty great famines in that country during the eleventh and twelfth centuries.[8]

In their misery, the famished populations of Europe resorted to all sorts of wild herbs, roots, and the bark of trees and during the winter practiced a kind of collective hibernation analogous to that of certain animals. Whole villages would spend four or five months of the year in a state of torpor, "lying down most of the time, moving as little as possible and then only to satisfy the most indispensable necessities."[9] As a survival of the customs and conditions of the Middle Ages, this practice of inducing artificial sleep continued in some parts of czarist Russia (where it was known as *lyoschka*) into our own century.

The discoveries of the great navigators in the sixteenth century made available to Europe the food resources of other continents [as well as the precious metals upon which most European nations grew rich]. Famines became milder and less frequent but continued nevertheless to do tremendous damage. In 1586, England was shaken by one of the worst famines in its history, and in 1662, arould Blois, in France, peasants pastured in the fields like cattle, gnawing thistles and roots. During various hungry years of the seventeenth century, E. Parmalee Prentice has said, "men and women with their mouths full of grass were found lifeless by the roadsides of Europe, and children in the cemeteries sucked the bones of the dead." Prentice says with reason that food shortages did not cease with the Renaissance in Europe but continued "with decreasing frequency in England, nevertheless with much suffering, even into the eighteenth century; and in France the lack of food, following the short crops of 1788, was one of the moving causes of the great Revolution of 1789."[10]

The eighteenth century was rocked by recurrent famines, and in the second half it seemed as though all possible adverse factors conspired to keep the continent in a permanent state of hunger. The starvation that reigned between 1769 and 1789 was without question a decisive factor in the outbreak of the French Revolution. In his detailed study of the Revolution, H. A. Taine pointed to hunger and misery as its principal causes. His description of the times is often unusually vivid and expressive, as this passage shows:

> Two causes excited and maintained the universal agitation. The first of them was the permanent food crisis. Lasting for 10 years and aggravated by the violence provoked by hunger itself, it served to inflame popular feeling to the point of madness. . . .

> When a river runs level with its banks, only a small rise is needed
> to make it overflow. Such was the misery of the 18th century.
> The man of the people who lives with difficulty, even when bread
> is cheap, sees death staring him in the face when the price goes
> up. [11]

Taine then goes on to present evidence of the collective
misery of the nation. In Normandy a quarter of the population was reduced to begging. The Town Council of Rouen
wrote to the king that the people could not pay the high
price of bread and remarked, "What bread it is, even for
those able to buy!" The number of indigents tripled in Paris,
and misery stalked both city and countryside. The Bishop of
Chartres testified that "men were eating grass like sheep and
dying like flies." [12] According to testimony of the period, "as
the 14th of July approached the hunger grew worse. Each
bakery was besieged by a multitude. Bread was distributed
with extreme parsimony. And this bread was generally black,
bitter, and full of clay. It caused inflammation of the throat
and pains in the stomach." And Taine adds that in the long
and agitated queues at the doors of the bakeries, dark
thoughts fermented. This was the background of the great
explosion, when a famished people scaled the walls by the
thousands, led on by the hope of better days.

The victorious principles of the French Revolution improved the lot of the people of Europe but did not bring
about the end of hunger. The abolition of serfdom assured
personal liberty but the landholding system changed very
little except in France. [13] Feudalism continued in full force; in
fact, many of its characteristics have lasted practically to our
own day.

The survival of monopoly landholding guaranteed the survival of hunger on the European continent. Nevertheless, the
growth of industrial capitalism in the last century, along with
the development of transportation and trade, has made outright famine more and more unusual in time of peace. The

last great calamity of this sort in western Europe occurred in 1846 in Ireland; a million people starved to death, and still more fled the country to escape the same fate. The Irish famine, occurring in the industrial era, can only be explained as the result of landlordism. The land of Ireland was monopolized by a tiny number of English conquerors, while practically the whole of the Irish population was reduced to a sharecropper status. It was the agrarian problem in its most acute form that caused the catastrophe of 1846 in Ireland.

Although actual famine disappeared except in time of war, the industrial revolution, and the concentration of the urban proletariat which it effected, created tremendous new problems of food supply. The result was a regime of chronic hunger. Great masses of the population in extensive areas of Europe were subjected to a permanently deficient diet. Like the famines of the Middle Ages, this chronic hunger is closely related to the peculiar social structure of the times. The chronic hunger in many parts of Europe is of central importance in understanding much of the more recent history of the continent, especially its political history. Here lies the explanation of many of Europe's wars and social agitations.

Michelet correctly said that the history of France up to the great Revolution, "with its crescendo of miseries accumulated from century to century, will never be understood until a terrible book has been written—the History of Hunger." [14] And E. P. Prentice observed that if this book were written, a new light would be shed on the history not only of France but of the whole world—because in all ages, and in all parts of the world, men have suffered from hunger.

The full history of hunger in Europe is an exceptionally rich line of investigation that awaits detailed study and objective interpretation. But to write such a history is not the purpose of the present study. This is a Geopolitics of Hunger, and geopolitics is concerned with the present, not the past. It is the study of living reality, the analysis of facts as they are at the moment when we live and observe them. Such historical events as we have noted in passing are intended merely to bring us to a vantage point, for it is often impossible to understand the present without some knowledge of the past, and in such cases geopolitics must resort to the historical method as a complementary approach.

In order to understand the food situation in present-day Europe, we must know something of conditions there before World War II and of the changes that have taken place during and since the war.

Years of Decision, 1930-1939

In 1929 the German philosopher Oswald Spengler gave a lecture at Hamburg in which he called for the revival of Germany and the country's preparation for a role of world leadership. The Nazi coup of 1933, which permitted Hitler to seize power, fulfilled part of this demand. Spengler then published his lecture in expanded form with the expressive title, "Years of Decision" (*Jahre der Entscheidung*). So far as the title went, Spengler's words were really prophetic—during the decade that followed his famous lecture in Hamburg, Europe, and in fact the world, lived through some of the most decisive years of their history.

During this period, the lamentable nutritional conditions of the majority of the peoples of Europe became known not only to a limited circle of specialists but to the world at large. Until then, it had been generally assumed that the problem of food supply in Europe was difficult but that a high level of industrialization, together with large-scale importations, kept the population pretty well fed. The experts of the Special Food Committee set up by the League of Nations in 1935 demonstrated that the situation was in fact quite different. Their investigations made it clear that Europe was a great

hunger area, with dense groups of the population permanently subjected to diets that were both insufficient and
incomplete. Great Britain was importing 66⅔ percent of
her food, Belgium and Norway 50 percent, Holland 30 percent and Germany 25 percent, but with all their efforts, these
countries were not supplying a balanced diet to their concentrated populations.[15] It was also found that even in such
countries as Hungary, Rumania, Poland, and Yugoslavia,
where there was an excess of food energy available for
export, the diet of the peasants was precarious indeed, even
worse than in the Western nations with agricultural deficits.

John Boyd-Orr studied British alimentation in 1936 and
concluded that about 50 percent of the people suffered from
inadequate diets.[16] This half of the population included the
10 percent with the lowest incomes, whose diet was deficient
in all the essential elements of nutrition; 20 percent with
somewhat higher incomes, whose diet was sufficient in quantity but lacked various protective elements; and another 20
percent with certain specific deficiencies of vitamins or mineral salts. The sensational revelations of Boyd-Orr and his
collaborators, concerning a people presumed to enjoy a living
standard among the highest in Europe, made a profound
impression and were even received with a certain reserve. But
a new investigation carried out in 1936 and 1937 under the
direction of Sir William Crawford confirmed the figures of
Boyd-Orr in full.[17] The truth was that England suffered on a
large scale from various types of specific hunger, such as
rickets, [xerophthalmia,] and alimentary anemias.

The famous "Medical Testament" that followed was
brought out by a committee of doctors in an English county,
the Local Medical Committee of Cheshire. It is one of the
most eloquent and unanswerable documents ever to describe
the grave effects of malnutrition on the biological characteristics of the British people. The 600 regional doctors, in a
statement that had world repercussions, said they were

charged by law with the prevention and cure of disease, that they were able to accomplish a certain amount so far as the cure of certain ills was concerned but that they could do nothing or almost nothing toward preventing them—because most ill health was due to the use of a permanently defective diet:

> Of the first item, the Prevention ... of Sickness, it is not possible to say that the promise of the Bill has been fulfilled. Though to the sick man the doctor may point out the causes of his sickness, his present necessity is paramount and the moment is seldom opportune, even if not altogether too late, for any essay in preventive medicine. On that first and major count the Act has done nothing. Our daily work brings us repeatedly to the same point: "This illness results from a lifetime of wrong nutrition." The wrong nutrition begins before life begins. "Unfit to be a mother"—from undernutrition or nutritional anemia—is an occasional verdict upon a maternal death. For one such fatal case there are hundreds of less severity where the frail mothers and sickly infants survive. [18]

This impressive document reveals the alarming amount of tooth decay found among children and the high incidence of various degrees of rickets, as well as of other diseases indicating a state of chronic malnutrition.

The bad nutritional condition of the British people was due, in part, to the limited amount of arable land available and to the consequent dependence on large imports from abroad. But the fact is that even the available land was not adequately used. The deficiencies of the British system of land use were making the situation much worse than was necessary. This was demonstrated during World War II, when emergency measures were adopted that changed the food situation completely.

Serfdom had been abolished at the end of the Middle Ages and the peasants were given land. But in modern times, and especially in the nineteenth century, small holdings progressively lost ground to large estates, and the result was an extreme concentration of land in the hands of landlords. Thus the latifundia were created and with them the class of farm laborers—juridically free but economically bound in strict dependence to the noble landlords. Henri Sée had this to say on the English agrarian system:

> The nobles do not work their lands but rent them out to farmer contractors. These contractors differ from the general farmers of ancient France in that they are agricultural entrepreneurs; and from the peasant farmers because they direct large-scale activities, and by their culture and living standards belong to the bourgeoisie. The results of this economic revolution have been extremely serious. England grows less and less cereals, because plowland has been converted into pasture to make it easier to manage.[19]

Spain is another country where hangovers of agrarian feudalism were responsible for one of the lowest nutritional standards on the continent. Various indications of dietary deficiency have long been recognized among the people of Spain. Pellagra is endemic in Galicia and Asturias, while goiter is common in various parts of the country.[20] But the real state of dietary deficiency in Spain has been decribed in scientific terms only fairly recently.

During the Middle Ages Spain was better fed than the rest of Europe. This was a result of the culture of the Arabs, who occupied a large part of the country and set up, particularly in the irrigated lands of the south, an intensive, diversified agriculture based on fruits and vegetables. The gardens and orchards of Moslem Spain that made Andalusia famous in the tenth century had a highly favorable effect on the regional diet by making it rich in protective elements—mineral salts and vitamins. In his book, *La Péninsule Ibérique au Moyen Age,* Lévy Povençal refers to the striking variety of produce in these Mohammedan gardens: oranges, dates, pomegranates, almonds, and figs were grown, as well as other plants in magnificent profusion.[21] W. Gordon East, in his *Historical Geography of Europe,* goes so far as to make the flat statement that in the middle of the tenth century, the agriculture of Spain was without a rival in Europe.[22]

Nevertheless, under the influence of various factors over the years, this excellent agricultural and nutritional tradition has been largely lost. It is hard to understand why a country as large as Spain, with almost 200,000 square miles of surface and only 25 million inhabitants*—an exceptionally low density of population for western Europe—should now be unable to supply its people with a balanced diet. But all becomes clear when we remember that with the Reconquista, feudal land relations were re-established and remain practically intact.

Fairfield Osborn attempts to explain the decadence of Spanish agriculture by the exhaustion of the soil and by the erosion of steep hillsides long ravaged by the flocks of nomad shepherds. The organization of sheep-raisers known as the *Mesta* enjoyed considerable political influence during the fifteenth and sixteenth centuries, according to Osborn, and contributed greatly to the destruction of forests and the ruin of the soil.[23] It is my impression, however, that the feudal land system has been a much more important factor than erosion in creating the miserable dietary conditions of Spain. No other country of Europe has preserved the great estates on such a scale as Spain, and this situation is directly contrary to the biological and economic interests of the majority of the population. Until the fall of the monarchy in 1931, Spain had a typically medieval agrarian system, with the best arable lands monopolized by a handful of great landlords.

The American writer Leland Stowe, studying Spain on the spot, said in 1947:

---

* 32 million inhabitants.

Before the Republic—as is still true under the Franco-Phalangist counterrevolutionary regime, and will be true under any conceivable restored monarchy—about 50,000 large landowners held a monopoly on more than half of Spain's land, including all of its richest portions. Some estimates numbered the big land-monopolists at not many more than 20,000. Thus the Spanish aristocrats, constituting one five-hundredth or less of the total population of some 24 million people, owned about 51 percent of the land; and wealthy farmers another 35 percent. About 1 million small farmers, with parcels of some 12 acres, held another 11 percent of the land. This left 1.25 million peasants, with barely one acre apiece, and representing 2.2 percent. And it left more than 2 million Spanish laborers landless, and at the mercy of whatever the grandees and other propertied landlords chose to pay them for working from one third to two thirds of the year.[24]

When the Republic was established, the agrarian question was one of the most acute that the government had to face. In certain regions such as Andalusia and Estremadura, an archaic property system kept more than 60 percent of the arable land out of use, while the remaining 40 percent was inadequately cultivated. Salvador de Madariaga remarks that "in these regions there were a few landlords with enormous tracts of land, surrounded by a landless proletariat whose subsistence depended on the whims of the lord's overseers."[25]

The Republican government attempted to solve the agrarian problem but never succeeded in accomplishing its basic objectives. The whole world knows what happened. Leland Stowe describes it as follows:

Then the Spanish Republic launched a modest beginning at redistributing a few great estates—with moderation to a surprising degree and with fair remuneration to the owners. Even this gradual and restrained effort was more than Spanish dukes and grandees, with their medieval mentality and pronounced lack of social conscience, would tolerate. The great feudal landlords, the army, the monarchists, and the Church united, as throughout a long past, and joined the counterrevolution headed by Franco and backed by Hitler and Mussolini. They won again. As far as landed privileges are concerned, Franco's Spain is still the Spain of Ferdinand and Isabella.[26]

With the outbreak of the Spanish Civil War in 1936, the food shortage became much worse, and famine created macabre scenes of starvation in violent colors against the background of chronic hunger. During the last two years of the Civil War, Spain suffered from the same types of hunger as had Europe during World War I, with the deaths from starvation hardly fewer than those on the field of battle. Dr. Pedro y Pons observed the extreme nutritional poverty of the civil population in the so-called "Red zone," the part of Spain occupied by the Republicans. This specialist reported that a majority of the population was forced "to accept a desperately monotonous and restricted diet—an unvarying fare of lentils boiled without oil, plus—part of the time—a scrap of bread."[27] Because of the scarcity of more nutritious foods and the astronomically high prices, "for many months the majority of the population got no fish, meat, eggs, milk, or olive oil." This majority had to limit itself instead to bread, soup, and lentils, or to chick-peas and wild plants. Bands of the starving combed the fields for roots and leaves with which to delude their hunger. Thistles, pigweed, and poppies cooked in brine were lifesavers at such a time. Again Europe had gone back to harvesting the weeds of the fields, once called the "market garden of misery."

When a diet is so extremely deficient in many nutritional elements, various serious conditions appear. Pedro y Pons registers them with an abundance of detail: hunger edemas, deficiency dysentery, deficiency bone diseases, nutritional anemias, and above all the terrible increase of pellagra, which took lives right and left. According to Ed Simonart, some

30,000 cases of pellagra were registered in Madrid in a single year.[28]

The prewar situation in Italy was not much better than that of Spain. The fertile soils of the north were densely populated, while the soils in the south were poor and badly eroded. In order to support its people at even a modest standard, Italy was for a long time the largest wheat importer in continental Europe, with a gross annual importation of some 80 million bushels of cereals. The needs of the Fascist armament program gradually cut down this figure, to the point where only a fourth as much—20 million bushels—was imported in 1935. This reduction of wheat importations had disastrous effects on the health of the Italian people, workers, or farmers. As a factory worker in Rome told me in 1938, there was only one thing to do: take up their belts another notch. The Italian diet had always been defective, overloaded with cereals and deficient in animal proteins and certain vitamins. And in the decisive years of preparation for war, it became still more precarious.

The conquest of Ethiopia did little to improve the situation. High freight rates added so much to the cost of products shipped in from the celebrated Italian Colonial Empire that they were out of reach of the poorer classes. Pellagra had practically disappeared from Italy after World War I, but with the lack of meat and other protective foods, it flourished again on a considerable scale.

Nutritional conditions reached the lowest level in the south, in the region the Italians called the *mezzogiorno.* There subsistence was particularly difficult because of the agrarian crisis created by the problem of the great latifundia, on which the peasants or *cafoni* were kept in a state of semislavery. The plantations produced wheat, beet sugar, oranges, and other foods but all this was exported to the more socially advanced centers of the country, while the southern peasant was reduced to permanent starvation. The

Italian novelist Ignazio Silone described the misery of southern Italy in his book *Fontamara,* which dealt with the Fuccino region, in Marcia:

> The beets of Fuccino constitute the raw material for one of the most important sugar mills in Europe. But for the *cafoni* who raise them, sugar is a luxury that appears on the table only at Easter, for the ritual cake. Furthermore, practically all the wheat of Fuccino is sent to the city, where it is used to make white bread, paste, cookies, and even special foods for dogs and cats, while the *cafoni* who cultivate it are forced to live, practically all the year, on corn. What the *cafoni* get from Fuccino may be considered a true and legitimate hunger income—an income that permits them to keep on living only, but never lets them get ahead.[29]

Prince Torlogni of Silone's novel, like the good plantation owner he is, never leaves any more for the peasants than is strictly necessary to keep them alive and working his land. All the rest he sends to market and converts into hard cash, so that he can live luxuriously in the capital.

Another book that faithfully portrays the southern part of Italy is *Christ Stopped at Eboli,* by Carlo Levi. He describes the food situation in Lucania:

> The rich eat a little bread and cheese, a few olives and dry figs. The poor eat nothing but bread throughout the year, with a raw tomato smeared on it once in a great while, or a little garlic or green pepper.[30]

With such a diet it is no wonder that the children of the region look, as Levi describes them, "pale and thin, all of them, with great, dark, melancholy eyes in their waxen faces. Their swollen bellies are like drums, stretched and mounted on thin and twisted legs."

Elizabeth Wiskemann rightly judges that "the regions of Calabria, Lucania, and Apulia are the Achilles' heel of Italy and perhaps of Western Europe as a whole. Their problem is basically agrarian, and it is intricate because of endless diversity."[31] And this hunger area has the highest birth rate in all Italy—another vivid example of the theory of hunger as a factor in population growth.

Now let us take a population group living at the opposite end of the European continent—in the extreme north—and see how well they were being fed in the years before the war. Surveys made in Sweden indicate that nutritional conditions there were quite a bit better than any we have noted so far but were still far from perfect. Various sectors of the population showed signs of deficiency. Some 15 percent of the individuals studied, for instance, were not getting enough total calories; 27 percent revealed a deficiency of Vitamin A, 36 percent of Vitamin B-1, 43 percent of Vitamin B-2, and 14 percent of Vitamin C. A League of Nations survey of medical and social conditions carried out in 1929 and 1930 demonstrated a close relationship between the above dietary deficiencies and the incidence of certain diseases of the blood and digestive tract.[32]

The economic structure of the eastern European countries was predominantly agrarian. However, in spite of an excess food production that made many of them exporters and suppliers of grain to western Europe, their populations suffered from all kinds of nutritional deficiencies. In Rumania, which is considered one of the principal wheat granaries of Europe, pellagra had never been wiped out. According to observations made by Dr. W. R. Aykroyd in 1935, 5 to 6 percent of the inhabitants of Moldavian villages were attacked by pellagra every spring. A nutritional survey in this area indicated that the habitual diet was extremely deficient in proteins, in calcium, and in vitamins. In Hungary, "the basic foods were bread, dry beans, beets, potatoes, cabbage, and bacon. Even those with means rarely ate beef and mutton, and pork only occasionally. Hardly anybody consumed milk, eggs, fowls, butter, green vegetables, and fruits. The overall diet, therefore, was extremely deficient in all the groups of protective foods. The F.A.O. found that the diet of Polish peasants consisted almost exclusively of potatoes and rye, with obvious deficiencies in proteins, minerals, and vitamins."[33] Rickets and xerophthalmia had been endemic to Poland and Hungary since medieval times.

How can we explain this lack of balance in these essentially agricultural countries between the productive capacity of the land and the food needs of human groups? Various factors stood in the way of the desired balance: the use of outmoded farming methods; a lack of financial assistance to the farmer; and the frequent disproportion between the low prices the peasant got for the product of his labor and the high price he paid for the industrial products he needed. There is no doubt, however, that of all the factors that maintained hunger in central and eastern Europe until the war, the most important was the top-heavy system of landed property. Enormous latifundia, hangovers of feudal times, existed side by side with tiny farms too small for family subsistence. Take Poland, for example, with its high density of rural population representing, in 1935, 61 percent of the national total. On the one hand there was excessive subdivision of land among the peasants; and on the other, the Polish government tells us, monopolization of 20 percent of the arable land and 50 percent of the forests in the hands of a tiny group of great landholders.[34] In 1921, according to Raymond L. Buell, 65 percent of Polish farms were of less than 30 acres—dwarf farms, that is, incapable of sustaining a family. In addition, some 4 million peasants had no land at all. This shortage of land for the peasants was a result of the fact that about 43 percent of the country's total cultivated land was taken up by the huge estates, belonging to 19,000 great landowners.[35]

However, the most notable hangover of feudalism—the most shocking and scandalous land monopoly in Europe, worse even than Spain's—was to be found, until World War II, in Hungary. For many years the Hungarian feudal nobility was the only political force of any weight in the country and so was able to keep its privileges, handed down from feudal times, intact. Out of 60 million acres of arable land in Hungary, according to M. W. Fodor, some 20 million, or a third, were the property of 4,000 landed proprietors. Studying the plantation system of Italy, Silone gave us Prince Torlogni, owner of all the land and wealth of an entire region. But he was only a fictional character. Leland Stowe, studying the system of latifundia in Hungary, gave us a list of the twenty-five greatest landowners in the country, with real, not fictional, names. The list ran all the way from Prince Paul Esterhazy, who owned the biggest estate in the nation—some 300,000 acres—down to the Hungarian Catholic Culture Fund, which placed twenty-fifth with a modest 45,000 acres. Aristocrats and members of the royal family stood out in the list of biggest landholders, along with the orders and institutions of the Roman Catholic Church. That is one of the reasons why the nobility and the clergy were always stubbornly opposed to any and all agrarian reform.

The living conditions of rural workers in these feudal domains were naturally extremely low. An American journalist, Theodore Adrica of the *Cleveland Press,* traveling through the country in 1938, noted that their average wage was about twenty cents a day, "in season, when they could work."[36]

These examples are enough to give a general idea of the food situation in Europe during the years of ferment before the great world conflagration, when Germany was preparing to make Spengler's prophecies come true. Even with all its dietary deficiencies, with a round third of the population living on a chronic hunger diet, Europe could not survive without importing huge quantities of food: 9 million tons of bread cereals, great quantities of forage for the cattle, fertilizers to feed the worn-out soil, and fats for food and for industry. The dependence of Europe on the rest of the world, so far as foodstuffs were concerned, was very great.

With the rapid growth of its population, the European continent needed a progressive expansion of imports to balance its dietary needs. Generally speaking, however, the economic situation of the European countries was precarious, and such a course, for the benefit of the human potential, was not politically feasible. What happened in various countries, instead, was a progressive reduction in the volume of imports. William Vogt said of this forced decrease of European food importations:

> Reduction in imports does not mean that the gap was being filled from European farms. It resulted, to a large extent, from a deterioration of diet. Corn, rye, and potato flour were increasingly used in attempts to arrive at national and continental self-sufficiency. There was a considerable cut in the use of feed grains, which brought about a decrease in animal foods. This prewar trend was already preparing the way for the Spartan—or Asiatic—measures to which Europe resorted during the war.[37]

It was following the great crisis of 1929, which rocked the economic structure of the whole Western world, that the greatest reduction in food imports by the European countries took place. "In 1933, the wheat imported into Germany, France, Italy, Poland, Sweden, and Czechoslovakia was less than $1/7$ of what it had been in 1924-28," says Henri Claude in his study of the effects of this tremendous depression on the international markets.[38] Agriculture, which had been stimulated by World War I and supplied with important new technical resources, had registered enormous expansion in the period 1920-29, but suddenly found itself face to face with the terrible problem of surpluses and production that was in excess for lack of consumer markets. The world economic crisis, by creating mass unemployment, had reduced internal consumption. Export opportunities were also reduced, since each country, trying to save itself from bankruptcy, put all sorts of hindrances in the way of the importation of foreign products. Then came a wave of economic nationalism, which worsened the living conditions of the poorer populations everywhere. Protective tariffs almost paralyzed commercial activity. The world could find no way out of the economic asphyxiation into which it had fallen. Hunger and productive abundance existed side by side, with no one able to find a way of harmonizing the economic interests of the producers with the biological interests and needs of the consumers. It did no good to produce food because "the world was plunged into economic depression with unemployment so widespread that consumers had to cut down their purchases of food." [39] A World Economic Conference was called in London in 1933, but the only recommendation to receive unanimous approval was that additional restrictions on production must not be further delayed—this in spite of the demonstrated existence of universal hunger and malnutrition.

In this anguished atmosphere, with the peoples of Europe weakened and worn out with chronic hunger, Germany initiated its totalitarian food policy as a necessary step in preparation for war. The Germans had discovered the importance of food as a weapon of war during the first world conflict, when the hunger resulting from the blockade had proved the most pressing factor in their capitulation. They now planned to take advantage of the decisive years in such a way as to avoid a repetition of the collapse of 1918.

German production supplied four fifths of the country's food needs. The first objective of the Third Reich's food policy, therefore, was to make up the remaining fifth through internal production and thus to achieve self-sufficiency. Toward this end, German scientists used the most modern agricultural techniques to get a maximum return from the available land. With Ratzel's old problem of *Lebensraum* again the order of the day, the greatest possible productive capacity had to be obtained from the given space. And in fact, between 1933 and 1940, Germany did increase domestic production by 15 percent.

It was necessary, too, to anticipate the deterioration in the productive mechanism that war might bring about and consequently to plan a rigorous food rationing system and to build up the required reserve stocks. In planning the rationing so as not to affect the health of the population, Germany had at its disposal the whole pool of knowledge made public by the League of Nations, as well as the direct experience of its own experts.

The Third Reich set up special legislation for total mobilization of food resources as early as 1933. All farmers, food processors, wholesalers, and retailers were placed under the strict control of a special agency, the Reich Food State or *Reichsnaehrstand*, which was given the job of directing the nation's battle of subsistence. Technically, the line of defense was secured by setting up food substitute industries to make ersatz products and through the psychological education of the people, who were disciplined to war rationing six years before the first shot was fired.

To set up great food reserves, Germany proceeded to sign a series of commercial treaties with neighboring countries that could supply the country with foodstuffs, particularly those of eastern Europe. It was during this crucial period, when the country was building up reserves for total war, that Germany applied a double diplomacy of promises and threats and succeeded in exchanging manufactured products and industrial equipment for Hungarian, Polish, and Rumanian grain, Danish pork, and Dutch butter and cheese. By applying this suction-pump policy to food supplies in neighboring countries, the Third Reich, between 1933 and 1939, absorbed 40 percent of the exports of Bulgaria, Greece, Yugoslavia, Rumania, Hungary, and Turkey, whereas previously the figure had not gone beyond 15 percent. Immediately after the occupation of the Sudetenland, in accord with the Munich pact, the Germans "compelled the hapless Czechoslovak Government to 'sell' its grain reserves of 750,000 tons. No payment was ever made."[40] Boris Shub said, with justice, that "the prewar trade agreements, successful because the democracies failed to find a counter-weapon to totalitarian Germany's economic Blitzkrieg against the granaries of Middle Europe, won for the Reich the first great battle of the war."[41]

When the war came, Germany alone had a favorable food situation, while nutritional conditions in the other continental countries, normally inadequate, grew correspondingly worse. From then on the gap became progressively wider. Germany was supplied with the spoils and confiscations of war, while its enemies were systematically robbed of their food reserves.

Europe a Concentration Camp

As soon as Germany invaded the various countries of Europe, it applied its policy of "organized hunger." According to Boris Shub, the master plan of the Third Reich was intended "to organize the pattern of privation for the peoples of Europe, apportioning among them in accordance with its military and political objectives, the short rations which remained after Reich priorities were satisfied." Shub's impressive documentary study of these events, *Starvation over Europe*, provides much of the data that follow.[42]

Along with racial discrimination, Germany thus established nutritional discrimination by dividing the populations of Europe into the well-fed, the underfed, the hungry, and the starving. The Germans themselves were really the only well-fed group; all the others were to be sacrificed so that there should always be enough food for the master race. According to a statement by the Reich labor leader Robert Ley, in 1940, "a lower race needs less room, less clothing, less food" than the German race. The collaborating peoples, who were engaged in tasks of vital or military importance for German security, received a diet that permitted them to maintain a certain degree of labor efficiency. Enemy countries were held to a regime of intense privation, so as to remove all will to resist, while certain racial groups, such as the Jews, were simply starved to death.

The Reich's "plan of organized hunger" had a solid scientific base and well-defined objectives. Here was a powerful weapon of war, with high destructive power, which was to be used on the broadest scale and with maximum efficiency. And that is just what the Germans did, leaving aside all sentimentalism and manipulating food supplies in keeping with the particular aims of this species of the "geopolitics of hunger," as Karl Haushofer and his clique of German geopoliticians might well have called it.[43] "For the first time in history, food control is being used not to ensure equitable distribution of available supplies, but as a weapon of slow and certain starvation in the plan to exterminate," the Polish journalist Maria Babicka wrote in 1943.[44]

An indispensable step toward the production of mass hunger was the confiscation of all food reserves within reach of German troops, the famous *Reichswehr.* One after another, the countries of Europe were sacked by the Nazis. When the Germans invaded Poland toward the end of 1939, a quarter of the country, comprising the fertile western plains, was incorporated into the Reich as the Warteland Province. This region immediately became the great granary of Germany. During the first two years of the war, Nazi military authorities took from this area 480,000 tons of wheat, 150,000 of rye, 150,000 of barley, and 80,000 tons of oats. Some 700,000 hogs were also collected on the plains of

Warteland. From the rest of Poland the Reich confiscated, in 1940 alone, about 100,000 tons of grain, 100,000 hogs, 100 million eggs, and 20 million pounds of butter.

In April 1940 came Norway's turn. Before the war this country had one of the highest nutritional standards in Europe; its fishing industry was one of the best in the world and its diet was extremely rich in marine foods. Norway's merchant fleet was the third largest in the world, and when Germany invaded Poland, the Norwegians, fearing a prolonged blockade of their coasts, set about increasing imports and establishing great reserve stocks of food. Large quantities of cod and other dried fish, flour, potatoes, rice, coffee, tea, and chocolate were accumulated against possible shortages. With their domestic production—fish, milk products, eggs, vegetables, and fruits—the Norwegians seemed safe from any threat of hunger. But, as Else Margaret Roed related in her dramatic study of the Norwegian food situation, one day the Germans suddenly appeared, brutally invaded the country, and took possession of all these reserves. "They descended upon us like locusts and devoured everything in their way. Not only did we have three or four hundred thousand greedy Germans to feed in Norway; the German transports which brought them to us sailed back laden with Norwegian food and other goods."[45] From then on, according to the Norwegian journalist, all these products, one after another, gradually disappeared from the market: "First eggs, then meat, wheat flour, coffee, cream, milk, chocolate, tea, canned fish, fruits and vegetables, and finally cheese and fresh fish—all disappeared down German throats."

The Netherlands suffered the same fate. The Dutch government had also accumulated large food reserves to protect the welfare of the people in case of partial or even total blockade. But in May 1940 came something much worse—the enemy invasion—and the so-called "crisis reserves" went to join the vast German food stocks.[46] During only the first week of the occupation, the Germans in the Netherlands confiscated some 18 million pounds of butter, 90 percent of the country's total reserves.[47] In the first two years of war, a quarter of the Dutch herds disappeared and a large part of their pastures were converted into fields for growing oleaginous crops. During this same period, the number of hogs dropped from 1.8 million to 490,000 and the number of chickens from 33 million to only 3 million.

A basic feature of the German plan was to confiscate livestock and to discourage all stock-raising in the occupied countries, under the pretext that cattle consumed foodstuffs that should be used for humans. So the Nazis carried off all the available meat and left the bran for the enslaved populations. This is another example of the inhuman application of Germany's pretended scientific principles. According to such a theory, famished Europe could not be permitted the luxury of raising stock because the transformation of vegetable products into meat represents a waste of energy. It was necessary to follow the example of China. And so Germany planned the Sinification of Europe, that is, the corruption and degradation of European living standards to the level of the pre-revolution Chinese diet.

Denmark, Belgium, France all brought their tribute to build up the great German stockpile. Some $10 million worth of ham, butter, and eggs were confiscated from little Denmark. As they penetrated the territories of the U.S.S.R., the Germans seized and sent back to the Reich everything that remained on the scorched earth.

The satellite countries, Germany's allies, received a treatment but little better, so far as food was concerned, than that accorded the enemy. The price their powerful friend demanded for continued protection brought these countries to the verge of starvation. The biggest victims of this "protection" were Bulgaria, Rumania, and Hungary, which were forced to furnish foodstuffs to the Reich well beyond the limits of possible production. Shub wrote in 1943, "The magnitude of their forced contributions to German silos and cold storage warehouses may be measured in their falling bread and meat rations; their governments are constantly reminded by Berlin that their people still eat too much to please the Reich."[48]

In addition to monopolizing their production, the Reich made the food supply of these countries more difficult by demanding a labor supply for German factories and thus robbing them of their agricultural workers. This labor levy was organized under Gestapo pressure and accompanied by all sorts of tragedies. They were recalled with bitter realism by the Rumanian writer Virgil Georghiu in his book, *The Twenty-Fifth Hour.*

Such was Europe, then, stripped by the Nazi locusts, devastated by bombs, paralyzed by panic, undermined by the fifth column as well as by administrative disorganization and corruption; and there starvation felt very much at home. Practically all the populations of Europe began a kind of concentration-camp existence. All Europe was one vast and somber camp. And in fact, the rationed diets of the civil populations were little different from those in the true horror camps—Bergen-Belsen or Buchenwald. These were diets of less than 1,000 calories daily, made up almost exclusively of rotten potatoes and poor quality bread.

Such extreme food scarcity gave rise to the nefarious black market, where all those who had any resources left tried to supplement their misery rations and make them easier to bear. It is clear that these black markets usually functioned with the tacit approval or the connivance of the occupation troops and were supplied with products diverted from their own military stores. Born of the occupation, stimulated by the Gestapo itself,[49] the black market also represented a technique for the organized looting of the private economy of the peoples subjugated by Nazi tyranny.

Even with the black market going full blast, as it did in France, where it reached the point of robbing the Treasury of more than 50 percent of the public revenues, the people continued to suffer terrible privations and to exhibit, more and more clearly as the days went by, the unmistakable signs of starvation. Not long after the invasion, the rationed Polish diet dropped to 700 or 800 calories a day, and the Polish people were reduced, Babicka says, "to eating dogs, cats, and rats, and to making broth from the skin of dead animals and the bark of trees."[50]

It is evident that the physical condition of populations on such a diet would necessarily decline to pathetic levels. Adults showed enormous loss of weight (10 percent to 30 percent), hunger edema, complete prostration, and inability to work; and children suffered a veritable stagnation in their growth. A scientific mission of the F.A.O. visiting Poland soon after the war found that children were 3 percent to 6 percent shorter than children had been before 1930 and that they weighed, on the average, 10 to 14 percent less. Other manifestations of starvation in Nazi-occupied Poland were acute anemias, goiter, and widespread rickets. At the end of the war, 70 percent of the boys and 58 percent of the girls showed signs of rickets, in greater or lesser degree.[51]

One of the most serious results of this acute malnutrition was the loss of resistance to all sorts of infections. Tuberculosis took the bit in its teeth and, like one of the horsemen of the Apocalypse, set out to devastate the entire country. When the armed struggle ended, it was found that 80 percent of the Polish children reacted positively to the tuberculin test and that some 15,000 children were broadcasting germs from open tubercular lesions.

The picture of hunger in the Netherlands, especially in the last year of the war, the winter of 1944-45, was even blacker than that in Poland. The Allies had liberated southern Holland in the fall of 1944 and plunged on into Germany, leaving the northern part of Holland, where the great cities of Amsterdam, Rotterdam, and The Hague are located, still under the German yoke. During this period the country's railroads stopped running entirely and nutrition reached an all-time low. The average daily diet, which had been 1,200 calories the previous year, dropped to about 800. Consumption of animal protein fell practically to zero. Total proteins varied between 10 and 15 grams a day and consumption of fats dropped abruptly from 30 to 2½ grams.[52]

This meant black starvation, with generalized edemas, extreme debility, and hunger diarrheas. Of the classic vitamin deficiencies, conditions of Vitamin A shortage were most characteristic; on the other hand, decalcification of the bones and acute anemias were frequent. Hunger edemas were so shockingly widespread that when this part of the country was liberated the number of sufferers was in the neighborhood of 40,000 in Rotterdam, 30,000 in Amsterdam, 17,000 in The Hague, and 15,000 in Haarlem. And in many other cities, there were thousands of poor creatures with faces swollen and deformed by this degrading mark of hunger.[53]

Under these circumstances the death rate, which had risen to 9 percent in the first year of the war and to 17 percent in the second, went up to shocking heights. According to Max Nord, so many people died that, inasmuch as "timber for coffins was scarce, long rows of corpses accumulated in the churches."

The desperate state to which hunger had brought the populations of northern Holland during this period can be judged from the impressive photographic documents accompanying Max Nord's book *Amsterdam during the Winter of Hunger.* The introduction contains these tragic words:

> Our thoughts go back to the winter months of 1944-45 when the isolated part of western Holland was living in bitter desperation and in the greatest need and longing for food and fuel.
> Here we really present the pains, sorrows, and griefs of the

individuals who were so desperate, hungry, and frightened that they could not and did not care that there were millions of people in the world suffering in the same way. The pain caused by the death of one's own son does not lessen because millions of sons of others were killed at the same time. The paradox is that people are governed by minds and brains—they live by their hearts and souls. That is why the atomic bomb had to fall; that is why the Allied Forces marched into Germany and left us behind without food and fuel to get through a hard winter under the Germans.[54]

The words of Max Nord are as thoroughly true as his photographs are trustworthy. His statement that millions of individuals in other parts of the world were suffering the same tortures as the Dutch is also true. The same conditions of starvation, to a greater or lesser degree, reigned in Belgium, in Norway, in Denmark, in Italy, in Greece, and in other occupied countries, and everywhere there was demanded the same high and obdurate tribute in human lives.

To round out the grotesque portrait of hunger on the European continent there remains only to add a stroke which makes it still more tragic. This final touch is the situation of that human group which, in all the occupied countries, always suffered more from hunger than all the other oppressed groups: the Jews. Starvation was one of the Nazis' chosen means for the extermination of the Jewish people: "German scientists have, therefore, devised a plan whereby slow starvation shall eradicate the Jewish population of Europe, destroying in time all who do not perish by other means."

The harvest of death from this process was dozens of times more abundant than that from gas chambers and firing squads. The massacre of Jews during the war was carried out, above all, by the terrible weapon of hunger, by starvation and its associated plagues and epidemics. Through certain data which Boris Shub very appropriately calls "hunger statistics," one can get an idea of what happened to the Jewish people.

In the Warsaw Ghetto, during the year 1941, some 50,000 Jews perished, or a tenth of the total population—"decimation in the precise, literal sense of the word," Shub remarks.[55] In Bohemia-Moravia, 14 percent of the Jewish population perished in the same year. In Vienna, the Jewish death rate in 1942 was ten times the prewar figure. These statistics give an exact idea of the tragedy of the Jews in Nazified Europe.

While the entire continent was writhing in hunger, Werner Klatt points out that the German people succeeded in holding their own nutritional standards up to 90 percent of their prewar level until practically the end of the struggle.[56] Only in the last year did the German diet fall, first to 2,000 calories, and then to 1,600. And only during the last months of the fighting did it also become qualitatively deficient.

Such, in broad outline, were the nutritional conditions of Europe when World War II ended in 1945.

Hunger, Legacy of Naziism

Among the fundamental freedoms asserted by the Atlantic Charter, signed in 1941 when the United Nations were in common struggle against Naziism, was freedom of the peoples from hunger. It was Point Three, known as "Freedom from Want." In order that this third freedom might really have effect in the critical period that would follow the war, the United Nations began to prepare advance plans for an adequate food supply for the countries of Europe after their liberation. At Hot Springs, in 1943, President Roosevelt called a United Nations Conference on Problems of Food and Agriculture. Here the first seed was sown for the future international organization, the F.A.O., which was given the job of promoting a more adequate distribution of foodstuffs and of laying down the lines of a world nutritional policy.

In the same year the United Nations Relief and Rehabilitation Agency, the U.N.R.R.A., was created, with the aim of bringing aid to victims of the war, especially in the way of food. During the war the United States, through U.N.R.R.A. and lend-lease credits, furnished foreign countries some $60 billion worth of consumer goods, principally food. About 90 percent of this aid was destined for the countries of Europe.[57]

With the end of the conflict it became clear that conditions in Europe were tragically unfavorable to a rapid economic recovery. They quite supported, in fact, the black predictions made by John Boyd-Orr during the war:

> When the fighting forces of the Axis Powers have been completely defeated, the United Nations will be in control of the whole world. It will be a shattered world. In some countries the political, economic, and social structures will be almost completely destroyed. Even in the countries least affected by the war, they will be badly damaged. It is obvious that the world will need to be rebuilt. This affords an opportunity such as humanity has never had before of building a world in which the great advances of modern science can be applied to the development of an organization of human society which will be not only free from war, but such that mankind can rise to a level of well-being and culture higher than that dreamed of by social reformers of past ages.
>
> The opportunity will be there, but the immensity of the opportunity is equaled by the immensity of the task. The task cannot be accomplished unless the free nations which have united in the face of the common danger of Nazi world domination remain united to cooperate in building "the new and better world."
>
> It may not be easy to keep the nations united for peace aims after the last battle is won. In the flush of victory there will be a tendency for the great nations to think more of their own nationalist and imperial interests than of the contribution they can make to the common world cause.[58]

One of the toughest postwar problems was to provide food for a Europe that had been torn and broken by six years of fighting. Several factors had led to a marked decline in food production and now stood in the way of recovery. Particularly responsible for the decrease of food production in Europe were a decline in productivity of the soil, due to lack of manure and fertilizers; a reduction in cultivated area; a relative scarcity of agricultural labor; and a shortage of farm tools and machinery. Acting together, in most cases, these factors had reduced agricultural production 40 percent below the prewar level. This decrease had still graver effects on Europe's food balance because the population of the continent, in spite of heavy loss of life, had increased by some 20 percent during the war.

The war was most intensely destructive to the countries of eastern Europe, but it was in the west that the problem of food shortage proved most difficult to solve. This was because of the greater density of population in this more industrialized part of Europe and because the countries in the western part of the continent had always depended on food imports from the countries to the east. When the war was over, western Europe found itself in the gravest nutritional situation of its entire history. A few figures about basic foods will give a clear idea of the dietary poverty that desolated the region:

Comparing 1945-1946 production with that of 1934-38, Raymond Delprat found that cereals had declined 50 percent, meat 36 percent, butter 30 percent, other milk products 57 percent, eggs 37 percent, sugar 30 percent, and potatoes 25 percent.[59] Besides, it was soon clear that western Europe could not count on the countries of eastern Europe to make up even the most serious of these shortages—because the interests of the two great powers that had seized economic control of the world, the United States of America and the Union of Soviet Socialist Republics, were opposed to commercial intercourse between the two worlds of their respective influence.

The Western powers, recalling that their prewar trade with the eastern part of the continent represented only 15 percent of their total exports, underestimated its importance. They soon recognized, however, that the barrier to commercial exchange between the two Europes set up by the iron curtain was one of the most serious handicaps to the economic recovery of the continent.[60] This lack of exchange was one of the reasons why the dismal famine situation of western Europe in the postwar period improved so slowly.

Before the war, the countries of eastern Europe furnished great quantities of cereals and other food products to the west, in exchange for industrial products. During the war, Germany withdrew the bulk of these foodstuffs from the east to supply her troops. Once the war was over, however, the eastern countries set out to expand their internal consumption and to raise their standard of living. Moreover, the eastern countries took exception to the fact that the Marshall Plan, which had been put into operation in the countries of western Europe, prohibited the export to eastern Europe of products classified as strategic. In reprisal, they refused to sell their agricultural products to industrial Europe. The eastern countries held this clause in the Marshall Plan responsible for the paralysis of east-west trade.

These adverse factors created by the war were reinforced by a ruinous coincidence. The years following the peace, 1946 and 1947, brought serious weather disturbances, droughts and frosts, which damaged crops on an enormous scale. After the last battle had been won and in spite of the really great efforts of those authorities responsible for planning rehabilitation and reconstruction, all these pressures kept Europe in the grim embrace of hunger for a long time.

The postwar phenomenon of hunger had its peculiar aspects in each part of Europe, but it was in Germany that the problem was most serious and hardest to solve. At the time that the Supreme Headquarters of the Allied Expeditionary Force was established in conquered Germany, it was assumed that by reducing consumption to the essential minimum, the German population could be supplied from local food resources. This minimum was set at about 2,000 calories a day but the food authorities soon discovered that the country's food reserves were a long way from permitting such a nutritional level, and they were forced to cut the daily ration to 1,550 calories for the normal consumer. This restricted diet was at that time considered barely adequate to maintain health on an emergency basis, and for a period not exceeding six months. But economic contingencies forced the occupation authorities to hold the German diet to that or an even lower level for some three years after the end of the war.[61]

In the second year of occupation—1946—the situation grew worse instead of improving, and in the British and American zones the average ration fell to 1,000 calories daily. In 1947, it dropped to 800 calories. To make matters worse, this diet with its overall caloric deficiency, representing only a third of ordinary physiological needs, was made up almost exclusively of bread and potatoes. There was an extreme scarcity of other nutritional substances, so that the consumption of protective foods declined to levels that were very dangerous for the health of the people. Daily consumption of proteins fell to about 28 grams, of which only 5 were of animal origin; and consumption of fats was reduced to 5 grams, whereas 40 to 60 grams a day are necessary for normal health. Supplies of vitamins and mineral salts were also severely limited, and as a result, a great variety of deficiencies were observed in Germany during the postwar period.

The nutritional situation became so dramatically unsatisfactory that the German people began to grumble and to suspect that the Allies were starving them purposely, in a spirit of revenge and in accord with a plan to exterminate the German race. It was then the Germans' turn to suffer exactly the same privations they had imposed on other peoples during the war, and it was natural perhaps that they should make the same accusations against the Allies that had been made against them by the Jews, the Poles, the Yugoslavs, and other "inferior peoples" who had been subjected to the punishment of "organized hunger."

In September 1947, the Nutrition Committee of German Doctors submitted a memorandum on the dietary situation in Germany to the Second United Nations Conference on Food and Agriculture. They offered proof of the desperate food situation and the nutritional deficiencies of the people and made an incisive appeal to the world to put a stop to the total destruction of the German people by starvation. The document was not presented to the General Assembly of the Conference but to the Consultative Committee on Nutrition, to which I had the honor to belong, and in it I felt the same tone of revolt, anguish, and despair that one saw in the document prepared in 1943 by Boris Shub, in which he described the general starvation of the people of Europe under the domination of the German hordes. The statement of the Committee of German Doctors begins:

> The German medical profession appeals to the conscience of the world not to tolerate any longer the alarming decline of the German people's health. The majority of the German population is now living on a scale of rations amounting to not more than one third of the minimum of food recognized by international authorities. Even the heavy worker rations, though just sufficient to keep men alive, are insufficient for the work these men are expected to perform. This existing chronic undernourishment has already produced an advanced reduction of the physical substance and has not only extremely diminished the German's physical efficiency but has also adversely affected his intellectual powers and altered his emotional structure. A starving man is

deprived of initiative: he is irritable, hypercritical, and incapable both of constructive work and of discharging his public duties. The German medical profession raises a warning voice against the inevitable physiological consequences of chronic starvation, and the potential dangers not only to the people directly affected but also to the moral standards and the security of the rest of the world.[62]

Then follows a description of the various manifestations of hunger rampant in Germany: hunger edemas; debility and loss of weight, which in adults sometimes reached over 100 pounds; and other symptoms and signs of the rich gamut of the "hunger disease." The German doctors ended their document with the following words:

> We, the German physicians, feel ourselves in duty bound to point out to the whole world that the things happening here are the very opposite to the "education for democracy" promised to us; truly, it is the destruction of democracy's biological foundation. What we are now witnessing is the destruction of the spiritual and physical substance of a great nation and nobody may disclaim responsibility unless he does everything in his power to save and help.

Thus the German doctors endorsed the people's view that the Allies planned to exterminate the defeated enemy by "organized hunger." A study of the world economic situation during the dramatic years of 1945, 1946, and 1947, nevertheless, reveals that the Allies were not in the least interested in exterminating the German race. It appears, rather, that the short rations to which the German people were subjected during this postwar period were a natural consequence of the destructiveness of war and of the breakdown of world economy brought about by the war. Adequate food stocks were not to be found within Germany, although large-scale importations of foodstuffs from the United States, a country that had doubled its cereal production during the war years, could have set the level of food consumption safely above the hunger line. But it must be remembered that when the hostilities ended in Europe, there were other countries which had been allies rather than enemies of the United States, countries which had joined in the common fight for the liberation of Europe and whose nutritional conditions were much worse than Germany's.

The war-devastated populations of Belgium, the Netherlands, France, and other countries were starving to death. It was only right that these countries should have priority over Germany in receiving what aid in the form of food North America was able to send to Europe. And under these circumstances, not much was left over for Germany. As to the worsening of the nutritional situation in 1947, this can be explained as a direct consequence of the previous year's drought, which greatly reduced the harvests not only in Germany but in practically the whole of Europe.

It must be recognized, however, that if the Allies could do nothing at the start to combat the epidemic of hunger that the Germans let loose on the European continent, which ended by infecting their own territory, they might still have undertaken administrative measures that would have hastened the economic recuperation of Germany and short-ened the period of postwar nutritional poverty. The Allies did little or nothing in this sense. In fact, their administrative policy in Germany, instead of ameliorating the miserable dietary situation, contributed to aggravate and needlessly prolong it. Observing the political blunders and adminis-trative mistakes of the Allies in Germany, the American author, William Henry Chamberlain, remarked, "To the worst world war has succeeded the worst world peace."[63] Another American writer, the war correspondent Howard K. Smith, said without pulling punches that "the story of the Allied occupation of Germany is a long, grating, complex tragedy of errors, relieved only very occasionally by any act of construc-tive intelligence."[64]

Various of these errors had grim repercussions on the food situation of the Germans. The first mistake was the division of Germany into different occupation zones, functioning as closed economic compartments. In a continent that for many long years had suffered the cramping restrictions of over 2,000 miles of customs barriers, nothing could have been more harmful than to add several thousand more within Germany itself.[65] Moreover, the dividing line between East Germany, occupied by the Russians, and West Germany, occupied by the Western powers, immediately became a grave obstacle to the supply of the western part, accentuating still more its deficit of food production, as shown by the following facts.

Before the war, while agricultural production in the eastern part of the country provided a daily per capita average of 2,400 calories, production in the western part reached only 1,700. In order to make up this considerable dietary deficiency in the more industrialized zone of western Germany, the region to the east of the Oder contributed annually about a million tons of cereals, a half million tons of potatoes, and a quarter of a million tons of sugar. These alimentary reinforcements were totally cut off by the division of Germany for occupation purposes. Moreover, the occupation of western Germany as it was initially set up, in three strips of territory administered separately by the United States, Great Britain and France, made matters still worse since it blocked the free flow of products within an area of multiform economic structure. The zone that suffered most in this regard was the British, including the highly industrialized Ruhr Basin, since it was the most densely populated (about 23 million inhabitants) and had the least farm production. Jean Chardonnet reported that the food production of this area did not meet more than 40 percent of its needs and monthly importations of 100,000 tons were necessary to meet the minimum requirements of the population.[66]

Another serious political error of the Allies during the first years of occupation was the plan to dismantle German industry. This involved a drastic limitation of heavy industry, forcing the country to base its economy on light industry, agriculture, and export of raw materials. The attempt to "pastoralize" Germany, in keeping with the Morgenthau Plan, was aimed at the industrial disarmament of this warrior nation and the development of agricultural and peacetime activities. It called for a 50 percent reduction in German industrial production, at the same time setting aside 3 billion marks' worth of exportable goods to cover importations necessary to the life of the country.

It soon became clear that with such limitations on industrial production the German economy could not be balanced. The British were the first to feel the economic weight of maintaining their zone on such a highly distorted basis. Although 130 million pounds' worth of food had to be imported every year, the zone's reduced exportation of coal, caustic potash, and lumber brought in only 50 million. The difference of 80 million pounds had to be made up by the British government. In the American zone, while imports amounted to $50 million, exports did not reach $2 million. Such facts were decisive in producing a modification of the erroneous policy of the excessive limitation of industry in a country as predominantly industrial as Germany had always been.

The attitude of the Allied powers on agrarian policy also led to serious economic results. They refused to consider a healthful reform right at the beginning and only carried it out on the basis of too little too late.

The Russians, just as soon as the German troops had surrendered, set in motion a policy of land expropriation. They confiscated all properties of more than 250 acres, as well as those of Nazi leaders and war criminals. At that time more than a third of the properties in eastern Germany contained more than 250 acres, so the law had a broad effect. The lands of 7,000 great estates, and 3,300 farms belonging to war criminals, totaling 500,000 acres, were divided into small lots and redistributed by the land commissions. In this way 500,000 new small properties of from two to twenty acres were established. The weak point of this radical and somewhat hasty land reform was the extreme subdivision of the land. Excessively small properties were set up, which those opposed to the reform said were "too large to die on and too small to live on."[67]

In contrast with this quick action of the Russians, the Western powers indulged in long and costly delays, trying to make up their minds what course to follow, and thereby greatly retarded the agricultural recovery of the region. The Western powers felt that they had to play along with the political forces of the Right, in order to unite with them against the rising threat of Communism in eastern Germany, and they consequently found it difficult to settle on a plan of agrarian reform. The principal argument against action was based on the fact that four fifths of the great landed estates of Germany were concentrated in the eastern zone, occupied by the Russians; therefore there was no need to redistribute the land in the western zone. The international observer Werner Klatt, who made a profound study of food and agriculture in postwar Germany, commented on this Allied policy:

> In these circumstances the Allied authorities responsible for Western Germany were inclined to consider land reform an untimely measure likely to delay the recovery of a highly dislocated economy and an unstable society. After the event it might appear that an early decision and a clear announcement of policy on this issue might have been more satisfactory than years of uncertainty, but at the time the rash action of the Russians and Communists in the east tended to weaken the position of the Allies and Germans speaking in support of land reform in the

west, and to strengthen the hands of those who, for one reason or another, were in favor of maintaining the *status quo*. The reform laws which grew out of this situation are a not too happy compromise of widely diverging views.[68]

It was not until a year after the Russians had carried out their agrarian reform in eastern Germany that the Americans announced a very moderate program. It consisted in expropriation by the state of a certain quota of the land of the great estates, varying from 10 percent in the case of farms of 250 acres up to 90 percent in the case of great estates of more than 3,550 acres. Thus the largest latifundium in the country was reduced from 12,000 acres to 1,900—which is still an enormous estate. The American reform never aimed, as did the Russian, at total expropriation of the land.

In September 1947, the military government of the British zone promulgated its land reform, in keeping with which nobody could own more than 375 acres of land. The agrarian reform in the French zone was also put into effect in 1947; it affected a small number of estates with more than 375 acres. Analyzing this dilatory and somewhat confused agrarian policy of the Allies, a policy manifestly influenced by the more conservative parties of the Right, Werner Klatt concluded that:

> . . . the delay tactics of the extreme right-wing parties in the west are as regrettable as the hasty, ill-considered reform of the Communists in the east. A realistic land policy will not do more than contribute in some way to the solution of some of the most burning problems of present-day Germany, but without it extremists will find it only too easy to tread unhindered the road to new economic and political disaster in the future.

The result of these and other accumulated errors was that the nutritional situation in Germany continued to be disastrous until 1949. Only then, after a monetary reform which partly corrected the worst effects of inflation, did the situation begin to work back toward normal.

Defeated Germany was not the only country where Hunger set up his European headquarters after the war. In the camp of the winners also, in Allied countries entitled to reparations, nutritional conditions continued in a sad state for a long time after peace was won. The case of France is typical. There the war, the occupation, and the liberation led to extremely unfavorable conditions for food supply. France continued to go hungry for a long time after the liberation and was shamefully preyed upon, too, by the corruption of the black market. The agricultural recovery of France encountered serious obstacles, outstanding among them being the extremely poor condition of its farmlands and the absolute lack of mechanized agricultural machinery.

The lack of fertilizer and a shortage of workers had contributed greatly to the degeneration of French farmland. The deficit in fertilizers reached alarming proportions; consumption of these materials absolutely essential to the life of the land fell from 4 million tons in 1939 to only 150,000 tons in 1945—about a sixth of the prewar total. The decline in farm labor was also notable. According to the Ministry of Agriculture, between 1938 and 1945, 100,000 farmers and farm workers left the land for good. In addition to this, 400,000 farmers were made prisoner during the war and 50,000 were killed, leaving huge gaps in the ranks of agricultural labor. As a result of the tremendous drop in production and the absolute lack of financial resources to buy foods outside the country, France was forced to go through long years of nutritional poverty after the war.

In the other countries of western Europe, the postwar situation developed in the face of the same obstacles, the same upsets and difficulties. Little seemed to come of all the efforts to achieve that coveted economic integration of the continent about which the economists, politicans, and diplomats of the United Nations talked so much. Each country tried separately to find some saving means of escaping from the closed circle of its own privations. In the case of England, a diet was prescribed that was narrowly limited in accordance with individual biological necessities. In the case of Holland, an attempt was made to amplify the country's cultivated area by wresting new land from the sea. The Dutch built gigantic dikes in the Gulf of the Zuider Zee, where extensive new polders added 500,000 acres of land to the country, 7 percent of the total area of the nation. Here enough food can be raised to feed 300,000 people.[69] But considering that the annual population increase amounts to 100,000, and that the losses of the Dutch Empire in the Far East withdrew appreciable food resources from the nation, the Dutch did not win any great respite in this way.

The miracle accomplished by England in not starving to death during the war, and in attaining a certain postwar balance, was a result of the ancient experience of this island people. According to students of agricultural problems in Great Britain, the fondest dream of old-time English farmers was always a "good war." The English economist F. W. Bateson explains this aspiration as follows:

> A war could be counted on to fill the farmer's pockets. The experience of the Napoleonic Wars—when wheat rose from 40s. to over 120s. a quarter, and barley from under 20s. to over 60s.—had been amply confirmed by the world war of 1914. A war that was a war—as distinct from an "episode" like the Boer War—stimulated demand, while at the same time restricting supply. On the one hand, there was more money about in wartime, and people were hungrier because they were working harder; on the other hand, imported foodstuffs were scarce and expensive because of shipping risks, and British prices, undepressed by foreign competition, attained to new and exhilarating levels.[70]

World War II filled up the bins of English agriculture, and even if it did not fill the pockets of the farmers, it served to stock the warehouses under control of the Ministry of Agriculture with great stores of food produced in the British Isles. Nevertheless, though the dietary situation was tolerable by

1950, it was far from reaching the level aimed at for the well-being of the British people.

[But the harsh situation of the immediate postwar years in Western Europe was not allowed to last because it threatened the balance of international security. The profound disagreements between the United States and the U.S.S.R. that had arisen before the end of the war became more and more marked, and so began the Cold War, which was to be a decisive influence on international political strategy for a decade. The Soviets already occupied a substantial portion of central Europe when the United States started seriously to contest their further expansion into the western part of the continent. There were even those who affirmed—the American diplomat-writer Adolf A. Berle among them[71]— that the Americans knew of a Soviet master plan aiming at immediate invasion of West Germany, which could easily have been occupied given its people's overwhelming despair in the face of postwar living conditions. In France and Italy repeated strikes that threatened national stability were stimulated, according to the American government, by Communist forces who found in the economic disarray of these countries an ideal climate for subversive agitation. The United States had to act quickly to maintain the line of division between West and East established at the Yalta and Potsdam conferences. Otherwise, it believed, the iron curtain would move across the continent and the West would be submerged under a Communist avalanche.

The instrument conceived to defend capitalist Europe from this threat was the Marshall Plan, created in 1947 in the form of generalized economic aid to the European countries devastated by the war. The U.S.S.R. was invited to be one of the recipients, but the Soviet delegation at the Paris Conference declared that the plan was a device of American imperialism and left the conference. The United States took upon itself the entire responsibility for aid to Europe. It was a question of life or death for Western capitalism, and for this reason the plan won rapid approval in Congress.

American aid to Europe reached the sum of $15 billion and made possible such an effective revival of the devastated economies that, even today, adversaries of aid to Third World countries emphasize the contrast between the success of such programs in Europe and their failure in other, more marginal areas, where people do not know how to make international aid work for them. They present this as a decisive argument against giving further aid to countries that are by themselves incapable of development because of their cultural structures and their environmental and social conditions. These opponents of aid to the Third World have eloquent figures on which to base their arguments: while the Marshall Plan involved only $15 billion, international financial assistance to the Third World over fifteen years has totaled $100 billion. But these capitalist isolationists forget that in Europe it was only a matter of reorganizing an economy that, though disabled, possessed a sound infrastructure and a competent and experienced work force, while in the Third World all that must be created out of nothing.

But let us return to Europe. Supported by the Marshall Plan the European economy recovered rapidly and the marks of hunger quickly diminished across the whole area. In a short time Europe had regained its prewar nutritional level (in 1950 the average diet provided between 2,800 to 3,000 calories per day), and with growing prosperity public health improved because of the relatively lower consumption of grain and other starches and the proportional increase in the consumption of animal products.

The creation of the European Common Market by the Treaty of Rome in 1958 gave a new impetus to the continent's economy, leading to a still higher nutritional level. The problem that most preoccupies the Common Market nations today is not one of shortage but of food surpluses, which are an obstacle to real regional economic integration.

It would be erroneous, however, to conclude from this that hunger has been completely eliminated in Europe and that abundance is universal. The continent still possesses several regions marked by hunger and certain groups still live in nutritional poverty despite the enormous economic and technical progress of the last twenty years. In Spain and Portugal the standard of diet is far below normal and several types of deficiencies, especially of proteins, exist at levels comparable to those in the Third World.[72] Certain sociologists and economists insist, not without reason, on counting these two European nations and southern Italy among the underdeveloped countries, though in southern Italy an intensive program has been set up to improve living standards, and the continuing export of surplus manpower to highly industrialized countries like Germany, Switzerland, and the Netherlands is contributing to progress in the Italian *mezzogiorno.*

Further, in the great urban centers of Europe, one can find shantytowns inhabited essentially by foreigners whose psycho-sociological world is characterized by malnutrition and hunger. Relatively recent studies show that in England 14 percent of the population still lives in a culture of poverty and that nearly 7 percent of the British suffer from hunger. In France, 10 percent of the work force—most of these North African immigrants, Senegalese, Spaniards, and Portuguese badly integrated into the mechanisms of national production—alternate between unemployment and hunger wages. Germany, the Netherlands, and the Scandinavian countries also have their zones of hunger, though they are proportionally smaller. This proves that beside the conventional Third World—the underdeveloped tropical-equatorial fringe—there exists another Third World with beachheads in Chicago, New York, Paris, and London. The dominant characteristic of this Third World, too, is hunger operating as a social calamity.

To make this study of hunger in Europe complete, I should go on to examine the People's Democracies of the

East. In preceding editions I did so but this time I will leave these areas aside, for I intend to devote another volume to analyzing them, along with the U.S.S.R., North Korea, and Vietnam. I have decided on this course because it is not possible to add to this book an enormous new chapter on the U.S.S.R. Such a chapter certainly has a place in a global study of hunger, for Russia covers one sixth of the earth's surface and hunger has always played a decisive role there, either as an obstacle to, or as a motive force for, social change. But the discussion would have to be so long and complex that it would seriously unbalance the book's general plan and destroy its conceptual unity.

When this book was first published, it was practically impossible to obtain enough precise information to permit an objective analysis of the U.S.S.R. Statistical data were lacking, and political obstacles and the obstinate reserve that characterized the country during the Stalinist period hindered impartial information from crossing the iron curtain. I was therefore unable to treat the problem of hunger there with the same objectivity and certitude that I tried to bring to the analysis of countries like India or Mexico, for example, where everything was presented openly.

Later, however, after deeper and more sustained reflection on this problem, I came to the conclusion that neither the paucity of information nor the unreliability of available statistics had caused my inhibitions about broaching the subject. It was something else: the method I had used to analyze the phenomenon of hunger was valid only when this phenomenon was considered as a fundamental constant in the structure of the capitalist world that had as its two economic poles the great monopolies and the economically marginal regions crushed by colonial oppression. To overcome this difficulty and to understand the problem of hunger in the U.S.S.R., I made four trips to that country after 1947. Traveling throughout its enormous territory, from the sub-

polar regions to the Black Sea and from the European frontiers to the Pacific, I made observations and collected testimony and documents that enabled me to form a much
clearer idea of the problem and thus of the need to treat it in
depth. In view of hunger's political implications in the light
of the Communist revolution and of the construction of the
world's first socialist society, I decided to devote another
book, to be called *Hunger and Socialism,* to this subject.
Completing this book has turned out to be much more
difficult than I had anticipated at the outset, and although
the work is quite far along, it will not be published for some
time. It is for this reason, however, that the new edition of
Geopolitics of Hunger, like the first edition, will not be
concerned with the problem of hunger in the U.S.S.R.

The reader may find an apparent contradiction here, since
I have been concerned in this book with the study of hunger
in other socialist countries such as China and Cuba, but the
contradiction is only apparent. It must be realized that this
book was conceived and written between 1945 and 1950, a
period when other countries that are socialist today were in
the process of changing from a capitalist to a socialist structure, and when, therefore, the influence of capitalism was
still very strong. But the U.S.S.R. had made this transition
thirty years earlier and I could not apply to its problems the
same method of analysis that I used for the rest of the world.
A different approach was required, for it must be borne in
mind that the application of the doctrines of historical
materialism in the social domain was an unprecedented
experiment. It is because I respect this experiment that I have
judged it undesirable to mingle the two different analytical
methods in this book and have reserved a separate study for
the U.S.S.R.]

Part III
A World
Without Hunger

7
The Advance Against Hunger

In the second part of this book, I mapped out the distribution of hunger in the world and I assessed the factors that govern it. In view of the evidence, collective hunger cannot possibly be called a natural phenomenon. Analysis has shown that it is caused much more by economic than by geographical factors; it is a social phenomenon which results, as a rule, from failure to make use of natural resoures or from improper distribution of consumer goods.

The fundamental truth can no longer be concealed from mankind; the world has at its disposal enough resources to provide an adequate diet for everybody, everywhere. And if many of the guests on this earth have not yet been called to the table, it is because all known civilizations, including our own, have been organized on a basis of economic inequality.

The civilizations of antiquity, as Kenneth Boulding notes, "were endowed with such a limited economic surplus that they could not have continued to exist except on a basis of extreme inequality in the distribution of wealth. In the last analysis, all ancient civilizations were only small islands of culture, rising out of an immense sea of poverty and slavery."[1] Down through history, until the great technical discoveries of modern times, it has not been possible to imagine a civilization that did not inevitably crush the majority of men into poverty.

447

Today the forces of nature have been harnessed for mass production. For the first time ever, a society is possible in which poverty can be abolished and with it, misery and hunger. The eradication of hunger is no longer a utopian scheme; it is a perfectly available objective. [The wealth of a world that has grown fabulously rich at those points where production is concentrated and that has available an impressive arsenal of techniques for the sound utilization of its material resources makes it technically possible for man to solve the problem of hunger for everyone on earth.] All that is necessary is a better adjustment of men to the lands they occupy and a better distribution of the gifts of the land among men.

There is nothing quixotic about the modern fight against hunger. It is a task that follows from any cold and realistic analysis of the world's political and economic situation. Only after we have rooted out the gangrenous focuses of human misery will we be able to articulate the mass economy into which we have so avidly thrown ourselves—without taking note of the fact that we were not socially prepared for the venture.

The high levels of production on which our industrial and post-industrial civilization is predicated demand a continuous expansion of the market. This can only come about through incorporating into the world economy the two thirds of humanity who live on its margins. Solely by raising the buying power and consuming capacity of these people can the other third of the world survive and prosper within its present economic and social structure.

The fight against hunger is the most urgent imperative confronting us today. It is a kind of cold war, quite capable of freezing up the sources of our vitality unless we have the skill and determination to win it.

It is a pity, in these circumstances, that the struggle for better living standards does not command universal support.

Many people are still taken in by the archaic and feudal notion that hunger and misery are necessary or inevitable. Contemporary political thought clings to the false idea that economic life is some sort of game, in which some must always lose in order that others may win. The struggle for prosperity will have to begin by clearing up that misconception; the science of economics must become an instrument for the balanced distribution of the good things of the earth, so that it will never again be defined, as Marx defined it in the last century, as "the science of human misery."[2]

The Collaboration of Nature

The first big victory over hunger will consist of a substantial gain in the world's food production. Basically, there are two paths to the attainment of this objective: increasing the size of the cultivated area and raising the productivity of land already in use.

It is certainly legitimate to hope for an extension of the world's cultivated area, particularly toward the tropics and the poles. According to Robert Salter, tropical red soils and subpolar podsols cover approximately 28 percent of the earth's surface,[3] but not more than 1 percent* of them are cultivated.

The cultivation of tropical soils is not at all a new sort of enterprise. In the Far East, considerable areas of red soil have been in use for a long time, but the reserves in Africa and South America are practically virgin. If, using Salter's figures, we were to make use of only 20 percent of our African and South American land reserves, some 900 million acres would be added to the world's cultivated area. Another 100 million acres could be found in Oceania. Assuming that only 10

* 3 percent.

percent of the reserves of Russian and Canadian podsols could be farmed, another 300 million acres would be added to the total. Salter asserts that with the 1.3 billion-acre land increase thus postulated, provided it were intelligently farmed, the whole world (including its estimated population increase) could be adequately fed. No one can deny that the returns from these soils are not of the highest, and they do wear out more easily than temperate soils. Still, by appropriate technical devices—particularly by turning back all residues and leftovers to replenish their fertility—such soils can be kept at reasonable levels of production, so that their use is economically justifiable.

There is certainly no lack of soil reserves for the rational expansion of food production. Even in the more fertile regions, great tracts of land still go uncultivated because the economic structure is deficient in stimulating agricultural production. With a little work and economic investment, a large part of the soil that is now considered exhausted could also be restored. Edward H. Faulkner, an agricultural revolutionary, denied [even before the end of World War II] that thousands of years of tedious natural processes are necessary to replenish depleted soils. He insists that man himself can restore eroded soils by relatively simple technical processes:

> We can recreate good soil wherever good soil formerly existed, and we can do so by machinery. . . . For the whole category of areas that have suffered merely water erosion, however severe, there is still definite assurance that as good soil as ever existed upon them can be restored. Much the same can be said of areas damaged by wind erosion or by excessive cropping and grazing.[4]

Orthodox soil scientists and agricultural experts consider Faulkner a heretic and a visionary who thinks that his methods will multiply agricultural production to five or ten times its present size. But observations from different regions of the world give a ring of truth to his "heresies."[5]

Brazil provides a striking example of the variability of soil productivity according to the specific agricultural practices of the given economy. In the great coffee-growing area of São Paulo, as one-crop coffee farming advanced westward across the dark soil of the uplands, many plantations were abandoned when their incomes dropped sharply due to the exhaustion of the soil. Coffee monoculture, in a nomadic search for richer earth, apparently ruined vast areas of fertile Brazilian land and left it quite useless. Some Japanese immigrants bought these lands for nearly nothing. They put their long experience with thankless soils to work and through a farm cooperative organization developed the cultivation of potatoes and vegetables. A magnificent green belt has thus grown up around the state capital, contributing so much to the food supply of this city of two million* that its nutritional standards have been markedly improved.

Another good argument in Faulkner's favor is the example of the Dutch, who have succeeded in making new agricultural soils out of the beds of the shallow seas that surround them. If it is possible to *create* new soils where none existed, it should be much easier to *recreate* exhausted soils or to build up those unadapted to agriculture. There ought to be less difficulty in correcting deficiencies than in constructing soil in the first place. One is forced to the conclusion that what may be worn out or unusable soil within the limitations of one type of agrarian economy could well be made use of under other conditions.

Soil productivity, of course, is not an absolute. Like population density, it is a variable, a function of the prevailing kind of economic organization. The soil has neither absolute productive limits—Vogt's "biotic potential"—nor absolute demographic limits. The relation of population to the soil has been handled with an inaccuracy and a blind empiricism

* Six million.

repugnant to the scientific spirit. Earl Parker Hanson is entirely right in pointing out that "such neo-Malthusians as Vogt seem totally unaware that it is never a land that is overpopulated in terms of inhabitants per square mile; it is always an economy, in terms of inhabitants per square meal."[6]

Cultivation has so far been limited to the most productive soils available, on the theory that while these could be had, there was no point in working the poorer areas. But once the soils of high productivity have been used to the limit, we shall be forced to go on to the intensive culture of medium and low-producing soils. The ultimate aim of agriculture, after all, if not simply the collection of exceptional profits but rather the production of goods necessary to the collective welfare.

The price of reviving productivity should not be considered an impassable barrier; it ought to be thought of as a social problem that can be overcome by reorganizing the economic apparatus, taking into account the necessity of paying prices high enough to warrant the production achieved.

A few years ago when artificial fungus cultivation was begun in order to obtain antibiotics such as penicillin, aureomycin, and terramycin, the cost of the process was found to be very high, but the project was not abandoned on that account. The antibiotics were magnificently efficient in combating innumerable infectious diseases, and their cost was not prohibitive in view of the benefits.

Now it is a demonstrable fact that food is the most potent of all the antibiotics, since it protects the organism in a general way against all kinds of germ attacks. If the world had a well-balanced diet in adequate amounts, we would have considerably less need for specific antibiotics or other drugs. This line of thought is the foundation for the statesmanlike view of those who join E. B. Balfour in looking at agriculture as a kind of medical necessity:

> Once agriculture came to be regarded as a health service, the only consideration in any matter concerning the production of food would be "Is it necessary for the health of the people?": that of ordinary economics would take quite a second place.[7]

The second method of bringing about a large-scale increase in our food supply is to raise the production per acre of our currently cultivated land. Certain countries have shown recently, particularly during the war, that an appreciable increase in the agricultural output per unit of surface is indubitably possible everywhere, through the application of the technological methods of modern agronomy. These methods, used in long-range planning, embody the essential characteristic of our era, that of the second Industrial Revolution. Whereas the first Industrial Revolution applied mechanization to the manufacturing industries, the second applies scientific method to enterprises of every sort, that is, it involves the widest application of science to all problems related to production.[8]

[Before discussing how science can aid man in this vital objective, however, let us survey the world situation today.]

Science: Collaboration or Intrusion*

It is now almost a commonplace to say that we are experiencing a universal revolution, unprecedented in both its worldwide scale and its explosive pace. Nonetheless, even though it is obvious that in the second half of the twentieth century the world is undergoing a metamorphosis of both appearance and reality, triggered by the vast technological changes that have taken place since World War II, many people still continue to think in categories that antedate the revolutionary explosion.

* The section that follows was not included in the 1973 French edition. It appears here for the first time.

There is no doubt that this conservative cast of mind, this resistance to altering one's way of thinking, represents a great danger for the world. First, in this time of drastic change man must transform himself in order to survive, and to transform himself he needs above all to form a new conception of the world to which he must adapt. But even worse, it is just these intellectual reactionaries—who have to some degree participated in the world's material revolution but refuse to take part in a revolution of the spirit—who control the destiny of mankind. They are the ruling elites in the world's decision-making centers. It is to them that science and technology have given overwhelming power, and they are the technically overdeveloped minority thereby able to dominate the two thirds of humanity who remain deprived of the benefits of social progress—the inhabitants of the Third World, the world's hungry.

Never has the world stood so in need of a renewal of thought, a new philosophy of action, as it does today when historical processes are accelerating at incredible speed. Nothing now evolves gradually; everything happens in sudden destructive explosions. The chain reaction of explosions in all sectors of human activity is the central feature of our time. We live in an era of explosions: the atomic explosion, the population explosion, the psychological explosion of the oppressed peoples, the radical explosion of youth in opposition to the pre-atomic generation. All around us, continuously, sudden and violent explosion plays a role of creative destruction, serving as a model of the new technical civilization in which all of us are inevitably involved, whether we wish it or not, for good or for ill. It is a universal revolution that, in a sense, is devoid of ethics and foreign to all ideology. In our time technology has become the theology of the West. In it have been blindly placed all hopes for world salvation, even while the world is threatened with total annihilation by the powers of thermonuclear energy also made available by science, to men whose minds can barely grasp such terrible strength, such unmeasured power.

Einstein was right that man will not be able to survive this flood of threats and hopes unless he creates a new way of thinking, a new political consciousness based on a new set of values that arise from an existential experience totally distinct from that of the beginning of our century. The first task, the first concerted effort needed to redirect our thinking, is to place ourselves in this new world and seek to understand how the explosions that represent the great historical realities of our time have come about. If we do not understand, if we fail to find a valid interpretation for the crisis through which we are passing, we shall inevitably be beaten down by the storm it creates and blinded by the dust of material ruins and the emotional fall-out produced by the prejudices and sentimentalism inherited from other epochs. Either we shall, through intelligence, be able to measure up to the task of synchronizing our movements with the rhythm of the world that surrounds us or the omnipresent social frictions will destroy us as human beings.

In this chapter I wish to offer an interpretation of one of the most explosive aspects of the current crisis: the imbalance of the natural and biological order within the context of the global ecological system. This catastrophic imbalance between the food requirements and the food resources of an expanding human race has a precise name: hunger, the scourge of universal hunger that grows worse every day.

One of the factors behind this deterioration of the world food situation is certainly the much discussed demographic explosion, to which is attributed a much greater and more negative influence on the process of development than it actually has. To understand the relation of population growth to the machinery of social and economic development and to hunger (which is only the biological expression of economic underdevelopment), we must first determine what the demographic explosion is and how it is produced.

Demographic curves result essentially from the relation between birth and death rates, that is, the number of people who are born and the number who die within the same lapse of time. It is generally agreed that until the tenth century, at least in the West, these two factors balanced each other and the population remained stable. Starting in the eleventh century the death rate began to diminish relative to the birth rate and the population began to expand. But this took place at a very slow, almost imperceptible pace: thus, from the eleventh to the sixteenth century the growth rate was 1 percent per decade. In the seventeenth, it grew to 2.7 percent per decade; in the eighteenth to 3.2 percent and in the nineteenth to 4.5. In the first half of the twentieth century, because of the widespread use of vaccination and other methods of preventive medicine, the death rate diminished more rapidly, life expectancy increased, and the population grew at a rate of 8.5 percent per decade. In 1950, following the last world war, the demographic explosion began. The population began to increase at a rate of 2.3 percent annually in Asia, 2.4 percent in Africa, and 3.5 percent in Latin America. Overall, the increase averaged 2 percent a year, which is 20 percent per decade—a startling rate, capable of almost doubling the world's population in thirty years. What has caused this sudden rise in the demographic curve? A real improvement in living standards, a universal economy of abundance? No. To answer this one need only recall that the phenomenon is most accentuated in Latin America, Asia, and Africa—the poorest, least developed, and hungriest parts of the world.

The demographic explosion in these areas results almost exclusively from a marked drop in the rates of infant and premature mortality brought about by the widespread use of survival techniques based, above all, on the massive employment of antibiotics and insecticides. It is progress in bacteriology, chemistry, and biology that has caused the radical change in the rate of world population growth. Thanks to antibiotics the rate of infant mortality, formerly alarmingly high in underdeveloped countries, has been strikingly lowered. Children have begun to survive in these regions where they once seemed doomed to die, because these products enable them to resist the attacks of infectious illnesses that decimated earlier generations. Let us take a few examples. In New Guinea before the era of antibiotics, 700 out of every 1,000 children died before reaching their first birthday. Today, this figure is 80. The likelihood of surviving is twelve times greater than it used to be. In Sicily the rate of infant mortality has fallen over twenty years from 300 per thousand to 30. Nevertheless, living conditions in New Guinea have hardly changed; wretchedness is universal, hunger is a constant in the lives of the people. The only difference is that, because of antibiotics, the children no longer die during their first year; they survive to die a little later, at ten, fifteen, or twenty. This is the principal cause of the so-called demographic explosion—which permits the survival of a large number of people who produce nothing or almost nothing but who augment the population and aggravate certain problems of underdevelopment, especially those of food supply.

Thus the demographic explosion is the product of the partial and consequently unsound application of an isolated technical achievement, unaccompanied by the use of other techniques that would foster real economic development and the integration of peoples whose poverty now relegates them to the fringe of society. But is it the real reason why hunger is a universal scourge? Does two thirds of humanity suffer from hunger today because of the overpopulation of the world? Is hunger produced by a surplus of mouths to feed on a planet with limited resources? In other words, is it an unavoidable natural phenomenon, an inevitability, as Malthus sought to prove when he published his law on population growth at the end of the eighteenth century? Today's science answers this question with a categorical no. I have tried to prove that this response rests on solid scientific bases.

Hunger is not a product of overpopulation; hunger existed on a grand scale before the postwar phenomenon of the demographic explosion. But the hunger that decimated the populations of the Third World was covered up, stifled, hidden, whereas today it is openly discussed and the problem has become a veritable international scandal. Moreover, not only did hunger exist in previous periods; it exists today in areas that are not overpopulated. Many hunger areas have low population densities: Africa and Latin America, for example, are underpopulated continents with an average of 24 inhabitants per square mile; well-fed Europe has 157. Was Malthus right when he predicted that hunger would provoke an apocalyptic disaster? He stated, in essence, that population increases geometrically while food resources increase arithmetically and that this would lead mankind to an inevitable impasse. The only conclusion he foresaw was widespread hunger that would pitilessly eliminate the surplus population.

Malthus' view is devoid of any scientific basis. His first major mistake was to consider demographic growth as an independent variable, whereas in reality it is subject to numerous influences from the ecological, natural, and cultural systems in which various human groups live. Population growth does not continue to infinity; it conforms to cycles connected with various structures in the natural and cultural environment. The concrete facts of history have completely destroyed the Malthusian theory. If it were correct and the increase had been as he predicted, the population of the world, about 1 billion when he published his theory, would be about 100 billion today—whereas in fact it is about 3.5 billion.

Population growth obeys a cyclical law. For a short time after the publication of Malthus' theory, a relative expansion took place, but by the middle of the eighteenth century a slowdown was already noticeable. Now we are again going through a phase of spectacular expansion, but this must be viewed as a cyclical episode, not as a permanent condition. Any long-term prediction about the size of the world's population can be no more than speculation, risky prophecy devoid of any scientific basis. Real planning for the future cannot be confused with prophecy or divination. An understanding of the factors that affect the workings of demography indicates, it is true, appreciable population increases for a certain time to come, because of the possibility of a fall in mortality rates. But we cannot tell how long growth may continue because ecological factors also influence birth rates, which may diminish naturally, thus re-establishing the balance and halting the demographic explosion. We know that the highest birth rates in the world are those of the underdeveloped and hungry peoples of Asia and Latin America. These high rates are based on a biological principle, teleonomy, which decrees that all living systems perform their functions with the rhythm and energy most favorable to the survival of the individual and, above all, the species. The defense of life exerts a powerful influence on all vital acts and behavior. Whenever a species is threatened, it increases its reproductive capacity and multiplies in order to neutralize the danger of extinction. This happens in both the vegetable and the animal kingdom. In China, the bamboo tree flowers best during periods of extreme dryness, scattering its seeds on the soil to protect the threatened species. Certain birds lay more eggs after a natural cataclysm. Statistics show that birth rates rise noticeably after wars particularly costly to human life. Such a rise was recorded in Eastern Europe after World War II.

The high birth rates of the underdeveloped countries follow the same biological law: they represent the natural effort of human groups to survive, for the mortality rates in these regions have always been high. Only if they produce a surplus of people—for most are born there to die, not to live—can these groups survive, and thus they follow the so-called anti-economic cycle of the demographic evolution characteristic of underdeveloped peoples.

Today, we have a detailed knowledge of the biosocial mechanism that makes low living standards and high birth rates inversely proportional. One of the most active elements of this mechanism is the insufficiency of food, especially the specific lack of biologically high-value proteins, a kind of hunger that results in increased fertility for both men and women. This explains why it is the badly nourished peoples, especially those whose diet is largely vegetarian, who have the highest birth rates. Basically, as I have explained earlier in this book, hunger is one of the determining factors of overpopulation, since it causes the birth rate to rise and consequently accelerates the rate of demographic expansion. If we modify the ecological situation of the underdeveloped regions, if we transform their special economic structure to ensure adequate supplies of food at the same time that the death rates are falling, we shall see nature act "teleonomically" and lower birth rates as they were lowered in Europe, the United States, and New Zealand—in all the regions that enjoy a high standard of living. The world's demographic growth will regulate itself naturally.

My theory that hunger acts as a cause of relative overpopulation is borne out not only by the results of experiments on laboratory animals but also by history. The evidence wholly confirms my position and totally disproves the pseudo-scientific assertions of neo-Malthusians horrified by the demographic explosion, which they view as a gigantic wave of colored peoples threatening the survival of the white race. Without distorting the facts, one cannot say that overpopulation causes hunger, for it is not the most populous countries that suffer most from it. Far from it: hunger exists in Brazil, with a density of only 24 inhabitants per square mile; Bolivia suffers from hunger with a mere 8.7 inhabitants per square mile; while Belgium and the Netherlands do not, though their respective population densities are 798 and 942 persons per square mile—one hundred times those of certain famished countries of the Western hemisphere. Even China and India, which have always been considered archetypal regions of hunger, have population densities of only 190 and 390 per square mile, far lower than that of European nations almost exempt from the problem.

By delaying the improvement of living standards for certain groups, the population explosion can certainly aggravate conditions of chronic hunger or famine but it does not create these situations. As a general rule, hunger is the result of unsound economic structures not of insuperable natural conditions. To try to justify hunger in the world by seeing it as a natural and inevitable phenomenon is only a technique of mystification, an attempt to hide the true causes: in the past, the colonial exploitation to which most of the world's peoples were subject, and in the present, the economic neo-colonialism imposed upon those countries with primary, dependent economies, that is, precisely those underdeveloped regions where hunger prevails.

Because of colonialist economic exploitation that, far from stimulating real, independent economic development, has actually blocked it and closed the path of progress to many peoples, two thirds of mankind still do not receive the 2,700 calories they need every day. It is even harder for them to obtain adequate amounts of the various other indispensable nutritional elements, especially amino acids, various mineral salts, and certain vitamins. We can no longer hide the fact that hunger, in all its various forms, is always the direct result of underdevelopment and that this situation, in turn, is not the inevitable outcome of natural forces but the product of historical circumstances. Underdevelopment results from misusing natural and human resources in a way that serves to impede economic expansion and those social transformations necessary to bring underdeveloped human groups into an integrated economic system. Only a global strategy of development, capable of mobilizing all the elements of production in the interest of the entire human race, can eliminate underdevelopment and hunger from the world. The solution lies not, as the neo-Malthusians contend, in radically reducing the population of our planet, but in enabling the population to make intelligent use of the potential that nature has placed at our disposal. Given the present state of scientific knowledge, we could derive much more benefit from natural resources than we are now doing.

Unfortunately, the battle for development has not yet been joined rationally and decisively enough. The disordered and spasmodic efforts made to date, under an inadequate policy of international cooperation, have led to failure, lending apparent support to the neo-Malthusians' macabre predictions of the world's imminent end in a cataclysm of hunger. Plans for international cooperation aimed at developing the Third World have not produced the intended results. Instead of narrowing, the gap between the rich and well-fed nations and the poor and hungry nations grows wider daily. There is little hope that in the short run the struggle against underdevelopment will lead to any significant improvement of diet in the poorer countries, and the possibility of banishing hunger from the world is still far off—especially in view of the growing imbalance between available food resources and the biological needs of a population increasing at a dizzy rate.

The problem requires the immediate attention of the world's leaders. It must be examined in the context of the overall economic picture, but beyond that, every means that can contribute to bettering the diet of those who live in the economically depressed regions must be used.*

* End of new material.

[One field in which we can expect positive results is the application of science and technology to the production and preservation of food. This scientific area, where biology, physical chemistry, ecology, and the biology of soils all come together, is the most promising weapon against hunger that now exists. As we have seen, it is science, by making possible the large-scale application of survival techniques (especially the widespread use of antibiotics and insecticides) that has led to the sharp decline of mortality, especially infant mortality, rates and thus to the demographic explosion. But while the number of mouths to feed has increased enormously, the world has failed to make use of other techniques that would allow these human masses to escape their present state of chronic hunger, to live instead of merely to survive. These techniques do exist, however, and could bring about a spectacular rise in agricultural production, making available natural products richer in essential nutritive elements and providing better ways of preserving foods so that the now disproportionately high waste of food could be avoided.

Obviously, just making food available in sufficient quantity and diversity to meet the world's nutritional needs is not enough. The problem of hunger is not merely one of insufficient food production. The majority of the world's population now lacks the purchasing power to obtain the food it requires. Financial resources must be made correspondent with biological needs. Nevertheless, improving the world's food-producing potential and establishing an intelligent distribution plan for foods in needy areas will represent a great step forward in the struggle against hunger.

Understanding the gigantic task that faces us, the tactics that must be employed, and the philosophy of action that must be brought to bear requires an objective synthesis of the present state of the problem, at least in its main lines. There is no doubt that we live in a world that suffers from the whole spectrum of hunger, from systematic deficiencies of the nutritive elements indispensable for the vital balance of the human organism. But within the complex and confusing picture, two features stand out as the most alarming aspects of the problem, demanding the greatest attention from those in authority: caloric insufficiency, that is, an inadequacy of the energy that man needs to maintain himself in vital balance, and insufficiency of proteins, or rather of their formative elements, the amino acids that are indispensable for building up the vital substratum of living protoplasm. Hunger can and must be considered, above all, in terms of these two forms: hunger for calories and hunger for proteins. For greater clarity, particularly as an aid to the nonspecialist's understanding, I shall examine these two aspects separately.

With regard to calories, the present situation is as follows: given average needs—2,600 calories per person per day—and the total population, the overall world demand for calories amounts to about 1 billion tons of food a year. Caloric needs must be met by a combination of vegetable and animal substances, with the former furnishing the more substantial portion. If we consider total food production—in both the developed and the developing countries—the caloric deficiency does not seem alarming; the deficit is only 15 percent of overall needs. If we view these two groups of nations separately, however, we see that while the rich, industrialized countries have a relative surplus of food, the poor, underdeveloped regions produce only 60 percent of the nourishment they need in terms of caloric content.

This is the present situation; the prospect for the future is much worse unless world nutritional policies are radically changed. With the dizzying rate of population increase, which is at its greatest precisely in those regions that are underdeveloped and hungry, the caloric deficit is on its way to a rise of overwhelming proportions. Sen, former Director-General of the F.A.O., has warned that to meet world needs for calories in twenty years, food production must increase by 175 percent.

The protein situation is even more disturbing. The lack of proteins of high biological value, capable of furnishing all the amino acids necessary for human metabolism, is undoubtedly the most serious aspect of the world's nutritional problem. Nigel Calder described it in his book *Eden Was No Garden:* "The main failure of agriculture can be summed up in two words that resound as a threat just as terrible as that of the hydrogen bomb or the bubonic plague: protein deficiency."[9] It has been calculated that, with intelligent planning, the production of some 34 million tons of animal proteins could satisfy the world's needs. Only about 20 million tons a year are now produced, however, 17 million from meat and 3 million from seafood. Thus the deficit amounts to about 40 percent of the actual need.

About 160 tons of vegetable proteins (of which grain is the principal source) are produced annually. This suggests that, in this area at least, no deficit exists, but actually half this amount is consumed by animals, leaving only 80 million tons for human nourishment. Since at least 120 million tons of vegetable proteins a year are needed by humans, here again there is an annual deficit—about 40 million tons. It should be pointed out that the 80 million tons used for animal feed is far from enough for this purpose. The lack is one of the fundamental factors preventing a satisfactory increase in the production of animal proteins.

Thus the people of the underdeveloped countries are locked into the vicious circle of being improperly nourished because they do not produce enough and of not producing enough because they are hungry. To improve their diet, it is essential to use all the techniques that can, on the one hand, raise the rates of agricultural productivity and increase total world production and on the other, by means of new procedures, make available food supplements of high biological value, especially complete proteins. If the minimum needs of the world's population are to be met in 1988, the production of these proteins must triple during the next twenty years. Attaining this rate of increase would make man victorious over hunger and would definitively unmask the Malthusian scarecrow that the menace of population explosion has brought forth from outdated economic theories.

Can this goal be attained? Technically there are no obstacles. The knowledge that man now possesses, if intelligently applied, would provide humanity with enough food of the necessary quality to insure its nutritional balance for many years to come, even if the population were to double, quadruple, or increase tenfold. The difficulties in resolving what is known as the Malthusian dilemma are not technical; they are political difficulties of much greater complexity.

This chapter, however, is limited to an analysis of technical resources—resulting primarily from discoveries in biology and physical chemistry—upon which mankind can draw to win the battle against hunger. Accordingly, I shall try to make a brief inventory of the most important tools at man's disposal for reshaping nature—or, in François Perroux's striking phrase, creating a second nature springing forth from the hand of man.

To increase food production in the countries of the Third World, science and technology can follow four different paths:

1. More informed and intense utilization of land, thanks to techniques capable of transforming unproductive soil into arable soil of high productivity.

2. The application of the knowledge of genetics and plant selection to increase the nutritional yield of this land, by modifying its chemical composition and consequently the nutritive value of certain products.

3. The application of physicochemical, microbiological, and biochemical methods to render nourishing such nonfood substances as petroleum, certain wood products, and residues from the sugar industry.

4. The extraction of great quantities of food from the sea. Let us analyze the different paths rational action could take. So far as land use is concerned, agriculture can be extended to areas that are not now sufficiently cultivated, as discussed at the beginning of this chapter. More important, soil productivity can be considerably increased by the systematic use of technical measures. The amount of land now under cultivation is small in relation to the amount potentially arable. It is estimated that at least 50 percent of the 34.6 billion acres of the land area of the planet could be cultivated using the procedures of traditional agriculture. But the area under cultivation today is only 3.2 billion acres, or 20 percent of the land available. It should also be pointed out that an important portion of the 50 percent considered noncultivable could be utilized by employing techniques that would correct or eliminate the natural factors that now prevent its use. It has even been argued that, with the scientific arsenal now at our disposal, all land could be cultivated. Everything depends on the economic factor: production is profitable on some land, while in other places it is possible but at present economically unfeasiable.

Where land is cultivable but is not presently being utilized, adequate methods must be employed to strengthen its biotic potential and thus to incorporate it into the world's food production facilities. Better use must be made of water, an essential factor in agricultural production; manure and synthetic fertilizers must be used to correct the physicochemical composition of the soil; plant species must be chosen for their ability to resist the hardships and deficiencies of the natural environment.

The extent of cultivated land is most limited in the underdeveloped countries. It is estimated that in the Third World only 8 percent of the land is worked, and the greater part of that is given over to nonfood products such as rubber, fibers, and tobacco, or to foods that are of minor nutritional value, such as condiments and stimulants (coffee, tea, cinnamon, etc.). Not much is left on which to grow food for the people of the Third World, whose numbers are increasing at such a rate that, according to the calculations of Professor Raymond Evell of the University of Buffalo, they will number 2.25 billion in 1980, that is, 1.5 billion more than now.

Here a controversial problem arises that deserves a detailed discussion: the question of artificial fertilizers.] The first point at issue is whether there are available in the world sufficient reserves of these corrective chemical elements. The second question is whether the use of fertilizers, admitting that it increases production in a quantitative sense, does not have a negative effect on the quality—whether there may not be a decline in nutritive value when fertilizer is used on a large scale.

The use of artificial fertilizers is limited to a certain number of countries, but the amount of these materials needed to maintain present world agricultural production has already reached tremendous proportions. The United States alone, to maintain food production during World War II, made use of an annual average of some 12 million tons of fertilizers, costing approximately $400 million. If the world's cultivated areas are to be increased by 1.3 billion acres of new soils, and if the present rate of use of artificial fertilizers per acre is continued, then, as Robert Salter calculated, eight times the present quantity of phosphates will be needed and eighteen times the present consumption of potash. Does the world possess enough reserves of these elements for use on such a scale? Or will nature turn out to be niggardly in this respect and so sabotage humanity's plans for expansion?

Let us see what Salter himself said on this point: "Even so, the known world reserves of phosphate would last more than 5,000 years and the known reserves of potash 500 years. The world has not been thoroughly explored for these minerals. Doubtless actual reserves exceed known reserves greatly."[10]

So there would seem to be no question as to the availability in nature of sufficient chemical fertilizers.

The picture is not so reassuring, however, with regard to their efficiency in maintaining soil health or in keeping up the nutritive quality of products and the health of the populations that consume them. There are some scientists like Dr. E. L. Bishop, former Health Director of the T.V.A., who look upon the use of artificial fertilizers as the most economical way of providing a constant restoration of soil fertility and a progressive improvement in human nutrition. But there are others, such as the late English scientist Sir Albert Howard, who regard the use of these artificial products as a veritable assault by civilization against the health of soils, plants, and men.

Howard's theory rests on the premise that synthetic fertilizers are a long way from furnishing soil with all the elements necessary to its complete restoration. This can only be accomplished by the use of natural manures and of agricultural methods more natural than those proposed by scientific Western agriculture. Howard called attention to the contrast between Western farming methods and the processes that nature uses to keep the soil in living, healthy condition:

What are the main principles underlying Nature's agriculture? These can most easily be seen in operation in our woods and forests. Mixed farming is the rule: plants are always found with animals: many species of plants and animals all live together. In the forest every form of animal life, from mammals to the simplest invertebrates, occurs. The vegetable kingdom exhibits a similar range: there is never any attempt at monoculture: mixed crops and mixed farming are the rule. . . .

And Howard insisted:

The main characteristic of Nature's farming can therefore be summed up in a few words. Mother earth never attempts to farm without livestock; she always raises mixed crops; great pains are taken to preserve the soil and to prevent erosion; the mixed vegetable and animal wastes are converted into humus; there is no waste; the processes of growth and the processes of decay balance one another; ample provision is made to maintain large reserves of fertility; the greatest care is taken to store the rainfall; both plants and animals are left to protect themselves against disease.[11]

Howard went on to accuse Western agriculture of being extremely antinature, what with machines replacing animals, one-crop farming in the saddle everywhere, and the use of artificial fertilizers becoming more general all the time. The great English agriculturalist said of artificial fertilizers:

Artificial manures are widely used. The feature of the manuring of the West is the use of artificial manures. The factories engaged during the Great War in the fixation of atmospheric nitrogen for the manufacture of explosives had to find other markets; the use of nitrogenous fertilizers in agriculture increased, until today the majority of farmers and market gardeners base their manurial programme on the cheapest forms of nitrogen (N), phosphorus (P), and potassium (K) on the market. What may be conveniently described as the NPK mentality dominates farming alike in the experimental stations and the countryside.

For Howard, the fertilizing practice that has developed out of Liebig's studies in chemistry "is based on a complete misconception of plant nutrition. It is superficial and fundamentally unsound. It takes no account of the life of the soil, including the mycorrhizal association—the living fungus bridge which connects soil and sap. Artificial manures lead inevitably to artificial nutrition, artificial food, artificial animals, and finally to artificial men and women."

Salvation might be found, according to Howard, in a return to more natural farming methods, particularly in the use of natural manures obtained from various sorts of organic matter. On the strength of his long agricultural experience in India, Howard recommended and publicized the "Indore

Process," which consists of composting animal and vegetable residues together with a chemical base which neutralizes their acidity. In a series of memorable experiments, he demonstrated that plants cultivated by his process were immune to innumerable pests and plagues and that the animals which ate them also showed surprising resistance to various epizootic diseases common in the Far East. In a speech delivered in Cheshire in 1939 (on the occasion of the reading of the famous Medical Testament which has been discussed in Chapter VI), Sir Albert Howard declared that nature and the peasants of India, in collaboration with the insects and fungi which he called "nature's own professors of agriculture," had taught people "how to grow healthy crops practically free from disease without any help from mycologists, entomologists, bacteriologists, agricultural chemists, statisticians, clearinghouses of information, artificial manures, spraying machines, insecticides, fungicides, germicides, and all the other expensive paraphernalia of the modern experiment station."[12]

Howard was without question an iconoclast whose overriding mental rebellion led him to deny categorically any and all value to modern agricultural technique. But there is undoubtedly a lot of truth in much of what he says. He is supported by certain objective facts.

On the one hand we have seen Chinese agriculture, based on the use of natural manures, endure for forty centuries without any demonstrable exhaustion of soil fertility. On the other we see how the United States, using fertilizers on a scale without precedent in the history of agriculture, has already exhausted more than 100 million acres of land in less than two centuries of cultivation. The living experience of China is a good antidote to the excessive enthusiasm of those who study agriculture in laboratories, forgetting that the natural habitat of plants is not a test tube but the bed of earth itself.

With the idea of making this Eastern experience available to the West, the American specialist F. H. King proposed to write a "Message of China and Japan to the World," to be added to his great book *Farmers of Forty Centuries*. Death, unfortunately, interrupted the preparation of this message, but from the finished portion the following significant passage has been published:

> It could not be other than a matter of the highest industrial, cultural, and social importance to any nation if it could be furnished with a full and accurate account of all those conditions which have made it possible for such dense populations to be maintained upon the products of the Chinese, Korean, and Japanese soils. Many of the steps, phases, and practices through which this evolution has passed are irrecoverably buried in the past, but such remarkable maintenance attained centuries ago and projected into the present with little apparent decadence merits the most profound study. Living as we do in the morning of a century of transition from isolated to cosmopolitan national life, when profound readjustments, industrial, educative and social, must result, such an investigation cannot be made too soon. [13]

The fact of the matter is that Western technique has a great deal to offer toward improving living conditions in the Orient, but at the same time the Orient also has weighty contributions to make to the human economy of the West. One of the most valuable of these contributions is the doctrine taught by the creator of the Indore Process. We really do not yet have sufficient data to tell whether the nutritive value of foods produced on artificially fertilized soils is or is not equal to that of foods grown on soils naturally rich in humus or restored with natural manure. But the facts seem to indicate that foods grown on artificially fertilized soils lack something or other of their full nutritional value. Howard was very sure that:

> . . . the verdict given by mother earth between humus made with animal residues and humus made with chemical activators like calcium cyanamide and the various salts of ammonia has always been in favour of the former. One has only to feel and smell a handful of compost made by these two methods to understand the plant's preference for humus made with animal residues. The one is soft to the feel with the smell of rich woodland earth: the other is often harsh to the touch with a sour odour. Sometimes when the two samples of humus made from similar vegetable wastes are analysed, the better report is obtained by the compost made with chemical activators. When, however, they are applied to the soil the plant speedily reverses the verdict of the laboratory.

It is reasonable to conclude that artificial fertilizers cannot restore soils completely, although they can be of inestimable service in making up some of the chief deficiencies. It is my opinion, however, that present-day fertilizers need a great deal more study before they are completely satisfactory. The science of soils is still far from coming of age; it is in just about the same situation as nutritional science was at the beginning of our century, before vitamins were discovered.

At that time, the science of nutrition was satisfied that the human body could be kept in balance with nothing more than sufficient doses of building materials and energy. When this principle was applied, however, by feeding chemically balanced synthetic rations to animals, it was found that all-around nutrition required something else again—something not to be found in a ration of synthetic proteins, carbohydrates, fats, and mineral salts. The missing ingredient—"X"—later came to be identified as the vitamins.

Something of the same sort must be wrong with the attempt to nourish soils with the mere mineral salts of artificial fertilizers. There is something about the process of vegetable nutrition that requires the presence of organic matter in the soil. Moreover, plant life does not depend simply on the chemical composition of the soil; there is also the question of its physical structure. With tropical soils, in fact, this is the most important factor. The agronomist Beinaert, with his broad experience of tropical African soils, always insisted that the ability of such soils to produce is a result of their physical makeup rather than of their richness in specified chemicals.

The colloidal complex is the prime element of soil fertility, as well as the greatest guarantee of its aeration and water-absorbing ability. From this fact follows the fundamental importance of conserving the soil's supply of humus. Without humus the plant can sprout, grow and bear—but something is missing in its life, just as it is in the lives of synthetically fed laboratory rats. Rats and plants so nourished easily fall sick and die for lack of natural resistance. Nobody has yet succeeded in keeping animals alive and healthy with exclusively synthetic food, and that miracle appears to be equally difficult with plants.

We can learn from the opposing views of Western agricultural experts on the one hand and the followers of Howard on the other that it is not only possible but necessary to combine the old methods and experience with the new. A combination of the practices preached by the two groups offers, perhaps, an ideal way to renew without destroying, to increase the quantity of production without permitting a qualitative decline in nutritive value.

One point is beyond all doubt. By the application of rational agricultural methods and by an increase in the cultivated area, it is fully possible to satisfy the basic nutritional needs of the world's growing population, without the Malthusian scarecrow hanging over the future of humanity like a tragic shadow. Indeed, such optimists as Colin Clark go so far as to say that there is no need to bring new lands under cultivation, that enough could be produced by scientific management of those already in use.[14]

Other scientists, who are even more optimistic than Clark, claim that even if all our soil reserves were gone, we could continue to feed ourselves by soilless culture. Following the studies of Dr. Sigfried Gericke, relatively successful attempts have been made to carry on agriculture in water enriched with the nutritive materials essential to plant life. During the war, American occupation troops on some of the sterile islands such as Ascension and Iwo Jima grew enough food in water to give great hope to the inventors of hydroponic cultivation.

But let's not be overly optimistic. Consumption levels must be substantially raised, not just maintained at their present levels. Incorporating all the soil in tropical and subpolar regions into the agricultural zone of the world must be envisioned.

[Utilizing tropical soils is not unprecedented; a portion of them have been actively exploited for a long time. Modern technology has made this exploitation even more rational and much more profitable. The discovery and application of growth hormones, which can protect certain crops from the weeds that proliferate in the tropics, has introduced a new success factor into tropical agriculture.

Toward the conquest of the subpolar lands modern genetics holds great promise. One of its marvels has been the development of plant varieties capable of living in the barest comfort, surviving and bearing with a minimum of heat and sunlight. A large number of these plants, which in the words of the Russian writer M. Ilin were sent to school to learn to live under the pole, have been suitably educated. They survive during extremely rigorous winters and bear fruit during summers that are too short for plants not steeped in this sacrificial mode. According to Ilin, "the agronomist Lysenko first had the idea of sending plants to school. The school receives them as seeds. Preparation consists of giving the seeds heat and cold, darkness and the necessary light, in predetermined proportions. When the preparation is finished, the plant is sent to the field." [15] With plants educated by Michurin, Lysenko and other seed teachers, Russia covered the formerly barren earth of the Siberian steppes. Today winter wheat, potatoes, cabbage, and turnips grow above the Arctic Circle. In Canada and Alaska, the limits of the agricultural zone have also been expanded at the expense of the boreal earth.]

Thus deserts of ice and impenetrable tropical jungles are being turned to gardens and orchards to assure a better provision for humankind, while the Malthusians go on setting up their sinister scarecrows, to little avail.

In the struggle against hunger, consideration should be given to incorporating into the agricultural tradition a number of wild plants that recent biochemical and nutritional studies have revealed as excellent sources of the principal nutrients. Studies at the Massachusetts Institute of Technology have discovered "a vast untapped food reserve" in the native flora of Central America. Upon examining some 200 specimens of regional foods in that part of the continent, the M.I.T. experts found that several were extremely rich in mineral salts and vitamins.

At the Institute of Nutrition of the University of Brazil, we have discovered, in the semiarid zone of the Brazilian northeast, plants that constitute the most abundant sources of calcium and Vitamin A in the whole world. The remarkable source of calcium thus brought to light is a bromeliaceous plant (*Bromelia laciniosa, Mart*). It can be made into a meal which contains fifteen times as much calcium as milk. [16]

The new source of Vitamin A is the oil of a palm, the *buriti* (*Mauritia flexuosa, Mart*), which contains 5,000 units of this vitamin per cubic centimeter. If such plants as these were cultivated on any appreciable scale, we would indeed have an arsenal of essential nutritive elements to arm us against specific hunger.

[Thus, an intelligent organization of agricultural production is all that is necessary to double the cultivated land area and food production of the Third World within ten years. If the water supply were adequately regulated in areas where it is excessive, like the alluvial basins of the Amazon or Congo rivers, as well as in those where it is insufficient, like the semiarid lands of the Middle East, immense grain harvests could be achieved, greatly improving the diet of these famished peoples. (Fertilizers would have to be used in conjunction with both irrigation and drainage.) This route is not the easiest and most economical for poor countries to follow, however. Rather than open up new territories without the proper machines to drain or irrigate them, it is better to utilize land that is already cultivated and inhabited and has the necessary organization for selling what is produced. The central problem, therefore, is to increase the ridiculously low productivity of such land. Two significant examples suffice: in India, where rice is the basic food, its rate of production is about 990 pounds an acre, while in Italy it is nearly two tons and in Japan more than a ton and a half, four and three times higher respectively. In India, fifteen cows are required to produce the amount of milk that a single animal gives in the United States.

The abysmally low productivity of agriculture in the tropical and subtropical regions is not, as is often believed, the inevitable consequence of unfavorable soil and climate conditions. It is essentially the result of primitive and unscientific farming methods employed there, while in the well-developed countries, agriculture proceeds as if the land were a biochemical factory powered by solar energy. If the transition to industrial production is to be made, it is necessary to move beyond the earth and man as God created them and make adequate use of new production factors. Over and above that, the land, as well as man, must be reformed and made more efficient. Among the factors that can help to raise productivity rates decisively are the following: the adequate use of fertilizers; the genetic selection of varieties that give the best return, qualitatively and quantitatively; the use of insecticides, herbicides, and fungicides; and the application of substances that accelerate the growth of plants and strengthen their photosynthetic power. All these techniques rest on a solid scientific basis and are of proven efficacy.

Let us return to the problem of artificial fertilizers and chemical correctives of soil composition. Few sciences have made as much progress as has the biochemistry of soils from the time of Liebig until now—and perhaps no other has been so little applied in the interests of mankind. Fertilizers play only a tiny role in the farming methods of underdeveloped areas. The average consumption of fertilizers in the underdeveloped countries is less than 5.5 pounds per acre, while it is more than 44 pounds in the advanced countries. The Third World now produces about 1.5 million tons of fertilizers and uses about 3 million, importing 50 percent of what it needs from the industrialized countries. But according to specialists, these areas should, at minimum, consume 15 million tons—five times more than they now use, or half the present world production.

Only by making up the soil's deficiencies with fertilizers will it be possible to double the production of food. The present rate of increase, an insignificant 2 percent a year, is not even enough to keep up with population growth, a fact that appears to give some support to the theories of Malthus and his modern disciples. Certain experiments undertaken in connection with the World Campaign Against Hunger categorically prove the economic value of fertilizers: in Turkey, by using 106 pounds of fertilizer per acre it was possible to raise the productivity of corn by 85 percent; in Lebanon, the application of 46 pounds of fertilizer per cultivated acre doubled the productivity of wheat; in Ecuador, the same quantity of fertilizer raised the potato crop by 71 percent.

These are eloquent examples, and these results were obtained by means of fertilization alone. The increase would have been much greater if, as has been done in Japan and the United States, fertilizer had been used in combination with the genetic selection of plant varieties. By themselves, fertilizers are often not very satisfactory from the economic point of view, which discourages the farmers of poor countries. In the United States, the combined use of fertilizers and certain varieties of corn produced by genetic experiment brought about a 100 percent increase in productivity from 1949 to 1950, despite a 13 percent cut in the area planted. This combination also explains the extraordinary milk productivity of certain varieties of cattle: a milk cow in India gives on the average 465 pounds a year; the figure is 8,770 for the Netherlands and 9,151 for Israel. Improvement of the herds is closely connected with improvement of the forage and secondary grains that are the essential foods for cattle. In the areas of both fertilizers and genetic selection the conquests of recent years hold out great promise. Today's fertilizers, unlike those in use over the last century, do more than merely restore the nitrogen, phosphorus, and potassium to overworked soil. Soil supplements and correctives also furnish elements that, while secondary in terms of quantity, are equally indispensable for the maintenance of the land's biological potential, the trace elements. The science of fertilizers has advanced perhaps even further than that of nutrition itself toward the correction of various kinds of soil deficiencies. Unfortunately, none of this is affecting the underdeveloped countries, primarily because the backward agrarian economy of these regions has ossified into a state where every act is considered a rite, untouchable and unchangeable. Furthermore, the fertilizer industry is profitable only in a highly differentiated industrial context; it needs to draw on a whole series of byproducts of other industries that are generally nonexistent in less developed countries. All these things conspire against the establishment of technically advanced agriculture in poor and nonindustrialized countries. As a first step, these countries' fertilizer requirements must be met through imports, a process that should be made as easy as possible by international organizations that are interested in genuine economic development for the Third World.

The most spectacular improvements in agricultural production have been obtained through genetic research on new varieties of grain, discoveries that are on the way to revolutionizing the world's food production. New varieties of corn, wheat, and rice are being cultivated in several underdeveloped countries with surprising results.

Corn, which is a basic food in a number of areas including Mexico, the *sertão* of northeast Brazil, and Rumania, has always been rightly considered an incomplete nutrient of little biological value, because it is low in protein and in certain essential amino acids, especially lysine. By means of hybridization, some American geneticists have developed a new variety of corn called "Opaque 2," which contains a valuable protein rich in lysine and in addition has a higher rate of productivity than the classic varieties. The International Center for the Improvement of Corn and Wheat, which has its headquarters in Mexico, is carrying on with this research, and its work offers great hope for a rise in nutritional levels in those areas where corn is the basic food. Financed by the Rockefeller and Ford foundations, the Center has also made sensational progress in wheat productivity through the creation of new varieties and has set up a kind of "bank" containing varieties of seeds suited to the ecological systems of different countries. One of these varieties, Mexican dwarf wheat, has been grown with startling success in several regions of the world, results that justify the twenty-five years of research in genetics that the Center has carried out. The possibility of doubling, tripling, or quadrupling the usual return per acre has led a number of undernourished countries to become interested in this miraculous hybrid and to import large quantities of the seed. In 1966, India imported 18,000 tons; Pakistan, 42,000 tons; and Tunisia, 23,000. Their hopes have been greatly surpassed, as we saw in the section on India. Another miraculous genetic development, produced by the International Rice Research Institute in the Philippines, has made possible a sixfold increase in productivity in certain rice-growing areas. The diffusion of all these varieties has been vigorously supported by the F.A.O. and especially by its director, A. H. Boerma, as an effective contribution to the struggle against hunger.

Another major step forward would be the intelligent use of the enormous food potential contained in the world's oceans, rivers, and lakes. This wealth, spread over three quarters of the surface of our planet, now furnishes only 2 percent of the calories man consumes and 10 percent of the animal proteins—insignificant amounts when we consider that, according to trustworthy estimates, the sea could annually yield about 100 billion tons of animal products (fish, shellfish, mollusks) and some 500 billion tons of vegetable matter. The abundance of the oceans is infinitely superior to that of the land. But today we take advantage of only a tiny fraction of this biological potential, and our methods of fishing and harvesting algae and plankton are, in fact, primitive, analogous to the ways in which food was gathered on land in pre-agricultural economies.

Fishing, which until quite recently was limited to the continental shelves, is only now beginning to extend to the deep seas, by means of factory ships that can deep-freeze the fish or use certain kinds of radiation to preserve them. Herein lies one of the greatest hopes for a solution to the nutritional problem, especially in the crucial area of proteins. The industrial production of a fish meal acceptable for human consumption is among the most important benefits that food technology can render to hungry peoples.

Much more rapid progress can be made in extracting wealth from the sea than in improving agricultural production, because it requires no break with archaic social patterns. The example of Peru proves the point. Peru's fishing industry, which not long ago was of secondary importance on the world market, was able in a few years to take first place, surpassing even Japan's. It grew at a rate of nearly 20 percent a year, while Peru's agricultural production was increasing at not more than 3 percent. The contrast is instructive.

Gradually, fishing will give way to something less haphazard and more organized: the planned breeding and raising of marine life. This will be done by seeding certain maritime areas, principally gulfs and bays, to grow plants that can nourish great numbers of fish and shellfish. This farming of the sea—marinoculture—will perhaps be more important in the near future than traditional agriculture. Israel's example indicates the dimensions of what will soon be possible on a world scale. Israel, which today holds the world record for productivity in inland waters, has over 12,000 acres of organized fish culture, producing an average of 810 pounds of fish per acre.

As well as the organized cultivation of land and sea, science offers other possible solutions to the food problem. One of the most important is the industrial production of nutritive substances: the transformation of inedible matter into food or the chemical synthesis of new substances. Today, using even such processes as extraction by vibration, almost pure proteins can be obtained from certain oleaginous seeds, from certain kinds of beans, and even from leaves and grasses. These methods are already in use in England and India.

At the present time, important quantities of proteins are being obtained by growing yeast, principally on a molasses base. In England, a variety of yeast is cultivated in the residue of potatoes, and the yield is 50 percent protein.

The most spectacular example of industrial biological

transformation is the production of proteins from a substance resulting from the distillation of petroleum. The first factory to produce food derived from petroleum is already in operation at Lavera, in the south of France, using a process based on experiments carried out, partly under my inspiration, by Dr. Champagnat. He obtained a product that is already fed to animals and will certainly be introduced gradually and without any risk into the human diet. Producing proteins from petroleum is not an expensive process, and it will be possible to do it in enormous volume, largely resolving the problem of protein deficiency. By a happy coincidence, a good number of the countries that suffer from this type of deficiency—Middle Eastern and Latin American nations—are major petroleum producers.

Until the photosynthesis of proteins can be effected, the greatest hope in the domain of synthetic products rests on the synthesis of certain amino acids that are now used to enrich low-value proteins. The General Electric laboratories in Schenectady, New York, are synthesizing various amino acids—some biologically, others chemically—and are doing so at a profit. This is a rapidly developing field that is opening up hitherto inconceivable possibilities for conquering hunger. Like other technical successes, it is being extended and amplified through research in nuclear physics.

Bioatomic research is making inestimable contributions in the development of new types of plants. Mutations provoked by atomic bombardment give rise to plants that not only produce better but also possess greater resistance to disease and to the hostility of the natural environment. Atomic science is also opening up important new methods of preserving food and avoiding the enormous waste of previous eras. Progress will be speeded in a variety of other ways by the employment in agronomy and nutrition of radio elements, or radioisotopes, which can be identified at the various stages of an experiment with soil or with a living organism. These trace elements have considerably advanced our knowledge in the area of photosynthesis, which may well produce the definitive answer to the nutrition problem.

I have tried briefly to indicate some of the possibilities that a technology based on the natural sciences, especially on biology and physical chemistry, offers for solving the most serious problem that humanity will have to confront in the coming years. In pointing out some of the uses to which certain important discoveries of modern science and technology could be put in the production of food, my aim has been to prove that the problem of hunger is not insoluble, that the Malthusian battle has not already been lost. There are practical and effective means to win it without subjecting mankind to any so-called natural obligation that requires artificially limiting world population growth. No justification exists for exerting a forced and artificial control over the birth rate. Attempts to do so appear to many peoples as discriminatory, a form of racist genocide that certain ruling powers are trying to impose on the groups that they dominate economically. Such a policy is dangerous, for it increases social tension and aggravates the risk that the world will explode in conflict.]

8
Geography of Abundance

No doubt remains that science and technology can play a decisive part in solving the problem of hunger. Production of foodstuffs can be increased to the point of satisfying fully the nutritional needs of all the human race. And the possible contribution of science would be greater still if students of biological problems had only received more stimulus and support from the ruling circles of our time.

The fact is that our mechanistic and utilitarian civilization has always relegated the biological sciences to a secondary plane. Major attention has been concentrated on the production of wealth; much more thought has been given to physical and chemical research than to the field of biology. The disparity between the successes achieved is apparent to all.

It must not be forgotten that men of science can work only if they are paid. They eat, dress, and have families like common mortals. And it so happens that these scientists get on a payroll only when their labors are of interest to somebody, whether it be an individual, an industry, or a government. Now governments, institutions, and employers, during the last century of Western culture, have been excessively absorbed in problems of economic exploitation and have in general shown no great interest in human problems as such. Man was treated as hardly more than an element of production, a cog in the economic machine. That is why there are a great many more paying positions for physicists and chemists than biologists.

Physical and chemical research are of prime utility to the commerce and industry that finance them, while health, which is the main beneficiary of biological research, pays no direct dividends. An English observer noted that in one industrial research laboratory alone—that of the Imperial Chemical Industries—the number of technicians working out new advances in the field of chemistry, in 1940, was a good deal larger than the total number of research biologists in the whole British Empire. It is obvious that the industrial chemists, with their larger numbers, better pay, and better equipment, are in a more favorable position to make discoveries and to hasten the progress of their science than the thin ranks of biologists, who are left to their narrowly personal enthusiasms and to their strange attachment to the study of problems that the leading elements of the world in general care little about.

Nevertheless, even with our limited knowledge of phenomena in the living world—with the present resources of agrobiological science—it would still be possible to carry out a veritable revolution in the field of food production. It would be possible, that is, except for the opposition of certain economic and political forces which stand in the way of large-scale application of scientific knowledge.

Planning for Plenty

To wipe out hunger, it is necessary to raise the productive levels of marginal peoples and groups and through economic progress to integrate them into the economic community. Such raising of productive levels depends on very many factors, the most important of which, no doubt, is the type of economic organization in which the individuals take part. Certain kinds of economic exploitation invariably impose infrahuman levels of productivity, far short of normal, minimum necessities. So long as these types of economic exploitation continue, hunger will continue to haunt our civilization, in spite of all our efforts.

The so-called "colonial" or "neocolonial" economy, under which the industrial powers get their raw materials at low cost and on this basis enjoy a marked prosperity, is one kind of economic exploitation that is incompatible with world economic balance. As we have seen in previous chapters, the world's great areas of endemic hunger are exactly those regions that are, or until very recently were, under colonial domination. They may be political colonies, such as the territories of Africa were, and in part still are, or they may be economic colonies as China was and as the greater part of Latin America remains, dedicated as it is to the production of raw materials to feed the industries of Europe and the United States.

Without a basic change in colonial policy, which would permit the colonial peoples to produce on a scale sufficient to satisfy their biological needs, there is no use hoping for a radical solution to the problem of universal hunger. Countries with dependent economies will go hungry just as long as they dedicate their best efforts to producing raw materials for export at low prices, because the play of world economic forces always tends to reduce the value of their labor in the interest of industrial profits. I should like to give a few examples of the greatly inferior acquisitive capacity of peoples in colonial situations. I shall take these examples not from true political colonies but from politically independent countries that continue to labor under a colonial economic structure.

Cuba was and continues to be one of the world's greatest sugar producers, yet in the 1940's a Cuban factory worker could buy, with his day's wages, only a quarter as much sugar as an average factory worker in the United States could buy with his daily wage, according to an investigation carried out by technicians of the National Planning Association of Washington, D.C. During the same period a factory worker in Colombia worked four hours to buy an amount of coffee corresponding to one hour's work in the United States—and Colombia was one of the leading coffee-producing countries.[1] [The systems of latifundia and low-salaried single-crop agriculture, which to some degree still exist in all colonial areas, produce an ideal growth medium for poverty, wretchedness, and hunger.] Colonial peoples have built their economies around one or two export products whose prices are always fixed by users in the mother country. At the same time, they have had to import an infinity of industrial products at prices also set by the mother country. As a result, the people have remained sunk in poverty. Only by freeing themselves from the colonial system can these hunger areas develop enough production to live on. They can do this not only by diversifying production but also by setting a fair price for raw materials and by working them up locally.

The problem cannot be solved by increasing individual productivity alone and so expanding the production of certain products. The article produced must be valued in keeping with the needs of the producers. This means that the prices of raw materials cannot forever be set on the basis of profit margins, through the play of competition for industrial products. They must be related to the cost of basic local necessities in the groups producing raw materials. A French economist was entirely right in calling attention to the dangers and disillusionment inherent in the belief that everything can be solved by a simple increase in productivity.[2] Productivity is no doubt the key to the problem, but it must be approached in terms of humanistic economics.

A case in point is that of Venezuela, where petroleum production per capita is among the highest in the world. But production of oil and nothing else has led to inflation of prices; that nominal wages are high, giving an impression of high individual productivity, doesn't prevent the country from being one of the great hunger spots of the world. Before the petroleum dynasty was established, the people of Venezuela produced meat and corn and fed themselves reasonably well. Today, however, to keep the population from starving, it is necessary to import [a major part of the country's food].[3] These imports cost all the apparent wealth brought in by export of oil, and still people do not have enough to eat.

In 1943, when the United Nations delegates at Hot Springs assumed responsibility for raising the living and nutritional standards of these peoples, they were perhaps not fully aware of the scale or the complexity of what they had undertaken. It took some time to find out how hard it was going to be to establish a really effective policy for the Food and Agriculture Organization, the agency they set up to attack the problem in its world-wide aspects.

In 1946 John Boyd-Orr, then director general of the F.A.O., submitted to the United Nations governments a proposal to create a World Food Board "to provide financial and other technical arrangements necessary to convert human need into effective demand in the markets of the world."[4] It was to be the duty of this organ to control the nutritional economy of the world; to promote stabilization of food prices; to buy and sell in the world markets, setting up food reserves and apportioning the surplus of given products to the areas that needed them most. Unfortunately, the proposal was never approved, and the F.A.O., for lack of specific powers, found itself limited to a kind of international consultative function, being, as LeGros Clark put it, "a world brain on all matters concerned with the production, the distribution, and the consumption of food and other products of soil, and the seas."[5]

This limited operation of the F.A.O. has placed difficulties in the way of carrying out its mission, and new proposals have consequently been brought forward in an effort to strengthen its activity in the field of world economic policy.

The danger of overproduction relative to world consumer markets arose toward the end of 1948, and in June 1949 the F.A.O. set up a Special Committee of Experts to outline a general plan of action on a world scale. What worried the F.A.O. leaders was the discovery that following the economic splendor of American agriculture during the war and the first postwar years, farm prices had begun to fall in 1948, so that cash farm income was running 10 percent less in 1949 than it had in the previous year. The Committee of Experts, which included such outstanding specialists as John Condliffe, Colin Clark, J. K. Galbraith, D. Ghosh, Gustavo Polit, and A. Radomysler, after considering all sides of the question, proposed the creation of an International Commodity Clearinghouse, with the aim of controlling the purchase and distribution of foods. The technicians justified their posposal as follows:

> We make this proposal because of agricultural surpluses, a threat that need never materialize if action is prepared now while yet there is time. This action, to be effective, must be international. National governments are equipped with the means of regulating farm prices and production; but national action is not enough. On the contrary, it can easily degenerate as it did in the 1930's into competitive dumping. Agricultural nationalism, experience has shown, can be more destructive than any other form of economic nationalism. What we propose is an international instrument of consultation and cooperative action in the commodity field, so that nations may join in concerted efforts to attack the common enemies of mankind—poverty, disease, and hunger—instead of each attacking the other's prosperity in a futile effort to defend its own.

After citing the world's commercial imbalance, the committee announced the necessity of carrying out an effective attack against this situation and toward the end set out five different fields of struggle:

There are five major fields in which an attack must be made. All are intricately connected and all are of vital importance. They do, however, have an appropriate time sequence and we list them in that order. The necessary measures are:

1. The maintenance of a high level of production and employment, particularly in the United States. In this case, as in others, the issue is not that the United States economy is less stable than that of other countries but rather that this economy is so critically important in that of the world.

2. The reduction of trade restrictions, including tariffs and quantitative and monetary restriction. In particular, the present dollar disequilibrium calls for measures to facilitate access to the United States market.

3. An increase in the standards of productive efficiency, particularly in countries of Western Europe.

4. The provision, by private enterprise and by national and international action, of large and continuing capital investments by the developed in the less developed areas of the world. This is necessary to finance the export surpluses of the former and the import surpluses of the latter.

5. The restoration of convertible currencies and multilateral transactions as the basis of world trade.[6]

This plan of action might well have had some effect if it had really been orientated toward the living conditions and vital needs of underfed human groups, and not treated merely as a temporary shot in the arm for overloaded export markets.

There can be no doubt whatever that one of the great drawbacks to this plan was its forced limitation to part of the world and the impossibility of extending it to include the U.S.S.R. and the other countries within the economic orbit of the Soviet world. The ideal would be to seek an understanding in this field of vital human necessities, so as to permit a broad utilization of world resources, the economic integration of all nations, and an improvement in the living standards of humanity as a whole. When those who are responsible for the destinies of the two halves of the world come to realize that world problems can hardly be solved on the basis of closed economies, then perhaps an era of greater understanding and tolerance will open up for humanity and cooperation may become possible on a truly universal scale.

One thing is certain—the best way to attain such cooperation is to reduce economic and social inequality by an adequate policy of development for the world's more backward areas. A world food policy, therefore, implies a sound policy of technical assistance to such areas, directed toward their genuine economic progress. Such technical assistance should not be limited to furnishing means and resources merely to enable them to produce more efficiently and more profitably the same raw materials that are now produced in colonial areas. Great Britain has already furnished this limited sort of technical assistance to various of its former African colonies and, far from improving nutritional conditions in those areas, has succeeded only in making them much worse. The technical assistance should be adjusted in accordance with the characteristics of each country and should aim at the integrated development of its natural resources for the benefit of the people as a whole. Proper technical help would mean rational and scientific use of the soil; restoration of worn-out land; industrialization of local products; plans for electrification, irrigation, and transportation—in short, a whole complex of projects that would liberate these areas from economic colonialism. The application of technology "in suitable forms and in assimilable doses," as the Milbank Fund study puts it,[7] is capable of bringing about the economic liberation of such regions and their transformation into zones of high productivity and full employment, within an expanding world economy.

Colonial Emancipation and Mutual Economic Interests

It is quite possible to make the transition from a colonial economy to a cooperative world economy based on mutual interests without the imperialist or colonizing countries going bankrupt. Everything depends on the attitude of the neo-colonial powers toward the new world reality. As colonial areas develop into great consumer markets, they will be in a position to contribute substantially to the consolidation of a more balanced economy, by absorbing certain surplus products of more highly developed areas. The American Revolution in freeing the thirteen British colonies did not injure the English economy but actually contributed greatly to its expansion. As soon as they were free, the former colonies became a prosperous market for British products, much ampler and more varied than the colonial market. "A growing U.S.," says Earl Parker Hanson, "did as much as India to create Britain's Victorian greatness."[8]

Latin America, Africa, and parts of the Far East constitute enormous potential markets which will begin to take their place in the world economy just as soon as their inhabitants, properly fed, can produce enough to reach a living standard in keeping with the technical possibilities of the modern age. Upon the improvement of living conditions in these areas now dominated by hunger and misery, therefore, depend the economic security and prosperity of the whole world. Under an economy of abundance, with adequate nutritional resources available to all human groups, a radical transformation will undoubtedly take place in the world's social structure. The Geography of Abundance will be matched by new social structures, which will guarantee the attainment of a new stage in the universal search for happiness and social well-being.

Two fundamental benefits will be achieved by seeing that everybody is well fed: the winning of health and the winning of security—collective victories over sickness and fear. Those ailments, one physical and the other moral, are the two most degrading characteristics of our civilization.

I have already had occasion to demonstrate, in various chapters of this book, to what a terrible degree disease holds back the march of social progress. Its damage is equally significant in economic terms. The losses due to disease in the United States, for instance, are calculated at $10 billion annually,[9]* and the annual cost of sickness in England reaches some £185 billion.[10]† These figures give some idea of the tremendous sums that ill health steals from the world economy. Now, it has been categorically demonstrated that a majority of the diseases to which humanity is exposed could be avoided, or at least greatly reduced in their incidence and effects, by an adequate diet. With freedom from hunger, human groups would also escape the oppression of fear, which often leads to attitudes that are incompatible with the dignity of human existence.

Biological Crisis and Political Crisis

There are those who try to explain the decadence of our civilization and its inevitable downfall as a progressive reduction in the number of individuals capable of bearing on their shoulders the enormous weight of our culture. This reduction is attributed to the biological and physical decadence of man, to his lack of strength and courage to face social reality. But this weakness and this fear are, in great part, results of the hunger or threat of hunger to which a great number of human groups in our time are exposed.

The fact is that many peoples, subjected to the dissolving action of hunger, surrender without a struggle to destructive

* $30 billion.
† £300 million.

and antisocial forces. We have seen how the siege of hunger delivered Japan over to fascism. The same mechanism led to the triumph of Naziism in Europe during 1930-40. With many individuals lashed by hunger, and the threat of hunger creating a general panic, it was easy for the "hypnotists of the multitudes," as Keyserling called the leaders, to knead the masses into a yielding dough. At that grave hour in history, certain European peoples felt themselves too weak to march forward with the dead weight of culture on their shoulders; they felt too weak to free themselves, by their own energies, from the moral asphyxia that surrounded them and so surrendered voluntarily to the urgings of the Fuehrers. Not knowing what to do with their hands, these poor slaves of misery gave in to the imperative gesture and, renouncing personality entirely, responded with the salute of submission. It expressed a voluntary loss of liberty, but it also gained them a momentary relief through flight from responsibility.

The collective psychosis that swept Europe at that time expressed a psychological crisis superimposed on a latent biological crisis. It was similar in many ways to a phenomenon observed by Pavlov in his experiments with conditioned reflexes in dogs. These animals could be so conditioned by the fear of hunger or of suffering that all their previous reflexes became entirely inhibited. The same thing happened to Europe, whose overwhelming anxiety complex has been well characterized by Pierre Janet in the following passage:

> Today the number of the depressed is enormous, individuals without sufficient energy to take an interest in public affairs, individuals in terror of social action. As a result they feel an overwhelming need for guidance and protection, and that is why dictatorships seem so attractive to them.

When Europe let itself be enslaved by the wave of Nazi fascism, it was giving way to an impulse to save its skin—"its dirty hide," Curzio Malaparte calls it, symbolizing thereby the instincts that cry out imperiously from within the animal-man, particularly the instinct of hunger. "Before, one suffered, killed, and died to save one's soul. Today man suffers and makes others suffer, kills and is killed, does magnificent things and beastly things, merely in order to save his skin," says Malaparte, in a mocking, grotesquely tragic tone.[11] This exaggerated love of one's own skin, this anguished impulse to satisfy the vegetative needs, derives from suffering, from fear, and from anguish provoked by the bitter experience of hunger. If society wants to recover its moral outlook, if it wants to see an increase in the number of men strong enough to fight, not only for their skins but for a world of democratic principles worthy of human beings, then it must first of all eliminate completely the degrading pressure of hunger.

An economy of abundance will take humanity a great step forward toward the quantitative, as well as the qualitative, solution of population problems. People will not only become abler and healthier; they will be better adjusted, numerically, to their natural and cultural resources. Among those human groups which today seem most exposed to the dangers of overpopulation, there will quickly come about a reduction in the exaggerated indexes of fertility, or, as Vogt puts it, their uncontrolled reproductive appetite, and the curve of demographic growth will tend toward an equilibrium of population.

The road to world survival, therefore, does not lie in the neo-Malthusian prescriptions to eliminate surplus people, nor in birth control, but in the effort to make everybody on the face of the earth productive. Hunger and misery are not caused by the presence of too many people in the world but rather by having few to produce and many to feed. The neo-Malthusian doctrine of a dehumanized economy, which preaches that the weak and the sick should be left to die, which would help the starving to die more quickly and which even goes to the extreme of suggesting that medical and sanitary resources should not be made available to the more miserable populations—such policies merely reflect the mean and egotistical sentiments of people living well, terrified by the disquieting presence of those who are living badly.

[After twenty years of bilateral and multilateral aid, public and private, after many attempts at technical assistance and successive injections of dollars into the Third World ($100 billion between 1950 and 1965), living standards there are farther than ever below those of the developed, industrialized countries, and the gap is continually widening. To talk of closing it is now utopian; rather, people speak in terms of building bridges over the abyss. Charles Iffland states that in the light of basic statistical data, aid to the poor countries is facing a dead end.[12] He is perfectly right.

Everyone seems to agree about the failure of the development programs. It has become clear that they rested on principles that doomed their effectiveness. Sustained efforts are now under way, aiming to uncover the weak points of the old approach and to conceive a new strategy of development that can save the world from the grave dangers represented by this growth disparity between two worlds that are contiguous but not integrated—the world of development and abundance and the world of underdevelopment and misery.

Certain serious errors were committed that caused the entire development effort to amount to little. The greatest error was to conceive the development process everywhere as analogous to the development of the rich countries of the West.

A kind of ethnocentrism led the majority of the theoreticians of development to base their ideas and build their systems on a conception of classical economics that was almost totally ignorant of the socioeconomic reality of the dependent areas. They forgot that there is no integrated world economy but only a Western economy full of contradictions, a socialist economy still being worked out, and, in the rest of the world, a system of buying and selling necessities. They did not concern themselves with the economic structure of the rest of the world; that was abandoned to the sociologists, or rather to the "folklorists." They forgot the human beings of these areas, with their traditional culture that is so distant and so different from Western civilization. Indeed, the West forgets human beings everywhere in its frenzy of productivity.

They thought that by injecting Western capital, discoveries, inventions, and innovations, they were going to change the traditional structures of the non-Western world and bring about development. The miracle did not happen. The illusion of assistance, the solution that seemed so simple in the first years, was followed by a sense of deception and pessimism, which led to the idea that the backwardness of the Third World is an almost insoluble problem. These countries are underdeveloped, said the Western pessimists, because of the force of circumstance, biological fatality, or geographic determinism, because of natural conditions that impede their access to truly independent development.

Was the distribution of wealth carried out automatically by what Adam Smith called the "invisible hand"—the power in liberal economics that was in charge of promoting the economic balance of the world? Unfortunately, the "invisible hand" has never acted for the good of mankind, and the visible hand of the privileged, ruling groups has always monopolized economic benefits, excluding great masses of people and leaving them in wretchedness and deprivation. Today, these peoples are called the "populations of the underdeveloped countries."

In fact, underdevelopment is not the absence of development but the product of wrongly directed development. It is not produced by some natural force, inexorably, but because of historic reasons—by the force of circumstance.

Development implies an increase of wealth and social change—both aimed at serving man. But we must recognize that this notion of development, although more complete than earlier notions of progress (the increase of wealth), is still not completely free of emotional prejudice nor is it scientifically precise. If development means—for all—the passage from a lower level to a higher level, there is still no unanimity about what criteria and values determine these different levels.

The failure to recognize fundamental needs leads to manufacturing false needs. Aspirations are injected from outside by the subtle system of advertising that is part of the consumer civilization in the "developed" countries. There is a sad formula that expresses this situation in the slogan of a large store: "Even if you don't know what you want, come in; we have it." We must form a clear notion of the goals of development. These are not only an increase of wealth nor even an increase of productivity per individual, as it is taken to be in official circles of the United Nations. It is something more complex that must embrace total human betterment through the enrichment of all the values of life. That is where a real policy of development can begin.

Conditions for a New Policy

It is not difficult to point out the weak points of world structures in terms of international cooperation for development, but I shall limit myself to the problem of international aid. First of all, what is called international aid—public grants and loans as well as private investments in developing areas—has always been insufficient, badly distributed, and badly applied. The United Nations recommendation that the rich countries devote at least one percent of their gross national product to international aid has not been followed by all the rich and well-developed countries. Only France has maintained a fairly continuous contribution of more than 1 percent. The United States and Great Britain, in all forms of aid, have never surpassed 0.5 percent of their gross national products. Even more disturbing, however, is the fact that the transfer of financial resources, which averaged a 15 percent annual increase between 1950 and 1961, leveled off at that time and now tends to decrease relative to the national revenues of the "donor" countries.

In addition, aid is generally bound, that is, conditioned on advantages demanded or expected in exchange for the assistance. But a number of developing countries are distrustful of this type of aid in speculative capital controlled by groups that will reap exclusive benefits.

Moreover, there can be no true social progress if individuals are not liberated from moral underdevelopment. Certain well-developed countries are, as Louis O'Neill describes them, "rich and underdeveloped."[13] The pre-condition for balanced world development is the development of man—the formation of capable and responsible people who will establish a real dialogue between the two worlds of abundance and poverty, two worlds that do not listen to each other now and understand each other less and less.

Among the criteria used in establishing priority for the insufficient investments made in the Third World countries has been a tendency to apply them almost exclusively to sectors that are thought to be "profitable"; that is, there has been a tendency to think about the production apparatus rather than about the human beings involved. This has led to the failure of all attempts at accelerated industrialization in countries where the weakness of human structures and the absence of a mass of consumers did not permit this economic adventure. Also forgotten was the fact that pre-capitalist societies are ritualist: each action is a rite. The introduction of a new technique cannot be separated from a new system of thinking. Fortunately, international aid donors are beginning to recognize that there are not two sets of investments: the profitable ones that lead to immediate production and the unprofitable ones that improve human conditions through education and health.

A new science has been born—economic psychology— which has a somewhat broader vision than classical economics and has led to the formation of an economics of education, an essential element in the formation and increase of human capital. An international politics of development should start with the formation of human capital, because only through human labor can wealth be created. Economic vitality is created in direct proportion to the quantity and quality of this specific production factor—human beings, the motive power of the economic machine.

Father Louis Joseph Lebret used to speak about the urgent necessity of moving toward the conversion of man:[14] on the one hand, changing the consciousness of men geared to power and domination, and on the other, creating a mentality nourished by the taste and desire for progress and the determination to obtain the benefits of true development. Within this new concept of development, learning, education, and training must be seen as the essential and most profitable investment.

In this new strategy for global development, three goals are essential:

1. To struggle against the persistent tendency to exterior imbalance in terms of commercial relationships between the underdeveloped world that produces raw materials and basic products and the industrialized world where the finished products are manufactured.

2. To fight the deficit of savings in the Third World, crushed by indebtedness to foreign creditors.

3. To work against these countries' economic vulnerability to peripheral encroachments.

In working toward this new policy, Europe has a great role

to play and supreme interests to defend. In the strategy of world political forces, where the North American economy and the Soviet are confronting each other, Europe must create, in order to overcome its own difficulties and affirm itself, other viable economic centers in close cooperation with the Third World. It must bet on a polycentrism that is able to avoid world-wide involvement in the rivalry of the super-powers.

The path to safety is still open to mankind. We will travel it on the basis of the trust we must place in our own powers. "The sciences of man are great, but man is still greater," a modern thinker has written,[15] reaffirming the trust that we must in our own days conserve in the grandeur of the human species.]

Notes

Introduction

1. Food and Agriculture Organization of the United Nations, *Besoins Energétiques et Besoins en Protéines: Rapport d'un Comité Spécial Mixte F.A.O./O.M.S. d'Experts* (Rome 1973).
2. Ibid., p. 71. Also in Nations-Unies, *Conférence Mondiale de l'Alimentation,* Rapport No. 52, *Point 8 de l'ordre du Jour* (Rome, 1974), p. 65.
3. L. Joy, "Food and Nutrition Planning," *Journal of Agricultural Economics* 14:1 (January 1973), p. 17.
4. Ibid., pp. 4-5.
5. Joy shows that amino acid fortification is of no significant value, except in special cases, in repairing inadequacies in protein intake. This conclusion is implicit in the fact that a protein deficiency is unlikely to appear when caloric needs are satisfied. Yet protein enrichment has been hailed as a panacea, and huge amounts of money have been spent on the marketing of the associated technologies by U.S.A.I.D., "philanthropic" foundations (financed by agribusinesses), and international organizations.
6. F.A.O./W.H.O./U.N.I.C.E.F., Protein Advisory Group, "Review of the Specific Proposals Contained in the ACAST Report," *International Action to Avert the Impending Protein Crisis* (U.N., 1971).
7. Michel Cépède, Hugues Gounelle, *La faim* (Paris: Presses Universitaires de France, 1970), p. 76.
8. Jacoby, in *Le Monde Diplomatique* (October 1974), notes that

international organizations are infiltrated by multinational corporations, particularly in the case of the F.A.O. and the agribusiness complex.

9. Ibid.

10. F.A.O., *Besoins Energétiques*, p. 81.

11. Ibid., p. 9.

12. The consumption of animal proteins implies a high intake of fats (see U.S.D.A., *Composition of Foods*, Agriculture Handbook No. 8, 1963, for data). In countries with high per-capita income, half of the energy intake comes from fat either in the form of vegetable oils or of fats involved in the consumption of *animal* products. Moreover, sugar (that is, energy devoid of any other nutrient) supplies an increasing proportion of the energy intake, up to 20 percent. Cereals (bread, rice, etc.) play a small and decreasing role in diet. Commenting on these tendencies, the nutritionists of the F.A.O. and W.H.O. write: "The rising incidence of diseases linked to nutrition (diabetes, obesity, heart and coronary diseases) raised the question of whether these tendencies are not detrimental in the long run." Indeed they are! (*Besoins Energétiques*, pp. 9, 21, 23.) Moreover, modern techniques of intensive feeding produce meat with an abnormally high content of hazardous saturated fats; "modern" meat, in fact, does not contain the necessary proportions of unsaturated fats! (*Science et Vie*, May 1975, p. 30.)

13. Most of the data are taken from Nations-Unies, *Conférence Mondiale de l'Alimentation*, pp. 66-79.

14. M. Ojala, Assistant Director of F.A.O., has produced such figures for the Colloque du CENECA (Paris, April 1975).

15. J. Klatzmann, in *Nourrir 10 milliards d'hommes*, (Paris: Presses Universitaires de France, 1975), p. 64, computes the cost of diet in various parts of the world. If 1 represents the cost of the Indian diet, the U.S. diet, in contrast, costs 6.3. These costs are calculated on the basis of market prices and do not take into consideration the "cost" of a starving person.

16. Nations-Unies, *Conférence Mondiale de l'Alimentation*, pp. 77-78.

17. Klatzmann, *Nourrir 10 Milliards*, p. 53.

18. Ibid.

19. Nations-Unies, *Conférence Mondiale*, p. 79.

20. In 1958, de Castro wrote a book on the cycle of crabs in Recife.

21. Michel Cépède, "Biographie de de Castro," *Encyclopedia Universalis.* My biographical notes draw on Professor Cépède's article and on documents supplied by Mrs. de Castro.

22. John Boyd-Orr studied the wretched nutritional conditions of the British lower classes in the 1920's. He was the first head of the F.A.O. but he, along with André Mayer, the head of the Executive Council, lost his position in 1947 when the F.A.O. was reorganized along governmental lines. Boyd-Orr and Mayer wanted a world food policy, not just a program that would dispose of supluses and leave commercial exchanges undisturbed. (See, for example, Michel Cépède, F.A.O. Conférence Commémorative Générale, Rome, November 16, 1970, for a short summary of the history of the F.A.O.) John Boyd-Orr was awarded the Nobel Peace Prize in 1949.

23. Tibor Mende, *De l'Aide à la Recolonisation* (Paris: Editions du Seuil, 1972), p. 1.

24. On the plunder of India, see the brief discussion in Paul Baran, *The Political Economy of Growth* (New York: Monthly Review Press, 1957), pp. 144-50.

25. De Castro's overviews on the development of agricultural production may be supplemented by one of René Dumont's books (*Lands Alive* [New York: Monthly Review Press, 1955], for example). Dumont, more than anyone else, has grasped the technical potential of agricultural systems and the immense possibilities for increasing food supply all over the world.

26. Ray Goldberg, *Agribusiness Coordination* (Cambridge: Harvard University Press, 1968), p. 10.

27. Federal Trade Commission, National Commission on Food Marketing, Washington, D.C., 1966, pp. 6-7.

28. Intervention de M. Ojala, Colloque CENECA, Paris, April 1975.

29. This section is based on *Comité d'Information Sahel*, Introduction (Paris: Maspero, 1974).

30. This does not mean that the colonial world could actually *afford* to export grain or oil seed. Nevertheless, in many instances food products were still being exported at the very height of a famine.

31. Nations-Unies, *Conférence Mondiale*, p. 102.

32. J. P. Chabert, M. Marloie, P. Spitz, and B. Valluis provide an estimate of reserve productive capacity in *Céréales, Pénuries Naturelles*

ou Pénuries Sur Commande, (mimeograph; Paris: Institut National de la Recherche Agronomique, 1973), p. 4.

Chapter 1

1. Food and Agriculture Organization of the United Nations, *World Food Survey* (Washington, 1946, 1952, 1962).
2. Sigmund Freud, *Totem y Tabu* (Buenos Aires, 1924).
3. Cornelius Walford, *The Famines of the World* (London, 1879).
4. Pitirim Sorokin, *Man and Society in Calamity* (New York, 1942).
5. Stefan Zweig, *Freud* (Paris, 1932).
6. Elisée Reclus, *Nouvelle Géographie Universelle* (Paris, 1876-94).
7. Jack Drummond, *Problems of Malnutrition and Starvation During the War* (Nottingham, 1946).
8. Julian Huxley, *On Living in a Revolution* (London, 1944).
9. José Ortega y Gasset, *El Libro de las Misiones* (Buenos Aires, 1940).
10. Holmer Shantz, in *Conservation of Renewable Resources* (Philadelphia, 1941).
11. *Biologie et Développement: Hommage à Henri Laugier* (Paris, 1968); and Nigel Calder, *Eden Was No Garden* (New York, 1967).
12. Ibid.
13. Nikolai N. Mikhailov, *Nouvelle Géographie de l'U.R.S.S.* (Paris, 1936).
14. Frank Boudreau, "Nutrition as a World Problem," *Transactions of the New York Academy of Sciences,* series II, 8:3 (January 1946).
15. Thomas R. Malthus, *Essai sur le Principe de la Population* (1788).
16. Alfred Sauvy, *Richesse et Population* (Paris, 1944).
17. Imre Ferenczi, *L'Optimum Synthétique de Peuplement* (Paris, 1938).
18. Wallace R. Aykroyd, *Human Nutrition and Diet* (London, 1937).
19. William Vogt, *Road to Survival* (New York, 1948).
20. J. D. Black and M. E. Kiefer, *Future Food and Agriculture Policy* (New York, 1948).
21. Fairfield Osborn, *Our Plundered Planet* (Boston, 1948).
22. Russell Lord, *Behold Our Land* (Boston, 1938).
23. George Soule, David Efron, and N. T. Ness, *Latin America in the Future World* (New York and Toronto, 1945).

24. F. W. Bateson, *Toward a Socialist Agriculture* (London, 1946).

25. Encyclopédie des Sciences de l'Homme, *L'Aventure de Demain* (Paris, 1968).

26. Jeans, James, et al., *Le Progrès Scientifique* (1958).

27. H. A. Keyserling, *The Travel Diary of a Philosopher* (London and New York, 1925).

Chapter 2

1. Walter Mallory, *China, Land of Famine* (New York, 1926).

2. R. Cilento, "Underdeveloped Areas in Social Evolutionary Perspective." Paper presented at the round table of Milbank Memorial Fund, 1947.

3. Frank Boudreau et al., *International Approaches to the Problem of Underdeveloped Areas* (Milbank Memorial Fund, 1948).

4. Max Sorre, *Les Fondements de la Géographie humaine, I: Les Fondements Biologiques* (Paris, 1947).

5. Pierre Gourou, *Les Pays Tropicaux* (Paris, 1947).

6. Lucie Randoin and Henri Simonnet, *Les Données et les Inconnues du Problème Alimentaire* (Paris, 1937).

7. E. J. Bigwood and G. Trolli, "Problème de l'Alimentation au Congo Belge," in *La Science de l'Alimentation* (Paris, 1937).

8. Lucien Febvre, *La Terre et l'Evolutione Humaine* (Paris, 1922).

9. Alfred Niceforo, *Les Classes Pauvres: Recherches Anthropologiques et Sociales* (Paris, 1905).

10. Rigoberto Aguillar, *Estudios Sobre las Avitaminoses y las Perturbaciones del Crescimiento en los Niños Avitaminosicos* (Mexico, 1944).

11. Lydia J. Roberts, "Nutrition in Puerto Rico," *Journal American Dietetic Association* 20:5 (May 1944).

12. Kenneth C. Beeson, *The Mineral Composition of Crops, with particular reference to soils in which they were grown* (Washington, 1941).

13. Gerald F. Winfield, *China, the Land and the People* (New York, 1948).

14. J. L. McClendon, *Iodine and the Incidence of Goiter* (Minneapolis, 1939).

15. Josué de Castro, *La Alimentación en los Tropicos* (Mexico, 1946).

16. C. A. Talberg, *American Journal of Physiology* (1922).

17. E. Parmelee Prentice, *Hunger and History* (New York and London, 1939).

18. Serguis Morgulis, *Fasting and Undernutrition* (New York, 1923).

19. Wallace R. Aykroyd, *Human Nutrition and Diet* (London, 1937).

20. Victor Heiser, *La Odisea de un Médico en 45 Países* (Buenos Aires, 1943).

21. Robert P. Parsons, *Trial to Light: A Biography of Joseph Goldberger* (New York, 1943).

22. Damião Peres, "Vasco da Gama," in *Les Explorateurs célèbres* (Paris, 1947).

23. Karl B. Mickey, *Health from the Ground Up* (Chicago, 1946).

24. Pitirim Sorokin, *Man and Society in Calamity* (New York, 1942).

25. J. Franklin B. Schielle, I. Bozek, and A. Keys, "Observations on Human Behavior in Experimental Semi-Starvation and Rehabilitation," *Journal of Clinical Psychology* 4:1 (January 1948).

26. Eugène C. Jacobs, "Effects of Starvation on Sex Hormones in the Male," *The Journal of Clinical Endocrinology* 8:3 (March 1948).

27. Alfredo Ramos Espinosa, *La Alimentación en México* (Mexico, 1939).

28. J. R. Slonaker, *American Journal of Physiology* 71, 83, 96, 97, 98, 123 (1925-28).

29. F. C. Russell and I. Leitch, *Diet in Relation to Reproduction and Viability of the Young* (1948).

30. *United Nations Statistical Annual* (1967).

31. Anton J. Carlson and Frederick Hoelzel, "Effect of Segregation and Isolation Before Mating on the Fertility of Rats," *The American Journal of Physiology* 163:3 (December 1950).

32. Maria A. Rudzinska, "The Influence of Amount of Food on the Reproduction Rate and Longevity of a Suctorian (*Mokophrya infusionum*)," *Science* 113:2923 (January 5, 1951).

33. Lawrence Galton, "Less Feed, Higher Profits," *Country Gentleman* (May 1952).

34. H. A. Teitelbaum and W. H. Grant, "Effect of Starvation on Sperm Count and Sexual Reflexes," *Science* (August 1958).

35. Robert C. Cook, "Puerto Rico's New Look," *Population Bulletin* 11:2 (April 1955).

36. G. E. MacGinitie, *Distribution and Ecology of Marine Invertebrates of Point Barrow, Alaska* (Washington, 1955).

37. V. Webster Johnson and Raleigh Barlowe, *Land Problems and Policies* (1954).

Chapter 3

1. Kingsley Davis, *Population Trends and Policies in Latin America* (Austin, 1946).

2. S. E. Harris, *Economic Problems of Latin America* (New York, 1944).

3. For more details on these different nutrition zones, see: Arturo Guevara, *El Poliedro de la Nutrición: Aspectos Economicos y Sociales del Problema de la Alimentación en Venezuela* (Caracas, 1944); José Maria Bengoa, *La F.A.O. y la Politica Alimenticia* (Caracas, 1947); Jorge Bejarano, *Alimentación y Nutrición en Colombia* (Bogota, 1941); Pablo A. Suarez, "La Situación Real del Indio en el Ecuador," *America Indigena* (July 1945); Emma Reh, *Paraguayan Rural Life: Survey of Food Problem* (Washington, 1946); Salvador Allende, *La Realidad Medico-Social Chilena* (Santiago, 1939); Josué de Castro, "As Areas Alimentares no Brasil," *America Indigena* (June 1945); Varela Fuentes and A. Munilla, *Algunos Aspectos de la Alimentación en Uruguay* (Montevideo, 1946); Pedro Escudero, *El Presente y el Futuro del Problema Alimentario en Bolivia* (Buenos Aires, 1947); Pedro Escudero, *Alimentación* (Buenos Aires, 1934). Other detailed information on regional aspects can be found in the reports of the two Latin American conferences on nutrition called by the F.A.O., the first at Montevideo in 1948 and the second at Rio de Janeiro in 1950.

4. Moisés Problete Troncose, *El Standard de Vida de las Poblaciones de America* (Santiago, 1942).

5. Josué de Castro, *Alimentaçao e Reça* (Rio de Janeiro, 1936).

6. Escudero, *El Presente y el Futuro del Problema Alimentario en Bolivia.*

7. G. Soule, D. Efron, and N. Ness, *Latin America in the Future World* (New York, 1945).

8. Josué de Castro, *La Alimentación en los Tropicos* (Mexico, 1946).

9. Emilio Llorens, *El Subconsumo de Alimentos en América del Sud* (Buenos Aires, 1942).

10. Josué de Castro, "As Areas Alimentares no Brasil."

11. Josué de Castro, *O Problema da Alimentaçao no Brasil* (3rd ed., Rio de Janeiro, 1939).

12. Soule et al., *Latin America in the Future World.*

13. Escudero, *El Presente y el Futuro del Problema Alimentario.*

14. M. Steggaerda, "Statures of South American Indians," *American Journal of Physical Anthropology* 1:1 (1943).

15. Raoul Lecoq, *Avitaminoses et Déséquilibres* (Paris, 1939).

16. A. R. Espinosa, *La Alimentación en México* (Mexico, 1939).

17. Andrade Lima, *Un Aspecto Regional de Antropologia Escolar* (Recife, 1941).

18. de Castro, *La Alimentación en los Tropicos.*

19. Tennent and Silver, "Perdas de Vitaminas pelo Suor," *Arg. Bras. de Nutr.* (May 1946).

20. D. Cereceda, *La Alimentación Española* (Madrid, 1934).

21. J. V. Santa Maria, *Esquema de la Situación Alimentaria Chilena.* Paper presented to the first Latin American Conference on Nutrition, 1948.

22. Reh, *Paraguayan Rural Life.*

23. R. Aguillar, *Estudios Sobre las Avitaminosis y las Perturbaciones del Crecimiento* (Mexico, 1944).

24. Lydia J. Roberts, "Nutrition in Puerto Rico," *Journal American Dietetic Association* 20:5 (May 1944).

25. Reh, *Paraguayan Rural Life.*

26. A. I. Benavente, "Public Health in Bolivia," *Bulletin of the Pan-American Sanitary Bureau* (January 1942).

27. Thales de Azevedo and A. Galvão, *Una Pasquisa sobre o Suplemento Nutritivo em Escolares* (Bahia, 1945).

28. M. Uzin, "Géophagie," *La Médecine Chez Soi* (February 1938).

29. Reh, *Paraguayan Rural Life.*

30. Ramón Carcano, *800,000 Analfabetos* (Buenos Aires, 1933).

31. C. A. Talberg, *American Journal of Physiology* (1922).

32. Graham Lusk, *The Elements of the Science of Nutrition* (Philadelphia and London, 1928).

33. H. Koster, *Travels in Brazil* (London, 1817).
34. Grenfell Price, "White Settlers in the Tropics," *American Geographical Society*, no. 23 (1939).
35. Josué de Castro, "Metabolismo das Vitaminas nos Tropicos," *Trabalhos e Pesquisas do Instituto de Nutriçao* (1949).
36. Pedro Escudero, "Etude Economique de l'Alimentation de l'Ouvrier de Buenos Aires," *Rev. Sud-Américaine de Méd. et Chirugie* (March 1933).
37. Firmo Dutra, "Borracha," *Brazil—1939-40* (Rio de Janeiro, 1940).
38. R. Passmore, *Nutrition and Health in Children in Five Countries in South America* (International Children's Emergency Fund, 1948).
39. J. Barros Barreto, J. de Castro, and A. de Castro, "Inquérito Sôbre as Condições de Alimentaçâo Popular no Distrito Federal," *Boletin do Min. do Trab. Ind. e Com.* (January 1939).
40. Escudero, "Etude Economique . . ."
41. A. Palácios, *La Defensa del Valor Humano* (Buenos Aires, 1939).
42. Alvaro Lôbo, "Bocio Endemico e Doença de Chagas," *O Hospital* (June 1942).
43. Arruda Sampaio, *Aspectos do Bocio Endêmico na Infância e na Adolescência* (1944).
44. Soule et al., *Latin America in the Future World*.
45. William Vogt, *Road to Survival* (New York, 1948).
46. Pierre Gourou, *Les Pays Tropicaux* (Paris, 1947).
47. F.A.O., *World Food Survey* (1946).
48. Soule et al., *Latin America in the Future World*.
49. Celso Furtado, *Desenvolvimento e Subdesenvolvimento* (Rio de Janeiro, 1961).
50. Dutra, "Borracha" in *Brazil*.
51. *Programa de Açao Econômica do Governo 1945-1965* (Brazil, 1964).
52. Antonio Dias Leite, "O Programa de Açao Econômica do Governo em Face da Realidade Nacional," *Carta Econômica Brasileira* 2:5 (May 1966).
53. Antonio Dias Leite, *Caminhos do Desenvolvimento* (Brazil, 1966).

54. C. M. Wilson, *Central America: Challenge and Opportunity* (New York, 1941).

55. Francisco Bulnes, *El Porvenir de las Naciones Hispano-Americanas ante las Conquistas de Europa y Estados Unidos* (Mexico, 1889).

56. E. Quintana, "La Alimentacion Popular en Centro América," *Memoria del V. Congresso Medico Centro-Americano* (El Salvador, 1942).

57. Francisco Miranda, *El Maiz* (Mexico, n.d.).

58. E. Quintana, "El Problema Dietético de Caribe," *America Indigena* 2:11 (April 1942).

59. A. Ramos Espinosa, *La Alimentación en México* (Mexico, 1939).

60. R. Aguillar, *Estudios Sobre las Avitaminosis* . . .

61. Medieta y Nunez, *La Economica del Indio Mexicano* (1938).

62. Fairfield Osborn, *Our Plundered Planet* (Boston, 1948).

63. F. J. Clavijero, *Historia Antigua de México* (Mexico, 1944).

64. G. de Reparaz, *Historia de la Colonización* (Buenos Aires, 1935).

65. Soule et al., *Latin America in the Future World.*

66. Ibid.

67. J. Calvo de la Torre, *Inform. de Conferência Latino-Americana de Nutriçao* (1948).

68. Vogt, *Road to Survival.*

69. Holland Thompson, ed., *Lands and Peoples,* vol. 3 (New York, 1932).

70. Bartolomé de las Casas, *Brevisima Relación de la Destruccion de las Indias* (1552).

71. Alexander von Humboldt, *Voyage aux Regions Equinoxiales* (Paris, 1804).

72. Georges Hardy, *Géographie et Colonisation* (Paris, 1933).

73. C. K. Meek, *Land, Law, and Custom in the Colonies* (2nd ed.; London, 1949).

74. Davis, *Population Trends and Policies in Latin America.*

75. F. Milanez, *Importancia y Alcance de las Enfermedades por Deficiencia Nutricional en Cuba.* First Congreso Nacional de Alimentación, Havana, 1945.

76. P. G. Minneman, "The Agriculture of Cuba," U.S. Department of Agriculture, *Foreign Agricultural Bulletin*, no. 2 (1942).

77. Soule et al., *Latin America in the Future World.*

78. Leland Jenks, *Our Cuban Colony* (New York, 1958).

79. Oswaldo Morales Patino, "Primero Encuesta Sobre la Alimentación de la Familia Obrera Cubana," *Boletin Oficial del Seguro de Salud y Maternidad* (November 1939).

80. Antonio Clerch, *Rapport Présenté à la Première Conférence Latino-Américaine de la Nutrition* (Montevideo, 1948).

81. J.-P. Sartre, *Fundaçâo Sôbre Cuba* (Rio de Janeiro, 1960).

82. For information on the agricultural reform in Cuba, see P. M. Sweezy and L. Huberman, *Cuba: Anatomy of a Revolution* (New York, 1960).

83. René Dumont, *Terre Vivante* (Paris, 1961).

84. *Una Politica per la Piena Occupazione* (1958).

85. Blas Rocca, *Los Fundamientos del Socialismo en Cuba* (Havana, 1961).

86. Scott Nearing and Joseph Freeman, *Dollar Diplomacy* (New York, 1925).

87. See Luis Cardóza y Aragón, "Guatemala Despues de la 'Gloriosa Victoria,'" *Cuadernos Americanos* (1964), review by Dr. Jesús Silva Herzog.

88. E. G. Young, "A Dietary Survey in Halifax," *Canada Public Health Journal,* vol. 32 (May 1941).

89. J.-E. Sylvestre and H. Nadeau, "Enquête sur l'Alimentation Habituelle des Familles de Petits Salaires dans la Ville de Québec," *Canada Public Health Journal,* vol. 32 (May 1941).

90. J. Patterson and E. W. McHenry, "A Dietary Investigation in Toronto Families Having Incomes Between $1500 and $2400," *Canada Public Health Journal,* vol. 32 (May 1941).

91. W. R. Aykroyd et al., "Medical Resurvey of Nutrition in Newfoundland in 1948," *Canada Med. Ass. Journal* (April 1949).

92. Committee on Nutrition in the Colonial Empire, *Summary of Information Regarding Nutrition in the Colonial Empire* (London, 1939).

93. L. J. Regatz, *The Fall of the Planter Class in the British Caribbean (1763-1883)* (New York, 1928).

94. William Ripley, *Races of Europe* (New York, 1902).

95. Price, "White Settlers in the Tropics."

96. J. C. Waterlow, "Fatty Liver Disease in Infants in the British Indies," *Medical Research Council Report No. 263* (1948).

97. R. Guerra y Sanchez, *Azucar y Poblacion en las Antillas* (Havana, 1944).
98. V. T. Harlow, *A History of Barbados* (Oxford, 1926).
99. E. O. Lippman, *Historia do Açucar* (Rio de Janeiro, 1942).
100. Price, "White Settlers in the Tropics."
101. Lippman, *Historia de Açucar.*
102. Michel Vaucaire, *Les Révoltés de la Bounty* (Paris, 1947).
103. A. Gerbault, *A la Poursuite du Soleil* (Paris, 1929).
104. Committee on Nutrition in the Colonial Empire, *Summary of Information Regarding Nutrition . . .*
105. Soule et al., *Latin America in the Future World.*
106. Report of the Census of Puerto Rico (1890), cited by Soule et al., in ibid.
107. R. Pico, "Land Tenure in the Leading Types of Farming of Puerto Rico," *Economic Geography*, vol. 15 (1937).
108. Ellsworth Huntington, *Principles of Economic Geography* (New York and London, 1940).
109. Preston James, *Latin America* (New York, 1942).
110. Eric W. Zimmermann, *Report on Puerto Rico*, cited in Soule et al., *Latin America in the Future World.*
111. Manuel Maldonado-Denis, "Puerto Rico: An American Showcase for Latin America," in Horowitz, Castro, and Gerassi, eds., *Latin American Radicalism* (New York: Random House, 1969).
112. James, *Latin America.*
113. H. C. Sherman, "Glimpse of Social Economics in Puerto Rico," *Puerto Rican Journal of Public Health and Tropical Medicine* (December 1930).
114. E. B. Hill and J. R. Noguera, "The Food Supply of Puerto Rico," Agric. Experiment Station of Rio Piedras, *Bulletin No. 55* (August 1940).
115. Lydia Roberts, "Nutrition in Puerto Rico," *Journal American Dietetic Association* 20:5 (1944).
116. Maldonado-Denis, *Puerto Rico.*
117. Committee on Diagnosis and Pathology of Nutritional Deficiencies, Food and Nutrition Board, "Inadequate Diets and Nutritional Deficiencies in the United States," *Bulletin of the National Research Council,* no. 109 (November 1943).
118. H. W. Odum, *Southern Regions of the United States* (Chapel Hill, 1936).

119. E. Q. Hawk, *Economic History* (New York, 1934).

120. Odum, *Southern Regions of the United States.*

121. Hawk, *Economic History.*

122. E. Lipson, *Economic History of England* (London, 1931).

123. Hawk, *Economic History.*

124. Odum, *Southern Regions of the United States.*

125. Gunnar Myrdal, *An American Dilemma: The Negro Problem and Modern Democracy* (New York, 1944).

126. W. Shepard, *Food and Famine: The Challenge of Erosion* (New York, 1945).

127. Charles Kellog, *The Soils That Support Us* (New York, 1943).

128. J. Goldberger and E. Sydenstricker, "Pellagra in the Mississippi Flood Area," *Public Health Report* 42:44 (November 1927).

129. Robert P. Parsons, *Trail to Light: A Biography of Dr. Joseph Goldberger* (Indianapolis, 1943).

130. Committee on Diagnosis, "Inadequate Diets and Nutritional Deficiencies in the United States."

131. J. B. Youmans, "An Assessment of the Nutrition of a Rural Population in Tennessee," *American Journal of Public Health* 31:7 (July 1941).

132. Ibid.

133. Russell Wilder, "Our Food Front," *Survey Graphic* (November 1943).

134. John Gunther, *Inside U.S.A.* (New York, 1947).

135. Ibid.

136. J. K. Galbraith, *The Affluent Society* (New York, 1958).

137. *Hunger U.S.A.*, report by the Citizens Board of Inquiry into Hunger and Malnutrition in the United States (1960); and *Données* (December 1969).

138. Ralph Lapp, *The Weapons Culture* (New York, 1968).

Chapter 4

1. G. B. Cressey, *Tierras y Pueblos de Asia* (Buenos Aires, 1946).

2. W. H. Mallory, *China, Land of Famine* (New York, 1926).

3. John Lessing Buck, *Land Utilisation in China* (Nankin, 1947).

4. G. F. Winfield, *China: The Land and the People* (New York, 1948).

5. G. B. Cressey, *Geographie Humaine et Economique de la Chine* (Paris, 1939).

6. B. S. Platt, *Chinese Methods of Infant Feeding and Nursing* (1938).
7. Winfield, *China: The Land and the People*.
8. F.A.O., *Rice Diets—A Nutritional Survey* (Washington, 1948).
9. *The Chinese Year Book* (Shanghai, 1936-37).
10. Weston A. Price, *Nutrition and Physical Degeneration* (New York, 1940).
11. J. C. Thompson, "Food Problems of Free China," *Nutrition Reviews* 1:9 (July 1943).
12. H. D. Fong, *The Post-war Industrialization of China* (Chungking, 1942).
13. John Robbins, *Too Many Asians* (New York, 1959).
14. Fairfield Osborn, *Our Crowded Planet* (London, 1962).
15. O. E. Baker, "Agriculture and the Future of China," *Foreign Affairs* (April 1928).
16. Winfield, *China: The Land and the People*.
17. A. Warwick, "Farmers Since the Days of Noah," *The National Geographic Magazine* 51:4 (April 1927).
18. David N. Rowe, *China Among the Powers* (New York, 1945).
19. T. Lynn Smith, *Population Analysis* (New York, 1948).
20. Thomas Doubleday, *The True Law of Population Shown to Be Connected with the Food of the People* (London, 1853).
21. Raymond Pearl, *The Natural History of Population* (London, 1939).
22. J. C. Waterlow, "Fatty Liver Disease in Infants in the British West Indies," *Medical Research Council Report No. 263* (1948).
23. A. H. Smith, *Moeurs Curieuses des Chinois* (Paris, 1927).
24. Roger Bastide, *Eléments de Sociologie Religieuse* (Paris, 1935).
25. Franz Schurmann and Orville Schell, *The China Reader* (New York, 1967).
26. Mallory, *China, Land of Famine*.
27. Frederick Schuman, *International Politics* (3rd ed.; New York, 1941).
28. G. T. Trewartha, *Japan: A Physical, Cultural, and Regional Geography* (Madison, Wis., 1945).
29. E. R. Hughes, *L'Invasion de la Chine par l'Occident* (Paris, 1938).
30. F. P. Chambers, C. P. Grant, and C. C. Bayley, *This Age of Conflict, 1914-1943* (New York, 1943).
31. Maurice Lachin, *La Chine Capitaliste* (Paris, 1938).

32. "L'Accession de la Chine au Rang de Grande Puissance," special edition of the review *Comprendre* (Venice), no. 19 (1961).

33. Marthe E. Berlels, *Tradition et Mutation dans la Grande Révolution Prolétarienne en Chine* (1968).

34. L. W. Trueblood, "The Complexity of India and Burma," in *World Political Geography* (New York, 1948).

35. Wallace R. Aykroyd, *Human Nutrition and Diet* (London, 1937).

36. S. Chandrasekhar, "Problemas Demograficos de la India y Pakistan," in *El Correo de la UNESCO* (April-May 1949).

37. S. Chandrasekhar, *India's Population* (New York, 1946).

38. André Philip, *L'Inde Moderne* (Paris, 1930).

39. E. Reclus, *Nouvelle Géographie Universelle* (Paris, 1875-1894).

40. Fairfield Osborn, *Our Plundered Planet* (Boston, 1948).

41. C. C. Furnas and S. M. Furnas, *The Story of Man and His Food* (New York, 1942).

42. Cressey, *Tierras y Pueblos de Asia.*

43. P. K. Wattal, *The Population Problem in India* (Bombay and London, 1934).

44. A. Huxley, *Tour du Monde d'un Sceptique* (1932).

45. Philip, *L'Inde Moderne.*

46. Rev. Père Vath, *Histoire de l'Inde et de sa Culture* (1937).

47. Gonzalo de Reparaz, *Historia de la Colonización* (Buenos Aires, 1922).

48. R. C. Dutt, *Economic History of India* (London, 1908).

49. Council of Chatam House, *A Food Plan for India* (London, 1945).

50. Government of India, *Economic Survey, 1967-68.*

51. Gilbert Etienne, *L'Agriculture Indienne ou l'Art du Possible* (1966).

52. On this subject see the following works, which were published recently: René Dumont and Bernard Rosier, *Nous Allons à la Famine* (Paris, 1966); William and Paul Paddock, *Famine 1965* (1967); Clifford M. Hardin, ed., *Overcoming World Hunger* (1969).

53. René Deléluse, "Le Dégel de l'Agriculture Indienne," supplement no. 5 to *Faim et Développement,* no. 57 (March 1969).

54. See the article by Pierre Marchand in *Réalités,* no. 2 (October 1965), and Maurice Guernier, *La Dernière Chance du Tiers-Monde* (Paris, 1968).

55. Roget Livet, *Géographie de l'Alimentation* (Paris, 1969).

56. John Laffin, *The Hunger to Come* (1966).
57. Robert Brooks, "Can India Make It?" *Saturday Review,* August 9, 1969.
58. Livet, *Géographie de l'Alimentation.*
59. Robert Brooks, "Can India Make It?"
60. Trewartha, *Japan.*
61. Pitirim Sorokin, *Man and Society in Calamity* (New York, 1942).
62. R. Ruellan, *La Production du Riz au Japon* (Paris, 1938).
63. G. V. Jacks and R. O. White, *Vanishing Lands* (New York, 1939).
64. Ruellan, *La Production du Riz au Japon.*
65. E. Dennery, *Foules d'Asie* (Paris, 1930).
66. Trewartha, *Japan.*
67. G. C. Allen, *A Short Economic History of Modern Japan, 1867-1937* (London, 1946).
68. E. M. Haddley, "Trust Busting in Japan," *Harvard Business Review* 26:4 (July 1948).
69. Tadasu Saiki, *Organisation Sociale de l'Hygiène Alimentaire au Japon* (Paris, 1937).
70. William Vogt, *Road to Survival* (New York, 1948).
71. Schuman, *International Politics.*
72. Jerome B. Cohen, *Japan's Economy in War and Reconstruction* (Minneapolis, 1949).
73. Supreme Command of Allied Powers, "Japanese Economic Statistics," *Bulletin,* no. 38 (October 1949).
74. A. Buchan, *Annual Changes in Population of Japan Proper,* Economic and Scientific Section, G.H.Q. Supreme Commander for the Allied Powers (Tokyo, 1948).
75. Editorial, "Prospects of Japanese Recovery," *The Economist* (London), September 4, 1948.
76. "Le Japon," *Cahiers de l'Encyclopédie du Monde Actuel,* no. 16 (February 1967).
77. Livet, *Géographie de l'Alimentation.*

Chapter 5

1. Ralph A. Graves, "Fearful Famines of the Past," *National Geographic Magazine* 32:1 (July 1917).

2. Jacques Nouvel, "La Crise Agricole de 1945-1946 au Maroc et Ses Conséquences Economiques et Sociales," *La Revue de Géographie Humaine et Ethnologie,* no. 3 (July-September 1948).

3. G. E. Pearcy et al., *World Political Geography* (New York, 1948).

4. Ellsworth Huntington, *Civilization and Climate* (New Haven and London, 1939).

5. William Vogt, *Road to Survival* (New York, 1948).

6. Fairfield Osborn, *Our Plundered Planet* (Boston, 1948).

7. E. F. Gauthier, *Le Sahara* (Paris, 1928).

8. A. Grenfell Price, "White Settlers in the Tropics," *American Geographic Society Pub. No. 23* (1939).

9. Paul Leroy-Beaulieu, *De la Colonisation Chez les Peuples Modernes* (Paris, 1882).

10. A. Gilles de Pélichy, "L'Homme Clanique et le Prolétaire en Afrique Noire," *Idées et Forces,* no. 3 (April-June 1949).

11. F.A.O., *The State of Food and Agriculture* (Washington, 1948).

12. E. Gauthier, *L'Afrique Blanche* (Paris, 1939).

13. A. Giberton, "Alimentation des Indigènes d'Algérie," *La Science et l'Alimentation en 1937* (Paris).

14. Paul W. Harrison, *The Arab at Home* (New York, 1924).

15. Nouvel, *La Crise Agricole de 1945-1946.*

16. Jean Dresch, "Villes Congolaises—Etude de Géographie Urbaine et Sociale," *Revue de Géographie Humaine et Ethnographie,* no. 3 (1948).

17. Weston A. Price, *Nutrition and Physical Degeneration* (New York, 1939).

18. E. J. Bigwood and G. Trolli, "Problème de l'Alimentation au Congo Belge," *La Science et l'Alimentation* (1937).

19. Committee on Nutrition in the Colonial Empire, *Summary of Information Regarding Nutrition in the Colonial Empire* (London, 1939).

20. Pierre Gourou, *Les Pays Tropicaux* (Paris, 1947).

21. Georges Hardy, *Géographie et Colonisation* (Paris, 1933).

22. G. G. Seligman, *Les Races de l'Afrique* (Paris, 1935).

23. Editorial, "South African Food Supplies," *The Economist* (London), October 18, 1947.

24. Report of the Carnegie Commission, *The Poor-White Problem in Africa,* 5 vols. (1932).

25. T. Gilman, "Malnutrition and Pellagra," *South Africa Nutrition Review* (December 1947).

26. René Dumont, *L'Afrique Noire est Mal Partie* (Paris, 1962).

27. Gabriel d'Arboussier, "L'Afrique, Continent en Mutation," *Courrier de l'UNESCO,* (June 1967).

28. See the series of F.A.O. publications on the world food situation.

29. Roger Livet, *Géographie de l'Alimentation* (Paris, 1969).

30. d'Arboussier, "L'Afrique, Continent en Mutation."

Chapter 6

1. H. Weigert, V. Stefansson, and R. Harrison, *New Compass of the World* (New York, 1949).

2. Hubert d'Hérouville, *L'Economie Européenne* (Paris, 1949).

3. United Nations, *Rapport sur l'Economie Mondiale* (Lake Success, N.Y., 1949).

4. Henri Pirenne, *Historia Economica y Social de la Edad Media* (Mexico, 1941).

5. F. Cruschmann, *Hungersnöte im Mittelalter,* cited in P. Sorokin, *Man and Society in Calamity* (New York, 1942).

6. E. A. Southard, "Famine," *Encyclopedia of the Social Sciences,* vol. 3 (New York, 1937).

7. Cornelius Walford, *The Famines of the World: Past and Present* (London, 1878).

8. E. Parmelee Prentice, *Hunger and History* (New York, 1939).

9. Adam Maurizio, *Histoire de l'Alimentation Végétale* (Paris, 1932).

10. Prentice, *Hunger and History.*

11. H. A. Taine, *Les Origines de la France Contemporaine, volume III: La Dissolution, l'Anarchie.*

12. Maurizio, *Histoire de l'Alimentation Végétale.*

13. Henri Sée, *Esquisse d'une Histoire du Régime Agraire en Europe aux XVIIIe et XIXe Siècles* (Paris, 1921).

14. Prentice, *Hunger and History.*

15. H. E. Erdman, "The Food Problem," *The Outlook for Postwar Europe* (Los Angeles, 1945).

16. John Boyd-Orr, *Food, Health, and Income* (London, 1936).

17. E. W. H. Cruickshank, *Food and Nutrition* (Edinburgh, 1946).

18. L. J. Picton, *Medical Testament* (New York, 1949).

19. Sée, *Esquisse d'une Histoire du Régime Agraire.*

20. Salvat Navarro, *Tradado de Higiene* (Barcelona, 1936).

21. Lévy Provençal, *La Péninsule Ibérique au Moyen Age* (Leyde, 1938).

22. Gordon East, *Historical Geography of Europe* (Paris, 1939).

23. Fairfield Osborn, *Our Plundered Planet* (Boston, 1948).

24. Leland Stowe, *While Time Remains* (New York, 1947).

25. Salvador de Madariaga, *España—Ensayo de Historia Contemporanea* (Buenos Aires, 1942).

26. Stowe, *While Time Remains.*

27. Pedro y Pons, *Enfermedades por Insuficiencia Alimenticia Observadas en Barcelona Durange la Guerra (1936-1939)* (Barcelona, 1947).

28. Eduard Simonart, *La Dénutrition en Guerre* (Brussels, 1947).

29. Ignazio Silone, *Fontamara* (New York, 1934).

30. Carlo Levi, *Christ Stopped at Eboli* (1947).

31. Elizabeth Wiskemann, "Poverty and Population in the South," *Foreign Affairs* (October 1949).

32. Société des Nations, *L'Alimentation dans ses Rapports avec l'Hygiène, l'Agriculture et la Politique Économique.*

33. F.A.O., *Report of the Mission for Poland* (Washington, 1948).

34. Ministry of Foreign Relations, *Information on Poland* (Warsaw, 1947).

35. R. L. Buell, *Poland: Key to Europe,* cited in Stowe, *While Time Remains.*

36. Leland Stowe, "Hungary's Agrarian Revolution," *Foreign Affairs* (April 1947).

37. William Vogt, *Road to Survival* (New York, 1948).

38. Henri Claude, *De la Crise Economique à la Guerre Mondiale* (Paris, 1945).

39. F.A.O., *World Food Survey* (Washington, 1946).

40. Inter-allied Information Committee, *Rationing under Axis Rule* (London, 1942).

41. Boris Shub, *Starvation over Europe* (New York, 1943).

42. Ibid.

43. R. Strausz-Hupé, *Geopolitica—La Lucha por el Espacio y el Poder* (Mexico, 1945).

44. Maria Babicka, "The Current Food Situation Inside Poland," *Journal American Dietetic Association* 19:4 (April 1943).

45. Else Margrete Roed, "The Food Situation in Norway," *Journal American Dietetic Association* 19:12 (December 1943).

46. L. A. H. Peters, "The Contemporary Food Situation Inside Holland," *Journal American Dietetic Association* 19:4 (April 1943).

47. Editorial, *The Times* (London), August 13, 1940.

48. Shub, *Starvation over Europe.*

49. J. Debû-Bridel, *Histoire du Marché Noir* (Paris, 1947).

50. Babicka, "The Current Food Situation Inside Poland."

51. F.A.O., *Report of the Mission for Poland.*

52. J. H. P. Jonxis, "Nutritional Status of Dutch Children in Wartime," *Nutrition Review* (April 1946).

53. Frederick J. Stare, "Nutritional Conditions in Holland," *Nutrition Review* (August 1945).

54. Max Nord, *Amsterdam Tijdens den Hongerwinter* (Amsterdam, 1947).

55. Shub, *Starvation over Europe.*

56. Werner Klatt, "Food and Farming in Germany," *International Affairs* 26:1 (January 1950).

57. H. K. Smith, *The State of Europe* (New York, 1949).

58. John Boyd-Orr, *The Role of Food in Postwar Reconstruction* (Montreal, 1943).

59. R. Delprat, "L'Europe Devant le Plan Marshall," *Economie et Humanisme,* no. 37 (1948).

60. A. Chomel, "L'Asphyxie de l'Europe—Les Echanges Est-Quest," *Le Diagnostic Economique et Social,* no. 15 (June 1950).

61. Klatt, "Food and Farming in Germany."

62. F.A.O., *The German Medical Profession on the State of Nutrition in Germany* (Geneva, 1947).

63. W. H. Chamberlain, *The European Cockpit* (New York, 1947).

64. Smith, *The State of Europe.*

65. Alexander Galin, "Europe Split or United," *Foreign Affairs* (October 1950).

66. Jean Chardonnet, *Les Conséquences Economiques de la Guerre 1939-1946* (Paris, 1947).

67. Klatt, "Food and Farming in Germany."

68. Ibid.
69. Edgar Brown, *The History of the Zuiderzee Works* (The Hague).
70. F. W. Bateson, *Towards a Socialist Agriculture* (London, 1946).
71. Adolf A. Berle, *Tides of Crisis* (1957).
72. See Demetrio Casado, *Perfiles del Hambre* (1967) and *La Faim au Portugal,* edited by the Portuguese National Liberation Front (1968).

Chapter 7

1. Kenneth Boulding, *The Economics of Peace* (New York, 1945).
2. Raul Gomes, *Caminhos da Paz* (Curitiba, 1948).
3. Robert Salter, "World Soil and Fertilizer Resources in Relation to Food Needs," *Freedom from Want,* a symposium edited by E. E. Turk (1948).
4. Edward H. Faulkner, *Plowman's Folly* (New York, 1943).
5. James Rorty and N. Philip Norman, *Tomorrow's Food* (New York, 1947).
6. Earl Parker Hanson, "Mankind Need Not Starve," *The Nation,* November 2, 1949.
7. E. B. Balfour, *The Living Soil* (London, 1948).
8. J. D. Bernal and M. Cornforth, *Science for Peace and Socialism* (London, n.d.).
9. Nigel Calder, *Eden Was No Garden* (New York, 1967).
10. Salter, "World Soil and Fertilizer Resources in Relation to Food Needs."
11. Sir Albert Howard, *An Agricultural Testament* (New York, 1943).
12. L. J. Picton, *Nutrition and the Soil* (New York, 1949).
13. G. T. Wrench, *Reconstruction by Way of the Soil* (London, 1946).
14. Colin Clark, "The World's Capacity to Feed and Clothe Itself," *The Way Ahead* 2:3 (1949).
15. M. Ilin, *Les Montagnes et les Hommes* (Paris, 1946).
16. Josué de Castro et al., "Os Alimentos Barbaros dos Sertões do Nordeste," *Arq. Bras. de Nutrição* (February 1947).

Chapter 8

1. G. Soule, D. Efron, and N. T. Ness, *Latin America in the Future World* (Washington, 1948).

2. Editorial, "Productivité et Bonheur Humain," *Diagnostic Economique et Social,* no. 19 (November 1950).

3. Ricardo M. Ortiz, "Fundamentos Economico-Sociales de la Sub-nutrición en América Latina," *Forum del Colegio de Estudios Superiores de Buenos Aires* (1950).

4. John Boyd-Orr, "The Food Problem," *Scientific American* 183:2 (August 1950).

5. F. LeGros Clark, "The Scientist As Guide to Global Food," in *The Soil and the Sea* (London, 1949).

6. F.A.O., *Report of World Commodity Problems* (1948).

7. Milbank Memorial Fund, *International Approaches to Problems of Underdeveloped Areas* (New York, 1948).

8. Earl Parker Hanson, *New World Emerging* (New York, 1949).

9. I. S. Falk, *Security Against Sickness* (New York, 1936).

10. E. B. Balfour, *The Living Soil* (London, 1943).

11. Curzio Malaparte, *La Peau* (Paris, 1949).

12. Charles Iffland, *L'Aide aux Pays Pauvres dans l'Impasse* (Lausanne, 1967).

13. Louis O'Neill, *L'Homme Moderne et la Socialisation, Analyse Ethico-Sociale du Phénomène* (Montreal, 1946).

14. Father Louis Joseph Lebret, *Développement-Révolution Solidaire,* with the collaboration of R. Delprat and M. F. Desbrugères (Paris, 1967).

15. Hanson, *New Worlds Emerging.*

HIGHSMITH 45-220